Bermuda's
Architectural
Heritage

BERMUDA'S ARCHITECTURAL HERITAGE

SMITH'S PARISH

VOLUME FIVE

OF THE

HISTORIC BUILDINGS BOOK PROJECT

BERMUDA NATIONAL TRUST

2005

For the benefit of Bermuda, to preserve buildings, land, artefacts and
places of beauty or historical interest and to promote their appreciation.
Bermuda National Trust Mission Statement

© 2005 Bermuda National Trust
PO Box HM 61
Hamilton HM AX
Bermuda
Tel: (441) 236-6483
Fax: (441) 236-0617
E-mail: palmetto@bnt.bm
Web site: www.bnt.bm

ISBN 1-894916-53-0 (Laminated edition)
ISBN 1-894916-54-9 (Cloth bound edition)

Design and Production by Dace McCoy Ground
Printed in China

Cover illustration:
Frank Galsworthy, Boat Maintenance at John Smith's Bay, 1914
Courtesy Rosemary Glynn

Dedicated to
The Bacardi Group of Companies
during their
40th anniversary year in Bermuda
for their continuing support of
the Architectural Heritage
series of books.

Readers are reminded to respect the privacy of owners and occupiers of the buildings discussed in this book.

CONTRIBUTORS

WRITERS: TEXT   Diana Chudleigh
               INTRODUCTION Edward A. Chappell
               SIDEBARS   Edward A. Chappell, Architectural Assessments
                               Diana Chudleigh, On the Side
                               Richard Lowry, Archaeology
                               William S. Zuill, MBE, Family Story

EDITOR   David L. White, OBE
PHOTOGRAPHER   Robin Judah
LAYOUT & DESIGN   Dace McCoy Ground
ILLUSTRATOR   Barbara Finsness
FLOOR PLANS   Colin Campbell   Edward A. Chappell
                               Steve Conway   Adam Gauntlett
                               Deborah Darrell Mackenzie   Geoff Parker Jr.
                               Philip J. Seaman   Charles Tatem
                               Malcolm Wilson   Ted Wood

MAP WORK   Richard Lowry
BIBLIOGRAPHY   Hilary Tulloch
INDEX   Margie Lloyd
PROOF READERS   Gerry Brashier
                               Amanda Outerbridge
                               Hilary Tulloch

COMPUTERISED RECORDS Sue Simons
IMAGES COORDINATOR   Margie Lloyd
RESEARCH COORDINATOR Linda Abend
SCANNING   Clay Cade
                               Michelle Gallinger
                               Jeff Klee
                               Janet Murray-King

RESEARCHERS

Linda Abend   Suzanne Judah   Cecille Snaith-Simmons
Simon Baillie   Margie Lloyd   Hilary Tulloch
Diana Chudleigh   Lark Lombardo   Pat Waltham
Fay Elliott   Joan McKendry   Jinny White
Jean Jones   Diane Price   Joy Wilson-Tucker

READERS

Linda Abend   Betsey Mowbray   Sue Simons
Margie Lloyd   Louis Mowbray   William Sears Zuill

All of the above contributors gave their skills and time as volunteers for the Bermuda National Trust.

This book would not have been possible without the help of the staff and the resources of the Bermuda Archives, the Bermuda National Library, the Registry General and the Colonial Williamsburg Foundation of Virginia.

We would like to thank the many people who shared their knowledge, house deeds, family papers and old photographs with us and allowed us to photograph their homes.

Our thanks to Bacardi Limited
for their generous sponsorship of this series.

CONTENTS

Smith's Parish: *Courtesy Ministry of Works & Engineering*

Crest of Smith's Parish: *Courtesy Bermuda Press Limited*

Reading the Buildings of Smith's Parish

EDWARD A. CHAPPELL
DIRECTOR OF ARCHITECTURAL RESEARCH
COLONIAL WILLIAMSBURG FOUNDATION

Oleander Circle at Devil's Hole had a hall on the right and previously an unheated parlour on the left, both behind an enclosed porch.   *Photograph by Edward A. Chappell.*

The present book is the fifth in an ambitious series about the architecture of Bermuda's parishes, based on field work and archival research by National Trust volunteers. It has two related purposes, preservation and education. Obviously, the volume presents many of the most notable buildings in Smith's Parish, with the hope that recognition will cultivate appreciation and that residents and planners will care for these distinctive creations.

The work has an educational value beyond simple recognition of venerability and charm. Understanding how Bermuda's architecture developed and observing its changing relationship to buildings elsewhere helps to explain the evolution of society and the island's historical role in the Atlantic world. The nature of housing in late 17th and early 18th century Bermuda is especially important because discoveries here can contribute to recent architectural scholarship in Britain and North America, as well as at home. And if we are open minded, we will find developments of the last century are equally engaging.

Very little indeed is known about the buildings put up in the initial six decades of settlement, except that most were quite different from what later was considered typical Bermudian construction. Many 17th century buildings were constructed of wood, without stone roofs, and nearly all of them have disappeared with no more than an archaeological trace. About 1688, 487 of Bermuda's 579 houses were said to have been thatched, 63 shingled, and only 29 roofed with stone. Chances are that most lacked substan-tial foundations, so ravenous insects from below as well as great winds from above hastened their demise.

INVENTORIES AND SPACE

Records describing early Bermuda buildings with sufficient consistency to allow much meaningful characterisation are confined to probate inventories, the lists of the worldly goods left by deceased property owners. As in Britain and British North America, inventory takers sometimes recorded the names of the rooms where the furnishings were located. A generous number of room by room inventories survive from late 17th and 18th century Bermuda, many, but not all of them, for wealthy households. Considered in combination with the earliest surviving buildings, they suggest a closer association with the Chesapeake region of Virginia and Maryland than with other parts of the English speaking world, including the mother country itself. Conversely, some of the small Bermuda population appears to have been better housed than their mainland counterparts.

The inventories show that propertied Bermudians, of the circa 1670-1711 generation, lived in three to six principal rooms arranged on one or two floors. The primary room was called the "hall". People either entered directly into the hall or through a small projecting entry called a "porch". Most porches noted in the inventories were enclosed spaces with walls and windows rather than open to the air.

The 12 most complete room by room inventories compiled in

Smith's Parish between 1668 and 1711 describe houses that included a hall, and nine of them had a porch to separate the hall from people and weather outside. Of 62 Bermudian inventories in general for the era, all but one had a hall and 34 clearly had a porch. Listed furniture indicates porches in Bermuda were also informal sitting spaces more so than recognised elsewhere. When John Gilbert died in 1700, his porch contained a short cedar table, a backless bench and "1 old bass chare", as well as worn saddles, bridles and small cooperage. Visitors, particularly those of low status, could wait to be met in the porch, just as people were to do in open porches and on masonry stoops with built-in benches in subsequent centuries.

Halls served as the principal sitting and formal eating spaces, virtually always containing the best table and most chairs, stools, or settles. Governor William Sayle's house in Smith's Parish contained a cedar table, stools and chairs available to diners in 1671. John Gilbert's family and guests sat on nine "joynt stooles" to eat at a long table in his hall. In the next decade Thomas Smith and John Argent presided over similar hall tables, Smith's furnished with eight stools and Argent's with six.

The term "parlour" (more often spelled "parlor" in the inventories) was commonly used to designate a smaller inner room beside the hall. Nine of the 12 Smith's inventories contained a room specifically called a parlour, as did 33 of Bermuda's 62. This coincides with English and New England terminology more than with that of the Chesapeake, where the inner room was most commonly called a chamber. Parlours were high status bedrooms in much of England, though the term was used to encompass numerous functions of elevated quality. Some Bermudians used their parlours as bedrooms (21 of the 33 inventoried), though by the 1680s the best bedding was increasingly in another room, often a large chamber over the hall in two storey houses. In Richard Jennyns' 1691/92 inventory, the best sleeping accommodations were in the parlour. Moses Knapton's inventory was more characteristic, with the bed in the parlour less valuable than those in all three bedchambers upstairs. Trundle beds in the parlours of wealthy households emphasised that the inner room was more important as private sitting space than as a place to sleep.

Two or three "bedchambers" were sufficient for most of the parish's elite. Most of the 12 households had two, while William Sayle in 1684 had three and Richard Jennyns in 1691/92 had five, both in addition to a parlour containing a bed.

The term "dining room" was much less familiar in Bermuda, though apparently more common in Smith's Parish than in most of Britain and the mainland colonies. Five dining rooms appear in the earliest Smith's inventories, two of them seemingly on an upper floor (in Governor Sayle's and Jennyns' houses). Only three appear in the other 49 Bermuda inventories. The dining room was downstairs in Moses Knapton's big house, and it seems to have duplicated rather than replaced dining arrangements in the hall. Knapton's best table was in the front room, not the room his appraisers identified as specifically for dining. In fact, the Bermuda inventories generally point toward higher-status dining in the hall and suggest the dining room was used as informal eating space except when important visitors joined the family to dine in the hall. That the wealthiest Bermudians sought to separate private or lower-status dining from the hall indicates a notable concern for formality at the front of the house and often gave reason to place the common dining room closer to the kitchen.

"Entry" was the name used for lobbies or passages other than a principal porch. Entries often connected front rooms to rear wings, increasing separation between public and private spaces. "Outlet" is a term repeatedly used in the Bermudian inventories for small peripheral rooms, generally at the rear. Bermudians favoured this over the English terms outshut or outshot, for a small extension with a shed roof below the eaves of the main roof. The majority of outlets contained beds and they commonly were storage space for containers like bottles, boxes and chests, as well as an occasional rose still and beehive.

The old term "buttery" lingers in Bermuda and New England inventories longer than in those written in the southern mainland colonies. Indeed, the term is still widely applied in Bermuda to detached, unheated work buildings where food and drink were stored and sometimes butter produced. Earliest inventories in Smith's Parish (six of 12) seem to record butteries attached to the house and used to store food containers and utensils for its preparation. There are overlapping functions with "milk houses", though the latter more often contained churns, milk pans and tubs clearly related to dairy products. Both butteries and milk houses were more directly associated with the housewives' realm than were kitchens in affluent households.

Most inventories portray a superior lifestyle where meals were prepared at a seemly distance. Kitchens or cookrooms were accommodated in a rear wing, a cellar, or a detached structure. The Smith's Parish inventories always list them last among the domestic spaces, after outlets, butteries, etc., indicating their low status and removed location. Smith's Parish inventories generally list servants in or near the kitchens. Most bonded Native Americans and Africans living in the parish occupied kitchens, cellars and perhaps some lofts. No inventory lists designated quarters, except John Dickinson's for Verdmont, which notes servants' lodgings at the "outroom and buttery" in 1714.

This peripheral placement of cooking and servants parallels the pattern in the slave holding American South and is distinctly different from New England and, it seems, much of England. The New England scholar Abbott Lowell Cummings has argued that cooking remained at the core of even wealthy households there well into the 18th century. Cooking continued in the hall of English houses of the same scale through most of the 17th century. A defining characteristic of wealthy Bermuda households by the late 17th century is removal of cooking a substantial distance from the refined parts of the house.

KNAPTON HOUSE

Two inventories and a surviving building indicate how this collection of rooms could be assembled in two storey houses of the late 17th and early 18th centuries. The 1668 inventory for John Knapton reports that the "hall" and "parler" occupy the ground

Somerville on Middle Road was built about 1700 by the sons of John Gilbert for their stepmother Mary.   *Photograph by Edward A. Chappell.*

floor, and both contain a bedstead. Upstairs there are three rooms, a chamber over the hall, a bedchamber over the parlour and a third space "over the porch". The porch itself is not mentioned, so it was probably open to the air or unfurnished. A buttery and kitchen are listed but not located. As a two storey hall-parlour house with a porch at the front and the stair, buttery and kitchen conceivably attached at the rear, it matches rather closely the core of present Knapton House.

We should be cautious, however, in assuming an early description applies to a similar looking building now extant. The 1703 inventory of Moses Knapton seems more plausibly related to the existing house, but fewer upper chambers are listed in the inventory than exist in the standing house. One can read the present house as having a porch entry, a hall and parlour, a dining room and conceivably a kitchen in the rear wing, with chambers over all five ground floor rooms but not over an outlet behind the parlour. The scale of the rear wing and the absence of a cooking fireplace suggest it could have been rebuilt later in the 18th century.

Widow Gilbert's House

Another combination of document and house offers a more certain match, and together they reveal the architectural intentions of an early Bermuda landowner and his wife. Somerville is a surviving porch-entry, hall-parlour house with a single storey above a cellar. When compared to the 1699 will of John Gilbert, it offers a glimpse into the clients' and builders' design process.

Gilbert wrote a will the year before his death in 1700 that explicitly described a house his sons must build for their step-mother Mary in order to receive their inheritance. Gilbert conceived of it as a stone house with five ground floor spaces and three below, "The Hall Twenty and One foot Long the Parlor fifteene foot Long Sixteen Foot Brode Each, Two back Chambers Each fourteene foot Squaire & with Entry proportionable; and Porch

Twelve foot Square with Cellar under the Hall Parlor and Porch, with Two Chimneys Suitable and hearths and one of the Cellars and Chimney most Convenient Fitted for Kitchen."

The sons' builder constructed an antiquarian's dream house. A rectangular main block was built into the hillside, behind an enclosed porch and in front of a pair of wings containing two bedchambers. Four roofs covered these pieces, decorated with stone balls above multi-stepped parapets at the ends of the ridges. Exterior end chimneys served the hall on the west (left) and parlour on the east (right). The builders included a substantial cellar under the three front rooms and chose to locate the kitchen under the hall. The principal rooms and two chambers open into a little 9' by 5' lobby, the "entry" to which Gilbert referred. All five rooms were well finished, with plastered tray ceilings. In short, the sons followed their father's bidding in constructing a well-finished house with the required spaces.

Interestingly though, the room dimensions reveal a negotiation about shape. When the builders laid out the house, structural rationale won out over explicit specified dimensions and all five rooms were made slightly longer and narrower to reduce the floor joist and roof spans.

The Gilbert dower house resembles another existing single storey, porch-entry, hall-parlour Smith's Parish house. Rose Cottage has a larger hall (423 compared to 313 square feet) and parlour (364 compared to 247 square feet) and another central rear lobby connecting them to two rear wings, one with a kitchen as the rear room. A third single storey house, Oleander Circle, began life early in the 18th century with an enclosed porch in front of the hall and parlour and a third refined room centred on the rear, accessible from both front rooms.

These examples illustrate that by the late 17th century, wealthy Bermudians had developed a means of assembling a house that was two rooms long, a hall and a smaller bed occupied space beside it, often called a parlour. The hall was commonly entered through a porch. The model was flexible, allowing the porch to be omitted and for other rooms to be stacked above or placed at the rear. A rear wing could contain a stair if there was an upper floor, and it could also house a dining room and kitchen, though kitchens were also located in cellars, rear sheds and detached buildings.

As later houses like Tynes Place indicate, everything peripheral could be omitted, to make a house containing only a hall and chamber, with cooking in a cellar. Certainly less wealthy Bermudians occupied one and two room houses where they cooked for themselves in the hall, but early examples of such unpretentious dwellings have disappeared or have not yet been recognised among the present buildings of Smith's Parish.

ATLANTIC CONTEXT

Two aspects of the evidence are significant for understanding the nature of Bermuda society: the arrangement of the houses and the large number of survivors. English houses of similar scale were assembled in a variety of ways by the 17th century, but a common approach was to place a chimney between the hall and parlour, both reached via a lobby in front of the chimney. This lobby-entrance form worked well for Massachusetts Bay, Connecticut and coastal New Hampshire, in New England, as well as early Maryland and Virginia.

By the 1670s, wealthy Virginians and Marylanders moved away from lobby-entrance houses to favour arrangements like those seen in Bermuda with entry to the hall either directly from outside or via a porch, and cooking removed from the hall. Chimneys there, as in Bermuda, came to be placed on the outer ends. The shift is graphically illustrated by changes made to Virginia buildings, as in a Jamestown row of lobby-entrance houses where the central chimneys were later removed and relocated to the ends of each unit, and a direct entry was created.

That New Englanders continued to build centre-chimney, lobby-entrance houses through the 18th century is often ascribed to environmental determinism, that the punishing winters of the northern colonies bred affection for central chimneys and cooking in or immediately behind the hall. But changes to the Jamestown row illustrate that the Chesapeake preference for direct-entry houses had more to do with the order of the household than the escape of heat. Virginia archaeologist Fraser Neiman has argued that the direct or porch entry house flourished in slave holding regions because movement through the house was then centred on the hall, so that the property owners could monitor the actions of

The stairway at Verdmont, centred behind the hall and parlour, led to four upstairs chambers and an unfinished loft.

workers. Historian Cary Carson challenges this, suggesting that pursuit of gentility led wealthy Virginians to create a hall and parlour that worked en suite, as they moved cooking away from the core of the house. Hall-parlour houses were later built by families without slaves in other colonies like New Jersey. Yet, slave owning Bermudians' clear preference for porch-entry houses with suppressed kitchens links them to the Chesapeake and marks a significant move away from the common choices in contemporary England. Evidence that some Bermuda porches opened into both rooms supports Carson's interpretation.

The relatively large number of substantial porch-entry, hall-parlour houses surviving in Bermuda and described in the inventories is significant. Four remain standing in Smith's Parish and several dozen on the island in general, where the population was some 5,862 in 1698, with 547 in Smith's. This compares with only four surviving in all of Virginia and Maryland, whose combined population was 88,164 in 1700. The variation is magnified greatly if one considers the population of other major slave holding colonies like the Carolinas. The survival rate of early Bermuda houses resembles that of southeastern England or Massachusetts Bay and Connecticut more than the Chesapeake, and it illustrates the relative stability of the Bermuda economy by the late 17th century. In spite of vastly larger available land and numbers of settlers delivered to their shores, Virginia and Maryland remained extractive settlements dependent on the uncertain price of tobacco. Bermuda, the second successful English colony in the North Atlantic, turned from tobacco to shipbuilding and trading, which provided a more reliable basis for the accumulation of wealth and more reason to build expensive and survivable houses. Firmly established in the profitable decades following dissolution of the Bermuda Company in 1684, ways of building on the island were slower to change than in the mainland colonies.

VERDMONT

This conservatism was not for lack of precedent. Bermuda's grandest early house, Verdmont, built by John Dickinson sometime between 1694 and 1714, was clearly intended as a dramatic departure from even the superior houses of the island. Like Governor Samuel Day's publicly funded 1700 house (now the Globe Hotel) in St. George's, it was two rooms deep, two storeys high and unified under a single roof. Both in shape and siting, at the top of a hillside overlooking the South Shore, it followed the Euro-

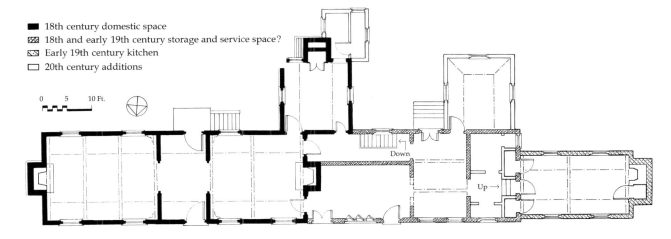

Hinson Hall floor plan, with a hall on the left of a passage, well removed from bedchambers, kitchens and storage spaces.   *Drawn by Edward A. Chappell.*

■ 18th century domestic space
▨ 18th and early 19th century storage and service space?
▧ Early 19th century kitchen
▢ 20th century additions

0   5   10 Ft.

pean model for fashionable houses that would eventually be called Georgian. The two houses set a standard that would only be attempted a century later and not exceeded until the Royal Navy built the vast Commissioner's House at Dockyard in 1823-32. Verdmont's bold stair and the placement of a fireplace in all eight refined rooms also exceeded the accommodation of its Bermuda contemporaries, so far as we know.

On the other hand, Verdmont can also be read as functionally similar to houses like Knapton House. Dickinson entertained well in his hall, with furnishings his inventory valued at £26. By contrast, a rear dining room was modest with furnishings worth £7. A parlour beside the front hall was used for sleeping, though the low bedstead and furnishings were worth only £4. The stairway, centred behind the hall and parlour, led to four first floor chambers and a loft. Dickinson's own chamber was over the hall, with a high bedstead worth £11 and total bedding worth £39. Second best was the chamber over the dining room, with bedding worth £10. So Dickinson used Verdmont much like his parish peers used their less stylish houses.

Formality, Slow in Ascent

Porch-entry houses remained popular well past 1700, but by the second half of the 18th century Bermudians were building porchless houses with a roughly centred passage between a hall and one or more other rooms. Passages had been used earlier between upper chambers in hall-parlour houses to avoid going through one bedroom to reach the other. Councillor Samuel Spofferth seems to have built single storey Hinson Hall on money from privateering as early as 1742, including a 9'1" wide passage between his hall and ground floor chambers. At Stilwell, a heated hall was located to the left of a 9' wide passage with two chambers in a row to the right. At Tanglewood Farm, a 6' passage separated a hall and chamber, eventually with two other spaces in a wing off the chamber. Unlike porches, Bermuda passages may have served only as circulation spaces. Neither the 1771 inventory for Hinson Hall nor the 1833 one for Stillwell list anything in

their passages. Late inventories from other parishes seldom mention passages known to be present, implying they were left largely unfurnished.

Eighteenth century Bermudians seldom built the emphatically formal edifices that made Britain a Georgian nation or that rich American colonists used to recast the landscape from the Carolinas to New England. Like Council President Henry Tucker in St. George's, most Smith's leaders were content to occupy what might be mistaken for cottages, usually on a single refined storey over rough cellars for cooking and storage. This reflects economic limitations in the later 18th century and their impact on community standards rather than remoteness from fashion, because a high percentage of male Bermudians were mariners who saw the great rebuilding of houses in other ports of Britain's empire.

It was in the first decades of the 19th century that dramatic change is evident among the surviving houses in Smith's and other parishes. British naval investment in Bermuda after the American Revolution and War of 1812, as well as privateering, enriched the island economy more than has been recognised, if we correctly read the buildings.

Early 19th century Bermudians experimented with different house plans, including direct entry into a large central hall, with smaller chambers to the sides and rear. Soon after 1809, Thomas William Smith occupied three first floor rooms over a full ground floor of storage spaces at Cotswold, reminiscent of a few merchant houses in St. George's and countless ones in the Caribbean. Design of the outer shell often remained organic, with chimneys and openings placed wherever needed, and decorative parapets apparently increasing in popularity. Smith set stone balls on his roof ridge, much as Somerville builders had done a century before.

What is most recognisable, though, is the formalisation of the best new houses throughout the parishes. The most expensive houses of the circa 1800-1825 era, like Villa Monticello, Villa Mont Clare and Magnolia Hall in Smith's Parish, featured symmetrical fronts, orderly circulation systems, refined finish in the best rooms and removed kitchens. At Villa Monticello and houses outside Smith's, an open front porch was flanked by small projecting rooms that enhanced the apparent harmony of the principal elevation.

The front door of such stylish houses usually opened into a passage between two reception rooms, with bedchambers and less formal sitting or dining rooms in rear wings. Rear lobbies and lateral passages provided access to the wings without intruding on the front spaces.

Multiple roofs continued to cover the various elements rather than a single roof encompassing the whole plan. Neoclassical mantels, doorframes and a few cornices decorated the most chic rooms in the parish, but builders continued to use old-fashioned surrounds for openings and exposed framing in middling houses and most private spaces even in the costliest houses.

KITCHENS, BUTTERIES AND PRIVIES

Historians arguing that slaves were better treated in Bermuda than elsewhere in the empire overlook the grim, dark cellars where early domestic workers laboured and often lived. The changing quality of workspaces reveal that by the 1820s workers and some owners recognised these as unacceptable. Enslaved 18th century cooks most often worked at hearths in cellar kitchens, like those at Somerville, Stilwell and Winterhaven. Light and ventilation were poor by the slaveholders' own standards. Verdmont and Rose Cottage show that kitchens could be detached or placed on the ground floor of rear wings by the 1710s. But it was the early 19th century that saw widespread construction of better kitchens and, to some degree, improved workers' quarters. These were primarily detached buildings with living space above or adjoining a cookroom on the ground floor.

A free standing cookroom with quarters was built as an alternative to the kitchen below the hall at Winterhaven about 1830. A detached kitchen with two rooms on the ground floor was included when Villa Mont Clare was constructed about 1812, and a two storey kitchen also accompanied construction of Cotswold. Separate workers' quarters distinct from kitchens are now rare, but J.C.S. Green's 1819 sketch of The Hermitage shows a duplex for two families of workers, each with its own doorway and glazed windows.

Moderately improved kitchens and associated quarters in Ber-

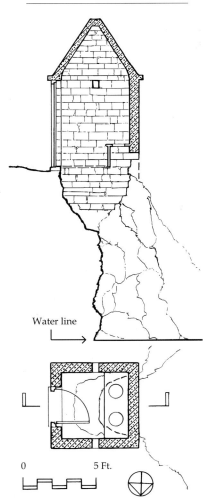

Early oven location

■ c. 1812
▨ Late 19th century
▧ c. 1900

0   5 ft.

Floor plan of a detached kitchen at Villa Mont Clare. *Drawn by Edward A. Chappell.*

Water line

0   5 Ft.

Peniston's Shipyard privy at Magnolia Hall. *Drawn by Edward A. Chappell.*

muda are part of a pattern that extends to slave holding regions in North America. Visibly raising their standards was an accommodation to growing abolitionist sentiment in Britain and the US, and it may have become a strategy for retaining Bermudian workers who gained freedom in 1834.

Removing the sounds and smells of kitchens from cellars also enhanced the refinement of reception rooms, like the halls at Somerville and Stilwell, and reflected the general effort by households throughout the 19th century to organise their functions and segregate refined space. For example, controlling how service was delivered became an important concern to comfortable residents of Smith's Parish. Owners made dramatic alterations like constructing stairways up through old chimneys and hearths to create internal routes from cookrooms to dining spaces, replacing arrangements that forced servants to carry food outside and in through the front door. When Sea View was built circa 1871, a direct route from kitchen to dining room consumed space that otherwise could have enlarged the principal rooms.

Efforts at refining domestic life included the removal of other work and storage. Buildings in Smith's and other parishes show that butteries ceased to be inconspicuous parts of landowners' houses. To a degree, they were replaced with free standing butteries as locations for food storage and production. The best of these were durable little structures with corbelled stone roofs rather than wood framed roofs covered with limestone slates.

The number of close stools and chamber pots in early houses may suggest that privies were not always as predictable a presence at Smith's Parish houses as they became by the later 19th century. Two settings in which durable privies resembling the pyramidal roofed butteries were built early in the century are at relatively wealthy households, and conversely, at workplaces with concentrations of labourers or soldiers. Boatyards at both Stilwell and Magnolia Hall had substantial stone walled privies built at the shoreline. The latter survives, in rustic condition, with a high corbelled stone roof and a seat located 14 feet above the sea.

GOTHIC BERMUDA

Academic architecture in the 19th century was peculiar throughout the larger European world in the degree to which it was reformulated by the study and incorporation of ancient idioms of design. Just as earlier Bermudians had employed Roman classicism only sparingly and selectively, as in quirky little pediments over the central door and rear window at Oleander Circle, few 19th century residents chose to build slavishly in the new fashions of Europe or America.

The greatest exceptions are the late 19th century Anglican churches, most explicitly the Cathedral in Hamilton, where every effort was made to create an Oxford Movement edifice virtually identical to English Anglican churches of its era. Bermuda's Anglican parish

The Gothic tower of St. Mark's Church. *Photograph by Carey M. Maddern,* 1981.

churches were more moderated by the island's building tradition, and often because they evolved through various building campaigns. They reveal how parishioners resisted high church liturgy, "smells and bells", and their full Gothic settings until half a century after their British beginnings. Ultimately, Anglican liturgy moved towards the Oxford norm, influenced, like educated speech, by formal English training, in this case, training of ministers.

St. Mark's evolution exemplifies the dramatic and late shift to ecumenical Gothic. The present church was built in 1846-1848 to replace the old parish church which generally resembled porch-entry houses. An 1870 view shows that the new church began as a larger but relatively simple box with ends of three bays and long walls of five, and by then it had acquired a south porch. The church had mildly pointed arches but pedimented gables and plain pilaster strips at the corners. Drama arrived when a great Gothic tower and altar projection were added and the main block richly medievalised. The pilasters were rebuilt as stepped buttresses, and their caps grew to be a Gothic cornice that wraps the building, including the choir. Windows were rebuilt in a sharper silhouette appropriate for stained glass and crowned with Gothic heads. The tower is the pièce de résistance, 102 feet high, with three levels of ziggurats above an open porch and lancet window arrangements, and a high spire braced lightly with diminutive flying buttresses. What makes the church look at home in Smith's Parish is the stucco, not the shape.

Inside, the old low vaulted plaster ceiling remained hung from the original roof frame, but the new choir was given a full Gothic treatment, featuring an exposed truss roof with long curved braces descending to stone corbels on the walls. Imported materials were favoured, so mahogany was used for west and chancel screens, altar rail and a delicate Gothic altar and pulpit heavily decorated by the gentleman carver Arthur Wilkinson. Stained glass completes the paean to English ecclesiasticism. The Trott family installed a window with plant materials in the style of William Morris, and the Zuills added one featuring angels with the large, poignant eyes of Jane Morris, muse of the pre-Raphaelites. Because of its low visibility, the vestry was left with its old noncommittal style, including plain corner pilasters.

ORANGE GROVE

There were earlier, more improvisational efforts to improve the appearance of Bermuda's architectural vernacular. One could argue that the worldly William Edward Zuill drew on eclectic sources to defy tradition when he created the core of the present Orange Grove about 1850-55. He housed a large reception room, rear circulation space and upper bedrooms in a single pedimented central block two storeys high, flanked by single storey wings. This three part composition was popular among some bookish Americans in the late 18th and early 19th centuries, and it ultimately derives from the 16th century Vicenzan architect Andrea Palladio through his 18th century English admirers. Zuill illustrated his preference for panache over practicality by making the roof slopes nearly flat over the wings so they could hide behind a classical parapet. He used bold Greek revival mouldings to enclose edges of the roofs.

The freely interpreted classicism is most explicit in the columns Zuill attached to the front. Like most later Greek revival work in Bermuda, these are simplified and crisp, partly because they are rendered in soft stone and stucco. No Bermudians followed Zuill's lead in Palladian composition, but the emphasis on broad flat surfaces and use of simple Greek based mouldings became standard in the late 19th and early 20th centuries.

ISLAND GREEK

Bermudians made international styles distinctively their own and sometimes maintained them much longer than elsewhere in the world. The modern popularisation of classical Greek architecture is usually said to begin with Englishmen James Stuart and Nicholas Revett's first publication of *Antiquities of Athens* in 1762, but in faraway Bermuda Orange Grove stands squarely in the first generation. Buildings influenced by the Greek revival were built here until after the First World War.

Bermudians generally eschewed the most characteristic elements like the small classical porches sheltering the front door on thousands of middle class houses in places as different as west London and upstate New York in the 1830s and 1840s. Rather, island builders favoured squarish houses with flat projecting bands vaguely resembling pilasters at the corners. Bermudians had occasionally used corner piers since the era of Rose Cottage, but the new ones were completely flat, usually connecting with horizontal bands at the tops of walls and edges of gables and without bases or caps. Eaves were buttoned up with plain stuccoed mouldings or bands. Imported timber made it possible to cover spans more than one room deep, permitting roofs to have a broad, relatively flat appearance in sympathy with the

Orange Grove's stuccoed porch and central block.   *Photograph by Edward A. Chappell.*

wall. Such roofs were convenient for a four room plan, often a living room, kitchen and two bedrooms. The result, often with no cellar, is an island creation, without direct counterparts in Britain or North America.

Inside, Greek revival design employed wide, smooth, unbroken surfaces for visual effect, in contrast to earlier neoclassical emphasis on delicately articulated woodwork. This was often accomplished in Bermuda and elsewhere by omitting cornices and chair rails, so that hard, carefully trowelled plaster extended up the walls and across ceilings, preferably flat ceilings, without interruption. In Bermuda, the same starched shirt aesthetic was expressed on exteriors with walls rendered in stucco kept perfectly flat and smooth, contrasting with the uneven, splotchy stucco common on even the best Bermuda buildings from genesis until the 1850s. Builders created smooth roof surfaces by setting two layers of slates with their edges butted together and staggered. Although smooth roofs never reached the popularity of the wall treatments, they illustrate how much effort could be expended to hide construction elements and make buildings appear less natural or traditional.

THE SUBURBAN HOUSE

Change to larger and more decoratively adventurous houses cannot be explained simply by new technological capabilities of

certain Bermuda builders, but those capabilities did facilitate change. Edward Peniston brought steam powdered production of architectural woodwork to Smith's Parish by the 1870s. His newspaper advertisements indicate that he made trim at what was sometimes called a "sash and blind factory". Mechanisation allowed builders like Peniston to produce elaborate interior woodwork and US style fancy wooden porches at a lower price. This and the importation of North American pine and fir helped some middle class Bermudians acquire larger and more decorated houses, to new international standards, though hand cutting of Bermuda stone seems to have resisted mechanisation.

Efforts at improving agriculture had met with limited success and land starved Bermuda began to focus on tourism in the 1890s. It was then that successful merchants and professionals formed a market for builders and suppliers like Peniston. Their houses were more splashy in appearance, more expansive in scale and more eclectic in ornamentation. Ultimate sources of their varied styles were British designers like John Nash, Charles Eastlake and Richard Norman Shaw, but the compositions were largely filtered through US and Canadian work of less famous pedigree and were outwardly modified to suit Bermuda stone construction and Bermudians' independent taste.

Veterinarian Elmore Reid Mercer and wife Julia Zuill Mercer's house called Aldie is a case in point. Mercer had studied at New York University and practised in New Jersey before returning to Bermuda about 1890 and building a fashionable house near Store Hill, on property that afforded space for sizable lawns and gardens. The house has two storeys on a high base and is picturesquely massed, with off centre wings intersecting at right angles and window bays projecting on three sides. Exterior finish is patently Bermudian, with smooth stuccoed walls, raised bands at the edges, and Italianate masonry brackets below a stone roof.

Interior accommodation was less regionally distinct. Indeed, it illustrates the aspirations of countless comfortable families beyond Bermuda. Aldie provided an open porch, an entrance hall made impressive with a machine elaborated oak stair, two addi-

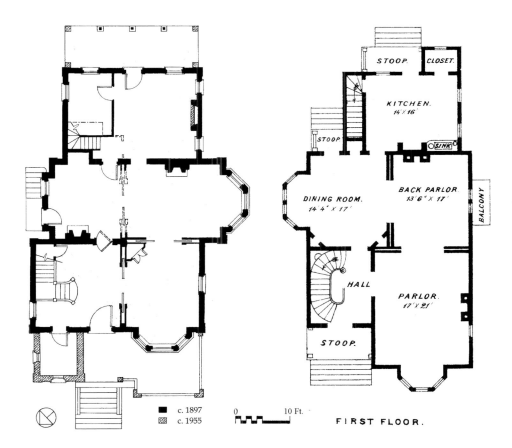

Ground floor plan of Aldie, left, drawn by Edward A. Chappell, and a "Suburban Residence", right, by New Jersey architect D.B. Provoost, published in 1873.

tional reception spaces, a family dining room, family bedrooms over the reception spaces, and a rear kitchen connected via back stairs to bedrooms for one or more resident servants. Large pairs of doors could slide into wall pockets to create a circuit of four sizable front spaces, sufficient for large parties.

Just how close this arrangement was to US houses of its scale can be seen by comparison with plans by the Elizabeth, New Jersey designer D.B. Provoost for a "Suburban Residence", published in 1873. While the exterior finish is completely different, the arrangement and scale of rooms is very similar. Glimmerview built by the Mercers' sister and brother-in-law is a larger example, even more orchestrated in its asymmetry, with several more rooms and a three storey tower that makes explicit reference to the Italian villa style. The point is the degree to which houses like Aldie and Glimmerview share a taste for how to structure family life and entertainment, rather than that the Mercers and their builder used the New Jersey plans.

Darrell's Store and House

Aldie and the grander Glimmerview represent idealised suburban houses on large lots sought by a few residents of the parish. The general desire for houses providing separate spaces for sitting, dining, cooking and sleeping was more pervasive among middle class Bermudians on both sides of the perceived colour line. Clarence Orester Darrell (1859-1922) was a successful black businessman who owned two stores in Flatts and one in Hamilton.

Both of his Flatts stores survive, a grocery in Smith's Parish and a dry goods store across the Hamilton Parish line. The former is a combination of store and residence, expressed in the building's form. It is L-shaped, with the store occupying the street frontage of a long façade facing Middle Road. The residence occupies the gable fronted two bays to the northeast (right) and, at least by the end of Darrell's life, the whole upper floor of the building. A separate doorway beside the shop front opened into a well lighted foyer which led to a dining room and kitchen on the ground floor and upstairs to a sitting room and four bedrooms, the best two opening onto a side porch. Darrell's granddaughter Gloria McPhee describes a good piano in the sitting room and a richly carved Jamaican mahogany bed in the couple's bedroom.

It is said that the building predates Darrell's ownership, but it served his spatial needs, and the details are an elaborated version of what he used when building a range of three workers' houses on Clarendon Road just over the parish line. The Darrell house/store was constructed in the restrained Greek style, with wide piers used at the corners and to frame the face of the house. Characteristically, simple masonry cornices seal the eaves and break out over the piers, making them resemble pilasters. The gable ends are finished with very low sloping parapets, just enough to seal the edges of the roof slates and to suggest a severe pediment.

The design grammar could be intensified for richer effect or simplified so that it relied solely on flat bands framing each wall.

Counter to Edward Peniston's profusion of machine sawn and turned exterior woodwork, the Bermuda Greek elaboration is spare, integral and supremely durable. Window frames are recessed in the walls and their sills are made of stuccoed stone.

In the decades after 1890, a Bermuda population swelled by Portuguese and Caribbean immigrants used the simple idiom to build orderly houses, stores and churches, ones that happened to contrast with the picturesque pre industrial houses occupied by most of the island's wealthy and poor. An African-Bermudian congregation used it for Harrington Sound Gospel Chapel in 1904, dressed with stucco keystones over round headed windows, and a white congregation did likewise with Gothic pointed arches at Wesleyan Centenary Methodist Church. Recent Bermuda National Trust president Wayne Jackson describes how black families with insufficient money to buy finished houses fêted teams of skilled and unskilled friends who would construct parts of a house in exchange for food and fellowship at weekends.

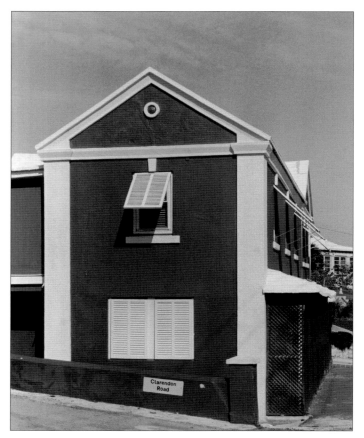

Clarendon was a combination of store and residence for businessman Clarence Orester Darrell. *Photograph by Edward A. Chappell.*

they clearly partook of the movement favouring relatively informal houses with direct entry into a living room, and incorporating a kitchen at the rear and one or two bedrooms, with a bath. Bungalows stimulated popularity of stuccoed porches with heavy masonry piers, making them an element in formation of the modern Bermuda house, still commonly built today.

Bungalows also merge seamlessly with 20th century houses and apartments in what can be seen as a resort idiom. Drawing inspiration from the Caribbean and coastal North America, and conceivably from English seaside resorts, it too is freewheeling in the use of concrete decoration, assembled as parts of porches or affixed to exterior walls. Such houses threw off the constraints of the more sober Bermuda Greek buildings, though at the cost of being less distinctly Bermudian. Neither showed much concern for the old ways of building.

BERMUDA BUNGALOWS

By the 1910s, builders offered for sale to middle class and some labouring Bermudians houses that were more festive, less sombre. Drawing selectively on British and American bungalows, they exposed the eaves, omitted wall piers, gathered windows into ensembles and extended low roofs to cover wings and porches. Living spaces were usually confined to one level, which extended into large room-like porches. Front rooms could be slightly more decorated, and the plans could be arranged to include inside bathrooms and interior access to habitable cellar spaces.

One influential aspect of bungalows was their celebration of personality. Even in homes for people of modest means, porches or front steps could take an idiosyncratic form. Hillsides like that at Flatts were aesthetically appropriate for simple bungalows such as the Burgess family's Villa Conti at 73 Middle Road, where steps snake up the hill toward a stuccoed porch. Furthermore, mainland bungalow developments also offered precedent for building houses closer together than many people had experienced in the Bermuda countryside.

Most observers would not think of such houses explicitly as bungalows of either the Home Counties or California stripe, but

BERMUDA REVIVAL

Tourism was nurtured into a principal support for the Bermuda economy in the 1920s when government spending and popular attention was focused on this resource. By the 1890s a market was created by affluent Americans who sought seasonal release from the irritants of urban life. Tourism cultivated new interest in old Bermuda buildings for multiple reasons. One obviously was the kind of tourists the island sought: educated and sophisticated travellers, primarily from the US. These were people who could choose a destination more distant than their own coastal retreats if the alternative had special cachet. Bermuda was closer than Europe, and it was seen as less formal, more restful than Britain and the continent. Yet as an outpost of the British Empire, it offered some of the same worldly appeal.

Experiencing regionalism was an important goal of vacation travel in the 1920s and 1930s and folk buildings were as essential as distinctive topography and endemic species. Nowhere was there an accessible and appealing destination whose British colonial culture was better expressed in its architecture than Bermuda.

It was an era when great efforts were made to study and preserve vernacular culture viewed as pre industrial, regionally distinct and threatened by modernisation. From Welsh farmhouses to Appalachian folk tales, regional culture became important to educated people. Harvard architecture professor John S. Humphreys brought Bermuda's old buildings into this realm when he published *Bermuda Houses* in 1923. In it, he presented picturesque images like the front of Somerville and the rear of Oleander Circle and called for new design recapturing the old manner. His call was answered in the 1930s, with

Steps lead up the hill toward a stuccoed porch at Villa Conti on Flatts Hill. *Photograph by Edward A. Chappell.*

Benjamin Chauncey Outerbridge and his wife Leah Montgomery in 1932 and designed by the architect George Houston Hutchings. Hutchings studied architecture at McGill University, and practised in Montreal and Boston before the stock market crash brought him home to Bermuda in 1929. Hutchings appears intent on overlooking no traditional precedent. One approached Outerlea through a timber arched gateway facing a roof with various curved and stepped gables. A masonry

the first generation of buildings for which there are numerous known architects and surviving drawings.

Not that Bermudians built many new buildings in the 18th century idiom specifically to attract sophisticated travellers and satisfy Harvard professors. Rather, the new focus on distinctiveness encouraged both residents and visitors to look approvingly upon what made the island distinctive, architecturally and otherwise.

Landscape painting is somewhat analogous. The island's character had inspired artists like Thomas Driver to paint landscapes scattered with buildings since the early 19th century. More famous artists began to come primarily to paint these scenes after circa 1890. In the following decades, visiting and resident artists focused more exclusively on simple old houses in their unadorned settings. The Bermudian sisters Catherine and Ethel Tucker produced art specifically for the tourist trade, most including a pretty stuccoed cottage set amid colourful foliage beside a quiet lane. The Tucker paintings were shaped and labelled, ready for postcard reproduction. Such popular art as well as superior romantic landscape painting and engraving flourished in newly touristic Bermuda, with the latter collected by Bermudians as well as their visitors. In short, the 1920s saw a heightened appreciation for what defined Bermuda visually and culturally, and educated Bermudians internalised these values.

Designers from varied backgrounds produced revival buildings in Smith's Parish. Lawrence H. Smart was a landscape member of the Royal Institute of British Architects who moved to Bermuda in 1926 and worked on Josephine Dodge Wilkinson's Coral Ledge beside Harrington Sound in 1930. Six years later he designed Channelway, a substantial two storey house for C. Vail Zuill, a manager of the Bank of Bermuda. Channelway is a more mature, well resolved building cast in a very creditable Vernacular revival style. Neoclassical mantels and a curved stairway gave the interior an eclectic flavour, but outwardly it could be mistaken for an unpretentious Bermuda house of the 1830s.

Channelway is more subtle than nearby Outerlea, built for

porch, pyramidal roofed buttery, moulded round window heads and a central chimneystack are presented like trophies along the front of the house. Outerlea belongs among the 1920s English and North American suburbs where Olde English, Mediterranean and Dutch Colonial style houses were built side-by-side in a manner characterised by the English humorist Osbert Lancaster as "Bypass Variegated". This generation of costumed houses usually provided five to eight rooms and several baths.

The range of people involved in revival of the old Bermuda style is further illustrated by Timberly. In 1938 an engineer named Cyril Hilton Smith designed a house for his friend and fellow Bermudian, Louis S. Mowbray, curator of the Bermuda Aquarium. Louis and Nellie Mowbray chose a hilltop site with a small rolling yard that offered 180 degree views of the North Shore and directly overlooked Gibbet Island. An old house had been cut into the back of the hillside and the Mowbrays left its picturesque ruins as a counterpoint to the Bermuda cedars. What appeared to be the porch was actually the front end of a transverse passage between bedrooms and a living room facing the yard. Smith gave this best room a tray ceiling and decorated its fireplace with Spanish tiles that Mowbray himself salvaged from the 1936 wreck of the *Cristobal Colon.* The house extended down the back of the hill, with a stair in the passage descending to the dining room and kitchen, so the two storey elevation was hidden from the front. Looking only at floor plans, one might guess the house was on the mainland as easily as Bermuda. What ties it and similar Smith's Parish houses to the island and its era is the simple use of white stucco on walls and roof, open eaves and a sympathetic, unassertive placement on the uneven hillside.

ONIONS AND CRAM

The canonical figure who hovers over the revival is Wilfred Onions, whose active career extended from about 1933 until his suicide in 1959. Onions went on an extended tour of Europe in 1933 after finishing architectural classes at McGill. Most of his attention in Europe, his notebooks reveal, was on Modernism.

There are only a handful of sketches of traditional English details; otherwise the pages are filled with careful notes on contemporary architects, their new buildings and their new concepts about planning. He was famously taken with the sculptural quality of the 1909-23 Stockholm City Hall, but was equally interested in the planning of small modern houses, and he carefully drew exhibition models by Walter Gropius and others at an influential Berlin exhibition.

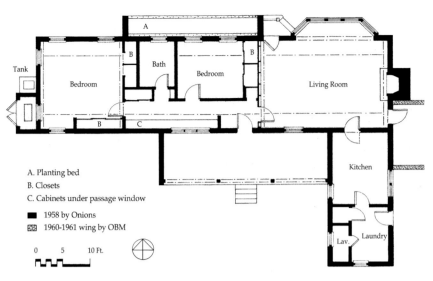

A. Planting bed
B. Closets
C. Cabinets under passage window

■ 1958 by Onions
▨ 1960-1961 wing by OBM

0   5   10 Ft.

Somersall floor plan. *Drawn by Edward A. Chappell after Wilfred Onions.*

in a class quite by itself, neither English, Spanish nor American, but emphatically of the islands themselves. The little stone cottages are masterpieces of simple and effective design, and many of the great houses are fine expressions of a stately and cultivated life." He says "nine-tenths of Bermuda is still unspoiled and singularly beautiful" and expects it will in-

After his return from Europe, Onions refocused on old Bermuda buildings, which he sought out and carefully measured with his family members and friends. This process of recording and learning merged with his modernist interest in simplicity and enabled him to design very handsome and unassuming houses for contemporary use.

Onions designed Channelway Cottage as a small second house for Vail and Janette Zuill in the early 1950s and was one of the defining contributors to a book of plans for relatively small houses, published by the Bermuda Historical Monuments Trust in 1948. He aided William E.S. Zuill with adjustments at Orange Grove and in 1958 he designed a two bedroom house for son William and his bride Joyce Zuill. The latter house, called Somersall, has a thoroughly modern plan, as informal as what Onions saw in 1933 Berlin. Its traditional details were chosen with freedom but deliberation and restraint, like a small sash window through which Joyce Zuill could watch the front porch and a large window bay from which the family and guests could take in the view from the Peak. No elaborate gables or faux butteries here. Onions set the standard for grammatical and understated houses that expressed a graceful informality.

The Bermuda Trade Development Board published a large folio in 1936, *Residence in Bermuda*, as a prospectus for foreigners, primarily US citizens, considering residence on the island, especially within an exclusive new development at Tucker's Town. It explains taxation and limited suffrage, discusses the relaxed lifestyle and liberally illustrates scenic landscapes and leisurely life available to a cultivated, affluent audience. All the buildings shown are in the old island style. The book concludes, remarkably, with comments by the prestigious American Gothic style architect Ralph Adams Cram and landscape designer Frederick L Olmsted Jr. Cram describes Bermuda as an almost perfect refuge for travellers and extols its indigenous domestic architecture, which he had admired for more than a decade. He respectfully writes that it "is

creasingly be a winter residence "for many from the mainland who appreciate this sort of society and environment, and I personally feel that all that is necessary to extend this usage is the curbing of ill advised building. There are many new houses recently erected in the islands, of great beauty and perfect propriety. The architects who are carrying on their profession there are, as they have proved, wholly competent to maintain and prolong the best traditions. All that is necessary is to let them have their way."

BERMUDA MODERNISM

Their way changed somewhat in succeeding years. A subject that has not received all it is due is the sometimes thoughtful use of modern design in the parishes, outside the city where Modernism put down roots. Beyond Onions' own interest in Modernism and tradition, one can see some connections between the two. The revival of the old Bermuda style of building was a means of banishing the seeming excess of ornamentation and unnatural symmetry of some late 19th century construction, and perhaps it offered a less proletarian alternative to bungalows. Buildings covered with a continuous white lime crust, over walls and roofs, and equally white interiors open above the walls unbounded by conventional ceilings have a certain minimalist quality.

The two idioms merge most literally at Stilwell where in 1968 Onions, Bouchard & McCulloch architects designed a modernist atrium house with a glass walled passage circling an open courtyard, incorporating the picturesque early house. The traditional front faces the North Shore and road. At the side and rear one encounters straight stuccoed walls, hardwood grilles and a plan traditional in Rome, not the Somers Isles. Clients Henry and Ronica Watlington resisted only the central fountain.

On a much larger scale, a square classroom building with three storeys of metal windows combined into shallow recessed bays with arched heads stands behind the Italianate face of the Whitney Institute. The school addition employs a favourite neoclassical way of arranging openings in a wall but is thoroughly clean and modern.

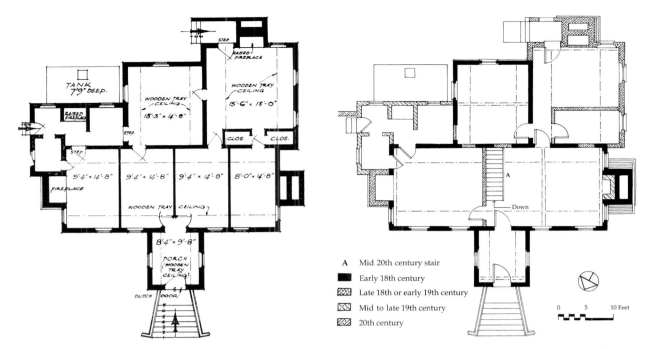

A	Mid 20th century stair
■	Early 18th century
▨	Late 18th or early 19th century
▨	Mid to late 19th century
▨	20th century

0   5   10 Feet

Oleander Circle ground-floor plan, left, drawn by D.M. Kirkpatrick as a model for new houses, in *Bermuda Cottage Plans*, published by the Bermuda Historical Monuments Trust, 1948, and right, by Edward A. Chappell to illustrate evidence for its development, 2004.

PRESERVATION AND SURVIVAL

The Bermuda revival, like most architectural resuscitations, was concerned with saving early buildings as well as re-establishing the traditional style. Both natives and expatriates began restoring Smith's Parish houses in the 1920s, including Knapton House and earlier work at Stilwell. Among the most serious and energetic antiquarians were Hereward Trott Watlington and Dr. Henry Campbell Wilkinson. Wilkinson was a physician who wrote books about Bermuda history and was a friend of William Graves Perry, senior partner in the architectural firm that planned the restoration of Williamsburg, Virginia, in the 1920s and 1930s. Watlington was a businessman and artist who collected Bermuda antiques, restored and remodelled old houses in the Bermuda style and restored a north Italian villa where he lived part of each year. Wilkinson restored the cruciform house Tankfield in Paget and Watlington influenced his nephew Henry Laing to restore the derelict Rose Cottage in 1965.

Together they led the creation of the Bermuda Historical Monuments Trust, predecessor of the present Bermuda National Trust, in 1937. The Trust's initial purpose was to acquire and protect especially intact examples of early architecture. In 1951, the Trust bought Verdmont, seen as significant and unspoiled by modernisation, including electricity and plumbing. It had, in the founders' words, the best Tudor stair in Bermuda. Watlington, Wilkinson and Onions formed a BHMT subcommittee that planned repairs and restoration. These focused on structural stabilisation and selective removal of features thought to denature the house, most visibly a two storey front porch replaced by a balcony designed by Onions. Since the 1950s, Verdmont has become one of the Trust's two principal house museums, both furnished with exuberant collections of Bermuda decorative arts.

The Trust has grown from its antiquarian beginnings into an organisation that owns 48 historic buildings and nine nature reserves. It is now the largest private landowner in Bermuda and is among the most influential of such organisations in the world, relative to the size of the population. The broadening reflects change in international perspective on preservation, with the recognition that whole landscapes and communities rather than solely the oldest or finest individual buildings are worth protecting in the face of wholesale development.

This is particularly true in Bermuda, an island of only 13,350 acres. The concluding remarks in *Residence in Bermuda* were written by Frederick Law Olmstead Jr., whose father designed New York's Central Park. Like architect Cram, Olmstead had visited Bermuda and loved what he saw. His final observations seem directed more towards Bermudians than prospective settlers, when he wrote that the island must maintain the intimate scale of the landscape to remain a refuge from the modern world.

Bermuda is now thoroughly modern, with traffic jams and high rise corporate headquarters, but the matter of scale remains central to the character of life here. Its roads, yards and gardens have a delicacy that links them to parts of England most often designated as conservation areas, not to the mass produced wastelands of North America.

Accelerating scale as well as the extent of development is a concern for Bermudians of varied income and architectural taste. Three aggressive driveways or one posturing condominium can spoil a hillside long considered part of Bermuda's visual identity. Ultimately, preserving a diverse architectural heritage and designing new buildings that are sympathetic in scale can combine with conservation of open land to form a mission that will benefit everyone, far into the future.

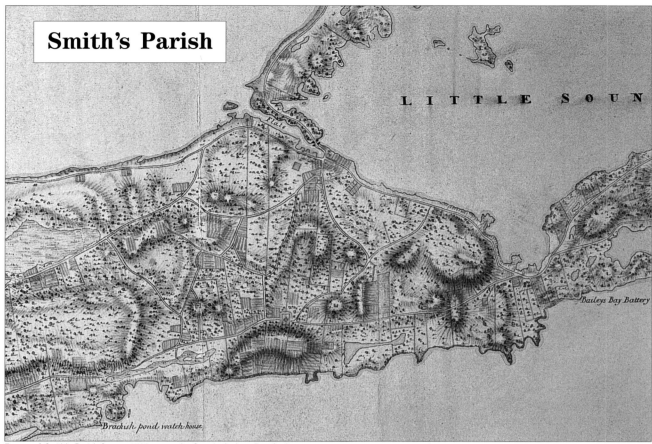

Smith's Parish

Extract of Smith's Parish from a 1793 survey by Captain Andrew Durnford. *'A survey of the Islands of Bermuda by Captain Andrew Durnford Royal Engineers assisted by Mr. Henry Lauzun, Draughtsman' 1793, (detail). The National Archives, Britain (TNA) MPH1/137 (WO 78/160).*

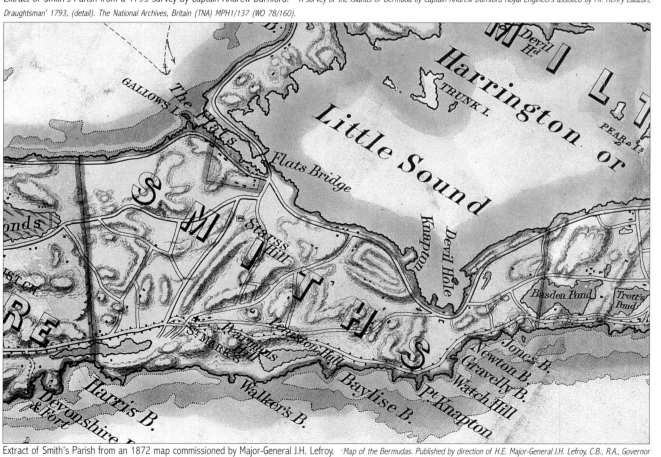

Extract of Smith's Parish from an 1872 map commissioned by Major-General J.H. Lefroy. *'Map of the Bermudas. Published by direction of H.E. Major-General J.H. Lefroy, C.B., R.A., Governor and Commander-in-Chief of the Bermudas' 1872 (detail). The National Archives, Britain (TNA) CO 700/BERMUDA14.*

1
Smith's Parish

A white road of crushed limestone, edged with wind blown cedar trees, leads to John Smith's Bay. This photograph of South Shore Road, west of John Smith's Bay, was taken by US serviceman Alexander P. Malecki who was stationed in Bermuda during the Second World War. *Emeralds On A Silver Zone, Early Colour Photography in Bermuda 1939-1960, 1992, page 21.*

Smith's Parish was named after Sir Thomas Smythe, or Smith, a shareholder in the Bermuda Company and a leading figure in British trading and colonial history. Historically it was called by the colloquial name of Harris' Bay.

The parish lies on the eastern end of the main island of Bermuda between Devonshire and Hamilton parishes. It stretches to the sea on three sides, to the North and the South Shore as well as to Harrington Sound, but somewhat curiously its boundary does not extend to Flatts Inlet. This seemingly obvious port was instead awarded to Hamilton Parish in the Richard Norwood division of the island in 1663.

Shareholders in Smith's Parish, in the Norwood allocation, were granted parcels of common ground on Flatts Hill (*see chapter 7*) as well as in the neighbourhood of what is now known as Captain Williams' Bay in the south. This allocation of half acre common ground lots was designed to encourage village development around convenient outlets to the sea.

Sir Thomas Smythe (circa 1558-1625), owned five shares in Smith's Parish, or Smith's Tribe as it was earlier called. His holding was in the centre of the parish and stretched from the southern side of Flatts Inlet to the South Shore.

In 1612 he was Governor of the Virginia Company, a joint stock concern, which sent the *Plough* with the first settlers to Bermuda and in 1616 upon the formation of the Bermuda, or Somers Islands, Company Sir Thomas Smythe became its first Governor. He served until 1621 and again from 1623 until his death in 1625.

The Bermuda Company met at his spacious house off Fenchurch Street in London. On his death he left much of his sizeable fortune to charity and several of his bequests are still in existence in England. The Sir Thomas Smythe's Charity, for instance, provides pension benefits to elderly residents of 26 parishes in the vicinity of Tonbridge and Tunbridge Wells in Kent.

Sir Thomas Smythe left £50 for the erection of a church in Bermuda, although there is no record of how this money was used. This was the time when the Assembly had decided to increase the number of churches from four for the whole island to one in every parish, so it is conceivable that his contribution went to the first church in Smith's Parish (*see chapters 7 and 11*).

The leading entrepreneur and shipping magnate of his day, Sir Thomas Smythe was head of every, and founder of most, of the English trading companies. He was Founder Governor of the East India Company and was also Governor of the Russia or Muscovy, Levant and the French companies. He served as Special Ambassador to the Tsar of Russia and was a major promoter of voyages to find a Northwest Passage to the Orient.

Smith's Parish Uncovered

Archaeology is the study of man's past through the objects and materials he leaves behind. In most cases this information is hidden, literally buried in the historic landscape and often all that may remain of a site is a casual reference in an archival document or a cryptic marking on an aged map. It is through archaeological research and excavation that Bermuda's "lost" history may be uncovered.

There are many examples of this sort of history in Bermuda and Smith's Parish is no exception. Once, a series of four fortifications, dating from the mid to late 18th century, defended its southern shore. We know from documentary sources that Newton's Bay Fort overlooked Newton's and John Smith's Bay, Albouy's Fort was situated on Albouy's Point and Harris' Bay Fort guarded Spencer's Point. However their exact locations remain a mystery because none of these structures have survived intact, if at all. Fortunately in the 1980s archaeologists re-discovered the ruins of the fourth site, Sears' Fort, entrenched above the cliffs at Pokiok and during these excavations they unearthed a small D-shaped redoubt of soft limestone partially built into bedrock.

Similarly, from church records we know that St. Mark's Anglican Church, completed in 1848, had two predecessors. The location of the first church, built of wood in the mid 17th century but destroyed by a hurricane in 1712, has yet to be positively identified, although Richard Norwood's *Book of Survey of 1662-3* places it on the Parish common ground, located on modern Flatts Hill.

The location of the second church, however, is not in question. Harris' Bay Church was built during the early 18th century in what is now the St. Mark's Church graveyard. Despite being built of stone, it met a similar fate to its predecessor when it collapsed during renovations undertaken in 1846. In 1998 a team from the Bermuda Maritime Museum, the Bermuda National Trust, the College of William and Mary and the church vestry carefully excavated a series of test trenches, without disturbing any of the existing graves. The partial stone foundations of the Harris' Bay Church were uncovered as well as the remains of a second unidentified building. The National Trust followed these excavations in 2004 with a geophysics survey of the graveyard using a magnetometer to detect any further subterranean features without the need for excavation. Ultimately the results were inconclusive and further archaeological research is required.

An excavation was undertaken at Winterhaven Farmhouse by archaeologists from Colonial Williamsburg in 1997 to try to ascertain the building's original appearance and possible construction date. The results indicated that the front steps, cellar and chimney were built at the same time as the house, while the ceramics recovered suggested an 18th century origin.

Geophysics surveys were also conducted at the Jennings Land burial ground to try to find an unmarked grave as well as at the gardens of Verdmont to try to locate the remains of timber outbuildings and the position of the original driveway. Again the results proved inconclusive but future geophysics trials using different methods are planned for 2005.

Excavation is usually the last stage of archaeological research, so recent projects have focused on surveying and cataloguing potential archaeological sites using Geographic Information System (GIS) technology. In Smith's Parish 33 houses listed in Richard Norwood's 1663 survey and 187 buildings included on Savage's 1898-99 Ordnance Survey were catalogued, while the sites of ten ruins, including Spanish Rock and a privy overhanging the North Shore, were also identified. This is not only an effective research tool for archaeologists, it is also an important preservation tool enabling archaeological sites to be assessed and excavated beforehand, should they be threatened with development. *R.M.P.L.*

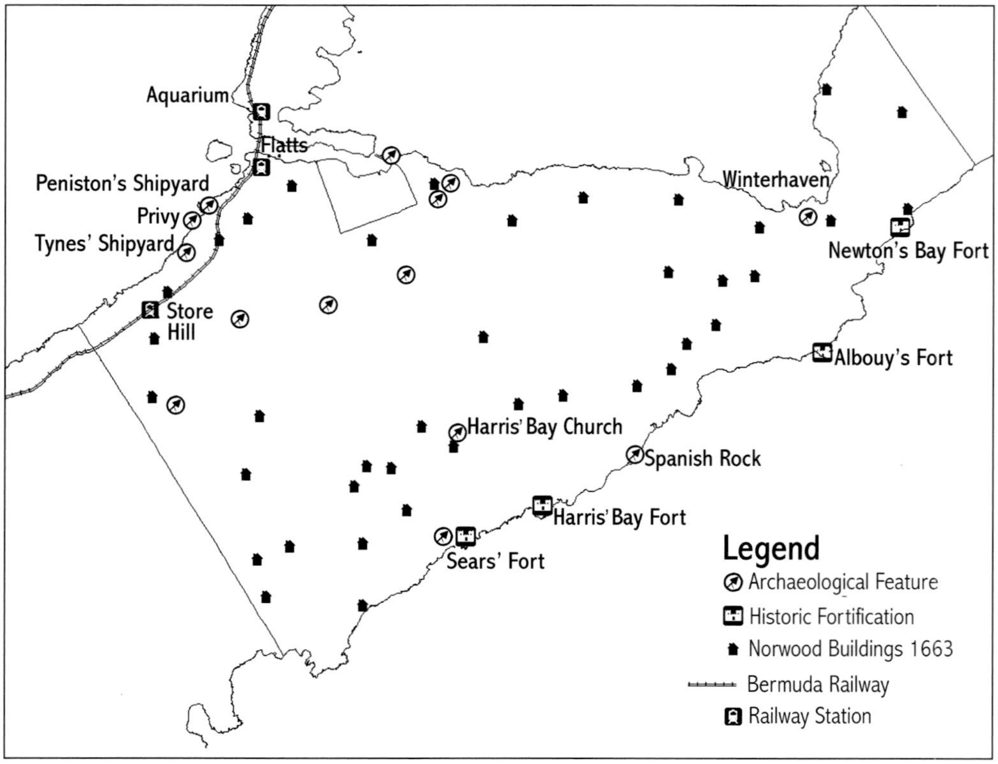
Aquarium
Flatts
Peniston's Shipyard
Privy
Tynes' Shipyard
Store Hill
Winterhaven
Newton's Bay Fort
Albouy's Fort
Harris' Bay Church
Spanish Rock
Harris' Bay Fort
Sears' Fort
Legend
Archaeological Feature
Historic Fortification
Norwood Buildings 1663
Bermuda Railway
Railway Station

Archaeological features in Smith's Parish. *Courtesy Archaeological Research Committee and the Ministry of Works and Engineering.*

An aerial view of Smith's Parish shows Gibbet Island, right foreground, and Flatts Inlet, centre. Smith's Parish extends to the right and Hamilton Parish and Harrington Sound are to the left. The St. James Court condominiums on Flatts Inlet had yet to replace the Coral Island Hotel, right. The condomimiums were built in the 1980s but it is not known precisely when this photograph was taken. *Bermuda News Bureau.*

Though the parish was named for a prominent foreigner, John Smith's Bay, a popular beach on the South Shore, was named after a Bermudian. It is called after John Thomas Smith (circa 1832-1924) who owned 12 acres and two cottages behind the bay.

John Smith moved from Hamilton Parish to Smith's when he bought the property in 1866 from Thomas Murray Trott of Winterhaven Farmhouse at Devil's Hole (*see chapter 9*). Smith was variously described in the records as a labourer, a constable and a planter. It is interesting that he was in the position to buy a substantial amount of land from one of the descendants of Samuel Trott of Walsingham (see *Hamilton Parish*) only a generation after emancipation.

The two cottages on the 12 acre property are now numbered 8 and 10 Ashwood Lane. Both have been extensively renovated, but the former was owned in 1989 by a fifth generation descendant of John Smith.

Ashwood Lane was originally known as Bay Road and was the only route from Harrington Sound to the South Shore until the road now known as Devil's Hole Hill was constructed. The old Military Road along the South Shore was not built until the 1870s

when land was purchased from the various property owners in its path, including John Smith.

The name of John Smith's Bay should more properly be ascribed to the small cove at the western end of the beach as the larger beach is called Newton's Bay. Despite being marked on the current Ordnance Survey as well as the older Savage Survey as Newton's Bay this beach has become popularly known as John Smith's Bay. Samuel Newton, who died before 1689, was the owner of the land stretching from John Smith's Bay to Devil's Hole at the time of the Richard Norwood survey in 1663.

Harris' Bay was the popular name given to the parish as a whole, although by the 20th century it appeared to refer to the area stretching from Devil's Hole on Harrington Sound to the South Shore.

All the original eight parishes (excluding St. George's) were given local names, usually after some prominent geographical feature. The names of the merchant adventurers who had established the colony and lent their names to its parishes were forgotten as distant figures in England. English governess Susette Harriet Lloyd in *Sketches of Bermuda*, published in 1835, wrote, "… all the parishes have two names, an

ancient and a modern; and they are called indifferently by either".

On the map surveyed by Lieutenant Arthur Johnson Savage in 1898-1899, Harris' Bay is printed as the alternate name for Smith's Parish. "Harrises Bay" was the name given on 17th century maps to an inlet on the very edge of the southern boundary of Smith's Parish with Devonshire Parish.

Text continues on page 20

Smith's Parish was named after Sir Thomas Smythe, or Smith, first governor of the East India Company.

Portrait of Sir Thomas Smythe, line engraving by Simon de Passe after J. Woodall, British Library imagesonline: 17527.

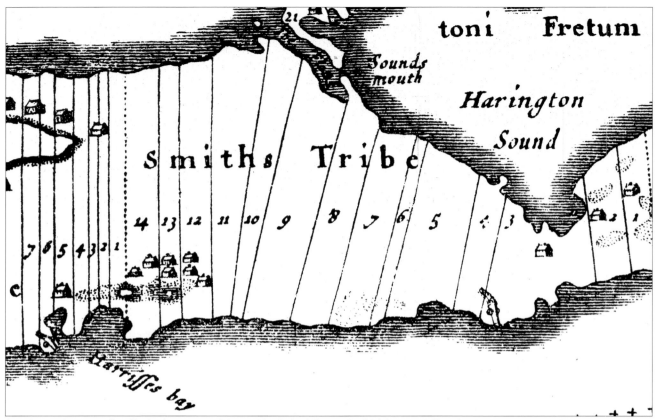

Seven houses cluster in a village like development around the marshland behind "Harrises Bay", left foreground. The only other houses shown on this early map of Smith's Tribe, or Parish, were in the vicinity of Devil's Hole, right. This map was copied from the 1618 Survey of Richard Norwood. *A Mapp of the Sommer Islands (detail of Smith's Tribe), Abraham Goos, 1626. The Adventurers of Bermuda, Henry C. Wilkinson, inside back flap.*

The pattern of settlement had changed by the time of the Richard Norwood Survey of 1663. Houses were no longer clustered together but instead were spread out on each share. *Richard Norwood: 'A Mapp or Description of Sommer Islans' (detail of Smith's Tribe). Copied from one in the State Paper Office, London, by Gabriel Mathias 10th of May 1739 and sent to Attorney General John Harvey Darrell in Bermuda in 1843. Neg.3747. Bermuda Archives: Maps & Plans Collection.*

The Savage Survey

These Architectural Heritage books and the earlier Historic Buildings Survey are based on a series of maps known as the Savage Survey. An extract of the map, surveyed from late 1897 to 1899 and published in 1901, is included at the start of each subsequent chapter.

The survey was led by Lieutenant Arthur Johnson Savage (1874-1933) of the Royal Engineers. He was a 23 year old British Army officer fresh out of training at Woolwich and Chatham in southeast England when he arrived in Bermuda in November 1897 to begin this task.

This was not the first military survey of the island but Savage's job was to produce a detailed contour map. The maps Lieutenant Savage produced were to serve Bermuda for more than half a century and were only replaced by a series published in 1966-1967 and produced with the help of aerial photography.

He arrived in Bermuda with a work party of three men: Corporal Pickford, 2nd Corporal Painting and Sapper Boyd. All were members of the Royal Engineers (RE) and trained at the Ordnance Survey in Southampton, England. They brought with them surveying instru-

Lieutenant Arthur Johnson Savage, Royal Engineers, photographed about 1895 aged 20, when he left the Royal Military Academy at Woolwich in England. *Courtesy Major P.J.A. Savage, RE, grandson of Lieutenant A.J. Savage.*

ments, including two seven inch theodolites, one 100 foot steel chain, one 100 foot steel tape, four four inch theodolites, one ten inch level and prismatic compasses.

Their first task was to train the British soldiers already on the island to assist with the survey work. The 2nd Battalion Worcestershire Regiment along with some Royal Engineers, known as Sappers, were stationed here at the time.

Bermuda's correct position in the world, or latitude and longitude, had first to be fixed. This was done at the East End on the clear starlit nights of January 15 and 19, 1898, with a seven inch alt azimuth theodolite.

A geometric method known as triangulation was used to survey the island. The work began on a stretch of straight road on the Causeway where Lieutenant Savage measured the base line for the first triangle using the steel chain and tape he had brought with him. A distant prominent point was chosen as the apex of the triangle and its distance calculated after measuring the angles with his theodolite.

Once the first triangle had been accurately plotted it was possible to establish a complete system covering the island. So great was the surveying party's accuracy that when it reached the West End it was

found that calculations were only 0.63 inches out.

Detailed fieldwork took place between February and November 1898, starting once again in the East End. Working within each triangle the surveying party entered details of buildings, fences, roads, scrub and arable land etc and plotted them on paper. So step-by-step, triangle-by-triangle, the information for the whole island was gathered. They travelled on foot or on horseback and were sometimes impeded by vegetation or rough countryside.

Results were sent to the Ordnance Survey office in England where they were plotted and traced by expert draftsmen and the resultant draft maps sent back to Bermuda for checking.

Place names were then inserted. A commission was set up to determine parish boundaries and all names were checked with at least three local authorities before being entered on the maps.

Lines of levels were taken along 98 miles of main roads between December 1898 and February 1899. Bench marks, or broad arrows, were cut on prominent stones or walls along the roadsides with the horizontal stroke across the top of the arrow indicating the level above mean sea level. Contours were then drawn on the maps at heights of 50, 100 and 200 feet.

The survey was completed in the spring of 1900. Lieutenant Savage and his party left Bermuda on April 3, 1900. Its total cost is not known nor who paid the bills. It was originally estimated at £1,100 of which Bermuda would bear half. The Survey of Bermuda Act of 1894 voted "a sum not exceeding £400 as a contribution", but it is not known how much Bermuda actually paid.

The map was published on the scale of six inches to a mile on six sheets. It went on sale at the Royal Gazette Stationery Store at two shillings per sheet. A comment in *The Bermuda Pocket Almanack* of 1909 noted that the map gave "the impression of a closely settled country".

After leaving Bermuda Lieutenant Savage went on to a notable army career serving in the Boer War in South Africa and in the First World War where he received the Distinguished Service Order (DSO). He was promoted to the rank of Colonel in 1923 and his last job before retirement was as officer in charge of Royal Engineers records at Chatham, England.   *D.C.*

It is marked on a map of 1626, based on the first survey done by Richard Norwood in 1618, and also on the Norwood map of 1663. However, by the end of the 19th century the bay had lost its early name and become known as Captain Williams' Bay.

Captain Williams' Bay is a small relatively inaccessible and little known inlet which lies immediately to the east of Sue Wood Bay in Devonshire. It probably got its name from two sea captains who owned nearby Tynes Place on Ap Owen Road (see chapter 3) for much of the 19th century. They were Captain Samuel Williams (circa 1784-1867) and his son Captain Benjamin Abraham Williams (1815-1893).

Smith's Parish contains a number of interesting natural features. Town Hill is the highest point of land in Bermuda and rises to 259 feet or 74 metres. It is the site of an early 20th century tower (see chapter 7) which now serves as the hub of an important electronic communications network. It is said to have been called Town Hill because from here, in Smith's Parish, the Town of St. George could be seen.

Harrington Sound, an almost landlocked arm of the sea, is shared by Smith's and Hamilton parishes. The only visible link of the sound to the ocean is through Flatts Inlet where the two parishes meet. This spot by Flatts Bridge was historically known as Sound's Mouth.

Various popular theories have been put forward to explain the existence of Harrington Sound. It was not formed in the mouth of a giant volcano or in a large cave whose roof has collapsed, but was a large inland depression within the greater land mass of Bermuda during the last ice age. This basin, which may have been forested, gradually filled with sea water as the ice melted and the sea level rose.

John Smith's Bay is amongst the most popular beaches on the eastern part of the main island. Spittal Pond (see chapter 10) is an important nature reserve and contains Bermuda's largest brackish water pond as well as interesting historic landmarks including the so called Spanish Rock.

Watch Hill on the South Shore is a small Government owned coastal park. Sears' Cave off St. Mark's Road is a na-

ture reserve and the property of the Bermuda Audubon Society.

Gibbet Island (see chapter 6) near the seaward entrance to Flatts Inlet is a stark reminder of a violent past. However, Smith's Marsh, the site of a major landfill, no longer exists as it was largely filled in with refuse in the 1960s.

Smith's Marsh stretched south of South Shore Road and into the property now known as The Pampas. Naturalist John Matthew Jones writing in The Visitors Guide to Bermuda in 1888 described the marsh as "a long narrow hollow filled with sedges, rushes, palmettos and diminutive shrubs. It is always wet, more particularly at high tides, as it has underground communication with the outer sea. In former days this hollow was higher than it is at present, as the presence of giant cedars, now lying prostrate under the boggy soil, sufficiently testify."

With its central location Smith's Parish was not strategically placed for the defence of the island. Only one fort can be recognised and that is Sears' Fort. It is located on the Pokiok estate almost due south of St. Mark's Church. Dr. Edward Cecil Harris in Bermuda Forts wrote, "It appears to have been built by the Bermudians about 1793, when (Captain Andrew) Durnford records a payment to 'William Sears for Land and Expenses in building a Fort'." It was partly cut into the rock and was half moon in shape. It formed part of a chain of small defences of the South Shore, four of them within Smith's Parish (see 'Smith's Parish Uncovered' page 16).

In 1618 Smith's Parish was owned by 14 shareholders. Settlement was based around Harris' Bay and Devil's Hole as shown in the map of 1626 (see map page 18). There were seven houses clustered behind Harris' Bay on the south facing slope of what is now known as Collectors Hill just to the north of the marshland and three near Devil's Hole which is close to a relatively sheltered harbour on Harrington Sound.

This pattern of early settlement followed the guidelines of the Bermuda Company to encourage village or town development: "… the spare land lying neare the fresh water in every Tribe shall be divided in proportion to every

share, and shall be orderly layd out, for the building of houses, and for gardens and other easements to bee adjoyned to them, that the people may live more comfortable as in townes together".

By 1622, when a note of shares was taken prior to the arrival on the island of Governor John Bernard, there were 80 people living in Smith's Parish, 41 men and 39 women and children. Sir Thomas Smythe had sent five able men to work his land accompanied by seven women and children.

By the time of the second Richard Norwood survey in 1663 the number of shareholders had doubled and the pattern of development had substantially altered (see map page 18). No longer were homes centred in villages but instead were scattered evenly throughout the parish, with generally one house per share.

Together with his 1663 map Richard Norwood produced a Book of Survey of 1662-3 listing the owners of each share, the names of the tenants and the type of building on each share. It is reproduced in the second volume of the 1981 edition of Memorials of the Bermudas compiled by Major-General John Henry Lefroy. From this Norwood work it can be seen that there were 33 houses in Smith's Parish in 1663. The majority were lived in by tenants. A total of 26 houses were described as "tenements", four were "dwelling" houses and three "mansion" houses.

The principal land owners within the parish in 1663 were Captain William Sayle (see chapter 2) who owned six shares and a mansion house near Harris' Bay; Captain Richard Jennynes (see chapter 6), after whom Jennings Land is named, also owned six shares and John Somersall (see chapter 7), whose mansion house was located above Flatts Inlet on the property now known as Orange Grove, owned five.

Around the middle of the 19th century the population of Smith's Parish was 442. A statistical return published in The Bermuda Royal Gazette, March 12, 1843 shows that there were 116 adult males living in the parish, 179 women and 78 boys and 69 girls.

Smith's Parish in the 1920s became home to many people displaced from Tucker's Town (see chapters 9 and 11) when families settled in the area

Lion Rock on the south side of Harrington Sound near Harrington Sound Road was once a notable tourist feature. Patton's Point is in the background. *Bermuda through the Camera of James B. Heyl, 1868-1897, compiled by Edith Stowe Godfrey Heyl, 1951, page 180.*

John Smith's Bay, as seen in this early 20th century photograph, was named after Bermudian John Thomas Smith who owned the land behind the bay. *Courtesy Tony Martin.*

Carriages line up outside the natural aquarium at Devil's Hole. This is a pre-1914 postcard. *'A tour to the Devil's Hole, Bermuda.' Courtesy Marilynn Simmons.*

around Pink Beach, Devil's Hole and Hermitage Road.

Smith's remains one of the least densely populated parishes, with the 2000 census revealing that there were 5,658 persons living in Smith's Parish out of Bermuda's total population of 62,590.

Shipbuilding and farming have long been the occupations of the inhabitants of Smith's Parish. Shipbuilding took place on the rocky North Shore (*see chapter 6*) and on the shore of Harrington Sound.

Farming continues to be, an important occupation in Smith's Parish. The Model Farm was established at what is now the Pokiok housing development. It was an ambitious experiment in the 19th century by Governor William Reid to encourage Bermudians in the up-to-date methods of agriculture.

Tobacco was the early export crop from Bermuda but little record of tobacco farming remains, although in the 1668 inventory of John Knapton of Knapton House (*see chapter 9*) tobacco valued at £7 is listed in the cellar along with a "tobacco wheele". Aloe was grown around Devil's Hole in the 19th century. Today Smith's Parish still has a fair amount of arable land and its farmers continue to produce a wide variety of vegetables.

Dairy farming has always been important in Smith's and three farms remain. The two largest are at Spittal Pond and at Outerlea (*see chapter 5*). There is a smaller dairy farm east of St. Mark's Church near Zuill's Park Road where there is also a goat farm. Gone, however, are dairy farms at Pokiok and The Pampas, which have been subdivided for housing, and on the land west of St. Mark's Church which was turned into an equestrian facility.

Sir Howard Trott, who was one of the early developers of Bermuda's tourism industry, lived at Rockmoor on St. Mark's Road (*see chapter 10*) but there have not been any large scale hotels built within the parish. Pink Beach on the South Shore is a traditional cottage colony. Deepdene Manor, now Manor House, was run as a guest house (*see chapter 8*) before being turned into condominiums, as was Palmetto Bay and there were a number of smaller tourist properties like Angel's Grotto on Harrington Sound and the Breakers Club at John Smith's Bay.

Devil's Hole natural aquarium on Harrington Sound Road is said to have been one of the island's oldest tourist attractions (*see chapter 9*) and the Folly Tower, on the top of The Peak (*see chapter 7*), was built to attract visitors.

The road network in Smith's Parish, as on the rest of the island, has evolved over time. In 1761 the main artery, the Island or General Highway from St. George's Island via the Ferry to Mangrove Bay, ran within Smith's Parish from Flatts Bridge up Flatts Hill and then down Verdmont Road to South Shore Road. This highway may in reality have been nothing more than a foot or bridle path as, despite attempts by Government to enforce a minimum width of 14 feet, nothing appeared to have been achieved six years later.

In 1767 the Governor, according to Dr. Wilkinson in *Bermuda in the Old Empire*, "had to recommend its postponement and state his belief that paths six or eight feet in width would have to do for the time being and until more urgent matters had been cleared". Dr. Wilkinson added, "the Smith's parishioners wrote that money was too short with them to maintain a wide road".

A railway operated in Bermuda briefly between 1931 and 1948 and the track ran along the north of Smith's Parish parallel with North Shore Road. There was a station near the foot of Store Hill which handled freight, probably farm produce, as well as passengers. There was also one at Flatts which

A peaceful scene as a horse and carriage pass along the old white road at Canton Point near John Smith's Bay on South Shore Road. *Bermudiana, Ronald John Williams, photograph by Walter Rutherford, 1936 edition, page 168.*

Harrington Sound Road curves around the water near Devil's Hole. Turtle Island can be seen left. This photograph was taken early in the 20th century.   *Courtesy Tony Martin.*

Farming has always been an important occupation in Smith's Parish.   *'Onions' 1899. Charles Coit Album. Neg 2694. Bermuda Archives: PA881.*

Bermuda Construction

Earliest Smith's Parish houses like Somerville, Rose Cottage (*see chapter 4*) and Verdmont (*see chapter 2*) reveal that much of what now is considered traditional Bermuda construction was firmly established by circa 1700, if only for the most costly buildings. The tradition was partially based on English practice, but had already become distinctly Bermudian.

This involved first clearing and cutting away the bedrock to begin foundations and cellars, then raising walls with sawn limestone blocks. Partitions could be constructed of stone or studs with plaster. Hewn cedar floor joists were set into the stonework and, as necessary, supported midway in the span by larger hewn members called summer beams. The feet of hewn and sawn rafters were attached to hewn plates on tops of the walls, but the rafters or short added kick rafters passed down further to support the eaves and remain exposed below.

Rafters were joined at the ridge and triangulated with slender collar beams, secured with simple lapped joints. Rooms could be made loftier by omitting ceilings entirely or, as at Somerville, plastering up to the collars, making faceted shapes now called tray ceilings.

Spindly sawn cedar lath were nailed to the backs of the rafters and roughly 1" thick slabs of Bermuda stone were laid over them, lapped from eaves to ridge. The walls and roof covering were then either stuccoed or finished with lime wash so often that both became essentially monolithic.

Parts of Somerville's original roof survive and they suggest that around 1700 builders remained sufficiently uncertain of the roof surface that they pegged through random slates to make them hang securely on the lath. The pegs hooked over the edge of the lath, like lugs on tiles, rather than passing through them like nails holding shingles. Later builders would add pegs only when parts of the roof broke and began to move.

Roofs could be hipped or gabled, with the surface carried up to parapets at the top of end walls. Somerville was handled in the latter fashion, with stone balls set at the top of the stepped parapets and somewhat hidden by the exterior chimney shafts.

E.A.C.

Somerville roof section west end: *Drawn by Edward A. Chappell.*

---

served the village as well as the Frascati Hotel. Land owners, who gave up land for the track, were also permitted to have private halts and there was one at Stilwell (*see chapter 6*).

Smith's Parish contains a number of interesting buildings. Verdmont (*see chapter 2*) off Sayle Road, a museum of the Bermuda National Trust, was built by John Dickinson, and is a fine example of a very early 18th century mansion house built in an international style rather than Bermudian vernacular.

Hinson Hall (*see chapter 4*) off Middle Road was also located on John Dickinson's property and was a more typically Bermudian one room deep house with a hall, chamber and centre passage plus a detached kitchen. It was constructed in the mid 18th century for Dickinson's son-in-law Samuel Spofferth. Nearby Somerville (*see chapter 4*) off Middle Road was built to order from the will of John Gilbert as a dower house for his widow Mary.

Store Hill (*see chapter 5*) contains an interesting sample of late 19th and early 20th century houses designed by local architects. They range from Aldie

and Glimmerview at the top of the hill, which represent brief flirtations with American inspired design, to Channelway Cottage at the foot of the hill designed by Bermudian architect Wilfred Onions in the vernacular revival style.

Flatts Hill (*see chapter 7*) can almost be described as the village centre of Smith's Parish and was the site chosen by many leading men of the community to position their homes - from John Somersall in the 17th century to businessman Clarence Darrell in the late 19th and early 20th centuries. Here too stands Dean Hall which has remained continuously in the same family.

Although Flatts Inlet lay in the hands of the shareholders of Hamilton Parish, the south side of Harrington Sound was within Smith's Parish (*see chapter 8*). Here, not far from Flatts Village, are two elegant houses, Villa Monticello and Villa Mont Clare, which were owned by Frances Mary Whitney in the late 19th century. Along with her husband deputy US consul William Whitney, she lived in both. They spent the summer at Villa Monticello and the winter at Villa Mont Clare. The footbridge over Harrington Sound Road at-

tached to the Boat House is a well known landmark. The Boat House of Deepdene, now the Manor House apartments or condominiums, was designed by Thomas Hastings of the well known American design partnership of Carrère & Hastings.

Devil's Hole, a traditional hub of settlement, contains two early cruciform houses, Oleander Circle and Knapton House, as well as Winterhaven Farmhouse which was acquired by the Government in 1974 (*see chapter 9*).

Smith's is considered to be one of the central parishes and a prime location because of its proximity to the capital city and business centre of Hamilton.

It is a parish with a great sense of community spirit. Its parishioners built their own school, Whitney Institute (*see chapter 11*) with its landmark tower, and provided land and labour to construct their own community projects. Essentially rural, with considerable remaining open space, it was never the wealthiest of parishes but local craftsmanship in the various churches testifies to the generosity of the people of Smith's Parish. ❋

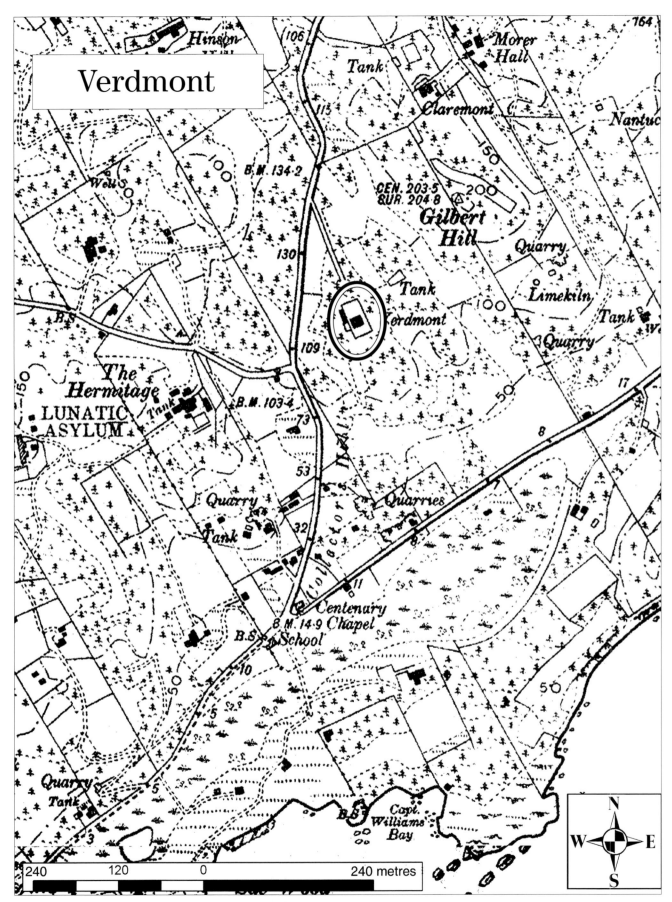

Verdmont

Surveyed and Contoured in 1898-1899 by Lieut. A.J. Savage, RE. Published at the Ordnance Survey Office, Southampton, England, 1901.
Courtesy Works & Engineering.

2
Verdmont

Verdmont, an early 18th century house, is run as a museum by the Bermuda National Trust. The design is symmetrical with a central front door. The small balcony above the door was designed by Wilfred Onions in 1955 and replaced an earlier two storey porch.

Verdmont located on the corner of Verdmont and Sayle Roads is often described as the jewel in the crown of the Bermuda National Trust and rightly so. It must have been an amazingly sophisticated house for the New World when built at the very beginning of the 18th century for John Dickinson in remote Bermuda. The fact that the money to build it is said to have come from a pirate venture in the distant Indian Ocean only increases its magic and mystery.

It stands high on a hill in Smith's Parish with a sweeping view over its property to the Atlantic Ocean, an outstanding position at a time when most houses were built in sheltered rather than impressive sites. The house is set in a walled garden with the land beyond originally extending to more than 93 acres. It was a mansion house set in an estate such as might have been found in England or on the east coast of America but built to Bermuda scale and in local materials for a Bermudian who had made his fortune.

The house has been lived in by an interesting cast of characters and has passed through a well documented and largely female chain of ownership. Verdmont descended through the heirs of its builder John Dickinson for 150 years until it was sold in 1860 to bachelor farmer Rupert Hugh Spencer. It remained in the hands of his heirs for almost a century until it was acquired as a museum in 1951 by the Bermuda Historical Monuments Trust, forerunner of the Bermuda National Trust.

Among the interesting people who lived at Verdmont after John Dickinson were Collector of Customs Thomas Smith, who married Dickinson's granddaughter, portrait painter and judge John Green, who married Smith's daughter, and its last occupant Lillian Wood Joell, who lived in Verdmont during the first half of the 20th century without the benefit of electricity or modern plumbing.

The estate was also home for more than 120 years to a number of slaves who tended the house and its surrounding acres.

It is thought the name Verdmont, meaning "green hill", was chosen during the time when the property was owned by Mary Green and her husband John. The house was certainly called

This aerial photograph shows Verdmont surrounded by a formal walled garden. The former kitchen and service building, now known as Verdmont Cottage, is at the rear of the house, left. Verdmont is located on the top of Collectors Hill and overlooks the South Shore.

Verdmont in John Green's death announcement of 1802.

The original footprint of Verdmont has survived intact into the 21st century but not without some changes, mainly internal, made by successive owners over the three centuries of the house's existence.

The two storey rectangular house is symmetrical in intent although not precisely in execution and built in a style that was later to be known as Georgian. The front door on the south side of the house is several inches out of its true centre whilst the back door is way out to allow for the cedar staircase.

There are four rooms on both the ground and upper floors and four chim-

---

Died, at his feat at Verdmont on Friday the third inft. the Honorable and Worfhipful John Green, Efq. many years a member of his Majefty's Council, and Judge of the Vice Admiralty Court for this Colony. A gentleman whofe upright character has been long too well eftablifhed to require any panegyric.

The announcement of John Green's death gives the name of Verdmont to the house. *Bermuda Gazette, September 11, 1802.*

---

neys. All of the chimneys have double flues so each of the eight rooms has a fireplace. These sturdy projecting chimneys are unmistakably Bermudian in character and are joined on their outer surface by a wall enclosing closets.

The symmetrically placed sash windows of Verdmont have simple but unusual rectangular moulding on the top and sides. The windows are single hung, only the lower sash being movable and needing to be propped open with a stick. They have heavy wood muntins and are early examples of sashes with 12 over 12 panes of glass.

The house is two rooms deep which must have taxed the roof builders of its day as traditionally Bermuda's early homes were one room deep. The precise form of the original roof is not known as it has been heavily restored. The present two tiered roof, which provides additional height and light to the attic, is of unusual design for Bermuda.

An octagonal cupola is believed to have been built on the roof. This may have been original to the house because the three storey stairs seem to lead grandly up to the top floor, or it may possibly have been installed by a later

owner. Thomas Smith as Collector of Customs would have wished to keep his eye on ships seeking to evade duty by offloading some of their cargo before checking in with the authorities in St.

Simple masonry moulding around the top and sides of the windows at Verdmont provide an unusual detail. The sashes are made up of 12 panes of glass over 12 panes between heavy wooden muntins.

William Sayle

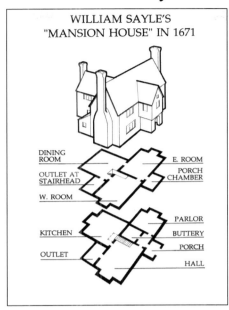

WILLIAM SAYLE'S "MANSION HOUSE" IN 1671

DINING ROOM

OUTLET AT STAIRHEAD

W. ROOM

E. ROOM

PORCH CHAMBER

KITCHEN

OUTLET

PARLOR

BUTTERY

PORCH

HALL

William Sayle (died circa 1671) owned the land on which Verdmont stands. However, his November 17, 1671 inventory reveals that the house he lived in was of a different shape to Verdmont and Richard Norwood's *Book of Survey of 1662-3* states that his mansion house stood on share number 23 rather than share number 27 on which Verdmont would have stood.

He was an important figure in the history of English colonisation. Not only was he Governor of Bermuda on three separate occasions, he also led an expedition from Bermuda to establish a colony in the Bahamas and another to the Carolinas where he became its first Governor.

Although his house contained a similar number of rooms to Verdmont and was two storeys high with a garret, the room layout indicates William Sayle's house was a different shape from Verdmont. It was built in an earlier cruciform style rather than the two room deep plan of Verdmont. Cary Carson, Vice President of Research at Colonial Williamsburg, has produced a conjectural drawing of Sayle's mansion house in Smith's Parish. The fate of his house is not known but few 17th century houses survive in Bermuda.

Richard Norwood's *Book of Survey of 1662-3* lists William Sayle as owning shares number 23, 26, 27, 28 and 29 within Smith's Parish. His mansion house on share number 23 was in the vicinity of Harris' Bay on the South Shore (see map on page 18). His other shares were occupied by tenants.

The 1671 inventory of William Sayle reveals a prosperous household as befits a governor.

William Sayle was variously given the title of Captain, Colonel or Governor according to his office at the time. His first wife was called Margery and the couple had three children Thomas, Nathaniel and James. He married for the second time in 1662 to the widow Frances Pitt.

He was Governor of Bermuda in 1640-1642 and 1643-1645 during the reign of Charles I of England and again in 1658-1663.

With England in the hands of Commonwealth or Protectorate the conflict between Royalists or traditionalists and the Roundheads or independents spilled over to Bermuda. William Sayle was a supporter of the Puritan or Independent movement and resolved to leave Bermuda and set up a new colony in the Bahamas.

In 1648 he left the island on board the *William* with a band of 70 settlers bound for Eleutheria (now Eleuthera) in a bold move to found the first independent republic in the New World. However his ship foundered on a reef off Eleuthera and provisions were lost.

William Sayle along with eight others sailed in the ship's shallop, a small open boat, to Virginia to obtain supplies. He was successful in reaching Jamestown and obtaining provisions. However, the new colony faltered and Sayle became disenchanted, leaving Eleuthera in 1656 and eventually returning to Bermuda where he was once again appointed Governor.

In 1669 an expedition to establish a settlement in what is now South Carolina was driven into Bermuda by bad weather. While here its leader Sir John Youmans relinquished his command and William Sayle was appointed to succeed him. He led a successful expedition and was in 1670 appointed the first Governor of the Carolinas. He died shortly afterwards having achieved success and high office in three English colonies.

His house no longer exists but he is remembered in the name of Sayle Road which leads to Verdmont.   *D.C.*

William Sayle's mansion house in 1671.   *Courtesy Cary Carson, Colonial Williamsburg Foundation. Drawn by Jeffrey Bostetter.*

George's. Two "spying glasses" were amongst his effects in his 1782 inventory.

The framework for this octagonal structure can still be seen amongst the 20th century roof timbers in the garret, a room under the roof space, which is another unusual feature for a Bermuda house. The cupola must have been unique as it was not until the 19th century that square towers, now called widows' walks, became popular.

The cupola is said to have been hit by successive storms and Verdmont's roof is believed to have been repaired following a hurricane in 1926 and then redone in 1954 following its purchase by the Bermuda Historical Monuments Trust.

There is no covered entry porch although there was a two storey porch with a simple gable roof on the front of the house shown in mid 20th century photographs. This consisted of an upper wooden verandah with gingerbread railings on top of cylindrical stone pillars which flanked the front door. Perhaps the pillars dated from early in the 19th century whilst the upper verandah appeared to be late Victorian. This porch was replaced by a small balcony in 1955.

The service buildings are at the back of the house. Today the detached kitchen and storeroom on the northwest and a two seat privy on the northeast are all that remain. However, John Dickinson's 1714 inventory attached to his will reveals that there were more. Listed are an "out store room and kitchen", presumably the present Verdmont Cottage, but there was also an "outroom and buttery" which provided "servants lodgings" and a "cabbin" in which wood was stored. An "outlett and 3 cellars – North Side" was listed but this was probably in Flatts.

The present driveway to Verdmont is on the north and leads to the rear of the house. This would not always have been so, but it is not known precisely

The fine three storey cedar staircase at Verdmont dates from the time when the house was first built by John Dickinson. *Courtesy Willie Graham, Colonial Williamsburg Foundation of Virginia.*

how access was gained to the south front. There is no carriage listed in either John Dickinson's or Thomas Smith's inventories so visitors probably arrived on foot or horseback at the formal front entrance. A pair of mounting blocks stand either side of the south steps. However, in the second half of the 19th century and during the 20th when the house had lost some of its grandeur the rear entry was used.

The narrow access road, cut through the rock from South Shore Road, is not marked on the Savage survey conducted in 1898-1899 but it is on a 1951 plan so it probably dates from the first half of the 20th century

when the house was owned by the Joell family.

John Dickinson (died 1714) acquired the land on which he was to build his home from Nicholas Trott about 1694. This was soon after his marriage in 1693 to wealthy widow Elizabeth Fyfield. The money to buy the land and build the house is said to have come from the proceeds of a highly successful pirate expedition led by Rhode Islander Captain Thomas Tew.

The story of the *Amity* is told by Dr. Henry Campbell Wilkinson in *Bermuda in the Old Empire*. Captain

Tew arrived in Bermuda in 1691 and purchased a share in the Bermuda sloop the *Amity*. In an incredible voyage he sailed across the Atlantic Ocean and around the Cape of Good Hope into the Indian Ocean and then up the east coast and around the Horn of Africa to the Straits of Bab el Mandeb at the entrance to the Red Sea where the sloop lay in wait for a convoy of six Arabian ships. Captain Tew had obtained a commission "to cruise against the king's enemies", according to Dr. Wilkinson, though this Arabian venture smacked more of piracy than privateering.

The *Amity* carried eight guns and a crew of 45, each of whom worked for a share in the proceeds. The tallest ship of the Arabian convoy was said to be heavily armed and carried 300 soldiers but Captain Tew boldly ran his ship alongside and boarded. According to Dr. Wilkinson, "The (Arabian) ship was carried without loss to the pirates. The booty was so immense that, notwithstanding waste, it yielded £3,000 a man. There was also a store of powder. Tew wished to attack the other ships in turn, but the crew objected, for they now desired nothing as much as a frolic ashore. The *Amity* was accordingly headed for Madagascar."

Henry Fyfield, the first husband of Elizabeth Dickinson, and her father Colonel Anthony White (died circa 1709) were among the Bermudian shareholders in the *Amity*. Dr. Wilkinson wrote, (the Bermudian shareholders received) "some Spanish bullion... together with broken gold and gold dust and... a substantial sum in Lyon dollars and Arabian gold". He added, "Arabian gold showed its face on the island for a while notwithstanding the efforts of its first recipients to be discreet." " Indeed, every effort was made to hush up the whole matter as far as it could be in so small, intimate, and inquisitive a community."

The precise date of construction of Verdmont is not known. The land on which the house was to be built was purchased in 1694 when John and Elizabeth Dickinson were newly married and flush with money. It would have taken time to build and it was completed by the time of John Dickinson's death, as revealed in his 1714 inventory, so it would be fair to say Verdmont was built some time between 1696 and 1714.

It is not known what inspired the design of the house but Dickinson must have been influenced by international trends in architecture. As a ship owner he may have travelled to New England, the Chesapeake or the Caribbean. The interior of the house has changed in a number of ways since it was home to John and Elizabeth Dickinson but the cedar staircase, the great chamfered cedar beams still visible in some of the ceilings and at least two of the fireplaces remain as a testament to the fine workmanship they inspired.

The origins of John Dickinson are obscure. He was a merchant and ship owner. The sloop *Elizabeth and Mary*, named after his daughters and valued at £400, was listed amongst the possessions in his inventory.

He was also Speaker of the House of Assembly from 1707 to 1710 and interested in the island's botany. Jill Collett wrote in *Bermuda Her Plants & Gardens*, "He was the man who sent the first collection of plants from Bermuda to Mr. Petiver in London which later became part of the Sloane Herbarium." It is fitting that the gardens of the museum have been planted with annuals, shrubs and trees that would have been available in Bermuda during the 18th century.

John Dickinson and his wife Elizabeth had two daughters, Elizabeth (died 1733) and Mary (died 1789). His unmarried sister Alice Dickinson also lived at Verdmont along with her slave Bess.

The house was relatively simply furnished in John Dickinson's time and contained comparatively little furniture identified as cedar, other than chests with lock and key, presumably used for storage of valuable items. The inventory (*see appendix 1*) attached to Dickinson's will and dated December 14, 1714 provides a valuable insight into the rooms of the house and their use.

The hall, the room on the southwest corner of the house, was the principal receiving room. Entry was made directly into the hall as there is no passage at the front of the house although there is one at the rear. The hall was simply and basically furnished. There were 12 pictures hanging on its walls and a number of tables and chairs, a

Verdmont photographed in the 1950s by Frederick Hamilton. The early 18th century house had a two storey porch on its south front which was removed in 1955 after its acquisition by the Bermuda Historical Monuments Trust. *Verdmont, Smith's Parish, The Bermudian magazine, June 1952, page 20. Courtesy family of the late Edmund M. Gosling.*

The southwestern chimney with its double flue served both the hall on the ground floor and the chamber above. Verdmont has four double flued chimneys serving fireplaces in all eight rooms. The room on the ground floor was the hall of John Dickinson, the builder of Verdmont, whilst his bedchamber was above. These were the largest rooms in the house.

This is the rear of Verdmont and is used as the museum entrance. The door is placed off centre, spoiling the symmetry of this view of the house, because of the early cedar staircase inside. The double hipped roof with a monitor in between, which gives greater light and height to the attic, is an unusual and later feature.

settle and couch as well as a large looking glass. There were no rugs, linen or silver in the room but it did contain two small hand guns.

John Dickinson's parlour on the southeast was a more private room used by the family. It contained a "low bedstead bed" as well as a couple of cedar chests, small tables and chairs. There were three pairs of money scales and weights in this room as well as a great quantity of silver valued at £78.4.0.

The dining room at the northwest contained one small table and ten "woren" or worn chairs. It did not appear to be a formal entertaining room. There were a number of practical utensils which included six pairs of smoothing irons, a spice mortar and pestle and a pair of bellows and "tongues". It is said this was the room in which the fireplace was used for warming food cooked in the detached kitchen. The fireplace in this room today with its raised cooking hearth may be the same as in the time of the Dickinsons as it does not appear to have been made smaller, unlike most of the others.

Possessions in the "northermost chamber", known in the museum at the beginning of the 21st century as the library, were not itemised although the relatively high total of £50 was put on them. It is not known why. Perhaps this was the chamber of Alice Dickinson.

Upstairs, the southwest chamber over the hall presumably served as the bed chamber of John and Elizabeth Dickinson. This would have been the largest room as the passageway to the balcony had yet to be created. The most expensive bed valued at £11 was in this room along with a quantity of linen, a dressing box and a looking glass.

The room over the parlour, known in the museum today as Mrs. Green's

Descendants of John Dickinson
Simplified family tree

John Dickinson m. Elizabeth Fyfield
(died 1714) (née White)

Elizabeth Dickinson
(died 1733)
m.
Perient Spofferth
(died circa 1727)

Elizabeth Spofferth
(died 1789)
m.(1) Robert Brown
(died 1752)
m.(2) **Thomas Smith**
(died 1781)

Mary Dickinson
(died circa 1789)
m.
Samuel Spofferth
(died circa 1770)

Elizabeth Spofferth, who married secondly Collector of Customs Thomas Smith, inherited Verdmont from the estate of her grandfather John Dickinson, the builder of the house.

Site and Form

South Elevation: Verdmont

The house built by John Dickinson before 1714 is among the earliest surviving formal houses in the British American colonies. It can be read as a Georgian house in its form and siting, in spite of predating the first George by a decade or two. Probably it is the best known house on the island and is seen as among the most characteristic Bermuda buildings, though few similar houses were ever built on the island. Indeed its form and disposition run counter to the norm of Bermuda buildings from the 17th through to the 19th century.

Dickinson chose for its location a dominant position at the top of Collectors Hill, facing down 2,000 feet to the Atlantic, with a panorama of rolling topography on both sides. It gave the impression sought by many 18th century gentry house builders that the resident owned the visible world — now made poignant by the development of houses closely scattered across the view.

The wild natural prospect contrasted sharply with a formalised setting immediately around the house. By mid century, lawns were levelled front and rear, the front (south) one supported by a retaining wall topped with rusticated stone piers holding a wood fence that partially screened the lower scene, throwing emphasis on the dramatic water view. A nearly symmetrical five bay wall made the south face clearly the front, unlike the uneven north wall facing a kitchen, storeroom and slave quarters. An octagonal cupola on the deck of a hipped roof cultivated the dominant appearance of the house and gave Dickinson an opportunity to offer further lofty and privileged views to his family and guests, and dis-

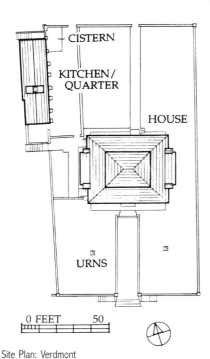

CISTERN

KITCHEN/ QUARTER

HOUSE

URNS

0 FEET 50

Site Plan: Verdmont

tracted attention from the two chunky Bermuda style chimneys projecting from both sides.

The house has rooms stacked two deep like the houses that wealthy individuals increasingly constructed throughout the English speaking world from the late 17th into the 19th century. This seems distinctly non Bermudian, particularly covering the whole with one large roof rather than two or more narrower roofs. On the other hand, the plan resembles the arrangement of surviving 18th century cruciform houses in that the front rooms are two fine spaces of unequal size, and that the upper floor was reached via a stair in space centred on the rear. At Verdmont, one enters directly into the 21' by 16'10" hall, and the 17'7" by 17' parlour is to the east (right).

The relationship of the hall and parlour to the front rooms in houses like Walsingham and Inwood is emphasised by original floor framing overhead: Dickinson's hall has a pair of summer beams set at right angles and the parlour has a single one running side to side. All the other spaces have joists supported on a single summer beam, except the space above the hall, which again has crossed summers. These are now among the few first period features visible inside the house. Originally the overhead framing and floors were all exposed. Recently evidence was found that the framing and floor above the hall was finished with a paint containing Prussian blue pigments. This strongly expressed structure overhead was highlighted by colour, perhaps contrasting with plain whitewashed walls. Both rooms open into a central rear passage with a stair that rises to the first floor and attic. Originally the first floor plan mirrored the ground floor with what presumably was Dickinson's best bed chamber over the hall. Fireplaces were wrapped with heavy Baroque mouldings like those widely admired and copied in Bermuda for new fireplaces since the 1930s. But Verdmont reflects an international taste at least as much as it does Bermudian. A feature that connects Verdmont more to the international mercantile community than to Bermuda is the extent of its fireplaces. All eight rooms were provided with fireplaces, contrasting with the very selective use of heating devices in even the best rooms of most early Bermuda houses.

There is no cellar, and cooking seems to have been segregated in a separate building until the 20th century. The present cottage to the north, at the edge of the rear lawn resembles detached kitchens and quarters associated with large 18th and early 19th century houses in the Caribbean and southeastern United States, and it, too, was used to house domestic slaves and work.

E.A.C.

Illustrations courtesy Cary Carson, Colonial Williamsburg Foundation. Drawn by Jeffrey Bostetter.

The fireplace in the dining room at Verdmont has a raised hearth for warming food cooked in the detached kitchen. This fireplace remains as it was when the house was built and has not been made fashionably smaller like many of the others within the house.

bedroom, was simply called "the storeroom over the parlour" in John Dickinson's time although it did contain one "high bedstead bed" but otherwise it held a variety of possessions ranging from "a halfe barrell flowr" to "parcell silver fringe".

It is difficult to know in which room the two girls Elizabeth and Mary slept. The "chamber over the dining room" contained the second most valuable bed along with a warming pan. There was also a "low bedstead" in the garret which may have been occupied by a servant.

Livestock were listed "in the field" in Dickinson's inventory. There were three horses, the most expensive described as a black horse was presumably Dickinson's. An unusual and highly valued animal was a "stagg", which must have added considerable class to his country estate and astounded the neighbours.

John Dickinson did not enjoy his fine home for long. In his will written on August 4, 1714, soon be-fore his death, he left a life interest in his property to his wife Elizabeth Dickinson.

Elizabeth Dickinson was to spend a long widowhood in the house and although her precise date of death is not known, she outlived her oldest daughter Elizabeth. She lived in Verdmont along with her sister-in-law Alice, Elizabeth and her husband Perient Spofferth and their two children and, until her marriage, her youngest daughter Mary.

John Dickinson left his sister Alice "the room or chamber she now useth, with suitable conveniences, clothing, meat, drink, lodging and washing during her natural life". He also left instructions for the "necessary accommodation for her negro Bess so long as she continues serviceable in the family" and he specified that his property was to be divided between his two daughters on his wife's death. Elizabeth was to get his house and 50 acres south to the sea and Mary (died 1789) the northern share on which Hinson Hall (see chapter 4) was to be built.

His daughter Elizabeth Dickinson (died 1733) married Perient Spofferth in the same year as her father died. The couple had two children Dickinson and Elizabeth Spofferth. Mariner Perient Spofferth (died 1727) was the son of Samuel Spofferth Sr. and his brother Samuel Spofferth Jr. was prominent in local affairs.

A 1733 inventory (see appendix 2) of Elizabeth and Perient Spofferth reveals the couple had a fairly modest list of household possessions, presumably because they lived along with her mother although Elizabeth was due to receive upon her marriage, under the terms of her father's will, a quarter of the possessions listed on his inventory

Her mother, Elizabeth Dickinson, outlived her. The fate of Dickinson Spofferth is not known but the estate passed to John Dickinson's granddaughter Elizabeth Spofferth.

Elizabeth Spofferth married first Robert Brown, a merchant of St. George's. He died in 1752 and in September 1755 she married widower Thomas Smith.

As the husband of Elizabeth, Collector of Customs Thomas Smith (died 1781) was to become the next influential owner of Verdmont. He had four daughters from a previous marriage. They were Elizabeth, known as Betty, Mary, known as Polly, Honora, known as Peggy, and Catherine. There were no children from the marriage of Thomas and Elizabeth. His daughters were to inherit the property thus breaking the direct line of Dickinson descent.

It was not possible to trace the ancestry of Thomas Smith. It is difficult to know whether he was a Bermudian or had been appointed from London. He had an important position as Collector of Customs and was a representative of the British Crown in Bermuda

Above: The double doors at Verdmont lead between the two front rooms and may have been installed by the Smiths. They are probably the earliest set of such doors in Bermuda and may be earlier than any known in America. *Courtesy Willie Graham, Colonial Williamsburg Foundation of Virginia.*

Right: This ornate carved and painted mantel in the southwest chamber was probably installed during the time when Elizabeth and Thomas Smith owned Verdmont.

Collector of Customs Thomas Smith (died 1781) married John Dickinson's granddaughter the widowed Elizabeth Brown née Spofferth in 1755. *Oil on canvas, unsigned, attributed to John Green circa 1775, gift of Hereward Watlington. The Bermuda National Trust: Verdmont Museum.*

Descendants of Thomas Smith
Simplified family tree

First wife m.(1) **Thomas Smith** m.(2) Elizabeth Brown
(died 1781) (née Spofferth, died 1789)

Mary Smith   *Elizabeth Smith*
(known as Polly)   (known as Betty)
(died 1803)   (died 1784)
m.   m.
John Green   *Henry Trott*
(died 1802)   (died 1805)

Samuel Henry Trott
(died 1817)

John Henry Trott
(1805-1892)

There were no children from the marriage of Thomas Smith and Elizabeth Brown, the granddaughter of John Dickinson. Verdmont passed to the descendants of Thomas Smith's first marriage, firstly to his daughter Polly who had married John Green and then to her nephew Samuel Henry Trott and then to Samuel's son John Henry Trott.

with the job of collecting duties authorised by the British Parliament and transmitting the proceeds to the Commissioner of Customs in London (*see chapter 3*). His office was in St. George's, the sole Customs port until 1794. It would have been a long journey to work although Verdmont did stand near the General Highway which ran from Verdmont Road to Flatts Bridge and then to St. George's via the Ferry.

Thomas Smith left his mark on Verdmont in which he lived from 1755 to 1781. Little seems to have been done to the house during the widowhood of Elizabeth Dickinson so it was probably time for Thomas and Elizabeth Smith to modernise and redecorate in the current fashion.

He was obviously of an artistic bent and was aware of the latest fashion in architecture and interior design overseas or perhaps he was influenced by his son-in-law, artist John Green. An unsigned portrait of Thomas Smith is hanging at Verdmont and is traditionally attributed to John Green. It is not known whether Smith was independently wealthy or whether it was his second wife's *Amity* gold which funded the substantial improvements to the house.

Thomas Smith also owned Tucker House in St. George's for three years before selling in 1775 to President Henry Tucker. Perhaps it was purchased as a lodging whilst he was about his official duties in St. George's. He obviously had a good eye, for Tucker House like Verdmont was to become a museum owned first by the Bermuda Historical Monuments Trust and then the Bermuda National Trust.

Thomas Smith may have converted the hall and parlour of John Dickinson into a fashionable double parlour with the installation of wider glazed double parlour doors. With the doors open these two rooms provided a large space for entertaining, perhaps for card and music playing. The panelled folding interior window shutters may also have been added during this time.

Upstairs parlours had become fashionable so the Smiths may have converted what had been the Dickinsons' bed chamber on the southwest. It contained a bed and was still called a chamber in Thomas Smith's inventory although it also held a writing table and "arm'd" chairs. They probably reduced the size of the fireplace opening and installed a carved and painted mantel imported from England. A partition was built to create a passage leading to a balcony or porch, although the appearance of the porch in their day is not known.

The Smiths turned the chamber over the parlour, on the southeast side of the house which had been used as a storeroom in the time of John Dickinson into their sleeping room. This contained the most expensive bed valued at £32, the most costly piece of furniture in the house.

They either papered the walls in some rooms or intended to do so because "a parcel of paper hangings" was amongst the goods listed in Thomas Smith's 1782 inventory. Many of the fireplaces, except in the dining room and northwest bed chamber, were reduced in size and their cedar mantels replaced or reworked to fit the new openings.

Thomas Smith's inventory of December 1782 reveals that he and his wife Elizabeth had added many refinements to their home from the simple furnishings of her grandfather's day. There was very little cedar amongst their furniture, presumably because the bulk was imported. A harpsichord and card table stood in the hall. There was a clock in the parlour from which the bedstead had been removed.

A camera obscura was listed in the northeast bed chamber. This may have belonged to their son-in-law portrait painter John Green as it was a device used for projecting images to the back of a box to help sketch and paint detailed objects.

There was a round cedar table and five small Windsor chairs as well as three old low chairs in the dining room. It does not sound as if it was used as a grand entertaining room. The room now known as the library was a chamber "below stairs" and contained a fairly modestly valued bed.

Elizabeth Smith, John Dickinson's granddaughter, died eight years after her husband. She had no children of her own and divided the extensive Verdmont property, giving her stepdaughter Mary, known as Polly, the house and the land north of South

Mary Green, known as Polly (died 1803), was a daughter of Thomas Smith by an earlier marriage. She was the wife of John Green, the painter of the portrait. *Oil on canvas, unsigned, attributed to John Green circa 1780, gift of Hereward Watlington. The Bermuda National Trust: Verdmont Museum.*

Shore Road, whilst her nephew Samuel Henry Trott, the son of Polly's sister Elizabeth got the land south of the road but would eventually inherit his aunt's Verdmont portion as well.

John Green (died 1802) is thought to have come to Bermuda from Philadelphia in the mid 1760s. Henry Wilkinson in *Bermuda from Sail to Steam* wrote that Green was an Irishman from Clonmel, in county Tipperary in the south of Ireland. There was a Greene family with a branch in Clonmel, but it was not possible to identify John Green.

He was a portrait painter who was to marry the heiress of Verdmont where he settled before becoming a judge. He brought some changes to the house in line with the current fashion for neoclassicism and even more sophistication to the house contents.

He presumably met the Smith fam-

Portrait painter and judge John Green (died 1802) was the husband of Verdmont heiress Polly, daughter of Thomas Smith. *Water colour on ivory, circa 1765-1780, miniature self portrait, gift of Alice Butterfield. The Bermuda National Trust: Verdmont Museum.*

ily some time after his arrival and Thomas Smith's daughter Polly caught his eye. In 1774 Green travelled to London to study with Benjamin West whom he had known earlier in Philadelphia. Benjamin West (1738-1820), an American artist, had become a leading figure in London and was the historical painter to King George III and a founder of the Royal Academy.

In September of that year Green wrote a long letter to Thomas Smith telling of his experiences. While in London he performed a few small tasks for the Smiths such as getting a microscope repaired and trying in vain to sell Mrs. Smith's shell collection. In his letter he sent his "kind love to Mrs. Smith and all the ladies".

On his return he married Polly Smith and lived at Verdmont with his in-laws. It was perhaps at this time that he painted portraits of the four daughters of Thomas Smith, Elizabeth (died before 1784), Mary (died 1803), Honora (died 1782) and Catherine, which now hang at Verdmont.

John Green was to live the life of the country gentleman on his wife's family estate. He was a member of the Governor's Council and in 1785 was briefly appointed Collector of Customs as his father-in-law had been before him. The following year he assumed the

Text continues on page 41

This is the old detached kitchen and service quarters of Verdmont viewed from the west. It was built into the hillside in the traditional manner with a cellar. It is now known as Verdmont Cottage.

This massive chimney served as a cooking fireplace in Verdmont's detached kitchen.

Heavy buttresses line the east side of Verdmont Cottage. They supported a building which was used as a farm shed. It was removed by the Bermuda Historical Monuments Trust in 1955.

Interior Finish and Evolution

When first seeing Verdmont, one has the sense that it remains virtually unaltered, as though all succeeding owners were content to leave it as planned by John Dickinson and its builder. While it is true that relatively little of its architecture has been altered in the last 175 years, a closer look reveals that there was significant change in its first century.

The most distinctive original fabric now visible inside is upper floor framing, fireplaces, and the most remarkable stair in Bermuda. Only the stair remains virtually intact, but all these elements suggest a bold interior finish apparently more consistent throughout the house than later residents found acceptable, or than later Bermudians would employ in their other refined houses.

All eight rooms had heating fireplaces ranging from 5'3" by 4' to 4'8" by 2'2". The interior of these cavernous openings was plastered and apparently whitewashed. The openings were finished with large Baroque mouldings piled on almost a foot in width around three sides.

Subsequent generations would find Verdmont's interior too crude in general and lacking certain refined rooms in particular needed for respectable domestic life, both public and private. One would expect this most prominently in the reception rooms, front and centre. Later alterations made the extent of early changes slightly unclear downstairs but it appears Thomas Smith opened the hall and parlour to allow freer movement of guests, air and light by insertion of a 4'8" wide pair of glazed doors. The width is modest by the standards of the 1810s and 1820s, but this is the earliest set of doors placed between "double parlours" in Bermuda, and apparently earlier than any known in the mainland English colonies. Flexibility of room use and privacy remained concerns, however, indicated by small wrought iron hooks that once supported a curtain over the opening.

Smith's family also sought a small, refined private chamber on the upper floor. They partitioned the east side of the room to create a passage connecting the stair and a front balcony, and placed a door at the front end, opening into the new room as far as possible from the stair. It was furnished as the second best bedchamber in 1782. Here and elsewhere Smith or his son-in-law installed expensive two panel mahogany doors.

The fireplace in the new, cosier room was reduced from

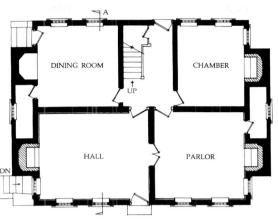
Ground Floor Plan: Verdmont

4'10" wide to 3', and was refitted with an elegant classical mantel. Rude old Baroque mouldings were pulled off and replaced with an architrave, frieze and cornice, all carved in the best professional style, probably in England. Leaves and acorns are wrapped with rippling ribbons between rows of eggs and leaves, originally all painted a shiny glazed blue. Crossed summer beams less than eight feet above the floor must have made this less seamless than a small Hogarthian parlour, but the only alternative was a lower ceiling, and elite Bermudians, again, maintained some affection for overhead framing.

High architectural taste of the post Revolutionary era was more intensely formal, exemplified by changes made by John and Mary Green or conceivably by Samuel H. Trott in 1803-1817. The paucity of Trott's inventory suggests the changes preceded him. Most attention was turned to the front entertaining rooms. Ceilings were plastered, walls were wallpapered from floor to ceiling, without chair rails, and fireplaces were simplified to plain classical mouldings around openings reduced from 5'3" to 3'10" and 3'8" respectively. Delicate cornices were added to the front rooms, their dentils fluted in a manner that disturbingly resembles teeth with dangling roots.

Elsewhere the remodellers added chair rails and board or plaster ceilings, only leaving the joists exposed in the upper rear rooms and left rear room downstairs, where they also left the old-fashioned bolections around the fireplaces. Oversized fireplace openings were left only in the left rear room, closest to the detached kitchen and quarters. Most of the doors were retrimmed with thin neoclassical architraves.

Restoration in 1954-1955 focused on repairing the damaged floor framing and re-constructing the roof. The roof had badly decayed, and the restorers rebuilt it entirely, being careful to save and piece together the 18th century deck frame, 7'10" above the attic floor, which preserved the evidence for an octagonal cupola about 4'6" in width, predating the upper hipped roof. The restorers' other objective was to nudge parts of the house back to an earlier appearance, most obviously in replacing the 19th century porch with a balcony designed by Wil Onions in the old Bermuda style, inspired by balconies shown on three houses in a rough circa 1731 drawing of St. George's.

E.A.C.

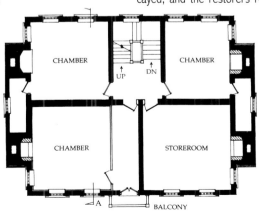
Upper floor plan: Verdmont

Floor plans of Verdmont: *courtesy Cary Carson, Colonial Williamsburg Foundation. Drawn by Jeffrey Bostetter.*

Born into Slavery

The last person to be born into slavery at Verdmont may have been Geoffrey. He was five years old on the eve of emancipation in Bermuda on August 1, 1834. Little is known about him, just his first name and age. His mother may have been Nancy, a 26 year old domestic servant, as she was the only female of child bearing age on the Slave Register belonging to the estate of Samuel Trott of Verdmont in 1833.

Slaves were listed with first names only so it is not easy to sort out family relationships. These Slave Registers were made in 1821, 1827, 1830 and 1833-1834 as Bermudian slave owners sought compensation from the British government as emancipation neared.

He was one of many slaves to have lived at Verdmont. The elegant house with its extensive estate would most probably have been built and certainly was maintained by slave labour for over 125 years. Fortunately we have good records of many of their names because they are given in the inventories left by some of the people who lived in the house in addition to the 19th century Slave Registers.

John Dickinson, the builder of the house in the early 18th century, possessed six slaves, four men and two women who lodged in the "outroom and buttery". All were listed in his 1714 inventory with a monetary value that no doubt reflected their skill or age. Robin and Peter were the most highly valued at £35 each. Prince was valued at £30, Sambo at £20, Ruth at £20 and Beck at £25. In addition there was also Bess, who is mentioned in his will, and who cared for his maiden sister Alice Dickinson.

Ruth and Beck presumably tended the house and kitchen while the four men may have been labourers or cared for the land and animals or may even have worked as sailors. A number of implements were listed in the inventory which the men would have used in their labours. These included a whip saw, an "iron spudd" or spade and "worne hows" or hoes. Whilst the women would have used the kettles, a grid iron, baking stone, "iron potts and pott hoocks", a frying pan and a chafing dish in preparing the family's food as well as the smoothing irons listed in the dining room.

John Dickinson's daughter Elizabeth who married Perient Spofferth lived in Verdmont along with her mother, also called Eliza-beth, after John Dickinson's death. The Spofferths' 1733 inventory lists Prince and Sue as well as four boys, two of them called Jack and the others Tom and Sam. The two adults would not have been enough to take care of the house and estate and it is assumed that her mother Elizabeth Dickinson also employed a number of slaves, presumably those listed in her husband's inventory or their descendants.

During the time of Thomas Smith and his wife Elizabeth, grand-daughter of John Dickinson, the number employed at Verdmont rose, increasing the population in the slave quarters at the rear of the house.

In Thomas Smith's 1782 inventory four men, three women, five boys and two girls are listed as slaves. The most highly valued man was Joe at £90. Mell valued at £75 was listed as being at sea. It was not unusual at this time for a slave to be away from home serving on board ship. The remaining two men were Daniel and Bacchus. The women were Rachel, Sue and Marian, the boys included Nat, Sam, Davy, Jim and Tom and the girls were Tish and Sall. It is difficult to know how much work children were expected to do but they were all valued quite highly so presumably they were productive members of the household.

The possessions of John Green, who married Mary or Polly as she was known, the daughter of Thomas Smith, were listed in a short inventory of 1803. He owned three slaves: Brutus and Prince, each valued at £40 and a girl Philis valued at £25. These three would not have been sufficient for the household but there is no record of his wife's possessions.

There were eight slaves registered to Sarah Musson Trott, widow of Samuel Henry Trott, in the 1821 Slave Register. All except 40 year old Tom, who was described as a sailor, were listed as labourers. There were four men: Dick, David, Prince and Peter, two women: Beck and Lattice and one 14 year old girl Nancy.

The Register for John Henry Trott in 1833 contained a total of six slaves, many being of the same name as in his mother Sarah Trott's listing. Tom was a mariner, Dick and Prince were labourers. Nancy and the two children Emma, aged 13, and Geoffrey were domestic servants.   D.C.

| RETURN OF SLAVES made by | | | | John. H. Trott | |
NAMES.	SEX.	COLOUR.	EMPLOYMENT.	AGE.	COUNTRY.
Tom	Male	Black	Mariner	5?	Bermuda
Dick	Male	Black	Labourer	46	" "
Prince	Male	Black	"	36	" "
Nancy	Female		Domestic	26	" "
Emma	"	coloured	"	13	" "
Geoffry	Male	"	"	5	" "

Five year old Geoffrey, bottom line, was listed in the records of the Registrar of Slaves as part of the household of John Henry Trott of Verdmont. *Return of Slaves 1833. John H. Trott, Agent for Samuel Trott. Neg. 3871. Bermuda Archives: Records of the Registrar of Slaves.*

position of Judge of the Vice Admiralty, seemingly abandoning his portrait painting. In 1789 his wife inherited Verdmont on the death of her step-mother Elizabeth.

As Judge of the Vice Admiralty, Green was responsible for hearing cases brought against privateers. He was accused of being too lenient with the Bermudians and too harsh with the Americans. This might have brought him popularity on the island but he was described as the "infamous John Green" and "Injustice of Bermuda" in a 1795 newspaper in Newburyport, Massachusetts.

A Boston newspaper of March 1795 quoted by Hereward Trott Watlington in an article in the *Bermuda Historical Quarterly* of Summer 1967 states, "We are sorry to inform the public that the business of privateering is carried on, if possible, with more keenness than ever before from Bermuda... The cargoes will certainly be condemned ... Such is the venality and wickedness of Green, the Judge of the Admiralty Court of those Islands, and formerly 'sign painter in Philadelphia' that it is immaterial to stand trial ..."

As a Justice of the Peace, Green was involved in yet another controversy, this time with Methodist missionary John Stephenson (*see chapter 11*) who was accused of fostering dissent by preaching to the slaves. According to Dr. Wilkinson in *Bermuda from Sail to Steam*, John Green remarked, "the slaves were 'kindly and humanely dealt with' on the Island, to which the missionary replied that he accepted the fact, but it was his duty to assist 'in saving their souls'. The justice then observed that the stranger had shaken hands with them and started social 'innovations' which could not be allowed."

In addition Green was also a farmer and in 1791 produced 80 bales of cot-

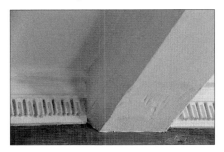

The large summer beam in the ceiling of the hall at Verdmont dates from the time of the builder John Dickinson. The dentil cornice was probably installed later.

This masonry urn in the south garden of Verdmont is one of a pair and may have been put there during the late 18th century when the house was lived in by Mary Green and her husband John Green.

ton grown on the Verdmont estate and on land he rented at Tucker's Town.

John Green was obviously influenced by the neoclassical movement sweeping London during his visit in 1774 and wrote in his letter to his future father-in-law of the influence of the ancient Greeks and Romans on art and architecture. He may have been responsible for the installation of the curved cornice with its strong dentil moulding in the hall at Verdmont. The two large urns in the garden may also owe their presence to him.

He lived a privileged life at Verdmont. Dr. Wilkinson in *Bermuda from Sail to Steam* wrote, "(John Green) kept a good house and table . . . He maintained a correct conservative standard of style so that he seemed to many people to present almost the pic-

ture of good fortune." In the announcement of his death in *The Bermuda Gazette* of September 11, 1802, it was written that he had died "at his seat at Verdmont" which gives the impression of one of Bermuda's nobility dying at his stately home although he and his wife only enjoyed three years together in the house without the presence of their in-laws.

The house and most of the possessions within it were his wife's, but a short 1803 inventory (*see appendix 4*) of John Green lists his personal goods. He was obviously responsible for introducing greater refinement into the house. He owned two flutes, a backgammon set, a china dinner service, prints and some books.

His wife Polly died within six months of her husband's death. There

Captain John Henry Trott (1805-1892) and his wife Harriet Brownlow Hurst (1807-1891) sold Verdmont following the death of their only surviving child Kate from typhoid in 1858. *Courtesy of William and Joyce Zuill.*

An inside view of the window in the hall, the main southwest room at Verdmont where there are panelled folding interior shutters. The dentil moulding on the cornice can be glimpsed above the window as well as the wood panelling, which is thought to have been installed to carry paper hangings.

were no children from this marriage and unfortunately there is no inventory of her possessions.

Verdmont became home to the Trott family for the next half century. Samuel Henry Trott

(died 1817), the nephew of Polly Green, quickly moved into the house and managed the Greens' estate. He was the son of her sister Elizabeth Smith who in 1772 had married Colonel Henry Trott (before 1753-1805), one of the heirs to the Walsingham estate (see *Hamilton Parish*).

Samuel Henry Trott was a magistrate and member of the Colonial Parliament. In 1804, a year before he acquired Verdmont, he married Sarah Musson (circa 1788-1866), daughter of James Musson Jr. of Frascati in Flatts.

Verdmont was to be filled with children as the Trotts' family regularly increased during their 13 year marriage and five were to survive to adulthood. The two previous owners, the Greens and the Smiths, had been childless.

Among their children was Mary Green Trott (1813-1892) who was in 1836 to marry British army officer Charles Ellard d'Esterre of the 30th Regiment. Their son James C.E. d'Esterre was to inherit many of the John Green portraits which were later returned to the museum by Hereward Watlington.

Samuel Henry Trott died prematurely. He had, according to newspaper reports, "suffered under a mental derangement for a long time prior to his death". Sarah Trott was to spend 47 years as a widow at Verdmont. Susette Harriet Lloyd, a young English governess who was in Bermuda from 1829 to 1831 with the family of Reverend Aubrey Spencer, Archdeacon of Bermuda, paid a visit to a Mrs. Trott at Verdmont, presumably Sarah, and was much impressed by the view and by the portraits.

In *Sketches of Bermuda* published in 1835 she wrote, "Last Friday we went on a visit to Mrs. Trott, whose house really deserves its name of Verdmont, for it stands in the midst of evergreen hills, and commands a splendid view over all the Southern coast… Mrs. Trott is related to Mr. Green, who was one of the Judges of the Admiralty Court, established here during the war. He appears to have been a very industrious artist, and many of his paintings are preserved with much care. Some of the portraits are really well done, and the rich hooped brocade dresses, Mechlin ruffles, and jewels, impress you with a favourable idea of the former wealth and consequence of the Bermudians."

The furniture of Rupert Hugh Spencer goes on sale at Verdmont. *The Royal Gazette, August 9, 1881.*

Captain John Henry Trott (1805-1892), son of Samuel and Sarah, took over the property from his father's estate in 1831 upon his marriage to Harriet Brownlow Hurst. He was Provost Marshal General from 1839 until 1887.

An inventory (*see appendix 5*) of his father's possessions made in 1835, some 18 years after Samuel Henry Trott's death, revealed that the paintings and prints of John Green had by now been consigned to the garret and were valued at a mere £6.13.11. Paper hangings of little value were listed in an inventory that was remarkably modest compared with those of John Dickinson and Thomas Smith.

Harriet Trott was to give birth to two daughters at Verdmont, and both were to die tragically young. Her first, Harriet Sarah Trott, died aged two. Catherine Packwood Trott, known as Kate, reportedly died of typhoid at Verdmont on August 31, 1858, aged 25.

Verdmont photographed from the south in 1939 by Walter Rutherford. The garden was overgrown and the house had fallen into disrepair. The two storey porch may be glimpsed, right. *Verdmont, Smith's Parish, photograph by Walter Rutherford. The Bermudian, August 1939, page 15. Courtesy family of the late Edmund M. Gosling.*

Following the death of Kate the Trotts are said to have lost interest in the house and moved to Hamilton. Verdmont and its land were first rented and then sold to planter Rupert Hugh Spencer.

Rupert Hugh Spencer (1820-1868) became the next owner of Verdmont which he bought in 1860 from John Henry Trott. He was a farmer and lived in the house along with his widowed elder brother, master shipwright John William Spencer (1807-1871), and his brother's two daughters (*see also chapter 10*).

The two girls, Ella Eliza (1846-1887) and Emma Elizabeth (1849-1919), were to inherit Verdmont as tenants in common from their bachelor uncle Rupert.

In 1875 Ella, who was about to marry Captain James Lusher, and Emma, who had married Stafford Nairn Joell, decided to divide their inheritance. They could not agree and resorted to arbitration.

Ella received the land south of South Shore Road plus her father's house while Emma was awarded her uncle's house Verdmont and the land north of South Shore Road.

In 1976 Vernon A. Ives, an American publisher who had retired to Bermuda, wrote an unpublished article on 'The Spencer-Joell family at Verdmont' for the Bermuda National Trust which forms the basis for the story of the family at Verdmont.

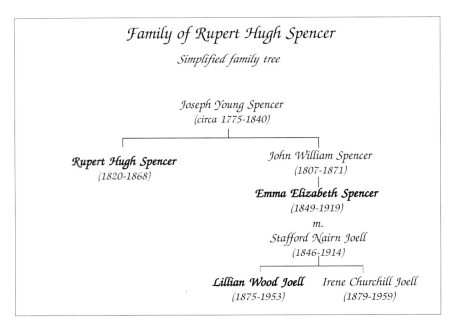

Family of Rupert Hugh Spencer
Simplified family tree

Joseph Young Spencer
(circa 1775-1840)

Rupert Hugh Spencer
(1820-1868)

John William Spencer
(1807-1871)

Emma Elizabeth Spencer
(1849-1919)
m.
Stafford Nairn Joell
(1846-1914)

Lillian Wood Joell
(1875-1953)

Irene Churchill Joell
(1879-1959)

Farmer Rupert Hugh Spencer, who purchased Verdmont in 1860, was a bachelor. The house descended to his niece Emma Joell, née Spencer, and then to her daughters Lillian and Irene.

Verdmont photographed in the 1930s when it would have been home to spinster sisters Irene and Lillian Joell.
Bermudiana, Ronald John Williams, 1946, page 102.

Emma's husband, Stafford Nairn Joell (1846-1914), was a planter and farmed the acreage north of South Shore Road whilst Ella's southern portion was probably let to a tenant farmer.

Vernon Ives wrote, "It is doubtful if the Joells took much interest in the history or architecture of the house. To them it was not their old family homestead, just a capacious, old fashioned home. They probably added the wooden verandah on the south side (now gone) and may have dug the water tank near the house to replace the hillside catchment 200 feet away. Fortunately, they did not modernise the buildings, which so often happened in Victorian times."

The Joells had five children: Emma Constance, Lillian Wood, Spencer Churchill, Irene Churchill and Edmund Willoughby. All but the youngest were born at Verdmont.

On Emma Joell's death in 1919 the bulk of the property including the house was left to her two unmarried daughters Lillian and Irene Joell. Her youngest son Edmund had the right to live in Verdmont until he married, which he never did. He drowned off the South Shore five years after his mother's death. Her oldest son Spencer had been given land on which he built Seamont in 1913 on Collectors Hill.

The two sisters, Lillian Wood Joell (1875-1953) and Irene Churchill Joell (1879-1959), were to live together at Verdmont. Irene however officially turned over her half of the Verdmont property in 1920 to Lillian although she continued to live in the house for the next 15 years before moving to Hamilton.

This left Lillian Wood Joell as the sole owner and occupant of Verdmont from 1935. She cooked on a kerosene stove in the dining room, pumped water by hand from the outside tank and used oil lamps and candles. She walked to Hamilton where she worked for 45 years in a law firm, known at the beginning of the 21st century as Appleby, Spurling & Kempe.

In 1951 Lillian Joell sold Verdmont and about 28 acres for £11,500 to her nephew Alan Paul Joell (1910-1960) and moved to Westmeath, a nursing home. Alan Joell was the son of her brother Spencer Churchill Joell of neighbouring Seamont.

However, before this conveyance had time to have been officially recorded Alan Joell on October 22, 1951, sold the house and surrounding 2.229 acres to the Bermuda Historical Monuments Trust for £8,000. Over the coming years he was to subdivide and sell off as building lots the remaining land which had belonged to this once great estate.

The Bermuda Historical Monuments Trust was to renovate the house and eventually open it as a museum in 1957. The Trust had been incorporated on May 1, 1937, and had purchased a number of historical buildings and nature reserves. A subcommittee of doctor and historian Henry Wilkinson, architect Wilfred Onions, known as Wil, and antiquarian and artist Hereward Watlington were formed to oversee the restoration.

The committee originally estimated the house would need £1,500 to put it in good repair as they believed the roof to be in good condition although some of the floors needed replacing. Among their first acts, as revealed in their minutes, was to order two fire grates from John Bell of Aberdeen and to discuss the planting.

The worst of the flooring was taken up and ground clearing started. However, in December 1952 Onions reported that some repairs were necessary to the roof and the rafters. Work on the roof by contractor and roof specialist Lionel Darrell did not begin until May 1954. Structural weaknesses were found and the job took longer and cost more than first estimated.

With the roof sound, interior work began at the end of 1954 under the supervision of Wil Onions with skilled carpenter Lawson Lambert. Windows and door frames were repaired and H-shaped hinges for the interior shutters ordered from London. The majority of the shutters had to be rebuilt. Electrical wiring was installed for the first time with a discreet outlet in each room although it was not to be linked to the mains until 1955.

In 1955 the building used as a farm shed alongside the detached kitchen was removed leaving its concrete floor to become a terrace for the cottage. The masonry wall on the east side of the shed was lowered to the same level as the existing garden wall. It is still possible to see where there were regularly spaced window openings in this Bermuda stone wall.

American architect Bryden B. Hyde, author of *Bermuda's Antique Furniture & Silver*, suggested in 1955 that a balcony be created over the south door to replace the two storey porch which was in a poor state of repair. The new small cedar balcony was designed by Onions. The main door frame on the south side of the house was also replaced.

The following year sash weights were installed in all the windows and the interior shutters completed and hung. Garden design was done by landscape architect Bayfield Clark.

The old detached kitchen with adjoining storeroom was turned into a curator's cottage using designs drawn by Onions. A bathroom and kitchen were added in the centre of the building and the floor in the south bedroom was raised and replaced. This was to be the home of the first museum curator of Verdmont, Lillian Fox.

Meanwhile Dr. Wilkinson was busy collecting and organising the furnishing of the interior and Hereward Watlington was overseeing the return of the John Green portraits to the house. The total cost of the restoration amounted to £4,000.

The Bermuda National Trust was established in December 1969 and took over the properties of the Bermuda Historical Monuments Trust including Verdmont and its furnishings. The Bermuda National Trust has continued to open it as a museum and to maintain the house in the manner established by the Historical Monuments Trust. Little more than essential repairs and maintenance have been done to the house although considerable work has been done in the garden.

A small car park was created on the northwest in 1991 and planting of native and endemic species has taken place on the eastern and southern slopes of the property whilst a small period fruit garden was established on the western hillside. The garden walls were restored and railings and a gate installed in 1993.

The cedar balcony on the south needed extensive repairs in 1992, and a tornado in 1986 and hurricane Fabian in 2003 damaged more than half of the slate on the upper roof.

The history of Verdmont is well documented and the house has been extensively studied although some of its secrets still remain to be uncovered. Architectural historians from the Colonial Williamsburg Foundation of Virginia have examined the house over the years and have contributed much to our understanding of its architecture. A brief archaeology test study was conducted in October 2004 (*see chapter 1*).

A preliminary survey was made of the interior paints and finishes but as yet no extensive study has taken place. Investigation by Welsh Color & Conservation Inc. in November 2003 revealed evidence of wallpaper, coloured paint on some of the interior woodwork and lime washes on the plaster walls.

Evidence of wallpaper was found on the undersides of the window sills and cornices in the two ground floor south front rooms. Frank S. Welsh observed "it seems logical to expect that these rooms were papered after the board walls were installed".

Although the cedar staircase balustrade and the mahogany doors have never been painted, evidence of a medium blue, a vibrant green and a reddish brown paint was found on some of the woodwork. Medium blue paint was found on the raised panel fronts of the original interior window shutters, the glazed double parlour doors and on the carved mantelpiece in the upstairs

Lillian Wood Joell was the last inhabitant of Verdmont.
Guide to Verdmont, undated. The Bermuda National Trust.

parlour. Vibrant green was found on some of the 18th century trim on the ground floor stair passage and reddish brown on the flat panel backs of the interior shutters. Investigation revealed that the cedar mantelpieces have been stripped of paint layers and further analysis is needed to determine whether or not they were originally painted.

Three centuries after it was built by John Dickinson Verdmont still stands much the same as it was when it was first constructed. Its acreage is much reduced, the neighbourhood more crowded and its view far less imposing. The families who lived in the house and the people who served them have gone to be replaced by curious visitors anxious to learn about its history. It has now served as a museum for nearly half a century having been opened on November 21, 1957, by the Governor, Lieutenant-General Sir John Woodall. 🌴

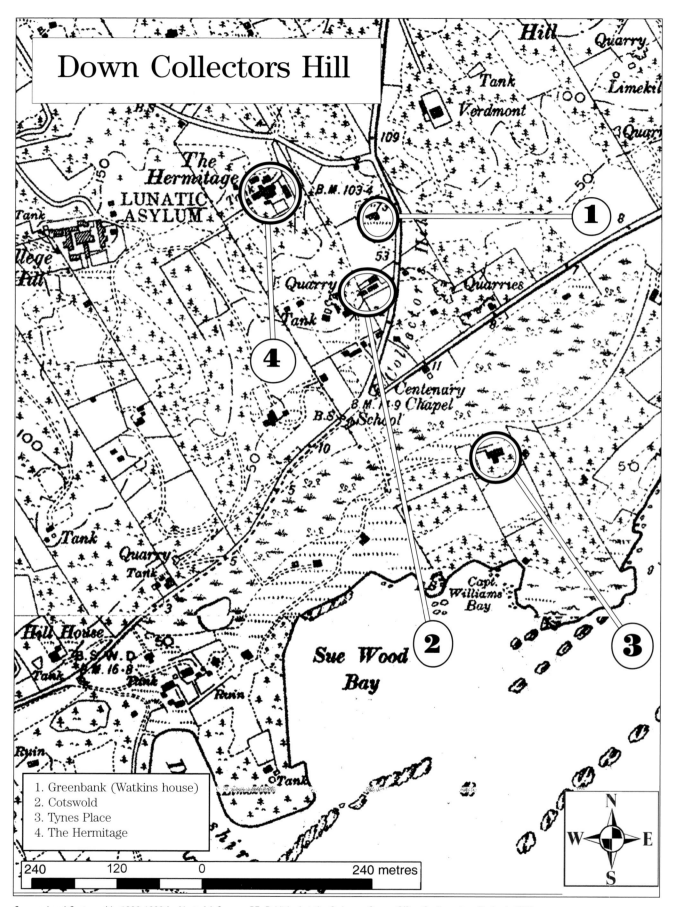

Down Collectors Hill

1. Greenbank (Watkins house)
2. Cotswold
3. Tynes Place
4. The Hermitage

240 120 0 240 metres

Surveyed and Contoured in 1898-1899 by Lieut. A.J. Savage, RE. Published at the Ordnance Survey Office, Southampton, England, 1901.
Courtesy Works & Engineering.

3

Down Collectors Hill

This tranquil scene was photographed in the early 1930s. The cart is being driven west down St. Mark's Road and is approaching the junction with Verdmont Road which leads into Collectors Hill. The rutted track in the background is now called Peets Point Lane. Vickers' Store, right, built about 1830 was largely demolished in 2002. The house in the distance, rear left, built in the early 20th century is still there although the porch has been filled in. *The Story of Bermuda, Hudson Strode, 1946, facing page 86.*

Collectors Hill, which runs from its junction with Verdmont Road near Hermitage Road downhill to South Shore Road, was close to the homes of at least three men who held the important job of Collector of Customs. Thomas Smith and John Green both lived at Verdmont on the east side of the road and Gilbert Salton at The Hermitage on the west.

The hill, which was part of the General Highway which led from St. George's Island via the Ferry and Flatts Bridge to Mangrove Bay in Somerset, could have been named after either or all of these men.

However, William Zuill in *Bermuda Journey* wrote, "The name Collector's Hill comes from Gilbert Salton, Collector of Customs between 1816 and 1839, who lived at the Hermitage near the top

of the hill. This house has now disappeared and the Collector is remembered only by the name of this difficult and tortuous hill and by a memorial tablet in St. Mark's Church."

Gilbert Salton was the Collector of Customs in the early 19th century whilst Thomas Smith was Collector during the mid 18th century and John Green very briefly succeeded his father-in-law during 1785 (*see chapter 2*). When it came to naming the road in the 19th century these earlier two may have been long forgotten.

Bermuda has always depended, and continues to depend, on duty collected on imports for its national income. In the first years taxes were collected by the joint stock Bermuda Company. After 1684, when the island became a colony, customs duties were

paid to the Commissioner of Customs in London. In 1778 the law was changed and customs revenue went straight to the local legislature, a move designed to defuse resentment following the American Revolution. Thomas Smith and John Green would have worked under the old system transmitting their proceeds to London, whilst Gilbert Salton was in office under the new.

The office of Collector of Customs lent its holder great dignity and importance. The collection of customs duties included responsibility for bonded goods such as rum and tobacco as well as the safeguarding of the cargoes of ships captured by Bermudian privateers whilst the fate of that cargo was decided in the Court of Vice Admiralty. In addition the Collector was also responsible for implementing the British

Greenbank, on the east side of Collectors Hill, photographed in the early 1920s by John S. Humphreys. This shows the rear wing in the foreground which may have been built later than the front of the house.   *Bermuda Houses, John S. Humphreys, 1923, page 253, plate 138.*

Navigation Acts. These were laws designed to control colonial trade.

St. George's was the sole customs port until Hamilton was declared a town in 1795. Thomas Smith and John Green worked in St. George's whilst Gilbert Salton's office was in Hamilton.

The 1782 inventory (*see appendix 3*) of Thomas Smith of Verdmont provides an insight into the contents of his office in St. George's. At the Customs House were official seals, scales and weights as well as a complete set of statutes. Four views of London decorated the walls, no doubt reinforcing his official position as Collector of His Majesty's Customs.

Collectors Hill has become a relatively crowded neighbourhood but a number of historic houses still exist. Verdmont, an early 18th century house now a museum owned by the Bermuda National Trust, is on the east side of the road and Greenbank and Cotswold on the west. Tynes Place is on Ap Owen Road, or as the road sign says A.P. Owen Road, which can almost be considered as a continuation of Collectors Hill on the south side of South Shore Road.

Greenbank, which was formerly known as the **Watkins house**, is at the top of Collectors Hill near its junction with Hermitage Road and not far from Verdmont.

It is a gable roofed L-shaped house which originally faced north up Collectors Hill. The main east to west block has a chimney at either end and there is a third at the end of the rear, or south, wing which is built over a cellar. All three chimneys differ in their stack mouldings and the location of shoulders, suggesting that they vary in date. It is probable that the one at the east end is the oldest and the one on the rear wing the next.

The house in the mid 20th century was partitioned for two families and there have been a number of changes and additions.

In 1789 cabinet maker Joseph Watkins (died 1813) owned four acres and a house in Smith's Parish. It is assumed that this was the house, or at least a portion of the house, now known as Greenbank which Joseph Watkins gave to his five daughters: Mary Watkins, Ann Homeyard Taylor, Elizabeth Davis, Sarah Watkins and Grace Peniston Watkins.

Three of the Watkins girls did not marry and continued to live at home. A comment in the Mercer/Zuill Notes in the Bermuda Archives, presumably written by William Edward Sears Zuill, states, "The Watkins lived in the fine old house which stands out boldly on the bank on the left as one mounts Collectors Hill. At this house, so Uncle Scott Pearman used to relate, William Trott (and one supposes, others of his generation) were taught to dance by Miss Gracie Watkins who lived there with her father. He was a carpenter and she turned the lathe for him."

Gracie Watkins was reputed to have played music for the dancers, according to William Zuill, on "a piece of thin paper over a comb".

Her father Joseph Watkins made spinning tops which were the craze amongst schoolboys of the early 19th century, especially when the tops were fitted with nails to destroy the opposition. John Harvey Darrell (1796-1887), who was to grow up to become Chief Justice of Bermuda, wrote in his jour-

An aerial view of Greenbank shows the original portion of the house, centre, with a gable roof stretching between the two chimneys. The rear wing, right, also has a chimney on its end. Modern additions are in the foreground.

nal of visits to the Watkins house to barter for tops.

John Harvey Darrell lived at the house called Cavendish in Devonshire (see *Devonshire*) and walked with his friends to the Watkins house first to take wood and then to collect tops made for him by Joseph Watkins.

He wrote in his journal, "Every now and then of a Saturday we used to make up parties to go to Watkins. Such of us as had no money (or very little) would carry Mr. Watkins logs of lemon and orange wood, guava and mangrove wood which we cut in the ponds and sea coast. The orange and lemon wood was rather brittle for making tops; the guava tougher but rather scarce; the mangrove was best of all for it was not only larger and heavier than the other kinds of wood, but the cleavage of the wood being in layers like the layers of an onion would not split open when picked into by the nail of another top...

"Old Watkins used to take these pieces of wood from us at certain prices, according to size and quality, payable in tops! He used to value his tops fitted with nails at one penny,

twopence, threepence and the largest and best at fourpence – currency."

Interestingly John Harvey Darrell wrote of the later near extinction of mangroves because the wood was "capital material for making the hubs and fellies of cart wheels". Carts, he wrote were "unknown in my schoolboy days". A felly was the exterior rim of a wheel.

Not only did the boys barter with the old man, they also traded with his daughters. John Harvey Darrell wrote, "The old man had two somewhat elderly daughters, whom we used to call Miss Molly and Miss Gracie. Their occupation was working palmetto plait into hats and other things they had to whiten with brimstone. Money was as scarce with them as it was with their old father . . ."

The boys would take broken pieces of brimstone given them by storekeepers in Hamilton and trade these for tops. John Harvey Darrell wrote, "The house door was not immediately in sight of the carpenter's shop door and while some of the boys were trading with the old man in the shop others

with brimstone would slip round to the house door, to deal with Miss Molly and Miss Gracie, who used to caution the boys against letting papa know anything about it and sometimes present them with an additional top as a bonus.

"As soon as the dealings were all over we used to set off on our return home but as we kept stopping along the way picking tops it was generally evening before we arrived at the Lane."

There were two washerwomen listed as slaves in the Watkins household in the Slave Register of 1821. They were 66 year old Nany and 22 year old Bess.

The Watkins house was by 1869 owned by planter Marcus Harvey (circa 1831-1883). He may have been responsible for adding the southern rear wing to the house. This wing is built over a cellar which was used as an ARP (Air Raid Precaution) shelter during the Second World War.

At the beginning of the 21st century, and more than 130 years later, the descendants of Marcus Harvey still live in the house which is now named Greenbank.

Cotswold

A two storey kitchen and service building, left, was separate from the main house of Cotswold. It was linked to the upper living level of the house, right, by a bridge or walkway, centre, in this early 20th century photograph. *Courtesy Sue Lusher.*

Cotswold is a two storey house that apparently confined the owners' living space to the upper floor, reached in the 19th and early 20th centuries by a stair set into the surviving porch overlooking the South Shore. Alterations confuse the evidence, but Cotswold expands the known spectrum of arrangement for Bermuda households with resident workers. The core of the house has a three room plan, with a 17'5" by 15'2" unheated room on the east (right) and a 14'9" by 15'2" heated middle room. A small 8'8" by 15'2" room on the west (left) is incorporated under the main hipped roof, its tray ceiling having three faces like the larger east room. There is now a fireplace in the west face of the chimney, in the small room, but one suspects it was inserted in the 20th century.

A bridge shown in a circa 1920 photograph connected this small upper room to a servants' room in a two storey building 9' to the west. This is a relatively large room — 17'4" by 12'3" — given its function, and is lighted by four windows. It appears always to have been open to the roof, braced by three tie beams, 6'6" above the present floor.

The ground floor of the house has large, rough longitudinal summer beams in both main rooms carrying rough old joists once covered with plaster. Apparently this was used for maritime and agricultural storage. A nicely finished summer beam under the bridge suggests some structure may have connected the kitchen/quarters from at least the late 19th century and it raises the possibility that the upper room once became a dining room for the owners.

The ground floor cookroom now has a 3'9" by 2'7" raised fireplace, probably reduced in the late 19th century, and an oven in the northwest corner with a cast iron "Number 14" door opening into the room and an exterior flue crawling up the west wall to reach the chimney. This room is 17'4" by 12'3".

John Humphreys in his book *Bermuda Houses* shows the present early porch with lattice below the upper handrail and enclosing the exterior stair. There are 4" square chamfered posts above and below, some of the lower ones with hewn shoulders as well as wrought angle irons supporting thin transverse summers.

A few datable details indicate this is an early 19th century house. There is a single tie beam in both main upper rooms, at the west (left) end of each, and these are planed and cut with single beads rather than chamfers. The door between the two main rooms has double architraves with circa 1800-1820 mouldings on both sides and the door from the middle room to the small space has a frame with corner beads but no rabbet, suggesting an old rebateless door. There are windows with plain board heads and recessed, beaded frames that have an early 19th century appearance. The roof is old fashioned, however, with a stone ball at the ends of the ridge.

This could be read as the "small house much in need of repairs, having a hall chamber and small closet with cellar underneath" that Sarah Smith owned and occupied before dying intestate in 1804, though it is far more likely to have been built by shipbuilder Thomas W. Smith, who bought the property in 1809 and owned it until his death in 1835. It remained in the Smith family until 1961.   *E.A.C.*

17⁴ x 12³   9⁰ x 12³ 8⁸ x 15² 14⁹ x 15³   17⁵ x 15²

OVEN BELOW

COTSWOLD, 21 COLLECTOR'S HILL, SMITH'S PARISH, BERMUDA : UPPER FLOOR OCT. 13, '03   6FT

Cotswold, field sketch: *Drawn by Edward A. Chappell.*

Cotswold is a little lower down Collectors Hill than Greenbank and continues to look like a timeless piece of old Bermuda although there have been some changes to make it suitable for contemporary living.

It was originally built with living accommodation on the upper floor and storage at ground level. It is hip roofed, one room deep and has a two storey wooden verandah overlooking the South Shore. Access to the upper level was earlier gained by an outside staircase built into the verandah.

A small two storey detached building stood immediately to the west of the main house. This contained a kitchen with a raised cooking fireplace and bake oven on the ground floor while the upper storey may have served as living quarters for slaves. This service building was earlier linked to the main house by a bridge or walkway on the upper level.

The five acres on which the house stood was intersected by Collectors Hill and there was a separate stable block on the other side of the road.

Cotswold appears to be an early 19th century house. It is just possible it may have been built for Sarah Gibbons Smith on land given to her by her grandmother Mary Packwood who was a midwife in Smith's Parish. Mary Packwood in her will written in 1744 left her granddaughter, who may have been a child at the time, 5½ acres along with her choice of ten cedar trees with which to build a house. Sarah Smith died in debt and intestate in 1804. Her house was sold by her executors to pay her debts.

The property changed hands a couple of times until it was purchased in 1809 by Thomas William Smith for £320. Cotswold as it stands today may more likely have been built by him than Sarah Smith.

Thomas William Smith (circa 1783-

Cotswold, an early 19th century house on Collectors Hill, was photographed in the 1920s by John S. Humphreys. A wooden staircase at the east end of the verandah provided access to the upper living level with space for storage below.   *Bermuda Houses, John S. Humphreys, 1923, page 263, plate 145.*

Cotswold on Collectors Hill seen from the east appears to be little changed from when it was photographed by John S. Humphreys in the 1920s (above). Gingerbread splats on the verandah have replaced the earlier trellis.

1835) was described in his will as a shipwright and was the grandson and one of the heirs of Nathaniel Tynes (circa 1744-1807) of Devonshire who was one of Bermuda's celebrated shipbuilders. He married his cousin Rebecca Skinner, who was also a grandchild of Nathaniel Tynes. They produced three sons. The youngest, Thomas Smith, was to become a Methodist missionary in Nova Scotia whilst the eldest predeceased his father.

The slaves, who would have lived in the detached kitchen building to the west of the main house, were listed in the Slave Register made on the eve of emancipation in 1833-1834. There were two carpenters, Daniel and Tom, one house servant, Jane, and three young children, presumably the children of Jane. The two eldest, Jacob aged seven and Emily Jane aged four, were already described as being house servants although the two month old baby Nancy was listed without an occupation.

Cotswold remained in the Smith family for the next 150 years descending to Isaac Smith (circa 1807-1870), the second son of Thomas William Smith, then to his grandson Adolphus Smith (1832-1916), his great-grandson George Ernest Smith and finally to his great-great-granddaughter Isabelle who married Joseph John O'Brien, known as Jack. In 1961 the house finally passed out of the family.

Tynes Place

Tynes Place: *Drawn by Barbara Finsness.*

The core of Tynes Place is a T-shaped house that grew incrementally, apparently from rear to front (south to north), built as a hall chamber house, then enlarged with another hall and chamber. Both accommodated work and workers in the cellar, in rooms less bright but sometimes more colourfully painted than those of the owners.

It seems to have begun life as a two room house facing east and west, with a 15'10" by 14'4" heated hall and a 7'8" by 14'4" unheated inner room (on the north). Below the hall is the original cookroom, a 15'9" by 13'8" space with a very rough work fireplace, 5'4" wide and 5'6" deep, chopped out of the limestone. Light was poor, possibly supplied only by a small window in the west wall. Apparently food was carried from an east door in the kitchen to the outside and into the hall where the owners ate.

If one accepts the will of John Tynes Sr. as applicable to this house, then before 1774 he added a second two room block, apparently that to the north, the present front. This contained a 20'1" by 14'4" west room and an 18'1" by 14'2" east room, each with a fireplace in an exterior end chimney. The front door now opens into the smaller of these rooms, conceivably having been moved when other rooms were subsequently added to the east. Below the larger north room is a second cellar room, 13'8" by 20'3", provided with a 4'5" by 3'1" fireplace, and probably intended as work and living space for Tynes' slaves.

John Tynes presumably planned one of the two north ground floor rooms as a new hall and the other as his new bedchamber. The latter intention as well as the relative date of the addition is indicated by his 1774 will which directs that his daughter Elizabeth Tynes should receive both "the bed and furniture which stands in the chamber called by the name of my chamber" and he gave to his daughter Anna Taylor "the bed and furniture which stands in the chamber called the old chamber".

A rear (south) room was added in the 19th century after cooking was no longer done below the old hall. Ingeniously, the new builders sealed off the original cellar fireplace and inserted a ground floor fireplace in the 4' by 2'2" flue passing behind the old hall fireplace. This rear room, now a kitchen, has a conventional Bermuda treatment, with tie beams exposed at the top of the walls and plaster carried up to collars partway along the roof slope.

The rest of the house is now treated the same, but climbing above the collars one finds that originally the four rooms were open to the roof ridge. The multiple layers of lime wash are most evident in the front spaces, where the end walls and masonry partition were painted with white and pigmented washes. Before being hidden by a ceiling, the interior stack of the east chimney was painted with no less than 11 layers of plain whitewash, then three layers of a brilliant yellow lime wash, followed by one layer of bright orange.   *E.A.C.*

The Smiths produced large families in what must have been a fairly modest sized house with living accommodation confined to the upper floor. Isaac had 13 children and Adolphus ten.

There was a mid 19th century proposal to alter the position of Collectors Hill. The House of Assembly in its Journal of Proceedings of July 21, 1854, recommended moving the line of the road towards the west, running "to the west of Mr. Isaac Smith (of Cotswold) and through the land of the late Miss Watkins (Greenbank)." The road at this time appeared to be known as Smith's Hill, possibly from the Smiths of Cotswold rather than Collector of Customs Thomas Smith of Vermont who died in 1781.

As Bermuda's economy changed from being dependent on shipbuilding to farming, so Cotswold evolved from being the home of a shipwright to a home for farmers with agricultural produce kept in its ground floor storerooms.

Interestingly the dwarf Canary Island banana *Musa cavendishii*, which is now grown almost exclusively rather than the taller variety, is a fairly recent introduction to Bermuda. According to E.A. McCallan writing in *Life on Old St. David's*, the dwarf variety was first introduced to Smith's Parish during the time the house was owned by George Ernest Smith. He owned Cotswold from 1908 to 1950.

In the middle and second half of the 20th century Cotswold was remodelled and the original storage rooms at ground level were incorporated into the house, an interior staircase constructed and the kitchen building joined to the main house. It was reslated but the roof finials remain.

Tynes Place is located near the South Shore off Ap Owen Road. Successive additions have changed the orientation of the house as it now faces north over Smith's Marsh.

Tynes Place is south of Collectors Hill and was built on the higher ground above Smith's Marsh (*see chapter 1*), near Captain Williams' Bay.

At the beginning of the 21st century Tynes Place has evolved into a T-shaped house which faces north, the oldest portion being the rear south wing. It is gable roofed and one room deep. The two oldest sections, in the south and west, are built over two previously unconnected cellars which provided a kitchen and accommodation for slaves. There are three sturdy chimneys, two of which also serve the cellars.

The slaves who may have lived in these cellars were described in the 1827 Slave Register as sailor Sam and domestic servant Sue. Four children were also listed, all with the occupation of domestic servant. They were Judy aged 14, Jack aged 12, Jem aged eight and Joe aged six. Judy and Joe continued to be house servants whilst in 1834 Jack had become a mason and Jem a gardener.

Tynes Place was almost in ruins in the 1930s and its roof was replaced in the mid 20th century. The old tie beams have gone to be replaced by boxed pine.

There are some late 20th century additions to the east.

It was called Tynes Place by its present owners after John Tynes, the presumed owner of the house in the late 18th century, although the deeds start with the ownership of Captain Benjamin Abraham Williams who owned the property in the late 19th century. The Tynes family of shipbuilders are traditionally associated with the North Shore although many of their descendants seem to have settled in the Collectors Hill area.

Tynes Place is said to have been owned by John Tynes Sr. (died 1774) who was described as a cordwainer (a shoemaker). In his will written in 1774 he left a house and three acres of land to his son John Tynes Jr. (died 1792), who was also a cordwainer. His three other surviving children, Thomas, Anna and Elizabeth, were given the residue of his estate.

In 1816 Tynes Place and three acres was acquired by mariner Captain Samuel Williams and the property was to descend through his family for the next 162 years whilst the nearby bay was to bear the family name.

Captain Samuel Williams (circa 1784-1867) married Ann Skinner in 1810. She was the sister of Rebecca, wife of Thomas William Smith of Cotswold, and a granddaughter of shipwright Nathaniel Tynes of Devonshire. Her brother, John Abraham Skinner, was the owner of nearby Cloverdale (see *Devonshire*).

Captain Samuel Williams purchased another parcel of land to the west of the Tynes Place property. It is possible he was engaged in whale fishing from his strategically placed position. Whales can still be seen off the South Shore as they pass Bermuda on their seasonal migration to feeding grounds.

In 1828 Captain Samuel Williams advertised his "valuable house and land

---

VALUABLE HOUSE AND LAND,
FOR SALE.

THE Subscriber intending to leave *Bermuda* Shortly, Offers For Sale, his House, and about 6 Acres of first rate Pasture, and Planting LAND, together with a great number of Valuable Palmitto Trees, on the same. The House is very Commodious, Containing a Hall, Parlour, 4 Chambers, 2 Pantrys, a Passage, and Wash Room adjoining, with a fine Tank in the rear, lately erected. From the House you have a fine View of the South Side of the Island, and is an uncommon healthy situation. The above would be particularly valuable to a person interested in the Whale Fishery, &c. The Premises can be seen at any time, and further Particulars made known on application to Mr. R. S. Musson, at Hamilton, or to the Subscriber

SAMUEL WILLIAMS.
Smith's Parish, February 11, 1828.

The Royal Gazette, February 12, 1828.

The Hermitage

The house has gone but is not forgotten as it is remembered in the road name and in a number of drawings. The Hermitage was the home of Collector of Customs Gilbert Salton and it stood on what is now known as Hermitage Close.

Scottish born Gilbert Salton (circa 1770-1839), a widower, arrived in Bermuda in January 1816 with his 18 year old daughter Jane along with his furniture, china, silver and portraits of himself and his daughter. It is assumed he built The Hermitage which stood on a 15 acre lot of land close to the boundary between Smith's and Devonshire Parishes.

The house can be seen in a number of sketches. There are two by James Charles Stuart Green an artist who must have visited Bermuda during 1819 as all his drawings, predominantly of churches, are dated in that year. One of these drawings is inscribed, "To Mr. Salton, Collector of Customs, my good and worthy friend."

The J.C.S. Green sketches, which belong to The Bermuda National Trust and are on display at Verdmont, show a single storey gable roofed house with a chimney at each end and a small porch over the front door. There are two substantial service buildings. Perhaps one of these was home to his housekeeper, Elizabeth Tynes, who was listed in the 1827 Slave Register as being black, aged 40 and born in the West Indies. It was unusual for slaves to have been listed with surnames in the register.

Another and later sketch of The Hermitage by Ella Tucker is found in *The Naturalist in Bermuda* a book written by Salton's grandson John Matthew Jones and published in 1859.

Gilbert Salton's daughter, Jane Helen Melville Salton (circa 1797-1833), married Sir Charles Thomas Jones, captain of HMS *Harrier* soon after the Saltons arrived in Bermuda and left the Island to live in Wales. It was her youngest son, John Matthew Jones, who was to inherit the house. He was the godson of Gilbert Salton's second wife, Alice, and made repeated visits to Bermuda. He was a barrister and also published *The Visitor's Guide to Bermuda* in 1876.

In 1828 Salton married Alice Jones Thomson (circa 1784-1877), the widow of the Reverend John Thomson rector of Sandys, Southampton and Warwick. She inherited The Hermitage and in turn left it to her godson.

A descendant who visited Bermuda in the early 1960s describes finding "the old house still standing but the estate had been subdivided into small lots with cottages. On a small rise southwest of the old house is an outcropping of limestone. I found carved in this rock 'I.M.I. 1873' — my grandfather John Matthew Jones's initials — in Latin."

In 1880 John Matthew Jones sold The Hermitage and eight acres to Jeremiah Scott Pearman (circa 1847-1932) who was in 1896 to inherit Mount Hope (*see chapter 11*). It is said that Pearman removed much of the fabric of The Hermitage to his home at Mount Hope.

Hereward Watlington in *Family Narrative* published in 1980 wrote, "it always seemed that Scott had some new project in hand: the glasshouses with their plants; the fountain which had been brought from The Hermitage on Collectors Hill (which house, I am regretful to say, my uncle had bought and cannibalised). The cedar doors went into wardrobes. It is true that the cries from the Mental Hospital made the place unattractive, and it was sold for housing of many of those people who had lived in Tucker's Town (*see chapter 11*) before the Mid Ocean colony was established, but it was a sad end to a house which had much charm and interest."   *D.C.*

Above: A drawing of the Hermitage by Ella Tucker appears in a book written by John Matthew Jones, the grandson of Gilbert Salton.
The Naturalist in Bermuda, John Matthew Jones, 1859, page 192.

Left: A driveway leads to the house of Collector of Customs Gilbert Salton.
The Hermitage, Bermuda Islands, belonging to Mr. Salton, Collector of Customs, J.C.S. Green, 1819. The Bermuda National Trust: Verdmont Museum.

Vickers' Cottage, on the corner of Verdmont and St. Mark's roads, was largely demolished the day after this photograph was taken.

for sale" describing it as "particularly valuable to a person interested in the whale fishery". He added that the house had "a fine View of the South Side of the Island and is (in) an uncommon healthy situation" as well as having "first rate Pasture, and Planting Land".

The house was described as being "very Commodious, Containing a Hall, Parlour, 4 Chambers, 2 Pantrys, a Passage, and Wash Room adjoining, with a fine Tank in the rear, lately erected".

However, he was obviously not successful in selling his property which descended in 1867 to his son Captain Benjamin Abraham Williams (1815-1893) who was a master mariner. He and his wife, Canadian born Maria Cutlip, had only one daughter, Maria Matilda Williams, baptised in 1849.

In 1890 Captain Benjamin Abraham Williams sold Tynes Place for £200 to Matthew Richey Smith. The new owner was a grandson of Captain Williams' sister Eliza Smith Williams who married Isaac Smith of neighbouring Cotswold.

Matthew Richey Smith (1858-1942) was the assistant overseer at the Lunatic Asylum, known at the beginning of the 21st century as St. Brendan's, which had opened in the former Devonshire College building in

The Hermitage Variety Store on Hermitage Road lost its traditional shop blinds soon after this photograph was taken.

1874 (see *Devonshire*). His daughter, Beryl Smith Boorman, who was to inherit the property in 1932, was responsible for the restoration of Tynes Place in the mid 20th century.

Collectors Hill remains as an interesting part of Bermuda's history which is rapidly changing. When research began on this book the small house in the picture at the beginning of the chapter was still in existence. Its photograph was taken, but the next day it was largely demolished. This house was built in approximately 1830 by grocer John Vickers (1799-1835). It was of traditional design with a sturdy chimney and windows close under the eaves.

Similarly a small shop, the Hermitage Variety Store, on nearby Hermitage Road was altered and lost its traditional shop blinds as this book was being produced. 🌴

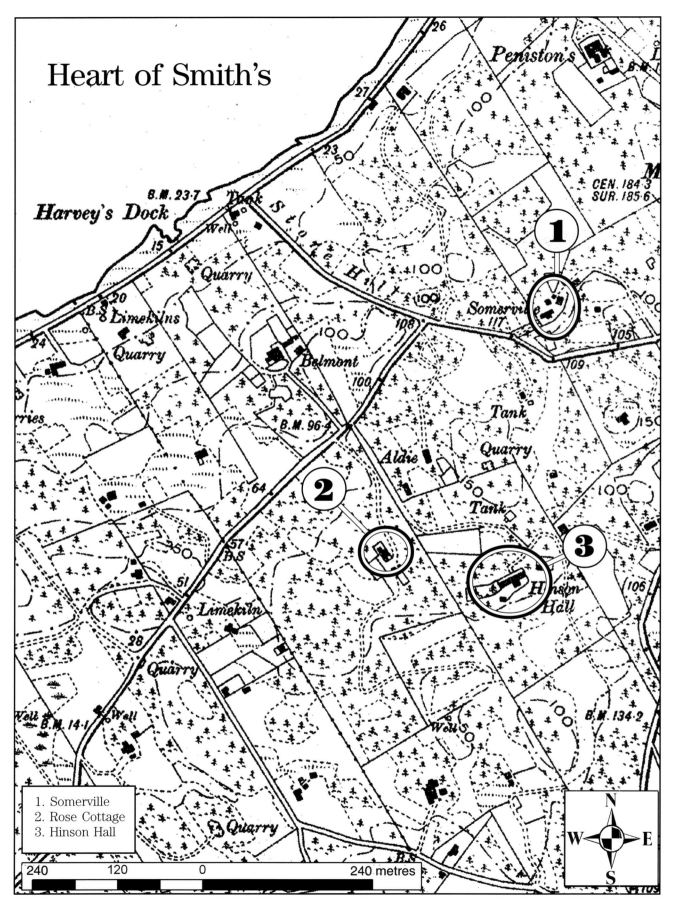

Heart of Smith's

Harvey's Dock

B.M. 23·7

Well

Quarry

B.S. Limekilns

Quarry

Belmont

B.M. 96·4

Aldie

Tank

Tank

Quarry

Somerville

Peniston's

CEN. 184·3
SUR. 185·6

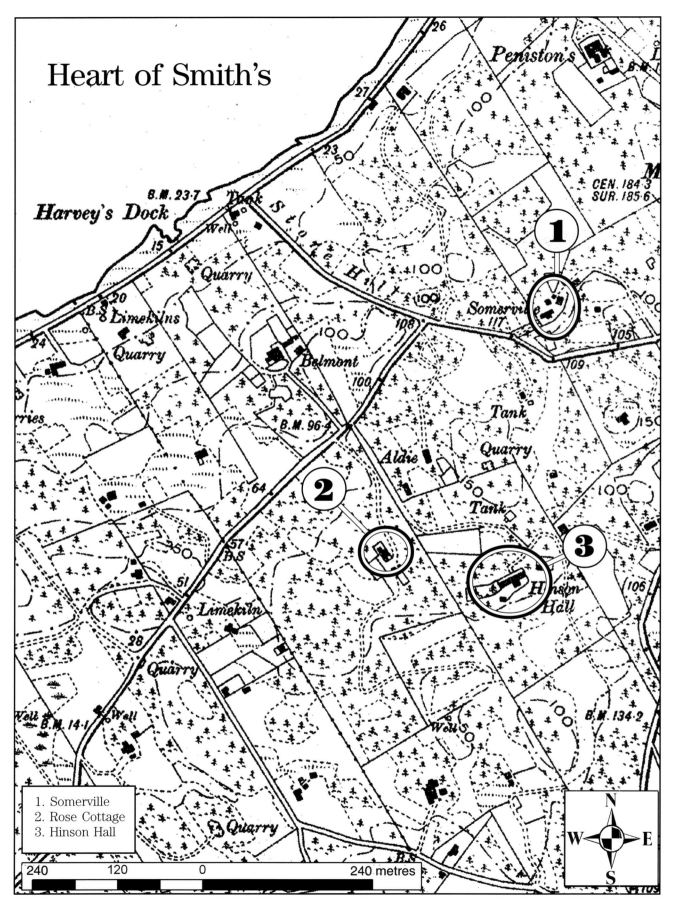

1

2

3

Hinson Hall

Limekiln

Quarry

B.M. 14·1 Well

Well

Well

B.M. 134·2

Quarry

Quarry

B.S.

1. Somerville
2. Rose Cottage
3. Hinson Hall

240   120   0   240 metres

N
W   E
S

Surveyed and Contoured in 1898-1899 by Lieut. A.J. Savage, RE. Published at the Ordnance Survey Office, Southampton, England, 1901.
Courtesy Works & Engineering.

4
Heart of Smith's

Somerville nestles in a valley in the heart of Smith's Parish. This water colour was done by an unknown artist about 1865. A room with a shed roof has been added either side of the original early 18th century dower house built for Mary Gilbert and a detached kitchen is visible to the right. *Courtesy Robert Fitzhugh Lee and Barbara Ann Lee.*

In the sheltered heart of Smith's Parish there are a number of 18th century houses. Somerville, Rose Cottage and Hinson Hall remain as interesting examples of Bermudian architecture. They were built on good planting land where they were secure from all but the worst of storms.

Somerville, an early 18th century house, was built to order for a stepmother by her stepsons. The original portion of the house is still recognisable as her home although changes were made during the 19th century. Rose Cottage was carefully restored from dereliction in the 1960s. Nearby mid 18th century Hinson Hall was built by a politician and privateer who married one of the Verdmont heiresses.

These three houses stand not far west of the triangle of land known, somewhat curiously because of its small size, as Zuill's Park. This was an area left over from public works in the mid 19th century at the intersection of Verdmont and Middle roads.

The park was created by William Edward Zuill, known as Billy (circa 1799-1872), of nearby Orange Grove who was one of the road commissioners at the time. His great-grandson William Edward Sears Zuill (1892-1989) wrote in *Bermuda Journey*, "William Zuill . . . had the idea of making it a shady place with a few benches where pedestrians could rest. Mr. Zuill did it all himself, and it soon got the name of Zuill's Folly Park, or shortly the Park."

There was actually no direct road to Hamilton from Flatts Hill before these road works as Hamilton was reached by the somewhat roundabout route of the General Highway which ran from Flatts Hill down Verdmont Road to South Shore Road. Middle Road, from Flatts Hill to Hamilton, was only created in the mid 19th century.

Somerville is a landmark building readily visible on a bend of Middle Road west of Zuill's Park and is one of the architectural gems of Bermuda.

The core of the house was built some time after 1700 although there are changes and additions made by sub-sequent owners. Somerville is doubly interesting because it was apparently built to specifications laid out in the will of shipwright, carpenter and wealthy landowner John Gilbert (died 1700). The connection between this detailed will (*see appendix 6*) and Somerville was first discovered by an early 20th century genealogist Julia Elizabeth Mercer (1862-1932), who lived at nearby Aldie (*see chapter 5*).

Under the terms of John Gilbert's will the sons of his first marriage, John Jr. and Joseph Gilbert, could not claim their inheritance until they had built a house for their stepmother, Mary. She was the daughter of Laurence Dill (circa 1630-1691) of Devonshire and was a widow with one son when she married John Gilbert. After building her house, John Jr. was to receive the house and land on which his father lived in Smith's Parish and Joseph a house and land in Devonshire.

Mary Gilbert was to have a five room stone house over a cellar kitchen on property which John Gilbert had recently bought from Nicholas Trott on

Somerville in the 1930s does not look much different from today. The chimney, centre, served both the hall and the old cellar kitchen. The windows were enlarged and metal grills were installed by John Harvey Tucker who lived here from 1818 until 1868. The semi circular grills over the cellar windows are inscribed with the letter "T" for Tucker.
The Story of Bermuda, Hudson Strode, 1931. Photographed by Walter Rutherford, page 261.

Norwood share 23 that ran from Gilbert Hill (which is east of Verdmont Road) to the South Shore.

The original portion of Somerville contains the same number of rooms, layout and chimneys as described in this will and the room measurements are approximately correct but it does not stand "on such a place on the said land as my now wife Mary Gilbert shall appoint". Records of Norwood share 23

strongly suggest (but do not prove) that no such house was built there.

The puzzle of the misplacement is made even more complicated because John Gilbert's will exists in partial form, only the first, second and last of 11 pages remain. The widow Mary was left with two very young children, Elizabeth and Thomas, and another on the way and it is probable that she, as guardian for Thomas, and the executors chose

to put the house where it is, on Gilbert land next to John Jr., instead of the more distant South Shore property bequeathed to son Thomas.

The house changed hands a number of times during the 18th century when in 1775 it was purchased for £300 by mariner Captain William Williams (died circa 1786). He left an inventory of his possessions itemised room by room. There were still the same num-

Somerville today with its stepped gable roof ends looks unchanged from earlier photographs. The L-shaped portion to the right was built for Mary Gilbert by her stepsons according to the instructions of their father's will. Thomas Heber Outerbridge who lived in Somerville from 1888 to 1942 was responsible for the two storey wing, rear left.

ber of rooms in 1786 although their use had altered.

John Gilbert specified Mary's house should contain a porch, hall, parlour and two back chambers. The first three rooms were to be built over cellars, one of which should be fitted as a kitchen. Five rooms and a cookroom are still listed in Captain Williams' inventory

The western chimney of Somerville with its double flue served the hall of Mary Gilbert on the main living level as well as a cellar cookroom.

although two are named differently. There was no parlour or second back chamber, instead there were rooms described as a hall chamber (which contained the most expensive bed) and a dining room. The change of use to a dining room no doubt reflected changing social needs since Somerville was the dower house for John Gilbert's widow.

Following the death of Henrietta Williams (died 1812), the widow of Captain Williams, the house was purchased in 1818 by John Harvey Tucker (1777-1868). He was to make considerable changes and additions and was the first to be recorded as calling the house Somerville.

Two rooms with a shed roof were added either side of the hall and parlour and a double parlour was created from the two front rooms. He introduced new larger windows with unusual metal grills. These were said to have been imported from England about 1840 and included the initial "T" for Tucker within the design of the grills covering the cellar windows. Ornate woodwork was installed around the interior of the window and door openings.

The detached building to the east

of the house was also probably added during the ownership of John Harvey Tucker. This would have replaced the original kitchen in the cellar under the house. It is possible that the two house servants Jinny and Sophy along with five children under the age of 11 at the time of the 1833 Slave Register lived in this building rather than the cellar as there appeared to be a trend around the time of emancipation to move the kitchen and service quarters outside the main house.

The kitchen must have remained separate from the house for some years because Keith B. Hudson in *The Bermudian* magazine of September 1933 wrote, "Not so many years ago, it (the Somerville kitchen) was within a range of outbuildings, the former slave quarters, and a daughter of the house retains childhood memories of rainy weather when it was her task to escort each dish with open umbrella as it made its perilous journey, in the hand of a servant, from kitchen to dining room."

A number of exotic trees were planted in the garden by John Harvey Tucker and in 1822 he added another half acre to the existing nine acre lot on which Somerville stood. This was a

Somerville

Specifications for his wife's house in John Gilbert's 1699/1700 will make Somerville a particularly important early Bermuda house. The house his sons had built for Mary Gilbert closely follows the description, with a porch, hall and parlour above a cellar and with two rear chambers reached through an 8'11" by 4'10" lobby that John Gilbert and numerous contemporary inventory writers called an "entry".

All four rooms and the porch always had tray ceilings with a single cambered tie beam exposed at the outer ends of all but the hall. The spaces above the ceilings show no evidence of having been left open to this ridge as in comparable 18th century Hamilton Parish houses. In short, the sons followed their father's bidding in constructing an expensively finished house with the required spaces.

Sufficiently well built to remain largely unchanged through the 18th century, Somerville was improved by John Harvey Tucker soon after he bought it in 1818 and by subsequent owners. Tucker refinished the front spaces with peculiar woodwork clearly made by the same joiner who fitted out a new third room behind the passage at the Henry Tucker House in St. George's in the same era. His builders reworked Somerville's openings using elaborate interior architraves with carved scrolls at their base and curved crossettes at the upper corner. There are no fewer than 32 scrolls and crossettes in the lobby, hall and parlour. The joiners were obsessive as well as productive, squeezing the fancy carving into uneven recesses of plaster on intersecting walls. The new doors were hung with heavy six panel Georgian leafs on butt hinges rather than more visible HL-hinges, and the windows were fitted with large 6 over 6 sash. The remodel-

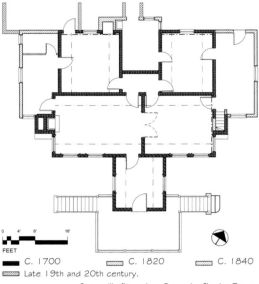

FEET
0   4'   8'   16'

■ C. 1700   ▨ C. 1820   ▨ C. 1840
▨ Late 19th and 20th century.

Somerville floor plan: *Drawn by Charles Tatem.*

ling included opening a 6'2" wide doorway between the old hall and parlour to create "double parlours", unified by the new woodwork.

The exotic quality of Tucker's remodelling extended to the three old cellar rooms, which were provided with half round windows, expressing the era's fascination with geometric shapes and resembling a similar transom over the reworked upper front door.

The circa 1820 remodelling included construction of a pair of long, shed roofed wings beside the old chambers and behind the chimneys. That on the east has a pair of wrought iron eyes set in the sloped plaster ceiling, suggesting storage, probably of food. The remodellers linked this space to the original cellar kitchen by aggressively closing the 4'10" by 3' parlour fireplace, cutting a doorway in the north wall of the chimney, and constructing a brick stairway that descends through the old hearth and foundation to reach the east cellar room. Their objective was to create a less visible route for delivering food to the dining room, then probably in Mary Gilbert's parlour.

The 6 over 6 sash windows seem to have been fitted circa 1840. Eventually an open wooden porch with Gothic ironwork was added to the front, and a third bedroom was added between the original rear wings. A separate two storey building was constructed on the hillside to the northeast, with a kitchen on the upper level and, it is said, a stable below. Substantial earth was moved, and a high retaining wall was built to level the front yard, and a balustrade was added, perhaps in the 1920s. The house survived the 20th century with expansion confined to a two storey northwest wing.   *E.A.C.*

small triangular parcel of land to the west between the house and the road, the site of the present driveway. The rubber tree is said to have been planted at the same time as the one in Queen Street in Hamilton. According to William Zuill in *Bermuda Journey*, "The handsome India rubber tree which shades the road is about a century old, having been imported with others in 1847 by Governor Reid, who had them distributed in various parts of the colony."

John Harvey Tucker was a lawyer and a member of an influential family. He was known as Lawyer Tucker. The refurbishment of Somerville from the simple dwelling of the widowed Mary Gilbert no doubt reflected his position

in the community and the architecture he had observed overseas. He was educated at Yale and at the Inns of Court in London.

Lawyer Tucker was the son of Speaker of the House of Assembly James Tucker (1745-1826) of Bellevue in Paget and a distant kinsman of President of the Council Henry Tucker of Tucker House in St. George's. His wife Mary (1780-1839) was the daughter of American loyalist William Browne (1737-1802) who was Governor of Bermuda from 1782 to 1788.

Politically he was reputed to have been opposed to his Tucker relatives who were said to have been involved in the so called Gunpowder Plot of 1775 in St. George's. In 1803 John Harvey

Tucker had defended Bermuda's rights to the Turks Islands in a pamphlet published in London and signed under the pen name of "Isocrates".

However, John Harvey Tucker was also a man of uncertain temper and fell out with his father, his wife, his children, his church and his neighbours. He is said to have dressed his children in red when his father died.

His wife, Mary, in a letter to relatives in Canada and published in Hereward Trott Watlington's *Family Narrative* wrote, "About two months ago, during an altercation between my husband and myself, which arose to violence on his part, all my children interfered, which so incensed him that he has turned his eldest daughter from

This is a rear view of the eastern chimney of Mary Gilbert's dower house. Weathered stone balls, or finials, are charming features on the gable ends of Somerville.

Rose Cottage on Kilderry Estate was in a ruined condition in the 1960s. This photograph taken from the rear shows the southwest wing, left. A room was added to this wing beyond the chimney in the 19th century. The front wing, right, had lost its roofs and several walls had collapsed. *Courtesy Henry Laing.*

his house; my second daughter and husband taking my part he has forbid again entering his house; and he has given several hints that as soon as the law will permit Emily, the third, nearly seventeen, shall share the same fate." There were four girls in the family: Mary Browne, Anne Harvey, Emily and Louisa Bryan and one son George Somers.

John Harvey Tucker refused to pay his taxes on the grounds the rector was not properly inducted. Every year a sale of a piece of furniture took place to settle the tax. He met a violent death aged over 90 when an intruder broke into his house and gagged him.

Somerville was purchased in 1888 by John William Richard Pearman of Mount Hope (see *chapter 11*) and it was to become the home of his daughter Mary Eleanor and her husband, dentist Thomas Heber Outerbridge (1847-1942). They had earlier lived at Whitby on Blue Hole Hill (see *Hamilton Parish*).

Thomas Heber Outerbridge lived at Somerville for 52 years until his death aged 94. He had a dental office over the store of Thomas S. Lightbourn on Front Street in Hamilton and is also said to have had a dental chair at his home. He was responsible for adding the two storey rear wing to the northwest of the house.

In an article in *The Bermudian*

magazine of January 1935, when Thomas Heber Outerbridge was aged 87, E. Carters McLaughlin wrote, "He (Dr. Outerbridge) finds walking, for instance, a congenial exercise, and therefore frequently goes on foot from Somerville, his home in Smith's Parish, to Hamilton – a distance of about four miles – to attend a meeting of the council. His duties performed, he just as frequently walks back home. On these expeditions, he carefully times himself, allowing forty-five minutes for the trip during the winter months and fifty-five minutes during the summer; the extra ten minutes during the hot weather are not because of a slackened speed, but to allow for a short period of rest en route." Thomas Heber Outerbridge was elected to the House of Assembly in 1882 and remained there until 1926 when he was appointed to the Legislative Council.

School teacher Bertha Loutrelle Outerbridge, daughter of Dr. Outerbridge, was the last member of the family to live at Somerville. She died in 1954. The acreage on which Somerville stood was subdivided during the ownership of the three Outerbridge children: Benjamin Chauncey Curling Outerbridge, Kate Langton Cox and Bertha.

The house on 1.736 acres was sold in 1957 to George Henry Russell although the northerly portion remained

as part of Chauncey's dairy farm (*see chapter 5*). Somerville was bought by its present owners in 1968 and has been lovingly tended ever since.

Rose Cottage is so like Somerville in the room layout of the original portion of the house that one wonders which house came first. Was Rose Cottage the pattern for the house which John Gilbert described in his will for his widow Mary or did it follow later?

The oldest sections of the two houses are almost mirror images of each other with Somerville facing south on the north side of Middle Road and Rose Cottage facing north on the south side of Middle Road. Like the original portion of Somerville the oldest part of Rose Cottage has an entry porch, two reception rooms and two rear chambers. The dimensions of the main rooms at Rose Cottage are however larger than at Somerville.

Rose Cottage stands somewhat incongruously on Kilderry Estate as an outpost of traditional Bermudian architecture amongst houses built in the latter half of the 20th century. It is a one storey gable roofed house symmetrical on its northern front with a chimney either end and a projecting porch. Unlike Somerville it is not raised over a cellar, although there is a cellar below the northwest room. An extension was

This shows a view of the east side of Rose Cottage following renovation in the 1960s. The new kitchen wing, centre to left of chimney, blends with the rest of the house. Pilasters were placed on its corners. *Courtesy Henry Laing.*

made to the rear of the southwest wing in the 19th century and in 1965 an addition housing a kitchen was built to the east.

The walled front garden is a charming feature with a pair of weathered lions on the gateposts. They are said to have been carved by William James Trott (1806-1872). The Savage map shows a long driveway leading from Middle Road along the eastern side of the house. To the south stood a two storey shed which burned to the ground in 1959 as well as a one storey cow stall. To the west of the main house stood a large barn that was a complete ruin by 1965.

The name of Rose Cottage was changed to Kilderry when it was rented by the Irish born headmaster of Whitney Institute, James Carters McLaughlin, from 1915 to 1929. The present owner changed the name of the house back to Rose Cottage although the estate continues to be called Kilderry.

Rose Cottage was in ruins and had been vandalised with doors, windows and mantle pieces removed when it was bought in December 1964 by Henry D.W. Laing, a grandson of Lucy Watlington née Trott (1868-1959) who was born in the cottage as was her father and her grandfather. In May 1966 Henry Laing wrote an account of its condition and restoration which he

updated in 1996. This provides a valuable historic record.

The porch chamber had collapsed, the main section of the house was without a roof, a number of wall sections had fallen and there was no flooring over the cellar.

Henry Laing undertook a careful restoration of Rose Cottage. He studied both the history of the house as well as its architecture with input from his uncle Hereward Trott Watlington (1902-1989), one of the founders of the Bermuda Historical Monuments Trust.

Plans for the restoration of Rose Cottage were drawn by C.E. Hinson Cooper. William Henry Van Putten and his brothers Lionel and Charles were employed as masons. Carpenter Lawson Lambert made the exterior doors, the windows and the board and batten interior doors. In 1995 Jose De Braga installed the two mantle pieces in the front rooms made from the sides of an old Bermuda cedar door frame.

Cleveland Ethelred Hinson Cooper (1909-1972) started as a master builder, overseeing a project from its design to its construction, although he was later to concentrate on architectural design. He trained with Ernest Hugh Watlington, a consultant engineer, and took a correspondence course in architecture. His office was on Front Street, first at the top of the Miles Meat Market building, now Ca-

lypso, and then in the now demolished Seon Building. Among the houses he designed were Coolshannah and Summerhill in Point Shares, and Ben Barra in Tucker's Town. He joined with architect James Gardner in the mid 20th century to form the firm of Cooper & Gardner.

The interior doors and their draught preventers, or pelmets, are a particularly charming feature of Rose Cottage. New cedar draught preventers, which were made by Lawson Lambert, were designed from one in the house and one found floating in an old tank at the south end of the west wing. Similar draught preventers exist at Somerville.

The old door and frame between the dining room and kitchen came from the home of the Dill family, Devonshire House now the Devonshire Recreation Club, on Frog Lane (see *Devonshire*). Replicas of this door were made for other doorways within Rose Cottage.

The half timber partition between the drawing and dining rooms was largely intact. It was made of hand split cedar laths with horse hair packed on either side before being plastered. Henry Laing wrote, "The half timbering in the Entrance Hall is fake and we simply mounted old pieces of cedar on top of the rafter feet where they rested on the wallplate."

Cedar from the estate at Woodside,

Anna Trott née Musson (1811-1883) and William James Trott (1806-1872). *Courtesy Henry Laing.*

the home of Hereward Watlington in eastern Paget, was used where new timber was needed for the roof.

The corner pilasters on the north corners of the drawing and dining rooms were in existence but Henry Laing wrote, "lacked definition so we simply duplicated the bases by inverting them at the top. We added two to the east wall of the 1965 kitchen."

The front porch was restored with reference to one at Lime House which is across the road from Old Devonshire Church.

It is difficult to date Rose Cottage. It would perhaps be fair to say that it was built around the same time as Somerville, probably in the late 17th or early 18th centuries. During the restoration of 1965/1966 a 1663 Charles II shilling was found in the northeast corner of the master bedroom under about eight inches of soil. This coin had a nail hole and this has led to a suggestion that the house may have been built soon after, perhaps around 1670. However, it is more likely that Rose Cottage may date from its ownership by Edith Jennings.

Edith Jennings (1676-1758) was the granddaughter of Captain Richard Jennings (died 1669) who at the time of the second Norwood Survey of 1663 owned the land on which Rose Cottage stands today. She was the daughter of John Jennings (died circa 1684) of Southampton, the second son of Captain Richard Jennings. Under the terms of her father's will Edith was to inherit a parcel of land of approximately 30 acres in Smith's Parish. An indenture conveying this property to Edith was made in 1701 but not proved until 1706.

She buried three husbands. The first was Jonathan Tucker (died circa 1700) with whom she had a son John Tucker. The second was a Mr. Stowe. There were two children from this marriage, Susanna and Joseph. The third was a Mr. Butterfield with whom Edith had a daughter Ruth.

In 1727 Edith Butterfield was assessed for property in Smith's Parish which seems to have descended to her Tucker heirs since in 1789 representatives of a Captain Thomas Tucker of Charleston, South Carolina, were assessed for 30 acres valued at £360 and a house at £250.

The ownership of Rose Cottage was difficult to trace during the period 1790-1818. It was apparently purchased in 1807 by William Sears (died 1830), but the lack of assessments and the extent of his holdings (*see chap-*

In the 1920s the front door on the north of Rose Cottage had been replaced by a window, left, and the projecting porch turned into a bedroom. The door was reinstated to its original position following renovation in the 1960s. *Courtesy Henry Laing.*

Rose Cottage

A single storey porch-entry house with some similarities to Somerville was extremely derelict before a major restoration in 1965 brought it to its present well brushed condition. Enough masonry and archaic framing survives to demonstrate that by the late 18th century, it consisted of two major rooms in front of two wings, one probably housing a kitchen in the rear, with circulation through a back lobby.

The scale is much larger than one expects, with the porch space being 14'4" wide by 15' deep. This first room has an off centre inner door with solid posts tenoned into the end tie beam, which also supports studs to make the rear wall rise straight to the roof collars.

This opens into a quite large (24'5" by 17'4") hall on the west (right). Restorer Henry Laing and his architect C.E. Hinson Cooper rebuilt the hall-chamber partition, based on remnants of the frame and the location of the tie beam between the two rear doorways. To the east (left) is the inner room 21' by 17'4". Both have slightly cambered tie beams confined to their end walls and are plastered up 11' to the roof collars.

Three gable roofed wings extend back, side-by-side and sharing inner walls, at the rear. The small central one, only 10'3" wide inside, served as a lobby between the two larger wings and the front rooms, like the smaller rear lobby at Somerville.

Some elements of all four openings survive, with chamfered door posts tenoned directly into the respective wall plates of the wings and the main block. Laing found no evidence for a door connecting the two front rooms.

An early cellar space at the northwest (right front) corner measures 23'2" by 11'10" with crossed summers, reinforcing evidence for the hall above. It also gives access to part of the unstuccoed rear wall, suggesting that at least the southwest (right) wing is original.

Only one ancient door leaf now survives, at the end of the front chamber (parlour). This is made of three vertical boards, with two thinner boards lapped into them, moulded on the face and secured with five bevelled battens on the plain rear. It is hung on strap hinges attached backwards so that the leaf closes flat against a joined frame. This door from the Dill house in Devonshire formed the basis for leafs replaced elsewhere in 1965.

The early Bermuda style was central to Laing and Cooper's restoration, with scrubbed beams, door pelmets and cast iron hardware liberally applied. They were sufficiently independent on occasion, however, to use elements like Chinese porcelain dishes and Dutch delft tiles freely embedded in plaster around the front fireplaces in favour of more academic joinery.

E.A.C.

Rose Cottage floor plan: *Drawn by Philip J. Seaman, Cooper & Gardner, from a plan by C.E. Hinson Cooper.*

ter 7) made this difficult to confirm. He left his daughters Mary Sears and Sarah Trott several tracts of real estate in Smith's Parish.

In 1805 Sarah Sears (circa 1786-1864) had married Captain John William Trott but he was lost at sea within a year or so. She is said to have lived with her father and son at Orange Grove in the early years of her widowhood. William Edward Sears Zuill (1892-1989) wrote in his papers, "It is said that she occupied the southwest bedroom and for weeks at a time would not leave her chamber. On the other hand she subsequently undertook to keep her father's accounts and write his letters . . ." Sarah Trott, known as Sally, moved to Rose Cottage probably following the settlement of her father's estate in the 1840s (*see chapter 7*) along with her half sister Mary, known as Miss Polly (circa 1781-1853), and her son William James Trott.

In 1831 William James Trott (1806-1872) married Anna Musson (1811-1883), a daughter of Samuel and Susannah Musson of Palmetto Grove in Flatts (*see chapter 8*). He was described as a storekeeper in an 1847 deed and a mechanic in his will. William and Anna had four sons Melville (1832-1868), Harley (1834-1897), Dudley (1837-1858) and Thaddeus (1838-1924).

The Slave Register of 1833-1834 reveals that there was only one 16 year old woman Rachel employed as a domestic for the Trott household but there were two men, Jim a mason and Tom a caulker.

As his family grew William James Trott enlarged the house by adding a kitchen room with an attic on the southwest and blocked up the front door in the porch chamber and turned it into a bedroom for his aunt Mary Sears. A fish pond was put in front of

the old doorway to divert visitors to two new doors into the dining and drawing rooms.

About 1858 Sarah Trott transferred 16 acres on the north side of Middle Road to her second grandson Harley Trott on which he built Belmont, later renamed Penhurst. According to her will this was originally part of the Rose Cottage property.

Sarah Trott died in 1864 aged 78. Her son William James Trott received a life interest in Rose Cottage which she left to her eldest grandson Melville Trott. William James Trott lived in Rose Cottage until his death in 1872, when his widow Anna went to live with her sisters Eliza and Georgiana at Palmetto Grove.

Thaddeus Trott continued to live at home for about five years following his marriage in 1863 to Louisa Margaret Pearman, daughter of John W.R. Pearman of Mount Hope (*see chapter*

Hinson Hall, photographed when it was home to Roy and Sarah Peniston from 1937 to 1945. This shows the old part of the house. The Penistons were probably responsible for installing larger windows and redoing the roof. *The Bermudian magazine, January 1939, page 15. Courtesy of the family of the late Edmund M. Gosling.*

11). Their three oldest children were born at Rose Cottage before he moved first to Eagles Nest in Devonshire, now part of the Cable and Wireless property, and then to Rockmoor which he built in 1877 (*see chapter 10*).

Helen May Fessenden (1866-1941), a daughter of Thaddeus Trott, wrote about her childhood memories of Christmas at Rose Cottage, "The family gathering was at our grandfather's. His children, in-laws and grandchildren even to the babies in arms all were bidden – easily a group of twenty-five or more. After church we were encouraged by the elders to play out-of-door games till the welcome call for dinner sounded. As we trooped into the dining room our unaccustomed eyes nearly popped out of our heads at the overwhelming bounty. The long table in stately array of silver and napery and beautiful with flowers and bowls of apples, oranges, nuts and raisins might well have come from fairyland."

Rose Cottage and its 33 acres continued to be assessed under Sarah Trott's estate until 1894. Melville Trott

died in Bridgetown, Barbados, in 1868 leaving two daughters, Carrie and Leila. His wife Laura Ophelia, one of the many children of Francis Peniston of Peniston's, later named Magnolia Hall (*see chapter 6*), resided in London but died in 1912 in Stockholm, Sweden. His two daughters Caroline Laura, known as Carrie (died 1933), and Leila Florence Trott (died 1934) returned to Bermuda after their father's death but later settled in England. Neither seems to have married.

In 1915 Thomas Heber Outerbridge (1847-1942) of nearby Somerville, bought Rose Cottage and its 33 acres. It was at this time that the property was rented to James McLaughlin and Dr. Outerbridge's son, Benjamin Chauncey Curling Outerbridge of Outerlea on Store Hill, used the land for pasturing his cows (*see chapter 5*).

In 1948 the children of Dr. Outerbridge sold the house with 23.4 acres to John Thomson Donaldson of the Channel Islands and Eric Pasold of England. In 1962 the property "together with the ruined dwelling house Kilderry" was sold to M.A. Gibbons, L.P.

Gutteridge and Elsa Gosling. Henry Laing in December 1964 purchased lot 6, the ruined house, with 1.662 acres at the newly subdivided Kilderry Estate. He later purchased the neighbouring lot with the ruined barn, lime kiln and one half acre where he built Sub Rosa in 1976-1977.

Hinson Hall stands on what was the northern portion of the Verdmont estate (*see chapter 2*). It is presently reached off Middle Road and the two houses seem far apart when the journey is made by road but both are clearly visible to each other across country.

The land was once owned by John Dickinson for whom Verdmont was built in the early 18th century. In his 1714 will he left the northern portion of his property to his daughter Mary upon the death of his wife Elizabeth.

Mary Dickinson married Captain Samuel Spofferth before 1731, her sister Elizabeth having earlier married his brother Perient Spofferth. It is very probable that Hinson Hall, although it has had a number of changes and is difficult to date because of the removal of much original fabric, was the house built for Samuel and Mary Spofferth sometime after their marriage.

A 1771 inventory of Samuel Spofferth's possessions listed room by room appears to relate to the present house. There was also said to be a window pane in the house until 1935 on which the initials of Samuel Spofferth were scratched.

Hinson Hall is an extremely long house because it consisted originally of a four room house at the east end and a detached kitchen at the far west with a storeroom in the centre. These were joined to form one long house which is one room deep with two rear wings, the older one to the east being built over a cellar. (*See floor plan page 5.*)

Captain Samuel Spofferth (died 1770), also spelled Spofforth, was active in politics and a member of the House of Assembly and of the Governor's Council but he was also a sea captain and privateer and often away from his political duties.

He was involved in privateering during King George's War (1739-1743), commonly known as the War of Jenkins' Ear since hostilities commenced between England and Spain following the cutting off of the ear of Captain Jenkins. During the course of this war Captain Samuel Spofferth obtained a Letter of Marque and Reprisal from Governor Alured Popple to apprehend any vessels and goods belonging to the King of Spain.

In December 1739 Captain Spofferth as commander of the private man of war *Popple*, which was armed with eight guns and manned by 12 men, captured a Spanish schooner off Curaçao. He sold the ship in Curaçao and the cargo in Bermuda. This venture was said to have netted each man £50 and about £1,000 for Captain Spofferth.

However, in 1742 according to Dr. Henry Campbell Wilkinson in *Bermuda in the Old Empire*, "Captain the Hon. Samuel Spofferth came ashore at Governor Popple's request and was made Surveyor General. Subsequently he was appointed to the captaincy of the Castle and thenceforth took over the problems of mounting the guns and supplying them with spikes and other hardware to make a ruinous discharge of canister against the sails of any vessels

A gathering of chimneys at Hinson Hall. In the foreground is the huge kitchen chimney while the double flued chimney to the rear or far right served the little chamber and cellar.

with the temerity to try forcing an entrance."

One wonders if this was the time when Samuel Spofferth built his home out of his privateering spoils and on land his wife had recently inherited upon the death of her mother Elizabeth Dickinson of Verdmont.

In 1750 Captain Spofferth once again obtained a privateering commission, this time from King George II. He had a new sloop, the 50 ton *Mary Ann*,

---

VALUABLE REAL ESTATE
FOR SALE
by Public Auction
on
Wednesday, March 18th, 1936
at 4.00 p.m.

The property known as
HINSON HALL
Smith's Parish
approximately 10 acres and old Bermuda House.

NOTE: The property will be sold as a whole or in 3 or 4 sections.

For further particulars, apply
SOMERS REAL ESTATE AGENCY

The Royal Gazette and Colonist Daily, March 17, 1936.

---

for this venture. Under the terms of the commission and during the American colonial war between England and France he was empowered to attack and take "any place or fortress upon the land or any ship or vessel, goods, ammunition, arms, stores or merchandise belonging to or possessed by the French".

There is no information on the success or otherwise of this venture but Dr. Wilkinson wrote, "for no sooner was peace proclaimed than back he came to resume his seat as a legislator, and not crestfallen either, since he took an early opportunity to have his old cronies in the council about his hospitable table".

Samuel Spofferth was said to be responsible for introducing the cardinal or red bird and sage or *Lantana* to Bermuda. Dr. Wilkinson wrote in *Bermuda in the Old Empire*, "Spofferth introduced the birds to Bermuda, for which we must be grateful to him. He also brought in the common sage from the Bahamas with a view to using it for firewood and so saving the cedar. But this purpose the sage did not serve; instead it soon became a nuisance, except that its berries were eaten by the birds, as Spofferth probably knew they would be."

In 1759 Samuel Spofferth purchased the lease of Brown's Island in Hamilton Harbour for £625. The island was later known as Godet's and is now called Hinson's Island. A substantial property owner, he was apparently in

Hinson Hall

Hinson Hall consists primarily of a string of rooms aligned end to end, probably beginning with a centre passage house. Fortunately, there is an inventory for Samuel Spofferth, a member of the Governor's Council, a document apparently describing this house in 1771 before it reached its present extent.

Front and rear doors open into Spofferth's 9'1" wide passage between two rooms, probably the 22'3" by 17'1" hall on the east (left) and 18'10" by 17'1" great chamber on the west, both with open or tray ceilings. Seven tie beams are cased in 20th century sheathing, but early wooden knees are spiked to those at the transverse walls, suggesting the passage partitions are in their original locations. Both rooms have fireplaces in exterior end chimneys. Off the southwest (right rear) corner is a 13'9" by 13'1" room, a likely candidate for the "little chamber", with a third fireplace too small to have been used for cooking. The rear room may be an addition intended to provide a more private bedchamber, and the inventory lists the finest furnishings in the little chamber. It has two early doors,

a full sized panelled door opening into the great chamber and a very small (1'8" wide) service door into a longitudinal passage in the western wing.

Two small doorways (2'3" by 6') also flank the great chamber fireplace, both with original four panel doors that close against thin beaded rectangular frames. The south door opens into the 5'8" wide longitudinal passage that now gives access to a cellar room (perhaps the original cookroom) below the rear wing and to a modern breakfast room. This passage has a ceiling of hand planed sheathing and plain joists too thin to span much more than the passage. It is tempting to interpret it as the "entry" in Spofferth's inventory, containing a cheap old bed and eight old chairs, and the room to the north as Spofferth's third chamber.

The 10'9" by 17'1" breakfast room could be read as early service space because overhead it has wide sheathing and lightly chamfered joists set into two large longitudinal summer beams. Above the joists, however, one sees the attic of a building extending some 38'

from the old great chamber, the former a space spanned by three early tie beams and apparently once open to the collars. It is conceivable that this began as an attached storehouse and was later partitioned by Spofferth and others to serve as bedchambers and service rooms.

Beyond the west wing is an early 19th century cookroom, 22' by 11'11", open to the collars and with three cambered tie beams. This has a large west chimney and could have replaced an earlier kitchen to the east. Extensive 20th century remodellings have removed much of the early finishes.

E.A.C.

This aerial view of Hinson Hall from the rear shows the oldest portion of the house, right, flanked by two chimneys at the east end of the long building. A large chimney at the left end of the photograph, near the pool, served the early kitchen. (*See also plan on page 5.*)

favour of moving the capital of Bermuda from St. George's to the area then known as Crow Lane (Pembroke Parish) and is recorded as voting accordingly in 1764.

Samuel Spofferth died intestate and an inventory of his possessions was made in February 1771 (*see appendix 7*). This reveals the layout and furnishings of his home in Harris' Bay (Smith's Parish) as well as a great quantity of possessions, including those on Hinson's Island.

Hinson Hall in Samuel Spofferth's

day consisted of a hall and chamber either side of a central entry with a rear wing known as the "little chamber" plus a detached kitchen. The hall was the principal receiving or entertaining room and was furnished with tables and chairs and three large mirrors or "looking glasses". The "great chamber", now a dining room, contained a bedstead with red and white chintz drapery plus a chest of drawers and desk made out of the now extremely rare native yellow wood. Samuel Spofferth's bedchamber must have been in the rear

wing, the "little chamber", because it contained the most expensive bed in the house, valued at £23.2.6 and hung with red and white calico.

A very large quantity of plate, china, earthenware, glass, pewter, tin ware and linen was listed in the house, no doubt reflecting his successful career. An interesting item in the inventory is "68 books (most of them old and much hurt)". His career in the local militia can be seen in his ownership of two gun carriages, shot, one fourpounder and powder horns.

Samuel Spofferth employed nine slaves: five men and a boy, August, Jacob, Lewis, John, Tom and Sam, and three women, Sarah, Ephy and Janey. August who was described as being "at sea" was the most highly valued at £75, no doubt because of his seamanship skills.

An interesting and personal footnote to the inventory reveals that there were a few small items which were not valued but were left for Mary Spofferth to dispose of privately. These included "Mr. Spofforth's wearing apparel and watch, the grey horse and side saddle and Mr. Spofforth's sword and cain".

Mary Spofferth lived on at Hinson Hall until her death in 1789 when her will specified that her estate was to be sold although she gave each of her children the opportunity to purchase the property. The Spofferths had five daughters: Elizabeth, Rebecca, Mary Ann, Frances and Alice, all of whom had married. It appeared that none of the daughters wanted or were able to purchase the old family home.

In about 1790, Joseph Hinson Sr. (died 1809) became the next owner. This is presumably when the property became known as Hinson's. He was part owner and master of a ship in November 1799 but little else is known about Joseph Hinson Sr. except that he married Margaret Albouy. He left his estate to his wife and after her death equally to his children: Nicholas, Joseph Jr., Patsy, Bernard Albouy and Margaret, known as Peggy, or their heirs.

His widow Margaret Hinson died in 1835 aged about 79 having outlived several of her children, leaving her son Joseph Jr. and grandson William Walter Kelly, the son of Peggy, as her heirs.

Mary Jane Hinson (1831-1903), daughter of Joseph Hinson Jr., was to eventually become the owner of Hinson Hall and its 20 acres of land. She is said to have bought out the interest of William Walter Kelly. She married Henry Morton Peniston and upon her death left her property to her two daughters Alice and Ada.

Alice, who married William Rogers, became the owner of the house and ten acres which she sold in 1924 to William James Howard Trott (1882-1971).

The house changed hands a number of times and was eventually purchased in 1937 by Roy Bryan Greyson Peniston (1896-1975). He was an

This shows the older eastern portion of Hinson Hall from the rear. The chimney to the right served the hall and that to the left the little chamber and cellar.

American citizen having been born in Atlanta, although his adoptive father Alonzo Peniston was a Bermudian. Alonzo Peniston ran the Frascati Hotel in Flatts, on the site of the present day St. James Court (see *Hamilton Parish*), before moving to the States in the 1920s. Roy Peniston ran a perfumery business, Peniston Brown. He perfected a formula for a perfume of his own fabrication named "One for Two" which was produced in Paris.

Roy Peniston purchased Hinson Hall at the time when there was an interest in Colonial revival architecture. This was a return to the style of the 18th century. The movement was spearheaded by Americans living in Bermuda who either restored existing 18th century houses or built in a traditional style.

He and his wife Sarah renovated Hinson Hall. They turned the formerly detached kitchen into a master bedroom. The Penistons were probably re-

sponsible for installing larger windows and redoing the roof. A bathroom was put in costing, at that time, the truly prodigious sum of £1,000 and conducted tours of the house were held solely for the purpose of showing off the new room. An article appeared in *The Bermudian* magazine of January 1939 featuring these renovations.

Hinson Hall was sold in 1945 to Henry John Balkwill Dunkley, a Hamilton merchant and member of the House of Assembly who owned many properties throughout the island. It was acquired in 1947 by his daughter Mabel Gray Dunkley who had married Stanley Henry Kugima.

In 2000 the house and 1.1 hectares were sold by the granddaughter of Henry Dunkley to its present owners. Although it has undergone a number of changes Hinson Hall lies amidst a peaceful rural landscape and is still recognisable as the home of politician and privateer Samuel Spofferth. 🌴

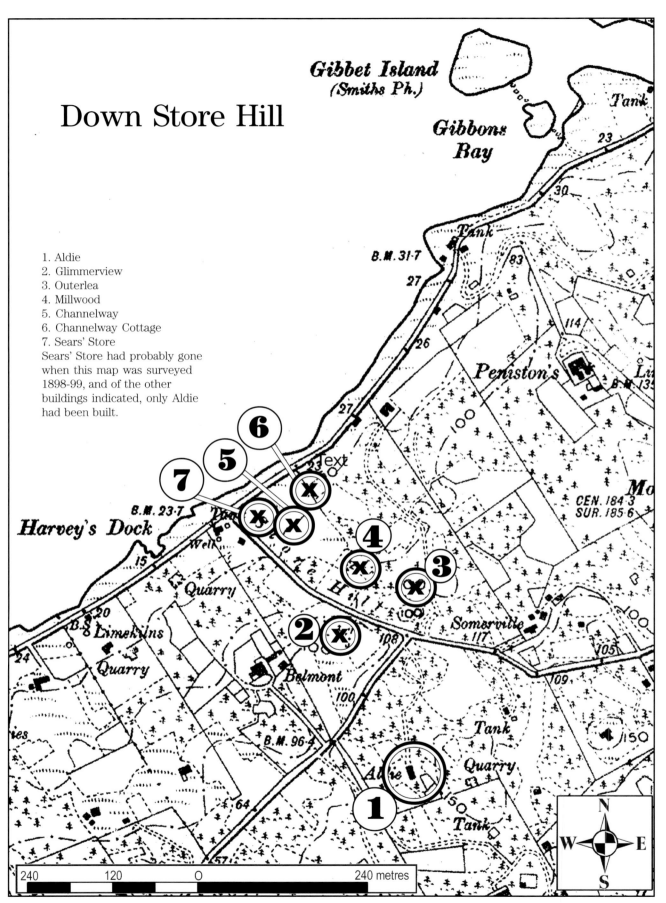

Down Store Hill

1. Aldie
2. Glimmerview
3. Outerlea
4. Millwood
5. Channelway
6. Channelway Cottage
7. Sears' Store

Sears' Store had probably gone when this map was surveyed 1898-99, and of the other buildings indicated, only Aldie had been built.

Surveyed and Contoured in 1898-1899 by Lieut. A.J. Savage, RE. Published at the Ordnance Survey Office, Southampton, England, 1901.
Courtesy Works & Engineering.

5
Down Store Hill

Milking time: A car stops to allow the cows to pass in the early 1960s on Middle Road near the dairy farm at Outerlea. *Emeralds On A Silver Zone, Early Colour Photography in Bermuda, 1939-1960, 1992, page 146.*

Store Hill runs north from Middle Road to North Shore Road and got its name because there was a store near the foot of the hill. It was owned in the early 19th century by Captain William Sears at the time when the shoreline opposite was the site of several busy shipbuilding yards.

The store, according to an 1830 survey map drawn by Colonial Surveyor Daniel Rayner Prudden (circa 1771 - 1852), stood east of the junction of Store Hill and North Shore Road, roughly in the northern garden of Channelway. The building was not marked on the map surveyed by Lieutenant Arthur Johnson Savage in 1898-99, presumably because it was no longer in existence. William Zuill describing a route along North Shore Road in *Bermuda Journey* in 1946 wrote, "(it) was a general store in the days when shipbuilding was a thriving

trade along the shore."

At the time of the second Richard Norwood Survey of 1663 this land, which stood on share 29, was owned by William Sayle, three times Governor of Bermuda. It was inherited by his granddaughter, sold to Nicholas Trott and by him to John Dickinson, the builder of Verdmont (*see chapter 2*). The land was then left to his daughter Mary Dickinson who married Samuel Spofferth of Hinson Hall (*see chapter 4*).

By the early 19th century the area through which Store Hill now runs was a parcel of land known as Bostock's and was owned by Captain William Sears (circa 1744-1830). A merchant, originally from St. David's, he moved to Smith's Parish in the late 18th century where he acquired extensive land holdings (*see chapter 7*).

In his will written in 1827 William Sears left the land "commonly called

Bostock's" along with the store to be split between two of his daughters Sophia Angelina Zuill and Frances Perot Hinson. Sophia Angelina, the wife of William Edward Zuill, known as Billy, of Orange Grove, inherited the western half on which Aldie, Glimmerview, Millwood and Channelway were to be built.

Store Hill was developed fairly late. It was not until June 28, 1842, that the House of Assembly Journal of Proceedings reported "the cross road leading by the late Mr. Sears' store is marked out and ready to begin". In June 1843 the Journal reported, "Road by late Mr. Sears' store has been made."

The hill contains an interesting collection of houses designed by Bermudian architects in the late 19th and the first half of the 20th century. Edward Peniston (1838-1903) was a Smith's Parish builder and designer (*see chap-*

Julia Elizabeth Mercer

Julia Elizabeth Mercer (1862-1932) of Aldie may have lived in an up-to-date house modelled after an American one but her heart was in Bermuda's past. Born at Orange Grove on Flatts Hill and the daughter of William Sears Zuill and his wife Anne Campbell Zuill, she collected antique Bermudiana and studied the history of its people.

She became the local expert on genealogy and researched countless documents in Bermuda as well as overseas in Barbados, Demerara and the US. In Bermuda she studied colonial, parish and private records. Her papers and publications are invaluable to current researchers and have assisted greatly with the writing of this book and others in the series.

An obituary in *The Royal Gazette* of August 3, 1932, noted, "Day after day she could be seen at the Customs House (in Hamilton), occupying a small corner of the table at the Audit Board, with one of the old volumes from the big iron safe before her, carrying on a work which she loved but which brought her only a trifling pecuniary reward."

The obituary continued, "Her papers, read before the Bermuda Historical Society, the St. George's Historical Society and the Nineteenth Century Club, were always anticipated with pleasure, for she had a particular gift for reading aloud which charmed her audience. Only last Thursday evening Mrs. Mercer read a paper before the St. George's Historical Society on the occasion of their Somer's Day celebrations."

Julia Zuill was educated in England at Vernon House in Kensington, London. She is reported in Samuel Cornelius Outerbridge's diaries as returning to Bermuda in September 1881. Presumably, because of the difficulty of long distance travel, she spent several years away at school.

She obviously collected a vast mound of papers and an attempt was made to put them in order in 1931 by Edith Vickers. It is not known who she was.

A letter written on March 30, 1931, by Edith Vickers with an Aldie letterhead notes, "The first move was to set aside one room in the house as an office for this work. Here two typewriters, a telephone and the numerous books, papers and files have been installed. There were 40 notebooks, some large, some small, filled with copious abstracts from official records — wills, deeds, deeds of gift, etc., as well as registers of births, marriages and deaths. In addition there was an enormous collection of loose papers, backs of envelopes, bits of memorandum pads, parts of old letters, and so on.

"The notebooks, some of which were worn and loosened, have been mended with transparent tape, firmly glued, and bound roughly to insure their holding together. They have been lettered from A to Z, and on from AA to RR, and have been paged numerically. The loose papers have been pasted into blank books and added to the above series, except for such papers as did not fit into these books, these have been filed in a large extension envelope, designated ZZ, and have been numerically paged.

"An index to all these notebooks and papers has been started, in which every reference to every name will be entered, with book and page, so that a complete record, genealogical, can be (got) at short notice. Books A and B, and a part of C, have already been indexed, and this tedious but essential work should be continued as rapidly as possible . . ."

Edith Vickers also referred to a plan by Julia Mercer for publishing a volume of "Wills in Bermuda". Approximately 500 abstracts of wills were typed and another 500 were to be added. Unfortunately Julia Mercer died before such a book could be completed.

Her nephew William Edward Sears Zuill, known as Will (1892-1989), (*see chapter 7*) was left her papers and he took upon himself the task of adding to them. They are known as the Mercer/Zuill Notes and exist in more than 80 notebooks in the library of the Zuill family at Orange Grove. In 1989 they were recorded on microfilm and are available at the Bermuda Archives. Often only snippets of information, these notes sometimes provide the vital clue when researching a family or a house.

Will Zuill passed on notes from his and his aunt's files to Tyler's *Quarterly Historical and Genealogical Magazine*, and extracts from the *Quarterly* became *Bermuda Settlers of the 17th Century*, which was published in 1982. He also wrote several books, including *Bermuda Sampler* and *Bermuda Journey*. *D.C.*

Julia Elizabeth Mercer of Aldie, an early 20th century historian and genealogist.

Photographer unknown. Neg.3628. Bermuda Archives: St. George's Historical Society Collection. PA2145.

ter 10) who may have had a hand in both Aldie and Glimmerview.

The houses on the east side of Store Hill display the work of architects of the first half of the 20th century. George Houston Hutchings was the architect of Outerlea, Cyril Hilton Smith designed and built Millwood, Lawrence Harrower Smart designed Channelway and Wilfred Onions, Channelway Cottage.

Aldie stands south of Store Hill but it was amongst the earliest houses on the land known as Bostock's, Windy Bank having been built earlier circa 1877. Aldie was built for Elmore Reid and Julia Elizabeth Mercer on a five acre plot before 1897 when it and its land were valued at £450. Julia Elizabeth Mercer née Zuill had inherited part of the western portion of Bostock's from her grandmother Sophia Angelina Zuill.

Aldie is a substantial late Victorian house said to have been modelled after one the Mercers lived in for several

Aldie is a late Victorian house modelled after an American one in Montclair, New Jersey. It is asymmetrical in form and picturesque in style. The original wooden porch on the front of the house was replaced by a masonry one in the second half of the 20th century. (*See plan on page 9.*)

years in Montclair, New Jersey. It is indeed decidedly un-Bermudian in appearance although it is built in local stone with a white Bermuda slate roof.

Outside the two storey house is asymmetrical in form and picturesque in style with heavy moulded gables. Originally there was a wooden porch both front and back. The two storey wooden verandah on the south remains whilst the one on the front of the house was replaced by a masonry porch during the second half of the 20th century. Otherwise there have been no additions or external changes.

Inside ornate wood moulding surrounds the window and door openings and there is an impressive oak staircase. The woodwork is reminiscent of much of the work done by Edward

Peniston in a distinctive Charles Eastlake style (*see chapter 10*). The window trim consists of square corner blocks incised with a simple flower design with reeded side and top mouldings. Much of the woodwork is said to be of bald cypress, a tree found in the swamps of southern USA. The woodwork has been carefully restored by its current owner.

The three chimneys are of interesting design and two of them serve small fireplaces that were originally intended for burning coal as the house was built at a time when coal was readily available on the island for bunkering steamships.

The house in true Victorian upper middle class tradition has a back staircase for the use of servants or the chil-

dren. A similar back staircase is also found in the Edward Peniston designed Rockmoor (*see chapter 10*) and in nearby Glimmerview.

Stables were located at the rear on the west side of the house. This is presumably where Dr. Elmore Reid Mercer ran his veterinary practice although he also had an office in the drug store at Mangrove Bay in Somerset which he

Aldie, located off Middle Road south of Store Hill, was built for Elmore Reid and Julia Mercer about 1877. The two storey verandah on the south facing rear of the house has turned balusters.

visited on Thursdays. The stables have now been converted into a house known as Las Palmos.

Elmore Reid Mercer (1856-1920) was the only son of Thomas Wood Mercer of Harrington Place in Hamilton Parish. His sister Eliza Estelle Skinner was to briefly live nearby at Glimmerview. Their father was a businessman and politician who represented Hamilton Parish in the House of Assembly for 28 years.

He graduated from New York University in 1881 and initially returned to Bermuda where he went into practice in partnership with Dr. Theodore

Outerbridge (1851-1930). Dr. Outerbridge of Sunnylands in Paget was one of Bermuda's earliest veterinary surgeons and a son of shipbuilder Joseph John Outerbridge of Shelly Bay (see *Hamilton Parish*).

In 1883 Dr. Mercer married Julia Elizabeth Zuill, the second daughter of William Sears Zuill Sr. of Orange Grove. The family moved to Montclair, New Jersey, where Dr. Mercer worked for a few years before returning to Bermuda where they lived at his wife's family home of Orange Grove whilst Aldie was being built. He set up a veterinary practice. In addition he represented Smith's

Aldie

Aldie, northeast side of house: *Drawn by Barbara Finsness.*

Built for veterinarian Dr. Elmore Reid Mercer and his wife Julia Mercer, nèe Zuill, Aldie represents up-to-date taste and domestic expectations Bermudians shared with American and British professionals by the 1890s. It provided several rooms that could be opened up for entertaining, four family bedrooms, and segregated rooms for live-in servants above a kitchen in the rear wing. These were packaged in a manner that gave the best rooms spatial character and the exterior a picturesque appearance. Subsequent owners have left the house sufficiently unchanged to keep it a legible building.

The front door opens into an entry hall made large by extending out the side exterior wall. Joinery is concentrated on the stairway constructed of American pine and oak: multi-panelled cabinetry, outsweeping steps, richly turned balusters and oversized posts with oak balls the size of boules. This stair connects all the Mercer family's spaces in the house: two reception rooms to the southwest (right), a more private room straight ahead and bedrooms on the upper floor.

Double doors were used to make entertaining possible on a large scale and to allow free circulation of air in hot weather. One set opens the entry and front room into virtually a single 31' by 16' space, and a second one permitted use of the two superior side rooms as what in the late 19th century were called double parlours. Carrying potential openness even further, a smaller third pair previously connected the rear parlour to the otherwise private fourth space, behind the stair hall. Triple sets of projecting windows increased light and air and gave stylish distinction to the double parlours. The pri-

vate third room was more practical than impressive, originally with two windows in a square projection. Two of the three rooms had small coal-burning fireplaces with wood mantels and multi-coloured tile hearths. (*See floor plan page 9.*)

Both rear rooms originally opened through a small lobby or directly into a kitchen on the south (right rear), with a pantry or servants' room beside it. The connections suggest that both middle rooms could be used for dining and the largest one reserved for more formal occasions. Backstage space extended to the upper storey, with a narrow board-sheathed secondary stair rising from the service lobby to a passage serving three small bedrooms, closets and the upper floor of the rear porch. An 1890s swinging but lockable door connected the servants' passage with two interlocking passages giving access to four larger bedrooms for the Mercer family. Three of the four benefited from the projecting bays with multiple windows.

The projections also gave sculptural quality to the outside, rising to faceted roofs off centre on the front and southwest (right) side and pedimented gables on the northeast (left). All the rear spaces were more modestly wrapped in a rectangular wing, but the whole house was unified by plain corner piers, watertables, strap courses and Italianate masonry cornices. This distinctly Bermudian masonry finish contrasted with American looking and perhaps US fabricated porches decorated with turned balusters and friezes until the front one was replaced by George Hill Wingate with a modern Bermuda style masonry porch about 1955.

E.A.C.

An aerial view of Glimmerview on the corner of Middle Road and Store Hill shows the asymmetrical house with its three storey tower, rear right.

Parish in the House of Assembly for 21 years and was a member of the Board of Education. The Mercers had four children: Anne Mercer (1881-1976) wife of Horace Lindeman Pearman,

The two storey verandah at Glimmerview with its cast iron pillars is reminiscent of the style of builder and architectural designer Edward Peniston.

dentist Thomas William Mercer (1883-1974), Howard Campbell Mercer (1885-1955) and Archibald Reid Mercer (1892-1971).

The Cornish family of New Jersey was invited to stay at Aldie during the summer of 1927. Julia Mercer, then a widow, was the great-aunt of the three girls, Alice, Harriet and Susan, who came along with their father and stepmother. They arrived aboard the SS *Fort Victoria* and were conveyed in style to Aldie by a carriage drawn by a team of Australian ponies and driven by their great-aunt Sophie Wilkinson.

A diary of this visit was kept by 13 year old Alice Cornish and an account of her experiences along with excerpts from her diary was written by William Sears Zuill Jr. and published in *The Bermudian* magazine in 1997. He wrote, "Aldie was a spacious house with six large bedrooms and a bathroom – the first to be installed in Smith's Parish . . . The house had a telephone and electric lights, and so was thoroughly up-to-date. The water was pumped by hand up to a gravity tank, a task which

fell on father Gilbert (Cornish) every evening."

Alice also wrote of a visit to Aldie by Eugenius Zuill of nearby Glimmerview and of a walk to collect milk "as usual" from the Pioneer Guernsey Dairy run by Chauncey Outerbridge of Outerlea.

In 1943 Aldie, and a barn and six and a half acres of land, was purchased by George Hill Wingate, the father of Bermuda's first conservation officer David Wingate. The house is now owned by a daughter of George Wingate.

Glimmerview, an early 20th century house, stands on the corner of Middle Road and Store Hill and with its square tower is a familiar landmark. It was not recorded on the Savage map which was surveyed between 1897 and 1899 but must have been built soon after, probably sometime between 1899 when 14 acres was purchased by James William Musson Skinner and 1904 when the land and house were sold to Eugenius

Glimmerview on Store Hill was built at the beginning of 20th century for James William Musson Skinner and his wife Eliza Estelle, sister of Dr. Reid Mercer of neighbouring Aldie.

Foggo Zuill.

It is an asymmetrical two storey house with a three storey tower and a verandah on its southeast front with cast iron pillars and gingerbread trim. Like Aldie, Glimmerview is characterised by heavy plaster mouldings and bay window projections whilst inside there is ornate Charles Eastlake style woodwork around the door and window openings. The main staircase has heavy turned balusters and an ornate carved newel post. With its rear staircase and formal front double parlour, the house was planned to accommodate servants and formal Edwardian living.

Glimmerview was originally built without fireplaces although it now possesses two chimneys. The first, at the rear, must have been added in the mid 1940s to vent the Aga stove in the kitchen whilst the chimney on the southwest was added in the late 20th century to provide a fireplace for the parlour. The tower, which seems to be such an integral feature of the exterior house design, also appears from inside inspection to be an addition. There is no ornate wooden moulding around the entrances to the tower and it does not appear to flow smoothly into the floor plan of the house. If it is later, it is not known when it was added although it may have been done when the house was purchased in 1904 by its second owner Eugenius Foggo Zuill.

Eliza Estelle Skinner, the wife of James William Musson Skinner, was the sister of Elmore Reid Mercer of neighbouring Aldie and she probably admired the design of her brother's American style home and wanted something similar. According to oral tradition the two houses were built by the same man, perhaps Edward Peniston who was the outstanding builder of the area. The two houses with their elaborate woodwork are indeed reminiscent of his style.

James William Musson Skinner, known as Jimmy (1856-1932), was the second son of John Skinner of the house now known as Cloverdale in Devonshire. He was a descendant of famed shipbuilder Nathaniel Tynes whilst his grandparents John Abraham and Letitia Skinner donated the land on which the Wesleyan Centenary Methodist Church (*see chapter 11*) was to be built.

Jimmy Skinner was later to become the proprietor of a livery stable in Pembroke. He married Eliza Estelle Mercer in 1880 and there were two children from the marriage, Mabel Frances and Willard Mercer.

Eugenius Foggo Zuill (1856-1930), the second owner of Glimmerview,

Glimmerview

A more imposing house than Aldie, Glimmerview partakes of similar aesthetics outside and functional arrangements inside. Being absent from the Savage map suggests it dates between 1899 and 1904. It is dramatically an asymmetrical house, with a two storey porch between a faceted projecting bay on the southwest (left) and a three storey tower on the northeast (right).

The porch has old-fashioned thin columns below and less classical Eastlake-like columns with multiple turnings above. Both levels have spindle friezes and railings, recently replaced. Exposed and beaded framing supports the upper porch floor, while the lower floor is masonry, paved with geometric tile in complementary earth colours.

The front door opens into a relatively small entry filled by a heavily turned and milled stairway that flows down to the door so emphatically that the visitor expects to climb right up to the bedrooms. Immediately to the southwest (left) are a pair of double parlours connected until 1995-1996 by a sliding pair of pocket doors. Glazed double doors originally opened from the rear parlour into an arcaded L-shaped porch.

On the opposite side of the entry is a dining room, with an arched opening to a smaller second space under the tower, well lighted by four tightly packed windows. The principal dining space borrowed light from the tower, augmented by some light from a glazed door to the porch. Behind the dining room was a less formal morning or breakfast room and beyond it a kitchen, these two rooms occupying a plainer rear wing and combined to create a kitchen in 1995-1996. Only the kitchen had a chimney or fireplace before 1995. Between the parlours on the left and more private space on the right was a back passage with a narrow stair and doors to the entry, rear parlour, morning room, and back porch.

Again there are front and rear passages upstairs, with a door between the two. The front passage opens into the two best bedrooms, one with a faceted front and the other with an arched opening to the tower, a romantic accoutrement. A simpler and lighter Eastlake stair rises from this inner space to a small room with elevated views available from six windows. The rear passage is less secondary here, balustraded with similar woodwork and giving access to three good bedrooms. The implication is servants at Glimmerview slept elsewhere.

E.A.C.

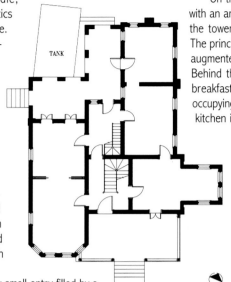

TANK

0 5 10 FEET

Glimmerview ground floor plan pre 1995: *Drawn by Ted Wood, Botelho Wood Architects.*

bought the house following his marriage in July 1903 to American widow Mary Adelaide Goodwin (circa 1853-1910). He married in the US and they went on an extended wedding trip returning to Bermuda in 1904 to find Glimmerview ready for occupancy. Perhaps the tower was added at this time. Edward Peniston (*see chapter 10*) had just died so his mill would not have been available to provide the woodwork.

Zuill's wife died after only seven years of marriage, leaving him to live as a widower in Glimmerview for 20 years. He was the son of Eugenius Augustus Zuill and his wife Caroline née Williams of Loyal Hill in Devonshire.

Eugenius Foggo Zuill was a planter and represented Devonshire Parish in the House of Assembly and was a member of the Board of Agriculture. He was a progressive farmer, experimenting with the latest crops and using labour saving farm machinery. He was said to

have been a keen opponent of the introduction of cars to Bermuda and a supporter of the railway project.

Young Alice Cornish, who was visiting her great-aunt at Aldie during the summer of 1927, described a visit by her father to look at the farming operations of Eugenius Zuill. Quoting the diary, William Zuill wrote in *The Bermudian* magazine, "He was reclaiming part of Devonshire Marsh, digging peat moss out of ditches, filling the ditches with stone, and then spreading the peaty soil on top and over the adjoining area. When the land had been raised enough to grow potatoes it was placed under cultivation – first a crop of potatoes planted in September and then celery, planted in February or March. This reached market in New York in May, just after the Florida crop had been sold. 'They take great pains with the crop,' the diary reports, 'using the best of seed and culture and commands a very high price - going as far west as Chicago. It is getting to be one of

Bermuda's best crops. Onions are dying out. The competition from Texas is too keen. Easter lilies are still a big crop, the bulbs being shipped all over the US'."

There were no children from the marriage of Eugenius and Mary Adelaide Zuill. He was 47 when he married and his wife about three years older. After the death of Eugenius Zuill the balance of his estate, after specific bequests, was left to his nephew Edmund Eugenius Zuill, and to Eugenius' brother Ormond Cox Zuill and his sister Margaret Adelaide Gilbert, known as Minnie. These three signed an agreement soon after he died. Edmund was to have Glimmerview and most of its contents and the other two were to have the land on the east side of Store Hill (*see Millwood and Channelway*).

Amongst the specific bequests was his gold watch and chain and property in Devonshire. This included two houses, one of which was Milner, be-

Outerlea, on the top of Store Hill, was built in 1932 and photographed soon after by Walter Rutherford. *Bermudiana, Ronald John Williams, 1936, page 143.*

queathed to Sarah Ann Jackson (born 1874) (see *Devonshire*).

Edmund and Frances Zuill were the next occupants of Glimmerview. John Edmund Eugenius Zuill (1898-1980) was the son of John Benjamin Zuill of Somerset. He was secretary/treasurer of the Bermuda Telephone Company for 40 years, joining the company in June 1928. Elizabeth Frances Zuill was the daughter of Dr. William Eldon Tucker, known as Willie, one of the sons of Archdeacon Tucker of Palmetto Grove (*see chapter 8*) and sister of the orthopaedic surgeon of London, Dr. William Eldon Tucker, known as Dr. Bill. She taught at the Bermuda High School for Girls, first as a teacher of gym, hygiene and religious knowledge, then as deputy and finally as headmistress.

It was Frances Zuill who added the Aga stove to the kitchen at Glimmerview. It was maintained alight winter and summer. Edmund Zuill kept horses, calves, an occasional house

cow, chickens and ducks. There was a two storey stable and carriage house to the northeast of the house. The field at the front of Glimmerview was used as a paddock, as a training area for standard bred horses and also for sport, particularly cricket. The spectacular royal poinciana tree planted on the east side of the paddock in 1930 was an important feature at Glimmerview and attracted visitors who stopped to photograph the tree. Frances and Edmund Zuill, aided by their housekeeper Helen Dillas, served fruit punch to them.

Glimmerview was sold following the death of Edmund Zuill in 1980 and became home to a nursery school for a while until it was purchased in 1994 by its current owners who restored it to a family home standing on almost four acres of land.

Outerlea, which lies at the top of Store Hill on the eastern side of the road, marks a return to a more traditional form of Bermudian

architecture than either Aldie or Glimmerview. It was built in 1932 for Benjamin Chauncey Curling Outerbridge, known as Chauncey, following his marriage in 1931 to Leah Montgomery. The couple lived at Villa Monticello (*see chapter 8*) for the first 18 months of their marriage before moving to Outerlea in September 1932.

The 1930s saw a return to the vernacular tradition and Outerlea incorporates many typically Bermudian features such as Flemish gables, eyebrows and a buttery roof. It is a one storey house designed by Bermudian architect George Houston Hutchings and built by Frank Edwin Hathway of Hathway Limited, a firm located in Flatts and also responsible for work at Deepdene, now Manor House apartments or condominiums (*see chapter 8*).

An article written in *The Bermudian* magazine in April 1933 by Keith B. Hudson noted, "in planning this house, the owners and the architect, Mr. George Hutchings, sought to design

A small walled garden with cedar posts framed the entrance to Outerlea. *The Bermudian magazine, April 1933, photographed by Walter Rutherford, page 10. Courtesy family of the late Edmund M. Gosling.*

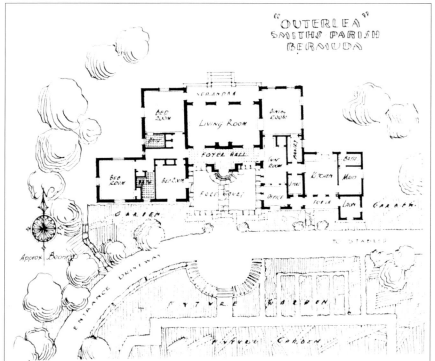

The design of Outerlea marked a return to a more traditional form of Bermudian architecture. George Houston Hutchings was the architect and this floor plan was drawn by Keith B. Hudson in 1933. *The Bermudian magazine, April 1933, page 11. Courtesy family of the late Edmund M. Gosling.*

a home which internally and externally embodied the distinctive manner of the old Bermudian dwelling". The writer continued, "The forecourt is framed in at the front by a fence and gateway of native stone and cedar, all very local in character, flanked on the west side by a bedroom wing and on the east by a sun room and office, whose purpose is explained by the owners' farming and official interests in the parish, which are served by a separate entrance away from the entrance proper to the home.

"The Bermudian style is chiefly expressed internally within the living room and entrance hall" where the ceilings are "beamed with cedar" which are "pegged". The floor of the living room consisted of boards "nearly a foot wide, and the joints filled with a coloured bitumen such as may be seen on ships' decking".

Hudson continued, "The house has the modern conveniences which have been common to American homes for years and are coming into general demand in Bermuda . . . It is new houses

The Pioneer Guernsey Dairy Farm at Outerlea in Smith's Parish photographed in the 1940s. A dairy farm is still located on the land. *Beautiful Bermuda, Frank R. Bell, tenth edition, 1947, page 220.*

like this one which carry on the tradition, the sentiment and that feeling for good domestic architecture which has made the simple old Bermudian homes so much appreciated and admired."

The architect, George Houston Hutchings (1880-1944) obtained a degree from McGill University in

Beautiful Bermuda, Frank R. Bell, tenth edition, page 601

Montreal, Canada, and worked in Montreal and then Boston before returning to Bermuda after the stockmarket crash of 1929. He set up his own practice in the Somers Building on Front Street in Hamilton.

The memorial erected in the Somers Gardens in St. George's, which celebrates 300 years of settlement as well as Sir George Somers, was amongst his earliest commissions. Hutchings designed a number of notable homes including the house on Frick's or Castle Point for Childs Frick, Kent House in Warwick, Halcyon in Pembroke, Mill Point in Fairylands as well as his own home Houston in Warwick.

The Art Deco Tennis Stadium in Bernard Park which was completed in 1932 was designed by George Hutchings as was the swimming pool, with its diving board so often featured in tourist promotions, at the now demolished Castle Harbour Hotel in Hamilton Parish.

George Hutchings, the son of Captain William Greig Hutchings, was born at Rhyllon on Brunswick Street in the City of Hamilton. He was a second cousin of brothers Nathaniel William Hutchings (1890-1974) and Joseph

Francis Hutchings (1892-1955) who were architects and builders. All three shared a great-grandfather, cabinet maker Solomon Joell Hutchings (circa 1769-1843).

Benjamin Chauncey Curling Outerbridge (1880-1978), the man for whom Outerlea was built, was born at Whitby in Hamilton Parish and was the son of Thomas Heber and Mary Eleanor Outerbridge née Pearman of neighbouring Somerville (*see chapter 4*). His first job was with *The Royal Gazette*, then he worked at the Agricultural Station until he became a farmer. He was a member of the House of Assembly for about 30 years and served as Deputy Speaker.

In 1915 Chauncey Outerbridge formed the Bermuda Green Vegetable Growers Association which he managed with James Hollis (see *Hamilton Parish*). It was a farmers' cooperative which exported produce to markets in New York and Canada.

He also ran what came to be called the Pioneer Guernsey Dairy at his farm at Outerlea and was the first to bring Guernsey cattle to the island. Previous breeds were Holsteins and Ayrshires. In 1920 he landed six pure bred Guern-

An old family photograph of Millwood taken in the 1930s when the upper verandah was infilled with windows. *Courtesy Sally Madden.*

sey cows in Bermuda. One of these was in calf to the US$100,000 Guernsey bull Don Diavola of Linda Vista. This calf, known as Bermuda Daisy, grew to be an exceptional animal producing as much as 29 quarts of milk a day.

Pioneer Guernsey Dairy was amalgamated with Dunkley's Dairy in 1964. The dairy farm still exists and cattle are grazed on land now owned by the Bermuda Government. The house, which has only had two owners, was acquired by its present owners in 1984.

Millwood is a little lower down Store Hill than Outerlea. It was designed and built in 1936 by Cyril Hilton Smith on land of his wife Dora Millwood Smith, a niece of Eugenius Foggo Zuill of Glimmerview. Cyril Hilton Smith had first built Millwood Cottage in which the family lived until the arrival of their second child.

The main house, Millwood, is an elegant two storey building. It has a spacious south facing upper verandah over an elegant colonnaded porch reminiscent of the British colonial style. Design is achieved through the form and proportion of the structures rather than through superficial details. The Smiths did much of the work in building the house themselves with the help of a Mr. Van Putten.

Cyril Hilton Smith (1902-1977) was an engineer and Director of Public Works. Born at Durnford House in St. George's, he was the youngest son of Joseph Inkerman Smith best known as the Police Magistrate of St. George's. Cyril Hilton Smith trained and worked overseas. In New York he worked from 1920 until 1922 as a draughtsman and in Spain from 1924 as a surveyor on the Santander-Mediterranean Railway. On his return to Bermuda in 1928 he worked for the Somerset division of the

Millwood on Store Hill was designed and built in 1936 by Cyril Hilton Smith. It has a large airy upper verandah above an elegant arched lower porch.

Bermuda Railway Company.

He rejoined the Bermuda Public Works Department in 1933 as assistant engineer and became the director in 1938. He was involved in the construction of the Severn Bridge, which once linked St. David's with Stokes Point in St. George's, and the Darrell's Island seaplane terminal building.

His hobbies were carpentry and sail boat design. He made almost all of the cedar furniture in Millwood including the mantels. He worked closely with Sir Eldon Trimingham on Bermuda dinghy designs and made many models, some of which hang in the Royal Bermuda Yacht Club. He was influenced by Nathaniel Herreshoff (1848-1938), a renowned American designer whom he knew.

His wife, Dora Millwood Smith née Gilbert (1899-1992) was the daughter of Margaret Adelaide Gilbert, known as Minnie (1865-1932), a sister of Eugenius Zuill of Glimmerview. The house acquired her middle name.

In 1988 Millwood was bought by its current owners who renovated the house in 1992 and returned the upper verandah to its original form.

Channelway stands near the foot of Store Hill with a panoramic view of the North Shore and overlooks the shipping channels into Hamilton Harbour and Dockyard. It was built in 1936 for Cummings Vail Zuill and his wife Janette, the cornerstone being laid on March 29, 1936.

It is a two storey T-shaped house designed in a traditional Bermudian manner. A gently curving staircase dominates the entry hall and a spacious verandah wraps around the house on the northern and eastern sides. Welcoming arms steps in the front lawn garden were added in 1957 and a garden room with an exterior sculptured frieze by Byllee Lang was built in 1965. A Canadian sculptress, she came to Bermuda in the late 1940s as a window designer for A.S. Cooper & Sons. Byllee Lang produced some memorable floats for the Floral Pageant and was responsible for the reredos in the Anglican Cathedral in Hamilton.

Lawrence Harrower Smart (1896-1965) was the architect of Channelway. A Scot and a member of the Edinburgh firm of Tarbolton and Smart, he arrived on the island in 1926 to work on the

An aerial view of Channelway taken in 1951 shows the extensive verandah sweeping around two sides of the house. The old store, after which Store Hill was named, stood in what is now the northern garden of Channelway. *Courtesy Mrs. C. Vail Zuill.*

The massive chimney at Channelway Cottage is strong and sturdy in the Bermudian vernacular tradition.

Channelway, designed by architect Lawrence Harrower Smart, was built in 1936. The garden room, left, with a frieze by sculptor Byllee Lang was added in 1965. *Pen and ink drawing by Richard Brooks, after 1965. Courtesy Mrs. C. Vail Zuill.*

Channelway stands at the foot of Store Hill and overlooks the main shipping channel into Hamilton Harbour.

Channelway Cottage, in the grounds of Channelway, was designed in the early 1950s by noted local architect Wilfred Onions.

replacement of the roof of the Anglican Cathedral. Lawrence Smart was also responsible for the design of the Roman Catholic St. Theresa's Cathedral as well as Coral Ledge. This house, built on the waterfront of Harrington Sound in 1930, heralded a revival of interest in Bermudian vernacular architecture (see *Hamilton Parish*).

Channelway was built by Henry Appleby Talbot. He was a contractor who also built housing on the US Base and the original Bermuda Electric Light Company building in Pembroke.

Cummings Vail Zuill CBE, JP (1906-1976) was the son of Ormond Cox Zuill (1869-1937) who inherited the land on which Channelway was to be built from his brother Eugenius Foggo Zuill of Glimmerview. C. Vail Zuill joined the Bank of Bermuda on January 1, 1924. He retired as chief general manager in 1972 having been with the bank for 48 years. He represented

Smith's Parish in the House of Assembly and was a member of the Executive Council for nine years and served on the Board of Agriculture and the Public Service Commission. He was a founder member and master of the Bermuda Paperchase Club, the local hunt club.

Channelway Cottage, in the garden of Channelway, was built in the early 1950s for Mr. and Mrs. C. Vail Zuill and was designed by Bermudian architect Wilfred Onions.

Wilfred Onions, known as Wil (1908-1959), who is believed to have worked as a student with Lawrence Smart, joined V.D. Bouchard in 1936. Onions is noted for his skill in Bermudian vernacular design and for being the architect of City Hall in Hamilton. In Smith's Parish he also designed Somersall (*see chapter 7*).

Channelway Cottage is a small

sturdy L-shaped two storey cottage designed to fit its exposed position overlooking the North Shore. Its traditionalism is expressed in its simplicity and proportions rather than the addition of decorative features.

Store Hill is thus an important showcase for a gradual evolution in architectural design in Bermuda over the first half of the 20th century. As the century opened Bermudians were looking to America for design ideas but with the coming of the Colonial revival movement in the 1930s and the advent of a number of influential local architects there was a return to a home grown style.

Aldie and Glimmerview at the top of the hill demonstrate the influence of American architectural ideas whilst at the bottom stands Channelway Cottage, unmistakably Bermudian in its simple form and scale. 🌴

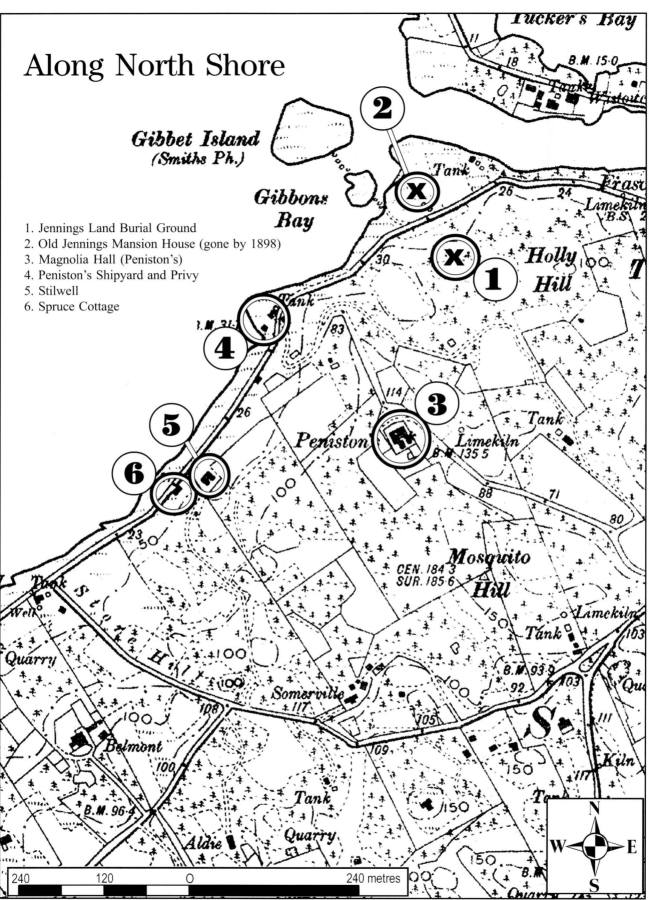

Along North Shore

Gibbet Island
(Smiths Ph.)

Gibbons Bay

1. Jennings Land Burial Ground
2. Old Jennings Mansion House (gone by 1898)
3. Magnolia Hall (Peniston's)
4. Peniston's Shipyard and Privy
5. Stilwell
6. Spruce Cottage

Surveyed and Contoured in 1898-1899 by Lieut. A.J. Savage, RE. Published at the Ordnance Survey Office, Southampton, England, 1901.
Courtesy Works & Engineering.

6
Along North Shore

Gibbet Island is now a peaceful landmark marking the entrance to Flatts Inlet. This oil was painted about 1955 by Earle N. Scherm. *Earle N. Scherm (1899-1959), oil on board. Courtesy Masterworks Foundation.*

Smith's Parish extends along the North Shore from just west of Flatts Village to west of Penhurst Park where Smith's meets Devonshire Parish. North Shore Road was earlier known as the North Longitudinal Public Road.

Flatts Inlet is not within Smith's Parish but is an outpost of Hamilton Parish. However, many of the major Smith's Parish landowners maintained wharfs and storehouses in Flatts as it was their natural outlet to the sea and overseas trade. Shipowner John Dickinson of Verdmont (*see chapter 2*) owned a wharf and store house at Flatts as did Samuel Spofferth of Hinson Hall (*see chapter 4*) and William Sears of Orange Grove (*see chapter 7*).

This north shoreline was an important shipbuilding site with slips along most of the flatter rocky areas. The quiet coast hides a busy industrial past. Shipbuilding was carried on along the waterfront at Peniston's Shipyard, below Magnolia Hall, and at James Tynes' Building Place, in front of Stilwell and Spruce Cottage. The slips can still be seen along the coast and are recognisable as smooth leaf shaped areas edged with holes where the posts, which cradled the hull during manufacture, stood.

Gibbet Island, sometimes known as Gibbons Island, is now a peaceful landmark marking the entry to Flatts Inlet, but it hides a violent past as it was one of the prominent public places chosen for the punishment of offenders during the early years of the colony.

As was the custom of the time, bodies of executed criminals were exhib-

Gibbet Island, Gibbons Bay, as seen from the North Shore Road above Flatts. Taken from a mid 19th century sketch by Miss L.L. Deudney. *The Naturalist in Bermuda, John Matthew Jones, 1859, page 130.*

ited on a gibbet, or gallows, to hold them to further contempt and to act as a deterrent. Often the body was quartered so that it could go on more widespread display in different parts of the island. Cobbler's Island off Spanish Point, Mangrove Bay, Stokes Point and Ordnance Island along with Gibbet Island were all such prominent places at harbour entrances.

Among the executions on Gibbet Island was that in 1681 of a slave known as Indian John, a slave to William Maligan of Flatts Hill (*see chapter 7*). He had planned to murder his master and mistress by stealing firearms, set-

ting fire to their house and shooting them as they rushed outdoors to safety. His plan failed, but he was hanged and quartered. In 1753 a slave named Quash killed his master John McNeil with a hatchet. He was tried, sentenced to death and hung from a gibbet on Gibbet Island. Legend has it that he hung in chains for many days before he died.

Flatts Inlet was an important harbour particularly at the time when St. George's was the only official port of entry. A portion of the cargo was often quietly offloaded at private wharfs before the ship put in for customs clearance at St. George's.

The inlet, however, became too shallow for larger ships in the early 19th century. A suggestion was made in the House of Assembly in May 1830 to link Gibbet Island to the shore by a wall in a bid to prevent Flatts harbour from silting up with sand. Francis Peniston, John Walker Sr. and Cornelius C. Hinson were voted £220 to do this.

The wall can still be seen running from the beach to Gibbet Island but it had a troubled history and may have done more harm than good. By May 1831 it was recorded in the Journal of Proceedings of the House of Assembly that bad weather had delayed progress and the money was almost spent. In July 1832 it was reported that boulders were constantly washed away and £60 more was voted for Flatts harbour in April 1833.

In the 19th century cattle were driven along the sea wall to graze on Gibbet Island. However, William Zuill in *Bermuda Journey*, first published in 1946, wrote, "It is thought that this road, by stopping the tidal current, caused the sand to bank up on both sides and largely contributed to the silting up of Flatts Inlet."

Jennings Land is now an exclusive neighbourhood of houses built in the 20th century but it was once owned by the Jennings family, early arrivals in Bermuda. Their name and a small

Peniston's, now known as Magnolia Hall, painted about 1830. *Courtesy William Peniston Starr, New Brunswick.*

Jennings Land Burial Ground

An ancient burial ground exists in residential Jennings Land in such a small and private place that many are unaware of its existence.

It overlooks the North Shore near the mouth of Flatts Inlet and lies a short distance from Jennings Road. It consists of two simple weathered and unmarked stone graves but an eyewitness remembers a third open vault visible in 1939 and it is possible there may have been more.

The larger of the two graves is roughly 3' by 8' and stands about 2'8" above ground on a plinth. The other is a mere 5" above soil level. They both have somewhat primitive and worn headstones, one almost cruciform and the other semicircular, but these may have been put in place when the burial ground was restored in the 1950s.

Graves dug partially into the ground but also extending above have become the standard form in Bermuda, possibly a response to the hard rocky ground and the lack of any great depth of soil.

The small plot of land on which the graves stand is now owned by the Bermuda National Trust, having been acquired from the Bermuda Historical Monuments Trust when the Bermuda National Trust was formed in December 1969.

The burial ground of 0.012 acres was conveyed for the token sum of £1 to the Bermuda Historical Monuments Trust on September 1, 1953, by Lucy, Lady Watlington, widow of Sir Henry William Watlington, and her sisters Mary Adelaide Trott and Mary Frances Emmeline Trott. The three were daughters of planter Thaddeus Trott (1838-1924) who owned 78 acres of Jennings Land and built his house Rockmoor (*see chapter 10*) on the southern portion of this estate.

Having acquired the burial ground, the Bermuda Historical Monuments Trust cleared the land, restored the graves and erected a rustic fence in 1955.

In the document conveying the land it was described as "the burial ground of the family of Jennyns". However, it is not known which members of the family were buried in these graves. In the early years of colonisation burial grounds were often on family land as the Anglican church struggled to become established.

The Jennings family came early to Bermuda. Richard Jennings aged 35 and his wife Sarah Jennings aged 18 are listed as immigrants in an appendix to *Memorials of the Bermudas* compiled by Major-General John Henry Lefroy, as bound for the island aboard the *Dorset* in 1635. He was to play a prominent role in the early history of the colony and was to become a major landowner.

Captain Richard Jennings (circa 1600-1669) was a member of the Governor's Council and Captain of the King's Castle. The Richard Norwood division of 1663 shows him as owner of two groups of shares in Smith's Parish. His mansion, or main house, stood on a four share tract which extended from "ye south side sea" to "Fflatts-mouth". The house was close to Flatts Inlet not far from the existing family burial ground. He owned a second parcel of two shares adjoining the border with Devonshire and a three share tract in Southampton.

Richard Jennings Jr. (died 1691), son of Captain Jennings, lived in a spacious two storey house in Smith's Parish and maintained a prosperous household as revealed in his inventory of 1691. He had three children, Richard, John and Sarah. His house contained eight rooms plus a kitchen, storehouse, cellar, buttery, milk house and corn house. He owned a considerable amount of bullion valued at £371 as well as cash of £422. Twelve negroes are listed in his inventory as well as "one Indian man arrived from Carrolina about seven yeares to serve called James". He was presumably an indentured servant.

The house of Richard Jennings Jr. has gone although a cruciform shaped mansion house is marked on an old plan. It is not known whether he inherited his father's house. Nor has the subsequent story of the Jennings family been traced. However, in 1813 Richard Downing Jennings of St. Thomas in the West Indies and his oldest son Joseph Clayton Jennings of London owned 75 acres of Jennings Land. In 1860 the property was purchased by Henry Morton Peniston and Harley Trott, brother of Thaddeus Trott.

This gift by the daughters of Thaddeus Trott saved for the nation this small burial ground when the former Jennings estate was subdivided for housing in the mid 20th century and respect for this spot by its neighbours has preserved this piece of Bermuda's heritage intact for future generations.   *D.C.*

A grave at Jennings Land Burial Ground: Drawn by Barbara Finsness.

---

unmarked burial ground are all that remain (*see sidebar*). Jennings Land was used as a 2,729 yard nine hole golf course in the early 20th century. Designed by American golf course architect Devereux Emmett (1863-1934), its first tee and ninth hole were within 50 feet of the Frascati Hotel, since replaced by the St. James Court condominiums in Flatts.

Immediately west of Jennings Land is Timberly, a house designed in the 20th century by Cyril Hilton Smith (*see chapter 5*) and built for Louis S. Mowbray, the son of the founder of the Bermuda Aquarium. The house was named after Henry Timberly the owner of the share at the time of the first Norwood survey of 1617.

Magnolia Hall stands in an extensive 28 acre estate immediately west of Timberly. Its property includes Gibbet Island and an old shipyard on the waterfront. The main house sits on top of the hill with a sweeping view over the North Shore and is reached by a long driveway. Today it is two storey. The second floor was added in the 1920s but the early 19th century house underneath can still be recognised.

The original house, known as Peniston's, was built for Richard F. Peniston (1760-1826) about 1815. An old photograph reveals Peniston's to have been one storey high and somewhat similar in appearance to Villa Monticello in Flatts (*see chapter 8*). Perhaps the same builder had a hand in both.

Peniston's was symmetrical on its

An aerial view of the Magnolia Hall estate shows its extensive grounds. The main house is seen, centre rear, with the Schoolhouse or the House at Pooh Corner and stables and carriage house to its rear. In the foreground are Pennystones, left, built in the 20th century and Magnolia Cottage, right, where numerous additions have been made to an older cottage.

front façade with a verandah extending between two projecting wings. It stood in a walled garden. There was heavy quoining on the corners and around the front door which is topped with a semi circular fanlight. Stables and a carriage house were at the rear

Matilda Starr (1810-1846) a daughter of Richard F. Peniston and her husband William Joseph Starr (1805-1869). *Courtesy William Peniston Starr.*

and an interesting lime kiln to the east of the house.

Richard F. Peniston was a wealthy merchant. He left a sizeable Bermuda estate owning more than 282 acres in Smith's Parish as well as considerable investments in the US. It is not known precisely how he amassed his fortune. Rumours were many. Hereward Watlington in *Family Narrative* wrote of a somewhat confusing tale, passed down through his family, of hidden treasure being retrieved from the auctioned cargo of wrecked ships.

He was obviously a shipbuilder as he owned a number of slaves skilled in the art of shipbuilding. They were listed in the Slave Register of 1821 and included Kitt a blacksmith, another man also called Kitt a carpenter, Jack a carpenter and Titus, Dick and Will all labourers. There were also four women employed as house servants, Ruth, Patience, Bessey and Doreas as well as 18 month old William.

Richard F. Peniston was the son of goldsmith Francis Peniston (1730-1785) and his wife Ann. He was the

Peniston's Privy on the waterfront below Magnolia Hall was built perched above the sea just west of Gibbons Bay and Gibbet Island. It served the shipyard and the ocean provided a natural form of flushing. (*See plan on page 6.*)

Peniston's was built as a one storey house about 1815 by Richard F. Peniston. This photograph was taken about 1912. A second storey was added after 1926.
Courtesy Elizabeth Zuill Cart.

Magnolia Hall, now a two storey house, was photographed in the 1930s by Walter Rutherford following additions by architect F.P. Hill and contractor G.H. Burland & Company. The garden walls and wings at either end appear to date from the earlier house. *Bermudiana, Ronald John Williams, 1946, page 117.*

Magnolia Hall photographed at the beginning of the 21st century appears little changed from early in the 20th century.

only boy amongst five girls, Elizabeth, Frances, Ann, Martha and Mary. He married Frances née Peniston (1755-1829) and they produced eight children, three sons and five daughters.

The oldest son, Francis Peniston (circa 1770-1854), inherited Peniston's. He was a shipbuilder and Peniston's Shipyard on the shoreline below the house must have been a busy place with a wharf and slipways. All that remains today is a gaunt and ruined privy which would have discharged into the sea.

In 1837 Francis Peniston built the 134 ton *Steadfast* for Daniel E. Gilbert. In 1838 he built the *Cygnet* which was intended as a mail boat for Barbados and in the following year the 140 ton *Flirt* for William J. Starr of Halifax in Nova Scotia. Starr was the brother-in-law of Francis Peniston having married

---

his sister Matilda in 1830. The *Halifax Royal Gazette* of April 10, 1845, reported the brig *Flirt* had made a couple of record breaking runs to the West Indies and Demerara. Although, as a letter writer to *The Bermuda Gazette* pointed out on May 6, 1845, the Canadian newspaper had omitted to write the *Flirt* was "of cedar and was built in Bermuda".

Francis Peniston was also engaged in shipping cattle from the US to feed the British military stationed in Bermuda and the convicts employed in building the Royal Naval Dockyard at Ireland Island.

This period of shipbuilding was post emancipation and it is difficult to know what form of labour was used in his yard. Perhaps Francis Peniston used indentured servants as on April 11, 1837, he advertised in *The Royal Gazette* that Richard Pritchard, an indentured servant from Bath in England, had absconded from his service. Under the indenture system a new arrival to the colony had his passage here paid by contracting out his labour for a number of years, usually seven.

Francis Peniston married twice, first in 1807 to Eliza Trott and secondly in 1828 to Mary Ann Gilbert. He had at

least 21 legitimate children. He was also reputed to be the father of John Henry Jackson (1822-1897).

Mary Frances Jackson (circa 1805-1865), a free black of Smith's Parish who was later to marry James Walker, was the mother of John Henry Jackson who was to become the founder of the family written about in the book *The Jackson Clan* by Vernon Jackson. John Henry Jackson became a highly successful businessman running a construction business, a sawmill, a livery stable, an undertakers and the Brunswick Hotel.

He was the father of John Henry Thomas Jackson (1846-1907) who was in 1887 to become the second black member of the House of Assembly. He represented Pembroke Parish. His many descendants have become leaders of the community. His grandson, schoolteacher Albert Jackson, became President of the Senate in 1987. Another grandson, Arnott Jackson, was the first president of Fidelity International Limited and a member of the Senate.

John Henry Thomas Jackson's great-grandson, Alex Scott, became Premier of Bermuda in 2003 and another great-grandson, Wayne Jackson,

The schoolhouse at the rear of Magnolia Hall is known by the family as the House at Pooh Corner. It was a reproduction of an old Bermuda cottage.   *Bermudiana, Ronald John Williams, 1946, page 118.*

became president of the Bermuda National Trust in 2002.

Francis Peniston died in New York in 1854 at the home of his son George F. Peniston who was a ship broker with Peniston & Company. Francis left his house with all the land adjoining to his widow Mary Ann Gilbert Peniston and for the use of his unmarried daughters. His widow lived on for another 30 years and his last remaining unmarried daughter, Anna Maria, died in 1899.

In 1900 the furniture of Peniston's was advertised for sale at public auction. At that time the house consisted of a hall, drawing room, dining room, breakfast room, pantry and four bedrooms. The kitchen and service quarters were not mentioned.

It was not until 1903 that Peniston's with 34 acres of land was advertised for sale. It was bought in 1905 by Ormond Cox Zuill (1869-1937), a son of Eugenius Zuill of Loyal Hill in Devonshire and a brother to Eugenius Foggo Zuill of Glimmerview (*see chapter 5*). Ormond Zuill worked as an influential member of the staff of Trimingham Bros. for 52 years.

The Zuills gave the house its new name of Magnolia Hall. Addison E. Verrill in 1902 wrote in *The Bermuda Islands*, "A large and fine tree (*Magnolia grandiflora L.*) grows at the Penistons. Flowers in June. Introduced from the southern United States." Their second son, Ormond Cox Zuill II, was born in 1911 at Magnolia Hall. The family did not stay long at their Smith's Parish home and moved to Pembroke although it would be almost 20 years before the property was sold.

In 1911 an osteopathic sanitarium opened at Magnolia Hall run by Dr. Campbell Black and Dr. Jessie Coons.

The extensive grounds around Magnolia Hall were landscaped by Lieutenant Commander Leslie Workman Howarth and his wife Jeannette. This is the Persian garden, an exotic area with a small pond near the house. *Bermudiana, Ronald John Williams, 1946, page 117.*

It closed in January 1917 when farmer Jose Jacintho Moniz, known as J.J., took over the tenancy. Bermuda vegetables, mainly potatoes and onions, were grown at Magnolia farm for shipment overseas. J.J. Moniz also operated a tomato canning factory in a building, which still exists, to the rear of the house. Here as many as 7,000 cans were produced in a day. There were 25 employees at work on the production line where tomatoes were peeled, tins sterilised, filled, sealed and labelled.

The Moniz family ran a store at 59 Front Street called California Fruit & Vegetable Market which exported farm produce, on commission, and canned vegetables. Despite their grand design, the family struggled financially and in June 1925 a public auction was held at Magnolia Hall of the goods and chattels of J.J. Moniz. An inventory of 1924 reveals the following rooms: kitchen, pantry, servants' room, six bedrooms, dining room, reading room and parlour.

The property had been purchased in 1923 by Ormond Ralph Loblein (1863-1935) who had built a chain of grocery stores throughout Bermuda and was a substantial property owner. In 1926 Loblein sold Magnolia Hall, a cottage and 36 acres to Commander Howarth.

Lieutenant Commander Leslie Workman Howarth (1890-1952) was a master mariner who spent 26 years at sea, the first eight of them in square rigged ships. He came originally from Cheshire in England. He and his American wife, Jeannette née Goodwin from Magnolia-on-the-Ashley in South Carolina, came to Bermuda in 1925. They leased Orange Grove on Flatts Hill from the Zuills before purchasing and then extensively rebuilding Magnolia Hall.

The Howarths added an upper floor and a wing for servants on the southwest as well as chimneys with fire-places. The house was more than doubled in size. Architect F.P. Hill of Point House in Somerset designed the additions. Not much is known about Hill except that he also designed the main house at Deepdene, now Manor House apartments or condominiums (*see chapter 8*).

Construction was done by G.H. Burland & Company, a firm founded by Gordon Burland who although he had a Bermudian mother first came to the island in 1922 as project engineer on the Bermudiana Hotel. G.H. Burland & Company was later to become Burland, Conyers & Marirea and is now BCM McAlpine.

Commander Howarth took up painting in his retirement and his naval pictures hang above the fireplaces. A small house at the rear of Magnolia Hall, formerly the schoolhouse but known as The House at Pooh Corner,

Goods and chattels

An inventory is a detailed list of goods and chattels. Probate inventories were often made when a deceased person's estate was being settled and ensured all heirs received their fair portion.

They are sometimes found attached to wills and recorded in the Books of Wills or, in the case of intestacy, in the Book of Inventories. Probate inventories are official documents, signed, witnessed and lodged with an authority, which was historically the Governor.

In addition to being useful when settling an estate, probate inventories today are a valuable research tool. Goods and chattels are sometimes listed within the room in which they were stored. It is these room by room inventories which are most useful for architectural research as it is often possible to determine whether the house still standing is indeed the one listed in the old document.

Inventories also throw light on the social and cultural history of their times. The quantity and variety of possessions in the inventory reveal the wealth and sophistication of the person who lived in the house. The slave owners' view on slavery is graphically illustrated as slaves were treated as possessions to be listed, with a monetary value, often in the cellar, kitchen or outbuilding in which they lived and alongside the equipment or livestock with which they worked.

The use to which rooms were put may also be determined from a room by room inventory. Beds were often to be found in every room in the house, but most likely in the rooms known as chambers. A dining room was a sophisticated addition to a house, not common before the second part of the 18th century but it is surprising how often they occur in early 18th century Bermuda.

Five inventories have been found for the Bermuda National Trust's museum at Verdmont (*see chapter 2 and appendices 1-5*), the first in 1714 and the last in 1835. The 1714 John Dickinson inventory and the 1782 inventory of Thomas Smith are listed room by room. It is thus possible to obtain an accurate picture of Verdmont and the activities of the people who lived in the house towards the beginning and the end of the 18th century.

The inventory for Hinson Hall (*see chapter 4 and appendix 7*) proves that the house still standing is indeed the one recorded in the 1771 inventory of Samuel Spofferth. It is possible to trace the movements of the executors as they made this inventory. Often executors start as they enter the house, but in the case of Hinson Hall, the executors probably met in the "little chamber" and then walked through the house from this back room listing and valuing all the many and varied possessions of Samuel Spofferth at the time of his death.

The Samuel Spofferth inventory also lists a variety of building materials giving us an insight into construction methods for both houses and ships in Bermuda in the late 18th century. House building materials include squared sawed stone, bricks, a wallplate, beams, rafters, cedar gutters, cedar and mahogany boards, shingles, lime and nails. Interesting in this list are the cedar gutters and the shingles. Shipbuilding materials included boat timber, tar and turpentine, lead and a stern post.

D.C.

Extract from the inventory of Samuel Spofferth of Hinson Hall, February 26, 1771. (*See page 184 for transcription.*) *Book of Wills, Volume 8, starting on page 523, February 26, 1771. Records of the Registrar Supreme Court.*

was extended to become his studio. It also functioned as a laundry and housed slate tubs and wooden ironing tables.

The land around Magnolia Hall was extensively landscaped by the Howarths although the walled garden at the front dates from the older Peniston's. There are a number of small formal gardens near the house which include a Persian garden and water gardens linked by brick walkways. A croquet lawn was added about 1968.

The property descended to the Howarths' daughter, Mary Jeannette Littlejohn, known as Marionette or Puppet (1925-2000), who added verandahs on the east and west of the main house in the late 1960s and early 1970s. The Magnolia Hall estate at the beginning of the 21st century is home to the descendants of Commander Howarth.

Stilwell sits above North Shore Road overlooking its former shipyard. It was a symmetrical one storey hip roofed house raised over a cellar which had a dirt floor until the mid 20th century. Welcoming arms steps lead to its centrally placed front

Stilwell was a symmetrical house, except for the chimney at the east end, with two windows either side of a central doorway. There are complex triple keystones over the windows and centrally placed welcoming arms steps.

door with a mounting block at the foot of the steps.

Despite its almost unchanged appearance from the road, Stilwell is much altered at the rear where additions made in the late 1960s have transformed it into a spacious and comfortable home for 20th century living. Entry is now made from the east side of the house.

It is difficult to give Stilwell a precise date. Perhaps it was built in the late 18th or early 19th century. The ownership of the land can be traced back to John Young at the time of the Norwood survey of 1663 and then to his daughter Sarah who married William Reynolds, a prosperous carpenter.

Stilwell was most certainly the home of shipbuilder James Tynes from 1801 until 1833 and whether it was built by him or by a previous owner, Captain John Steed Jr., who owned the property from 1791 until 1801 is a matter for conjecture. An inventory made in April 1833 following the death of James Tynes shows Stilwell at that time to be a three room house with a "back room".

The "hall" of James Tynes was elegantly furnished with a cedar sofa, a mahogany sideboard, a cedar round table, two looking glasses, a mahogany organ and 14 Windsor chairs as well as a dinner service and silver items. The "chamber" contained a cedar bedstead complete with bed curtains and a pine writing desk whilst a room described as the "hall chamber" also contained a cedar bedstead and was obviously furnished to function as a bedroom.

In the "back room" was cooking equipment as well as a number of items relating to shipbuilding. These include two cedar sterns, a cedar stern post, cedar timber suitable for building a vessel of 30 to 40 tons as well as whip saws, bevels and a grind stone.

There was originally a two seat privy or outhouse near the main house and another on the shoreline discharging into the sea. This second privy apparently served the shipyard which is described as James Tynes' Building Place on an old plan.

James Tynes (circa 1771-1833) was the son of famed shipbuilder Nathaniel Tynes (circa 1744-1807) of Devonshire. He married first Sarah in

1793 and they produced at least nine children, five girls and four boys. Sarah died in March 1827 aged 53 and in August the same year James Tynes married Ann Homeyard Taylor née Watkins. She was a daughter of Joseph Watkins (died 1813) of Greenbank (*see chapter 3*) on Collectors Hill and the widow of Devonshire mariner George Taylor. Ann Tynes died four years after their marriage.

A number of ships are recorded as having been built by James Tynes. These include the *Patriot*, a brig of 184 tons which the Wood brothers of Pembroke commissioned about 1808. The 169 ton war sloop *Morgiana* was also built by James Tynes & Co., as was a 45 ton yacht built in 1816 at a cost of £1,215 for Sir James Cockburn, who served a second term as Governor from 1817 to 1819. The Treasury in London was expected to fund this yacht.

The slaves of James Tynes were highly skilled in the art of shipbuilding. There was Tom, a caulker; Peter, a sawyer; Ben, a sailor; another Peter, a carpenter, and Sam, a labourer. Dinah and Sary were house servants. Some or all

Stilwell

Stilwell: *Drawn by Barbara Finsness.*

Stilwell, as it stands, is both a sophisticated 1960s response to traditional Bermuda design and an early house, front and centre.

The house began in the 18th or early 19th century as a rectangular block with five bays facing the North Shore: a cellar window and door as well as two upper windows almost evenly placed on each side of masonry steps rising from the north. The roughly centred door opened into a 7' wide passage between a heated 16'7" by 15' hall to the east (left), and one or two rooms occupying the 20' by 15' space to the right. The 1833 inventory of James Tynes suggests there were two west rooms, a "hall chamber" and "chamber".

A large interior chimney on the east unbalanced the house in a distinctly Bermudian fashion and apparently provided a cooking fireplace for the 16'6" by 14'7" cellar room as well as a smaller one for the hall. An arched opening in the stone jamb suggests there was an oven in the northeast corner of the cookroom, a space poorly lighted by a single 1'6" by 1'2" window. This and the larger adjoining storeroom were unfinished spaces with dirt floors, bare stone walls, and hewn summer beams overhead supporting roughly squared short joists laid over them, side by side.

An improved 15'4" by 14'2" kitchen with a fireplace and oven in a small exterior chimney was added over a water tank to the south-

east, perhaps in the middle of the 19th century, and at some date a narrower rear wing was added to the southwest, creating a slightly uneven U-shaped plan with five rooms, each opening directly into its neighbours without benefit of passage.

An American, Marjorie Critten, bought the house in 1938, enlarged it to the rear, moved here soon thereafter and entertained widely throughout the year. Miss Critten named the house for her mother, changing it from Vancefort. Henry Ponsonby Watlington and his wife Ronica bought the house in 1954, the year they married. They moved the two existing ground floor partitions to create a large living room on the east, entered from the front door, and a bedroom on the west. And they demolished the remains of an oven connected to the old southeast chimney.

Then in 1968, they worked with architects Jordy Walker and Fraser Butterworth of Onions & Bouchard to extend the west end of the main block and create a very modern house, enlarged to the south, with circulation space circling a central courtyard. The Watlingtons adjusted the plan but built it largely as designed with contemporary details like sliding plate glass windows and hanging cupboards in the kitchen. Self-consciously contemporary and literal minded use of the picturesque old Bermuda style join in a stylish mixture at Stilwell.

E.A.C.

of the slaves may have lived in the cellar of Stilwell.

As the century progressed shipbuilding declined and in 1824 James Tynes mortgaged nine acres and his house to wealthy merchant William Sears (circa 1744-1830) for £900. Tynes died in 1833 aged 62 before he was able to repay the loan and his estate was insufficient to cover his debts. In October that year his home was advertised for sale.

It would appear that the house did not sell and reverted to the estate of

William Sears (*see chapter 7*). It became the home of a daughter of William Sears, Frances Perot Hinson, and her husband Cornelius C. Hinson (circa 1785-1858), although they did not own the house. It was probably during this time that the property was accessed by a road leading off Middle Road through land west of Somerville. The old roadbed can still be seen to the rear of Stilwell.

Stilwell was to remain as part of the estate of Williams Sears until about 1882 when it came into the possession

The chimney to the far right on the front of Stilwell may have served a cooking fireplace in the cellar as well as the main living area. The near chimney, which has been extended, served a kitchen which was probably added after cooking ceased to be done in the cellar.

Stilwell was known as Vancefort and was U-shaped when this plan (detail shown above) was drawn in 1938 by C.E. Hinson Cooper. *Courtesy Hal and Ronica Watlington.*

home in which he planned to give amateur one act plays.

The house had gained two rear wings by the time of the Savage survey of 1898-1899 and a surveyor's map indicates that the house was U-shaped when it was purchased by Marjorie Critten in 1938. She was a wealthy maiden lady from Washington DC. She and her sister Mignon were friends of Alice Roosevelt, the daughter of US President Theodore Roosevelt. Marjorie Critten was said to have built bathroom facilities in the rear infill of Stilwell.

Stilwell was purchased from Marjorie Critten in 1954 by its current owners who have created a home with a traditional front appearance and a practical rear.

Spruce Cottage stands immediately to the west of Stilwell and is across North Shore Road from an early shipbuilding site. It was originally a gable roofed storehouse built into the hillside, two storeys at the front and one at the rear. It had a dome top water tank.

of Henry James Zuill (1859-1916) of Orange Grove, a great-grandson of William Sears. It was in 1915 to be owned by his son William Edward Sears Zuill (1892-1989).

It became the winter home of Colonel William Thomas Wood (circa 1865-1930), a retired New York lawyer and financier. Colonel Wood had acquired his title during service in the Spanish American War. He had extensive real estate holdings in New York City where he was the financial backer of theatrical productions. At the time of his death Colonel Wood had been finalising plans for a small theatre at his Bermuda

Spruce Cottage on North Shore Road, was an early 19th century storehouse. The original portion was the gable roofed simple two storey rectangular building. The two storey buttery, left, is a 20th century addition.

It was transformed into a picturesque Bermuda revival house by architect Bruce Barker when his then wife acquired the property in 1979. He added an arched entry porch and a bathroom under a buttery style roof and a hipped roof addition at the rear. It underwent major renovations in 2001 when the old plaster was removed and aluminium windows installed.

The plot on which Spruce Cottage stands was acquired about 1795 by Devonshire shipbuilder Nathaniel Tynes and transferred to his son shipbuilder James Tynes two years later. Presumably the storehouse, which appears to be a 19th century structure, was built by the Tynes family.

However, James Tynes of Stilwell mortgaged his property in 1824 and died in 1833 before he was able to repay the loan. Under the terms of that mortgage the property was next acquired by Joseph Jauncey Outerbridge (1771-1857), a merchant and a leading member of the community being among other things a member of the

Corporation of Hamilton and one of the judges of the Court of General Assize. He was of the Somerset branch of the Outerbridge family.

In 1847 two lots of land were advertised for sale by auction. One included a two storey house "well situated for a retail dry good or grocery store, or a school room" and the second lot was "an excellent spot for ship building".

In 1887 the property was purchased by Thomas Jackson (circa 1851-1910), who was then described as a mason from Devonshire although he was later to become a grocer and butcher. He was not related to the Jackson family of Pembroke. Thomas Jackson was also the owner of Mount Pleasant and Lime House in Devonshire (see *Devonshire*).

In 1929 his daughter Sarah Ann Jackson (born 1874) sold the two lots of land, one across the road on the waterfront and the other with a dwelling house, to Benjamin Chauncey Curling Outerbridge of Outerlea.

On *THURSDAY*, *the 30th Inst.*,
WILL BE SOLD,
BY AUCTION,
On the Premises,
At 11 o'clock,

TWO LOTS OF LAND, in *Smith's Parish*,—one of which has on it a Two Story HOUSE, 30 feet in length 15 feet in width, well situated for a Retail Dry Good or Grocery Store, or a School Room. The Lot measures 270 feet North and South, 36 feet on the East, and 24 feet on the West—bounding on the East, West and South on Lands of C. C. Hinson, Esq., and North on the Main Road.

The Second LOT is just below the above, and is an excellent Spot for Ship Building—Bordering North on the Sea, East on the Land of C. C. Hinson, Esq., South on the Road, and West on land of W. E. Zuill, Esqr., and measures 490 feet in length by 60 feet in depth.

☞ *Terms made known at time of Sale.*
MUSSON & DARRELL.
September 21, 1847.

The Royal Gazette, September 21, 1847.

Thus along this windswept North Shore Road lived Bermudians who toiled in the yards and made and lost their fortunes in the island's important shipbuilding industry which declined with the age of steam. 🌴

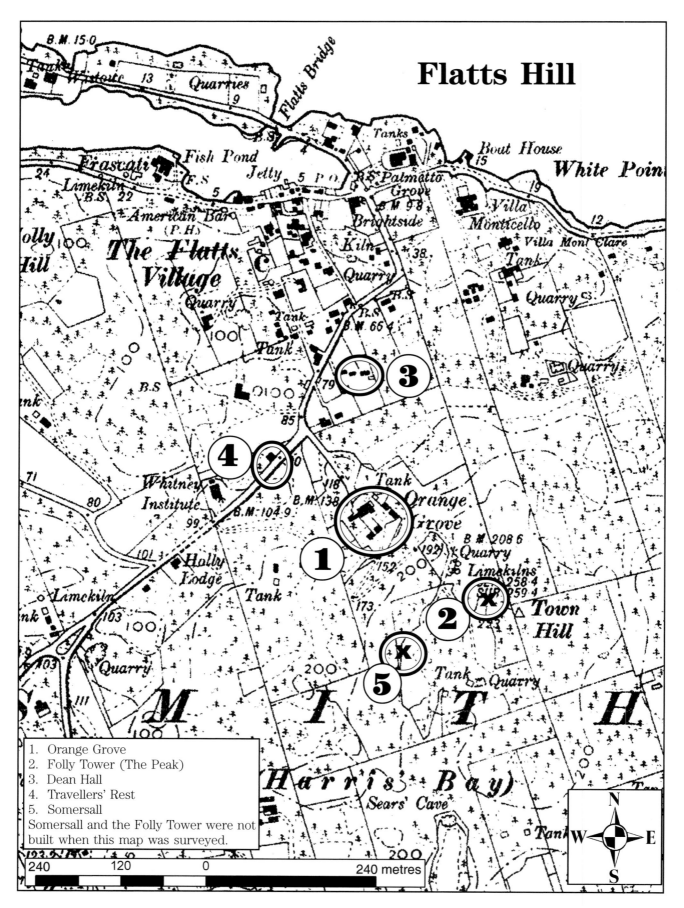

Flatts Hill

B.M. 15.0
Tanks
13
Quarries
9
Flatts Bridge
Tanks
Bout House
15
White Poin
Frascati
Fish Pond
Jetty
Palmetto Grove
Villa Monticello
24
Limekiln
B.S. 22
American Bar
(P.H.)
Brightside
B.M. 98
Villa Mont Clare
12
Holly Hill
The Flatts Village
Kiln Quarry
38.
Tank
Quarry
Quarry
Tank
B.S.
B.M. 66
79
③
Tank
B.S.
85
④
Whitney Institute
118
Tank
Orange Grove
B.M. 208 6
Quarry
71
80
99
B.M. 104.9
B.M. 138
152
B.M. 258 4
259 4
Limekilns
Town Hill
101
Holly Lodge
①
173
②
⑤
Tank
Limekiln
103
Tank
Quarry
Quarry
103
111
200
Tank
Quarry
⑤
M
I
T
H
(Harris' Bay)
Sears' Cave
Tank
200

1. Orange Grove
2. Folly Tower (The Peak)
3. Dean Hall
4. Travellers' Rest
5. Somersall
Somersall and the Folly Tower were not built when this map was surveyed.

193.
120
240   120   0   240 metres

N
W   E
S

Surveyed and Contoured in 1898-1899 by Lieut. A.J. Savage, RE. Published at the Ordnance Survey Office, Southampton, England, 1901.
Courtesy Works & Engineering.

7
Flatts Hill

Leading merchant Clarence Darrell, front left, and his family lived at Clarendon near the top of Flatts Hill. He is seen here in this old family photograph with his wife Henrietta, front right, and their children. Back row, from left, Hilgrove, Amy, Wilfred, Helen, Ambrose and Minnie. Front, from left, Clarence, Gladys and Henrietta Darrell. *Courtesy Hon. Gloria McPhee.*

Flatts Hill which rises above Flatts Inlet has long been an important site for homes of men who shaped the island's destiny. The Orange Grove property was home to the Somersalls, the Corbusiers, the Sears and the Zuills; Dean Hall to the Outerbridges whilst Clarendon was the home of leading merchant Clarence Darrell.

Flatts Hill is the popular name given to the portion of Middle Road which runs downhill to Flatts Bridge. It was also near what might be described today as a village centre of Smith's Parish which is at the top of

Flatts Hill around the current Post Office.

Here may have stood an early Smith's Parish church, according to the records of Richard Norwood. However, the precise location of this church within the parish has yet to be determined. Here were a couple of country stores as well as two schools, Whitney Institute and the Smith's School Room, and the old parish lock-up or Watch House (*see chapter 11*).

Clarence Orester Darrell (1859-1922) was an important force in the late 19th and early 20th centuries on Flatts Hill. In 1885 he purchased Clarendon,

a two storey building, which has been recently much altered, on the corner of Middle and Clarendon Roads. It was here that he opened a provisions business whilst the family lived behind and above the shop. He also ran a dry goods store on the corner of Middle Road with Paradise Lane. The store at the beginning of the 21st century is home to Twins Variety Store but the old sign for Clarence Darrell Dry Goods can still be seen tucked around the corner.

He was to gradually acquire considerable property on Flatts Hill and in Flatts Village (see *Hamilton Parish*). In the City of Hamilton Clarence Darrell

Orange Grove in the time of William Edward Zuill had a two storey central portion with flanking one storey wings. He was the first Zuill at Orange Grove and owned the house from 1843 to 1872. *Bermuda through the Camera of James B. Heyl, 1865-1897, page 115.*

ran a livery and grain business and was said to have been the largest importer on the island. Flags were flown at half mast when his body was returned to Bermuda aboard the SS *Fort George* after he died at St. Luke's Hospital in New York.

The waterfront of Flatts Inlet, which is within Hamilton Parish, was a commercial area, the site of warehouses and shipbuilding slips whilst the entrepreneurs lived on the heights above.

Orange Grove, which stands in a prominent position on Flatts Hill opposite Whitney Institute, has the appearance of a mid 19th century house although the history of the occupation of the site goes back to the 17th century.

It is a large and imposing two storey two room deep symmetrical house set on the hillside overlooking Harrington Sound. A Palladian style pediment above a balcony set on cylindrical stone pillars is a noticeable feature of the formal front of the house although entry is usually made at the rear.

Curiosities inside the house are the

The shop has gone but the sign for "Clarence Darrell Dry Goods" remains around the side of the Twins Variety Store on Flatts Hill.

pairs of vertical beams or buttresses within the downstairs rooms which may be remnants of earlier chimneys. The walls of the house are also unusually thick either side of the entry rooms.

The building now known as Calabash Cottage served as a detached kitchen and service quarters for Orange Grove. It was used as a barn and was converted into a residence early in the 20th century. It is named after a nearby calabash tree.

Sandbox Cottage, which appears to be a later addition to the property, was a stable in the early 20th century. It became a playhouse for children and then a residence for the gardener. It is named after a nearby towering sandbox tree.

William Edward Zuill, known as Billy (circa 1799-1872), was the first Zuill at Orange Grove. In 1855 he advertised Orange Grove as an "Eligible Country Residence. For rent or lease". The mansion house on 30 acres was described as "quite New, recently and substantially built, and in perfect order". Descendants of Billy Zuill have suggested he was using "advertiser's hyperbole".

This advertisement, however, appeared almost weekly in *The Bermudian* newspaper between January and early May 1855. Billy Zuill was then a merchant with business interests in Demerara and Baltimore. The advertisement was placed because he was "desirous of removing from the Colony early in the month of May".

The Bermudian newspaper, January 17, 1855.

Billy Zuill, who was baptised in St. George's, was the son of John Zuill (1758-1813), clerk to the House of Assembly. When his father's eyesight began to fail, young Billy aged about 12, took over his father's job. Here he met William James Sears (circa 1789-1818), only son of Captain William Sears (circa 1745-1830) of the property now known as Orange Grove.

At the age of about 14 or 15, Billy Zuill joined the very extensive family business of Captain Sears and became confidential clerk to young William James Sears. However, William James Sears died in 1818 aged 29 (see *Hamilton Parish*). In his will he entrusted Billy Zuill to continue the busi-

The Orange Grove property consists of the main house, centre, Calabash Cottage, front left, and Sandbox Cottage, front right.

ness in Flatts until the lease expired and left him a bequest of £1,000 on completion.

With this money, Billy Zuill in 1821 set off for Demerara, a former British colony and now part of Guyana, to found a business of his own but before he left he became engaged to Sophia Angelina Sears, known as Sophie (circa 1796-1873), a daughter of Captain Sears. The formal letter of proposal, dated January 31, 1821, still exists amongst the Zuill family papers. The letter tendering his "hand and heart for ever" was delivered by "our mutual friend and my confidant Mr. Trott" who was to convey Sophie's answer to Billy. It is not known which Mr. Trott was his confidant.

The answer was obviously favourable because Billy Zuill returned to Bermuda in 1824 when the pair were married, a day earlier than announced as they wished to avoid a big wedding. The family was indignant and the reception was held the following day in the long room of what is now Calabash Cottage.

The couple moved to Demerara.

Four children were born but only two, William Sears Zuill and Angelina Sophia Zuill, survived to adulthood.

In 1828 Billy Zuill registered his newly built brig *Herald* in Bermuda. She was reputed to have been built of cedar cut from the estate of William Sears. The *Herald* often carried rum, sugar and molasses from Demerara to Bermuda. On January 26, 1842, the ship brought 20 packages of furniture to the island, presumably the household effects of Billy and Sophie upon their return after 18 years overseas.

Captain Sears had died in 1830 but it was not until 13 years later that a survey of part of his estate was carried out. Sophie had inherited a share of her father's house as well as land extending to more than 30 acres.

Sophie and Billy agreed in 1843 to buy out her sisters' shares in their father's house. They named their new home Orange Grove and cultivated a citrus orchard and planted exotic tropical trees in the garden. Billy Zuill was elected to the House of Assembly in 1847 and became a commissioner for roads (*see chapter 4*).

Their son William Sears Zuill (1825-1867) took an active part in his father's business, travelling to Demerara and the US. He worked in the Baltimore office and later ran the Hamilton office. He married Anne Campbell Hayward in 1855. He died, aged 42, on June 17, 1867, while on board ship returning from a business trip to Demerara. His widow continued to live at Orange Grove with their young children, his parents and his sister.

Billy Zuill died in 1872 and Sophie

The Zuills of Orange Grove

William Edward Zuill, known as Billy
(circa 1799-1872)

|

William Sears Zuill
(1825-1867)

|

Henry James Zuill, known as Harry
(1859-1916)

|

William Edward Sears Zuill
known as Will
(1892-1989)

|

William Sears Zuill

Orange Grove

Mysteries lurk at Orange Grove in the form of 17th century references and early 18th century architectural fragments, but an advertisement of 1855 describes the present house as then newly built. William Edward Zuill broke with Bermuda tradition when creating what I think must have been a new house, using a three part Palladian design with a two storey temple fronted main block flanked by single storey wings covered by flat or low shed roofs that family memory describes as leaking soon after construction. Parapets shielded the low roofs from the view at the front, like Victorian false fronts, and versions of the cartoon Doric porch columns were engaged at the ends, under classical mouldings. Mouldings were also used to seal the eaves, originally and when grandson Henry James Zuill raised the wings to two floors about the 1880s.

The main block contains six ground floor rooms evenly stacked, with two essentially square spaces on both sides of a large entry hall and rear stair hall. The 1855 advertisement lists sitting, drawing, dining and breakfast rooms as well as four bed chambers and, perhaps in a recessed western (right) wing, a dairy, pantries, storeroom, bathrooms and kitchen. Confinement of upper space to the centre portion probably kept one or two of the bedchambers on the ground floor before the wings were raised.

Room finish provides an interesting example of refined mid 19th century taste. Following British and American style of the era, the walls were broad plastered surfaces uninterrupted by chair rails or cornices. This drew attention to natural finish, beaded framing and floorboards or sheathing overhead, an evocation of the construction

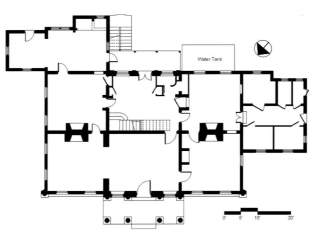

Orange Grove ground floor plan: *Drawn by Geoff Parker Jr.*

in older Bermuda buildings. Door finish conferred on the two smaller rear rooms a lower status, with that at southeast (left rear) the most modest. By the 1880s, however, there were four fine antique style mahogany fireplace surrounds, one in each of the corner rooms, creating another reference to older Bermuda taste. These contrast dramatically with small conventional Greek revival mantels upstairs, painted to resemble marble.

Businessman William Edward Sears Zuill modernised the house in the 1930s, by adding or remodelling a kitchen at the southeast (left rear) and reworking the service wing which was connected with Calabash Cottage immediately to the west. He was among the founders of the Bermuda Historical Monuments Trust and a friend of the architect Wilfred Onions. Onions designed a simple neoclassical stair that Zuill built to replace a less convenient stair in the rear hall in 1943.

The main house contrasts with Calabash Cottage, which began in the 18th century as a two room house and perhaps kitchen and that remains covered by a traditional hipped roof with stone balls at the ends of the ridge. It is said to have been employed variously as a school and a barn before W.E.S. Zuill returned it to domestic use. He may have installed some of the ancient 12 light window sash with small panes, salvaged elsewhere at Orange Grove. More of the old sash were installed when a north wing was added by the present William Sears Zuill, who was formerly director of the Bermuda National Trust.   *E.A.C.*

---

a year later. The house was left to their unmarried daughter Angelina Sophia Zuill and daughter-in-law Anne Campbell Zuill for life. At the death of the survivor the Orange Grove property was to go to their grandson Harry, the eldest son of William Sears Zuill.

Henry James Zuill, known as Harry (1859-1916), was 12 years old at the time of his grandfather's death. The executors of the estate held the property in trust for the boy. He and his sisters and brother were sent to school in England but during the holidays there were parties, picnics and family weddings. Mrs. Zuill's ball on February 3, 1882, was described as a splendid affair with about 150 people in attendance who danced all night.

In 1883 upstairs wings were added to the house and it took on the symmetrical Georgian appearance it has today. Previously Orange Grove consisted of a two storey central section flanked by plainer one storey wings (*see photo on page 102*). Builder and designer Edward Peniston (*see chapter 10*) estimated that the work to add the upstairs bedrooms would take six to eight weeks on each wing at a cost of £114, the owner furnishing all the materials.

In 1890 Harry married Eliza Pearman Trott (1864-1902), a daughter of Thaddeus Trott (1838-1924) of neighbouring Rockmoor (*see chapter 10*).

The rubber tree, a landmark opposite Whitney Institute, was planted, according to the recollections of Will Zuill, in 1900 or 1901 when relatives were visiting Bermuda from Philadelphia.

Harry Zuill died in 1916 aged 56 years. His estate was left in trust until all his children were 21, at which time it was to be divided into four parts of equal value. The youngest child, John Thaddeus Zuill, turned 21 on February 4, 1921, and in July of that year the property was valued.

William Edward Sears Zuill, known as Will (1892-1989), was to become the next owner of Orange Grove and its outbuildings plus two cottages, Calabash and Farm House. The property which included the Folly or Peak Tower

Orange Grove, a formal symmetrical house, has been home to several generations of the Zuill family.

(*see page 110*) stood on 21 acres with an additional adjoining four and a half acres. He was a senior partner at Pearman Watlington & Company, a member of Parliament for Smith's Parish from 1933 to 1938 and a member of the Legislative Council from 1942 until the late 1950s.

He was also a writer and historian and wrote many books and articles. Among his works was *Bermuda Journey* which was first published in 1946. It is a delightful guide to the island and was much used as a source in the writing of this book.

Will Zuill built up a notable library at Orange Grove and added to the genealogical papers of his aunt Julia Mercer (*see chapter 5*) and gathered a considerable amount of information on the history of his house. With his wife he created a fascinating garden, increasing the collection of trees, shrubs and exotic ferns begun by his great-grandparents.

During his tenure at Orange Grove a new cedar staircase, designed by noted Bermudian architect Wilfred Onions and made by carpenter Hamphiel Paynter, was installed in 1943 in the rear hall. It was built of cedar

cut from the property and replaced an earlier steeper staircase, although there was at one time a staircase at the front of the house. Will Zuill also created a cloakroom and telephone booth within this rear hall in the 1940s.

In 1926 Will Zuill married Christiana Susanna Bluck (1895-1981). They moved to Orange Grove in 1935 and raised their three children there. Christiana Zuill, known as Kitty, also contributed to the island's heritage through her writings on Bermudian traditions, crafts and cookery. Their eldest son William Sears Zuill is the present owner. He is a former editor of *The Royal Gazette* and was the first director of the Bermuda National Trust and author of *The Story of Bermuda and her People*, first published in 1973, and many other articles on the island's history.

Although Orange Grove as we see it today is largely the creation of the Zuill family, this site on the hill overlooking Flatts Inlet has long been an important position on which to build a house. The earliest recorded person to live here was John Somersall (died circa 1674) who purchased four

shares of land on September 4, 1654, from Perient Trott of London. This was tract 18 of the Norwood survey of 1663.

John Somersall was a member of the Governor's Council and a sheriff. A man of strong opinions, he was imprisoned in 1648 for his views on the new Governor, Captain Josias fforster, and again in 1663 when he was sent to London charged with abetting a disturbance and disobeying a Governor's proclamation on whale fishing.

In October 1667, on one of his visits to England, he married Joane Maligan (died circa 1683). This was a second marriage for John Somersall and a prenuptial agreement was signed as Joane was a wealthy widow with a young son, William.

When John Somersall wrote his will in 1671 he appeared to have fallen out with his elder sons, Samuel and John. He left his mansion house and two shares of land to his wife and in addition left two shares to his stepson, William Maligan, in lieu of half the "considerable amount his mother brought into the marriage".

There were numerous disagreements over the division of the land and the upkeep of the property. In 1680,

Mid 19th Century Changes to Orange Grove

My father put together a history of Orange Grove, and what follows are excerpts pertaining to the removal of the upstairs wings and their later replacement. Discussing the return of Billy and Sophia Zuill to live in Bermuda after building a business in present day Guyana and the West Indies, he continues:

"Mrs. Zuill, however, decided that the house was too big and she had the four bedrooms upstairs re-

An undated plan (detail shown above) for a new drive to Orange Grove shows the house without its second storey additions and Calabash Cottage, right, is much smaller than it is today. *Courtesy William and Joyce Zuill.*

moved, leaving two shed roofs with a double story over the central part of the house. Also the handsome winding staircase was removed and the present straight one installed in its place (since replaced by a cedar one). One of the granddaughters of Mrs. Sears, Mrs. Eudocia Cooper, said that this winding staircase led into a circular hall upstairs from which hall all of the bedrooms opened. This hall was used by the Sears family as a sitting room in the evening and the grandmother

went upstairs immediately after tea and the servants placed the whale oil lamps where they were required.

"The house was altered . . . but the shed roofs were never satisfactory and according to report 'leaked like a sieve'. Mr. Zuill, however, refused to have it altered, saying 'a little water won't hurt grandpa' . . .

"In 1883 the Executors of the estate of William Zuill Senior (Thomas J. Wadson, Dr. Thaddeus Outerbridge, Joseph M. Hayward and Anne Zuill (wife of William Zuill Junior, who had died) decided to rebuild the upstairs bedrooms which had been removed 40 years before because of the impossibility of keeping them watertight. Aunt Julia says 'I can well remember as a child having to go up a step ladder to put small basins and pans on top of the high post bedsteads to catch the leaking water.' "

William Sears Zuill

having passed one share of the land including the house to her son William, Joane Somersall left Bermuda to return to England.

William Maligan (circa 1655-circa 1689), the next owner of a house on the Orange Grove property, was the subject of an attack by one of his slaves, Indian John, who set the house alight with the intention of shooting the family as they ran out of the house. He was found guilty and executed at Gibbet Island (*see chapter 6*).

An inventory was taken of William Maligan's household effects in December 1690. Downstairs was a hall and "parler" and porch as well as a "little room" whilst upstairs were a parlour chamber, a porch chamber and a hall chamber. This room layout appears to suggest a cruciform house. There was also a "seller", a "new kitchin", an "old kitchin", an "out lett", a buttery, a "corne house" and a milkhouse.

William Maligan left his house to his wife Miriam (circa 1660-circa 1692) for life, after which their eldest son James was to inherit. Miriam Maligan died not long after her husband and the estate was entrusted to her father Colonel

William Peniston as her children were minors.

Their oldest son mariner James Maligan (circa 1676-1701) was lost at sea aged about 25 during a voyage in 1701. His estate was left to his wife Frances, a daughter of Colonel Anthony White (*see chapter 8*), with the stipu-

lation that if Frances had a child by James then the estate was to be divided equally between mother and child when the latter came of age.

A daughter, Miriam, was in fact born the year her father was lost at sea. She was raised by her mother and later by Frances' second husband Captain

This pastel of Sandbox Cottage was drawn, probably in the 1930s, by Frederick Lewis Allen (1890-1954), who was an American social historian and editor of Harper's magazine from 1941 to 1953. *Courtesy William and Joyce Zuill.*

John Gilbert, mariner and member of the House of Assembly.

The Gilberts lived in the Maligan family home and befriended the newly arrived French Huguenot Philip Corbusier with his two sons, Giles and Henry. After Philip's death the Gilberts asked his younger son Henry Corbusier, then about 20 years old, to live with them.

Henry Corbusier (circa 1700-1764) married Miriam Maligan and so began a period of ownership of about half a century by the Corbusier family which was to end with disastrous consequences for the close knit neighbourhood of Flatts Hill.

The young couple lived first in a cottage built for them on the northern boundary of the estate at Flatts and moved to the Maligan family home after the Gilberts died, probably in the early 1730s. Henry Corbusier was an active politician and a member of the Governor's Council.

Their son James Corbusier (circa 1722-1766) inherited the Maligan family home from his mother. In 1748 he married Ann Outerbridge and they had three sons and three daughters. The house and land were left to their eldest son Henry.

Henry Corbusier (circa 1749-1783) was involved in a terrible tragedy following a dispute with a neighbour, Richard Swiney, over some borrowed plates and glasses. The incident escalated and resulted in Swiney's death and in Corbusier being found guilty.

The argument arose after Henry Corbusier had gone to his neighbour's home and removed the borrowed items. Richard Swiney was enraged "that Mr. Corbusier had been there and taken away his plates and glasses" so, carrying a loaded pistol, he confronted Henry Corbusier at his house. There was a struggle and Richard Swiney was stabbed with a bayonet and died two days later.

The case went to the Court of Assize in December 1782 and the jury found Henry Corbusier guilty of "feloniously slaining" Richard Swiney. The Chief Justice ordered Corbusier to be burned, presumably branded, on his left hand. Disgraced, Henry Corbusier decided to sell his estate and leave Bermuda. He died the following year.

In August 1783 Bridger Goodrich (1757-1795) purchased the house and

Sandbox Cottage, to the south of the main house, appears to be a later addition to the Orange Grove property. Buttresses stand either side of the door with moulding above the windows.

Sandbox Cottage stands by a tall sandbox tree, right.

37 acres and in October the same year he bought a further 50 acres of adjoining land. He was a loyalist refugee from Virginia and had set up business in Bermuda in 1771. His family were merchants, mariners and ship owners who traded in the North Atlantic and by 1781 Goodrich led a growing privateering fleet from Bermuda. It is estimated that in the years 1778 to 1782 he made around £30,000, much of which he invested in property in Bermuda as well as England.

In 1778 he married Elizabeth Tucker (circa 1754-1799) and five of their six children were baptised in St. George's where they lived at Bridge House (see *St. George's*). In 1788 they sold the mansion house in Smith's Parish and 87 acres to William Sears of St. David's for £3,000.

Captain William Sears (circa 1745-1830) was a master mariner, successful privateer, merchant and ship owner when he purchased the Goodrich property but he was to recall later in life that he started as a young man with £40 "and I took unto myself a wife, gave her half of it, put the other half into a vessel and went to sea".

He had buried three wives before he moved to Smith's Parish and was a widower with two daughters, six year old Mary and Sarah, known as Sally and aged about two (*see chapter 4*). In 1788 he married Frances Perot (circa 1754-1841) by whom he had four children.

ARCHITECTURAL ASSESSMENT

Somersall

The architect Wilfred Onions designed Somersall for the newly married William and Joyce Zuill in 1958, a house they built on the Peak above and south of Orange Grove. The Zuills liked Onions' contribution to the Bermuda Historical Monument Trust's 1948 *Bermuda Cottage Plans* but wanted a design better suited to the site. Onions agreed to provide a new design for the couple but remarked that he was deeply involved with the Hamilton City Hall and would not be available for much construction oversight. Zuill contracted with the mason and marathoner 'Sir' Stanley Burgess and carpenters Lawson and Josey Lambert to build the house.

This is a small house providing the spaces common to such residences of the mid 20th century particularly in North America: a living room and dining space, a kitchen, two bedrooms, a bath, and a porch. Onions designed it much like a suburban ranch house in arrangement, but cast handsomely in the traditional Bermudian vernacular. It is an L-shaped house, facing the North Shore, with the small rear arm containing a kitchen beside a porch with stuccoed posts and a wood frame. The walls are stuccoed, of course, always painted pink, with oversized brackets at the ends of the open eaves and with buttresses added after hurricane damage at the downhill end.

Onions favoured a sizeable undivided space rather than formal separation of sitting and dining space, expressed both at Somersall and in the plan he drew for the *Bermuda Cottage Plans*. Here it is treated as a 22'8" by 15'10" room with a tray ceiling, and an off centre sitting area with a projecting window of five bays offering views to the water north and northwest. Beside this, at the far end of the room, is a sizeable raised fireplace with a freewheeling antique style bolection surround. (*See plan on page 12.*)

Natural finish cedar is used for cambered tie beams, a lintel over the bay, and low Bermuda style board doors looking into the living space, where exposed parts of the floor are also cedar. Ordinary imported pine flooring and mass produced woodwork are used elsewhere, as in a passage leading from the front door to two bedrooms and a bath on the west (left) end and the living room on the east. Fenestration is varied and organic, with sizeable windows lighting the kitchen, but a miniature sash opening onto the porch and a bank of three casements set high in the passage to allow for bookcases below.

About 1960-1961 William and Joyce Zuill added a wing to the east including a bedroom (usable as an office), lobby and bath designed by Onions, Bouchard & McCulloch architects. In 1964 they built a small detached schoolhouse further to the east, now a cottage called Malplaquet, designed by James Gardner with later interior by Stephen West.   *E.A.C.*

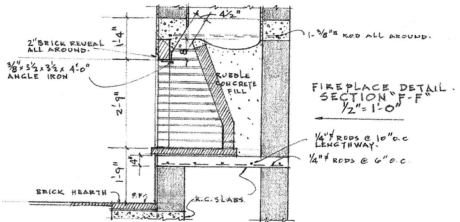

Detailed drawing of the raised fireplace at Somersall from Wilfred Onions' designs for William and Joyce Zuill, March 28, 1958, revisions May 1958. *Courtesy William and Joyce Zuill and OBM International.*

This small square building is now used for storage but was earlier a stable and may once have been a privy.

He died on January 28, 1830, aged 85 years a wealthy man. His land holdings in 1816 amounted to more than 160 acres in Smith's Parish.

An undated inventory of his personal effects reveals the layout of his house as well as his very substantial possessions. The house consisted of a hall, parlour, drawing room, four chambers and a passage upstairs. There was also a cedar room, a storeroom and a cookroom. This was much larger than the house of William Maligan inventoried in 1690. The possessions of Captain Sears included a substantial amount of cash in Spanish dollars and doubloons, gold, bonds and mortgages.

The slaves of William Sears, as listed in the 1821 Slave Register, consisted of three men, Canave and Ben, who were labourers and Brown, a boatman, and four women, Aurelia, Judy and Frances, who were house wenches, and Rose, a ground woman. There were three children, David aged 12, Caroline aged four and Rachel aged two. A poignant note reveals that 12 year old David was sold to William Jack and from him to William Watlington.

The only son of Captain Sears, William James, had died in 1818 aged 29 whilst his grandson, called James William Sears (circa 1817-1836), a medical student in Edinburgh, died aged about 19. This left four daughters: Mary Sears, Sarah Trott, Frances Perot Hinson and Sophie Zuill. It was Sophie and her husband Billy Zuill who reput-

Calabash Cottage lies to the west of the main house of Orange Grove. This photograph by Walter Rutherford shows the large calabash tree from which the cottage got its name.
The Story of Bermuda, Hudson Strode, 1932, opposite page 208.

Calabash Cottage was converted into a residence in the early 20th century when the bay window was added. Substantial additions were made later in the 20th century.
Courtesy William and Joyce Zuill.

Folly Tower

"The Peak", Bermuda

The Folly Tower, commonly known as the The Peak, stands on Bermuda's highest hill and was built as a tourist attraction in 1908. This view was used on an early 20th century postcard. *Donald E. Stephens Collection. Courtesy Bermuda Maritime Museum.*

High on Town Hill, the highest point of land in Bermuda, stands Folly Tower which is commonly known as The Peak. It was built in 1908 as a tourist attraction by Henry James Zuill, known as Harry, of Orange Grove. A visit to the Tower included a tour of the gardens of Orange Grove along with a maze, which no longer exists, planted on the flat land near the tower. It was advertised on a poster as "the highest point for 600 miles around".

It was built in the year when Americans were first able to buy property in Bermuda following a change in the law in 1907 and from that time on they began to come in increasing numbers, predominantly as winter visitors.

The Tower, however, was not a wild success as a tourist venue although there is a spectacular view of the northeastern end of the island from the top. The steep walk to the summit of Town Hill, which stands 259 feet above sea level, proved too arduous so donkeys were introduced to ease the climb.

Today the Tower stands as a landmark in Smith's Parish on top of a thickly wooded hillside and has assumed vital importance as a hub of Bermuda's wireless communications systems. It is rented by Telecom and a host of metal aerials rise above the old tower. The Tower today serves Bermuda's fast growing telecommunications industry. Internet communications, mobile phones, pagers and credit card services are all made possible by the masts around the tower.

Folly Tower is a plain three storey octagonal building with a viewing platform reached through a trap door. There was originally a spire with a flag pole at the top. It no longer exists.

Although the exterior lacks ornamentation, save for some moulding, the interior of the tower contains some interesting details. A wooden staircase curves gently around the inside. There are wood floors and moulded baseboards.

The interior of the window openings are framed in Charles Eastlake style wood mouldings similar to the window trim at Mount Hope. Charles Eastlake was a British born architect, furniture designer and writer who was particularly influential in the US. The windows have decorative corner blocks with reeded side and top mouldings.

Henry James Zuill (1859-1916), the builder of the tower, was the grandson of William Edward Zuill, known as Billy, and the grandfather of the present owner of Orange Grove.

He was a farmer but as a young man went to seek his fortune in the American west. According to the notes made by his sister Julia Mercer (*see chapter 5*), he lost his money in the venture along with other Bermudian entrepreneurs. She recorded a diary entry dated October 16, 1893, "Mr. Tucker tells me that the business Benny Watlington had in Boise City, Idaho, has broken down. His wife has come home with her two children, Englesbe Seon lost $5,000. Harry Zuill $10,000, believes that Trott & Cox had lost too." This was a time when there was a major financial crash in the US.

In 1890 Harry Zuill married Eliza Pearman Trott daughter of Thaddeus Trott of Rockmoor. She died in 1902 aged 37 leaving five children under the age of ten, including a baby girl who died a few months later. Most of the children went to live for a time with their grandmother at Rockmoor (*see chapter 10*) and the older ones attended a school run by their aunt Hattie Trott. The youngest boy, Thad, stayed with his paternal aunt Julia Mercer at Aldie (*see chapter 5*). The children would have been familiar with the tower and its visitors but could not have foreseen the technological advances leading to its use a hundred years later as a communications hub.

D.C.

---

edly called the estate Orange Grove and whose descendants live there today.

Dean Hall is hidden out of view off Middle Road near the top of Flatts Hill almost opposite Clarence Darrell's former property. It was built on a plot described in a survey plan drawn by Daniel Prudden in 1837 as "Harris's Bay Commons".

Surveyor Richard Norwood, in his division of the island in 1663, set aside 12 ½ acres on Flatts Hill as "a parcel of common ground". This was intended as an area of village settlement for the shareholders of Smith's Parish.

In his *Book of Survey 1662-3* Norwood wrote, "In these shares is ye Church and Church yard Smiths Tribe". However, Dr. A.C. Hollis Hallett in *Chronicle of a Colonial Church* wrote, "For Smith's Tribe, the list (of shares) and the map do not agree; the map shows it on Somersall's land, close to the present site, but the description puts it on common land next to, and north of, Somersall's share. Since . . . Somersall had conveyed some of his land to the parishioners for a church in 1656, Norwood's location of the church appears to have been in error."

Dean Hall is a two storey formal Georgian style building which faces north towards Harrington Sound. Its front façade is symmetrical with two windows either side of a central door and Flemish gables at either end. The single chimney on the east side of the house originally served a cellar as well as the two main floors. A detached two storey kitchen, which has since been joined to the house, stands at the rear.

Dean Hall is a formal two storey symmetrical house probably built early in the 19th century for William Henry Dean on land his wife Henrietta had inherited from her father Peter Gallagher. Wider stone was used on the lower storey, perhaps giving the building greater strength.

There is also an outhouse on the southeast which was in use until the mid 1940s.

The house was most probably built early in the 19th century for William Henry Dean and his wife Henrietta née Gallagher. They married in 1811 and Dean Hall has remained continuously within the family and is lived in today by sixth and seventh generation descendants.

The land on which Dean Hall stands was owned in the late 18th century by Peter Gallagher (circa 1744-1808). He was a tailor from the north of Ireland and the father of Henrietta Dean.

Little is known about William Dean (circa 1789-1818). He is said to have been an artist from Cornwall in England. The Deans had two daughters: Mary Alice Dean (1812-1882), who never married, and Eliza Susan Wood Dean (1814-1890).

In 1835 Eliza married mariner John Downing Outerbridge (1815-1879), a son of Captain William Thomas Outerbridge of Cedar Grove in Bailey's Bay (see *Hamilton Parish*). She left one half of Dean Hall to her eldest son Arthur and the remaining half to her

Scalloped Flemish gables decorate the roof ends at Dean Hall. The chimney is believed to have served fireplaces on three levels, in the cellar, hall and upstairs chamber.

other five children although she specified that her youngest daughter, Florence Lillian, was to have the chamber on the west end and the use of the front room under it.

Planter Arthur Outerbridge (1843-1911) and his younger brother Algernon Rees Outerbridge agreed that Algernon would purchase the remaining shares in the house for Arthur, who

in turn would leave all of his estate to Algernon. Arthur died following an accident when he was hit by a bicycle ridden by the Reverend Bridges of the Methodist Parsonage on Flatts Hill, so Algernon inherited the house.

Algernon Rees Outerbridge (1855-1912) was in his early days described as a writer and farmer. He went for a time to Demerara where he was the

Dean Hall

Using land inherited from the Irish tailor Peter Gallagher in 1809, Henrietta Gallagher and her husband William Henry Dean built Dean Hall as a house that was both formalised and distinctly Bermudian. Like countless stylish houses built in 18th and early 19th century Britain and North America, it is two storeys high and five symmetrical bays long, with openings slightly wider spaced at the centre. The plan was equally ordered, with an 8'5" wide central stair passage on both floors.

Being Bermudian, however, the builders terminated both ends of the long roof with old-fashioned scalloped gables and included only one chimney, its stack breaking through the east (left) gable and sculpted with grooves to suggest two flues. This placed the chimney in the marginally larger hall (16'1" by 14'6") and left the chamber or parlour (15'9" by 14'7") unheated. Apparently the chimney actually provided three fireplaces, one in a dark kitchen under the hall and a third in the upper east chamber.

Dean Hall: *Drawn by Barbara Finsness.*

Framing was exposed in a traditional Bermuda manner, with longitudinal summer beams projecting through the ground floor ceiling and smaller chamfered headers for the stair in the passage. Upstairs the three spaces were open to the roof collars, and tie beams passed front to back in the rooms, at the end walls and masonry partitions.

The house was substantially retrimmed circa 1900, and a single early doorway and three windows with 11/8" wide muntins survive on the upper floor. The door connecting the passage and upper chamber has a 2'11" by 5'11" opening framed with beaded, rebate-less posts tenoned into an unbeaded head that extends well past the posts.

A detached kitchen and quarter was added about 5' to the southeast at an early date. Measuring 16'6" long and 13'9" wide, it provided a relatively well lighted cookroom on the ground floor and living space above, both with fireplaces in a large exterior chimney at the back. The upper room is now reached by separate exterior steps, though it was connected to the house by the 1930s. *E.A.C.*

---

overseer of a sugar estate. Upon his return he worked at the Royal Naval Dockyard and the family lived in Sandys.

In 1890, Algernon married Maria Williams Smith (1866-1934), a daughter of John Newbold Smith of Morer Hall in Smith's Parish. Maria Outerbridge, who survived her husband for about 22 years, left Dean Hall jointly to her two daughters, Lillian Rees Outerbridge (1890-1973) and Enith Urma Outerbridge (1892-1967).

In 1909 Lillian married carpenter Nicholas McCallum Leeuwin Brunt Peniston (1880-1931), a son of master mariner William Hubbard Peniston. Lillian in 1932 was appointed sub postmistress of Flatts. Her younger sister, Enith, married US broker Edwin Marsh Schorb but returned to Bermuda following the breakdown of her marriage.

In 1935 the house was divided for the two sisters with Lillian downstairs and Enith upstairs, where there was already another apartment at the east

end of the house. Alterations and additions, including the removal of the staircase, were made at this time under the supervision of architect Lawrence Harrower Smart (*see chapter 5*).

Lillian Peniston left her half share of Dean Hall to her daughters, Lucy Dean Caton and Elsie Leeuwin Butland. Elsie had married Gilbert James Butland, a headmaster of Whitney Institute. The Butlands left the island and Elsie in 1976 conveyed her share to her sister Lucy.

Enith Schorb, who owned the upstairs portion but had lost her only son in the Second World War, also conveyed her half share of Dean Hall to her niece Lucy Caton.

The present owner and his wife have been the sole owners of Dean Hall since 1994 following the death of his mother Lucy Dean Caton in 1991. Although it has now been divided into three apartments, Dean Hall remains as a family home and small farm in a

quiet and secluded location off busy Flatts Hill.

Travellers' Rest stands on the side of Middle Road and is owned by Whitney Institute. Its verandah, projecting on to the pavement, is a familiar sight on Flatts Hill.

It is a mid 19th century gable roofed one storey house with a kitchen at the rear. Travellers' Rest is a small but extravagantly finished building. Heavy moulding surrounds the gable ends whilst there are large formal pilasters on each corner. It was probably built by Augustus Peniston about 1861 on land he had purchased from Nicholas Peniston who drowned in Harrington Sound in July 1860 while returning from a picnic at Trunk Island.

Augustus Peniston (circa 1795-1876) was the son of Ann Peniston (circa 1766-1850), a sister of Richard F. Peniston of Peniston's, now known as Magnolia Hall. He was the father of architect and builder Edward Peniston

The verandah of Travellers' Rest on Flatts Hill is a familiar sight as it juts out over the pavement of Middle Road.

It may be a small roadside cottage but Travellers' Rest is finished in an ornate fashion with heavy gable ends and corner pilasters.

(1838-1903) who was responsible for the Tower building at Whitney Institute (*see chapters 10 and 11*). It is conceivable that Edward assisted his father in the design of Travellers' Rest.

A carpenter, Augustus Peniston also owned Bridge House in Flatts (*see chapter 8*) and several other properties. He left Travellers' Rest to his daughter Ameria, the wife of Thomas J. Pearman, of Sunnyside in Shelly Bay (see *Hamilton Parish*).

The property was subsequently acquired by Jeremiah Scott Pearman of Mount Hope (*see chapter 11*) and in December 1921 he presented his fellow Whitney Institute trustees with the deeds for Travellers' Rest.

The cottage was then rented at £2 a month by Charles Harvey. Olivia James became the next tenant in December 1925 and her rent was increased to £2.10.0. The following year she requested a partition in the western room of the cottage.

Olivia James worked at Orange Grove, the big house over the road. Ann Zuill Williams, daughter of William Edward Sears Zuill, in her book *The Back Yard* wrote, "She was as much a mother to my Father as one could be because his mother died when he was so young. So he, his two younger brothers and sister were very dependent on Olivia for her warmth and love, and her discipline too, I guess." 🌴

Sound's Mouth

1. Bridge House
2. Palmetto Grove
3. Villa Monticello
4. Villa Mont Clare
5. The Old Johansen Homestead
6. The Boat House (Manor House apartments)
The Boat House was not built when the Savage map was surveyed.

240 120 0 240 metres

Surveyed and Contoured in 1898-1899 by Lieut. A.J. Savage, RE. Published at the Ordnance Survey Office, Southampton, England, 1901.
Courtesy Works & Engineering.

8
Sound's Mouth

Bridge House at Flatts Village seen in a water colour by Thomas Driver in 1823. The house stands on the side of the road not far from Flatts Bridge, left. The ground floor served as a shop.   *Thomas Driver, 'The Flatts Village, Bermudas', 1823 (detail). Neg.2537. Bermuda Archives: PA2190.*

Sound's Mouth was the name given to the area around Flatts Bridge where there is the only visible opening of Harrington Sound to the ocean.

A house at Flatts Bridge was first mentioned in 1681 when the trial of a slave called Indian John was held there (*see chapters 6 and 7*). The land in this area was owned by the Peniston family and the house of Anthony Peniston was the site of meetings of the Governor's Council in 1696 and again from 1702 until 1709. These meetings continued when it was home to Anthony's widow Elizabeth Peniston. The Court of Assizes also met at her house. The precise location of the house is not known.

There are a number of very special houses between Flatts Bridge and the little arched footbridge over Harrington Sound Road, which joined Deepdene to its Boat House. There is still a Bridge House at Flatts although Palmetto Grove, which stood at the head of the Inlet, was demolished in 2000.

Neighbouring Villa Monticello and Villa Mont Clare on Harrington Sound Road were home in the late 19th century to wealthy Bermudian heiress Frances Mary Whitney and her American husband whilst the Boat House of Deepdene, now part of Manor House apartments or condominiums, was designed by renowned American architect Thomas Hastings.

Bridge House occupies an historically important site as it commands the crossing point at the head of Flatts Inlet. There has long been a house in this position, perhaps the earliest belonging to the bridge keeper.

The present Bridge House may date from the beginning of the 19th century and is a two storey symmetrical hip roofed building standing on the edge of North Shore Road facing Flatts Inlet. It was earlier L-shaped with a detached kitchen at the rear.

There have been additions and changes in the 20th century, including the joining of the kitchen to the main house. The kitchen, with a cooking fireplace, was on the east side, nearest to Palmetto Gardens condominiums.

The position of Bridge House with its frontage on the main road has meant that it has been used as a commercial premises with a shop at street level and the family living upstairs. A wooden

Flatts Bridge spans the mouth of Harrington Sound. The bridge slid back to let boat masts pass. Bridge House can be seen on the roadside to the right whilst the small cottage, centre, close to the bridge is no longer in existence. This photograph was taken about 1900. *Outerbridge Album. Courtesy Bermuda Maritime Museum.*

building, once used as a restaurant and later as a sail boat club, stands between Bridge House and the condominiums.

Much of the interior woodwork of Bridge House has been removed so it is difficult to date the house, the earliest remaining is a double glazed door perhaps dating from the second half of the 19th century.

Bridge House in its present form can be clearly seen on a Thomas Driver water colour of Flatts Village dated 1823. The property was purchased by carpenter Augustus Peniston in 1822 and it is probable that he may have built the present house.

Augustus Peniston (circa 1795-1876) was the son of Ann Peniston (circa 1766-1850), a sister of Richard F. Peniston of Peniston's, now Magnolia Hall (*see chapter 6*). There is no

Bridge House at Flatts, left, drawn by R. Nelson in 1833 while on a journey from St. George's to Admiralty House in Pembroke. *'The Flatts'. Ride, Walk & Drive in Bermuda from St. George's to Clarence Hill, 1833. R.E. Nelson Album. Neg. 3869. Bermuda Archives: PA966.*

Bridge House in Flatts photographed in January 1899. The kitchen, centre, is detached from the main house. *Dwellings at Flatts Village' 1899. Charles Coit Album, Neg. 2659. Bermuda Archives: PA881.*

record of his father and he took his mother's surname. Augustus Peniston obviously prospered as he came to own a number of properties including Travellers' Rest on Flatts Hill (*see chapter 7*).

The introduction of a postal service on August 1, 1842, was an important step for Bermuda and Bridge House played a leading role as it became the site of the Flatts Depot of the post office. The service initially ran between St. George's and Hamilton via Government House. The mail coach also carried passengers.

Augustus Peniston married Anna Maria North in 1836 and the union

For Sale or Rent.

A LARGE HOUSE at present fitted up as a GROCERY STORE, with a WHARF in Front, on which is a small HOUSE, now in use as a DWELLING. The Premises are situated on the North Shore Road in the *Flatts Village*. They can be viewed at any time, and to a Purchaser the terms will be made moderate. Please apply to the Subscriber,

AUGUSTUS PENISTON,

Flatts Village, Aug. 7, 1860.

The Royal Gazette, August 14, 1860.

Bridge House at Flatts, rear, and a service building in the foreground. Flatts Inlet is in the background. The original house consisted of a main block facing North Shore Road and a rear wing, right. The chimney of the former detached kitchen is at the rear of the house on the left, front left of photograph.

Bridge House, photographed in the 21st century from North Shore Road, appears from this view to be little changed from earlier photographs and drawings.

produced three children: Cordova (1837-1868), builder and architectural designer Edward (1838-1903) and Ameria Ann (1850-1926).

Bridge House was left to their only daughter, Ameria Ann, who in 1872 married prosperous merchant Thomas J. Pearman (1847-1916). The couple lived at Sunnyside in Shelly Bay (see *Hamilton Parish*) and later at Daylesford in Hamilton, so Bridge House was let over the years to a number of tenants.

The Royal Gazette, April 3, 1881.

Millinery and dressmaking was carried on at Bridge House. In 1887, "The Misses Peniston" advertised they were prepared to execute all orders and hats and bonnets would be trimmed after the latest New York styles. It is not known which Misses Peniston worked at Bridge House. They may have been Emmeline Amelia and Annie Louise, daughters of Robert Thompson Peniston who died at Bridge House in 1885.

Another tenant was A. W. Reid Trott (1861-1934), a part owner of Winterhaven Farmhouse (*see chapter 9*) and proprietor of a grocery store at Lazy Corner (see *Hamilton Parish*). His daughter Mary Musson Outerbridge née Trott, who was born at Bridge House in 1895, was one of the group of young girls who were companions of visiting American writer Samuel Langhorne Clemens (1835-1910) who wrote under the name of Mark Twain.

In 1920 Bridge House was purchased by Henry James Tucker (1876-1950) and his wife Nella Louise. He was a son of the Reverend George Tucker

(1835-1908) of neighbouring Palmetto Grove and she a daughter of Thaddeus Trott of Rockmoor (*see chapter 10*).

Their son, Henry James Tucker Jr. (1903-1986), who was known as Jack and became Sir Henry Tucker in 1961, led a distinguished career in banking and politics. He became the Bank of Bermuda's general manager and was involved in the establishment of the island's exempt company business.

In 1964 Sir Henry Tucker was a founding figure of the United Bermuda Party and was made party leader the same year. In 1968 he became the first Government Leader under Bermuda's

The Royal Gazette, October 25, 1887.

Palmetto Grove

A gracious old Bermuda house once stood on the property now occupied by Palmetto Gardens and the Grove condominiums. It was called Palmetto Grove and was built for Samuel Paynter Musson, a member of the family which once dominated Flatts Village (see *Hamilton Parish*). The house, surrounded by its gardens, stood at the head of Flatts Inlet and its land extended across Harrington Sound Road.

Palmetto Grove was a large two storey rectangular hip roofed house with chimneys at the top of the hips. The roof was of painted imported slate. There was a two storey verandah facing Flatts Village. It was built after 1838 and its construction was supervised by William James Trott, husband of Samuel Paynter Musson's niece Anna (*see chapter 4*).

Samuel Paynter Musson (circa 1797-1873) was a son of Paynter

Palmetto Grove, which has since been demolished, photographed in 1949. *'Palmetto Grove' 1949. Frederick Hamilton, photographer, Neg.437. Bermuda Archives: The Bermuda National Trust Collection. PA207.*

Musson (died 1818) of Fairview in Flatts and his wife Ann, who was a daughter of Anthony Peniston who had earlier owned the land on which Palmetto Grove stood.

Samuel Paynter Musson left Bermuda to become a prosperous merchant in Bridgetown, Barbados, where he was senior partner of Samuel Paynter Musson & Co., an exporter and importer of produce. He lived in Barbados for 50 years and died there at his residence Stockton.

In 1847 Samuel Paynter Musson gave Palmetto Grove in trust for life to his sisters Frances (died 1850) and Susannah. Frances did not marry whilst Susannah had married her cousin Samuel Musson (1777-1872), a son of James Musson Sr. of Frascati.

In his will Samuel Paynter Musson left Palmetto Grove to his brother-in-law Samuel Musson and after his death to the four daughters of Samuel and Susannah, Susan Paynter Musson, Anna Trott, Eliza Musson and Georgiana Hinson (later Sauer). After their deaths the property was to go to Harley and Thaddeus Trott, sons of Anna.

Samuel Musson lived until he was aged 95. William Zuill in *Bermuda Journey* described him sitting under the mahogany tree which he had planted near the gateway, "when Mr. Musson was old and infirm he is said to have spent every fine summer day seated comfortably in an easy chair under its spreading branches. Beside the old man was a table on which was a huge earthern jug of sangaree, and behind him stood a manservant armed with a palmetto leaf with which he quietly fanned the air, thus keeping flies away from his master and from the jug. Whenever an acquaintance passed, the old man called him in to have a drink." The mahogany tree still stands although his house has gone.

Susan Musson and Georgiana Sauer sold their share to their sister Anna Trott. Eliza Musson and Anna Trott died at Palmetto Grove.

In 1876 the house was advertised for rent. John Thompson Peniston (1851-1919) ran a boarding house at Palmetto Grove. He also sold lumber, screws and ale from what was described in an advertisement in *The Royal Gazette* of December 10, 1878 as J.T. Peniston's Store at Palmetto Grove.

The wife of William Bradley, a stone cutter from Nova Scotia, also ran a boarding house at Palmetto Grove. They came to Bermuda about 1883 and William Bradley (died 1898) ran a Marble Shop at Flatts Village.

In 1893 the Reverend George Tucker (1835-1908) bought Palmetto Grove from the Musson estate. This was shortly after he had married his second wife Anna Emmeline Outerbridge (1862-1949).

The Reverend George Tucker was rector of Hamilton and Smith's Parishes from 1869 until 1887 and again from 1890 to 1907. He was appointed Archdeacon in 1896. George Tucker was the tenth and last child of Daniel Robert Tucker (1783-1861) and was educated at Yale University. He was known for his hospitality at Palmetto Grove. Dr. Henry Wilkinson in *Bermuda from Sail to Steam* wrote, "On one occasion there were forty sporting gentlemen for lunch to see the latest dinghies in Harrington Sound contest the Whitney cup."

Palmetto Grove was left to George Tucker's sons, William Eldon and Henry James, from his first marriage to Theodosia Trott. The property was sold in 1950 to The Palmetto Bay Company Limited, when it became Palmetto Bay Hotel. The hotel closed in February 2000 and condominiums have been built on the site although the promised hotel has not.   *D.C.*

Villa Monticello

Villa Monticello apparently acquired its name when it was one of two Bermuda homes of Frances Mary Hill and American US deputy consul William Whitney. The other was Villa Mont Clare, indicating the couple's European as well as Jeffersonian affectations. The term villa does have some relevance because both are stylish rural houses, and this one has a single refined storey over a service cellar. Hill and Whitney would have perceived a connection with Italian villas as sophisticated but compact rural retreats and with English and American tributes like Lord Burlington's Chiswick House built in the countryside close to London and Thomas Jefferson's Monticello in Virginia.

It was built as a formal Bermuda house early in the 19th century, probably by Robert Spencer Musson. There is an old tradition that the southeast (left rear) wing is a 17th century house based on its simple character, although it more resembles a backstage wing of a large circa 1810 house. The form of that house largely survives in spite of substantial additions and re-skinnings.

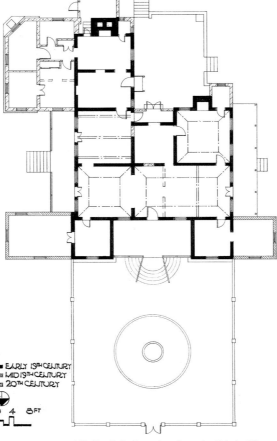

EARLY 19ᵀᴴ CENTURY
MID 19ᵀᴴ CENTURY
20ᵀᴴ CENTURY

0 4 8FT

Villa Monticello floor plan: *Drawn by Malcolm Wilson.*

The Musson house was conceived with an uneven H-shaped plan, symmetrical from the front but not the sides or rear. It has always been an expansive house with two small square rooms flanking a front porch, and rooms two deep looking onto side porches of the same Bermuda character, with chamfered posts tenoned into a plain plate. The airy sense of partially open space was extended by surrounding the front yard with a low wall supporting stone piers and a wood fence above, a technique used earlier to enclose the yard at Verdmont while keeping open a view toward the Atlantic.

Entering Villa Monticello's front door, visitors once found themselves in an 8'6" wide passage between two reception rooms, the larger one on the west (right). All three spaces had tray ceilings above high walls. The outer walls of both rooms are substantially glazed, with windows flanking doors that contain glass, compensat-

ing for shade cast by the deep front porch and blank walls created by the two projecting rooms. The glazed doors open onto original side porches.

Much interior woodwork was removed in the 20th century, but enough survives to suggest the small projecting rooms that flank the front porch were of relatively high status, conceivably used as withdrawing space and toilets for partygoers.

Like the porches, however, the decorative joinery is Bermudian in character, with a degree of informality in an elaborate setting. The door leafs in all the best rooms have five rather than six panels, accepting the marginally more economical choice of running a simple horizontal panel in the location often occupied by two small panels at the top of the door.

The best bedchamber appears to have been that at the southwest (right rear). It has a tray ceiling, the only fireplace near the front of the house and no access to the porch. It connected through a shed roofed lobby with its plainer mate on the east (left), which is accessible to the adjoining porch. Behind this are two smaller chambers, at least one originally spanned by whitewashed joists and boards. The

rear room has a fireplace in a back chimney that also serves the original cellar kitchen below. The two chimneys are similar, with ovolo moulded caps and steeply sloped shoulders, reinforcing the evidence that this is all of one era.

The cellar, only under the southeast wing, contains an impressive range of four service rooms, all now reached from a covered passage under 20th century additions and the east porch. A six foot wide fireplace served the dimly lighted cookroom, behind three rooms for storage and possibly quartering workers.

The front of Villa Monticello now has the stolid look of an 1860 or later house, created when a pair of rooms were added, one on the outer side of both small north rooms. The artful remodellers carried a parapet around these newly expanded front wings to frame the porch with heavy Greek revival abutments.   *E.A.C.*

---

new constitution. This office is now known as Premier.

He was born at Villa Mont Clare, where the family was living at the time of his birth. The daughter of Sir Henry Tucker now owns Bridge House and it has been renovated for use as a vacation home.

Villa Monticello is located next to Flatts Village on Harrington Sound Road. It is another example of an historically important site although the present house probably dates from the beginning of the 19th century.

It is a one storey house built over a

cellar. It has a traditional Bermudian appearance and the walled garden, at the front of the house overlooking Harrington Sound, is a particularly charming feature.

It is probable that Villa Monticello was built for Robert Spencer Musson after the settlement in 1799 of the es-

Front elevation of Villa Monticello facing Harrington Sound Road with its charming circular walled garden. The present house was probably built around the beginning of the 19th century.

tate of his wife's mother. In 1793 he had married Miriam Peniston (circa 1767-1852), a daughter of Anthony and Elizabeth Peniston who owned the land on which the house stands.

Robert Spencer Musson (died circa 1811) was a son of James Musson Sr. (1733-1818) of Frascati on Flatts Inlet, which has since been replaced by St. James Court condominiums (see *Hamilton Parish*). He was a master mariner and ship owner. He captained a number of ships including the sloop *Commerce* and the brig *Nimble*. He

For Sale or Lease.

The Subscriber being desirous of Re-moving near his Business in Hamilton, on account of Ill Health,

Offers For Sale or Lease,

His Present RESIDENCE, *"Harrington Retreat,"* at the Flatts Village. It is a convenient distance from Hamilton and St.Georges. The House, to which has lately been added Some Rooms, has every convenience to be desired for a Family-— There are TEN ACRES OF LAND, GARDEN well enclosed, CARRIAGE, GIG HOUSE and STABLE.—A Fine BATHING HOUSE, in that beautiful Basin of Water, Harrington Sound.

ROBERT S. MUSSON.
Hamilton, 1st September, 1863.

The Royal Gazette, September 1, 1863.

owned the schooner *Said Bridport* with his sister Susanna Musson, known as Cap'n Sukey (circa 1761-1845), along with his brothers John of Paynters Vale and Samuel of Palmetto Grove.

He died intestate and his son, Robert Spencer Musson Jr. (1798-1864), lived in the house with his widowed mother. Robert Spencer Musson Jr. was a senior member of the House of Assembly and a merchant on Front Street in Hamilton.

The house was known as Harrington Retreat and it is probable that Robert Spencer Musson Jr. added the two matching rooms at the front, possibly following his mother's death in 1852. A previous owner of the house, Yeaton Outerbridge, says the signature of "S. Harvey, mastercraftsman" is written on a beam of one of these rooms.

Harrington Retreat was advertised in *The Royal Gazette* of September 1, 1863, for sale or lease "to which has lately been added some rooms". However, Robert Spencer Musson Jr. died in what were described as "reduced circumstances", by Dr. Henry Campbell Wilkinson in *Bermuda from Sail to*

Steam, leaving his junior partner John S. Darrell (1835-1924) to assume the debts and reimburse the creditors (see *Hamilton Parish*).

In 1872 Harrington Retreat was purchased by Anthony Burgess Hill (1834-1877) of Radnor in Hamilton Parish. He was a son of John and Adriana Hill. He did not marry and left his estate to his sister Frances Mary Hill. Their mother, Adriana Hill, had also inherited a large fortune from her brother Anthony John Hill, known as Jack (1799-1868), which he had amassed in St. Croix and New York.

Frances Mary Hill (circa 1827-1901) married William Whitney US deputy consul in 1875 when she was about 48 years old. William Whitney (1821-1889) was born in New York although his family came from Derby, Connecticut, US. The Whitneys regarded the house now known as Villa Monticello as their summer home and each year the household moved next door to spend the winter at Villa Mont Clare.

The Whitneys entertained and kept open house for American and other visitors to the island. William Zuill in

This aerial view of Villa Monticello shows the formal walled garden, right front. There is a cottage, said to be a former carriage house, at the rear.

Bermuda Journey wrote, "The Whitneys had a barge. It was named *William and Mary*, after themselves, and was rowed by six men in uniform. Little excursions in the barge on Harrington Sound were a frequent form of entertainment by the Whitneys, and the Victorian elegance of the group seated in the stern contrasted with the oarsmen, whose sailor suits were set off by caps decorated with red pompoms reminiscent of the French sailor."

Following the death of Frances Whitney in 1901 Villa Monticello was left to historian Anna Maria Outerbridge (1848-1928), daughter of Dr. Thaddeus Outerbridge of Willoughby (see *Hamilton Parish*).

Villa Monticello was owned from 1968 until 1993 by Yeaton Duval Outerbridge, founder of Outerbridge's sherry peppers. This hot sauce was first produced in the cellar of Villa Monticello.

Although Villa Monticello was built at the beginning of the 19th century, perhaps the earliest house on this land belonged to Lieutenant Anthony White (died circa 1673). He is recorded on the Norwood survey of 1663 as having a dwelling house on Norwood tract 17, a 49 acre piece of land which extended south from Harrington Sound.

Lieutenant Anthony White was provost marshal and the only retailer for the sale of liquor in the Town of St. George. He apparently performed this duty in a sober fashion as in 1657 the Grand Inquest commended "Lieut. Anthony White the new marshall for his temperance and care in not suffering inordinate drinking, but rather doing all in his power to prevent it as much as in him lyeth".

The estate near Flatts was left to his son Colonel Anthony White (1644-circa 1709) after the death of his mother Honora (died circa 1677).

Colonel White, who served in the militia, was very active in local affairs. He was a member of the Governor's Council and was appointed a judge in 1691 and Chief Justice in 1706. He was one of the shareholders in the *Amity* (*see chapter 2*), a privateering venture in 1691 which smacked of piracy led by Rhode Islander Captain Thomas Tew, that netted its participants great rewards. Colonel White's daughter Elizabeth was the wife of John Dickinson of Verdmont.

Captain Leonard White (died circa 1731), the eldest son of Colonel White, was the next owner of the house. Attached to his will is a detailed room by room inventory.

The house of Captain White did not resemble the present Villa Monticello, but appeared to be two storey and cruciform in shape. Downstairs was a porch, hall, parlour and dining room, whilst upstairs was a room over the parlour, a room over the hall as well as a little room. There was also a buttery, "kitchin" and "sellers". An interesting entry in his inventory was a part share in a whale fishery.

The estate then passed to the Peniston family through a purchase in 1743 of a house and two shares "lately

Villa Mont Clare photographed near the end of the 19th century when it had acquired a verandah and an ornate garden and was home to Frances Mary Whitney. Collection Nicholas C. Lusher.

in possession of Captain Leonard White decd" for £1,400 by Jeremiah Peniston (died circa 1771). Elizabeth Peniston (died after 1788) was the next to be assessed for parish taxes for the estate. She was the widow of Anthony Peniston (died 1788), a son of Jeremiah.

An 1800 inventory of the property of farmer Anthony Peniston exists and it shows his house to have been two storeys, with a porch, two chambers and a dining room downstairs and a porch chamber and passage and two chambers upstairs. This sounds similar to the house of Captain Leonard White, but different from the present Villa Monticello.

The estate was divided between the 11 children of Anthony and Elizabeth Peniston, and so the land came into the hands of one of the daughters, Miriam, and her husband Robert Spencer Musson.

Villa Mont Clare is a large imposing two storey house overlooking Harrington Sound, immediately east of Villa Monticello. It has an impressive verandah and a garden laid out in an ornate elaborate style. The verandah was probably the work of builder and architectural designer Edward Peniston (1838-1903) of nearby Brightside in Flatts (*see chapter 10*). It bears some similarity to the verandah at Mount Hope (*see chapter 11*).

The house is believed to have been built about 1812 for John Burgess Hill and his second wife Elizabeth née Peniston on land owned by his father-in-law Anthony Peniston. The house, however, was much changed during the ownership of Hill's granddaughter Frances Mary Whitney in the late 19th century.

A small detached kitchen and service quarters at the rear of the house is a somewhat unsophisticated pres-

The detached kitchen at the rear of Villa Mont Clare has a large chimney. The box next to the chimney housed an oven. (*See plan page 6.*)

An aerial view of Villa Mont Clare shows the front of the house with the two storey verandah to the right and the small one storey detached kitchen, front left.

ence in this otherwise now very formal property. The old kitchen with its massive chimney resembles one, now in a ruined condition and without its roof, at Sea View on My Lord's Bay Lane, the former home of John Burgess Hill (see *Hamilton Parish*). There was also a carriage house and stables at Villa Mont Clare which have now been converted into a separate dwelling.

John Burgess Hill (died 1813), a son of Elisha and Miriam Hill, was a shipwright who is believed to have spent time in St. Eustatius when it was a centre for profitable arms trading before it was sacked by British Admiral George Rodney in 1781.

In 1795 John Burgess Hill married Frances Mary Peniston, daughter of Anthony Peniston, and after her death in 1811 he married her younger sister Elizabeth who brought up her sister's three children, Anthony John (1799-1868), Adriana Gilbert (1796-1877) and Frances Mary (1804-1861).

The only son, Anthony John Hill, was to inherit Villa Mont Clare. He was a very successful businessman in the West Indies and later in New York.

In 1865 Anthony John Hill gave

The imposing verandah, with its pediment, on the front of Villa Mont Clare may have been built and designed by Edward Peniston during the time the house was owned by Frances Whitney.

Villa Mont Clare

A rise in property assessment suggests that John Burgess Hill built Villa Mont Clare circa 1812, and the building itself indicates the great extent of Frances Mary Hill's rebuilding after she married William Whitney in 1875. It is said that she used the house seasonally, spending part of the year here and part nearby at Villa Monticello.

The roof outlines a U-shaped house with subsequent fill between the two south (rear) wings and addition of small flankers. It began as a five bay house with a centre stair passage, now two storeys above a cellar. The main stair is located at the rear of the passage, somewhat behind the rear wall of the front rooms, suggesting early integration of the wings and main block.

The only pre 1870s finishes one recognises are eight panels with neoclassical mouldings recycled as a front facing for the stair landing, probably the recycled panelling of the soffit, an enclosed stair with winders in the northwest (right front) corner of the southeast (left rear) room, some summer beams and some flooring.

The longitudinal summers in the front block and the southeast room (now a kitchen) project slightly

Villa Mont Clare, on Harrington Sound Road, photographed by James Heyl when the house did not yet have a verandah.
Bermuda through the Camera of James B. Heyl, 1865-1897, page 117.

through the ceiling plaster, and those in the front rooms and passage have small chamfers stopping just shy of the walls, indicating the front plan is unchanged. A summer in the southeast room is unchamfered.

A pre 1897 James B. Heyl photo from the north shows the house in a posh state after the Whitneys' remodelling, with a decorative retaining wall supporting a flat upper lawn planted with cedar trees, and a carriage house/stable at the rear of a west (right) drive. Interestingly, though, the rooms do not seem to have been grandly recast for receptions, with the exception of a 9' wide opening for folding

doors between the passage and west (right) room.

The front porch appears to date circa 1900, though traditional beaded joists and plates suggest the core may be older. A porch is not apparent in the Heyl photo.

A single storey 18'2" by 16'5" detached kitchen survives relatively unchanged to the southeast. An early partition divides it into a cookroom and a slightly narrower space presumably used for workers' quarters. The fireplace in an exterior chimney is flanked by a late 19th century oven used directly from the room and remnants of an earlier oven that opened into the fireplace. *E.A.C.*

The Old Johansen Homestead on Town Hill has a distinctive wooden verandah with a gingerbread balustrade. Greek style moulding can be seen on the corner of the house.

Carl Johansen came to Bermuda from the island of St. Croix and in 1880 married Almira Julia Eddison Pearman (1858-1936), daughter of Samuel Gilbert Pearman. Johansen also farmed the land around the Homestead.

He left the property to his wife and 11 children with the stipulation that "the Homestead to be included in the lot of Samuel R.W. Johansen at his mother's death". Samuel Raymond Wayson Johansen (died circa 1968) was coachman to the Howarths of Magnolia Hall (*see chapter 6*) and later a taxi driver. Carl Johansen also left a room in the Homestead to Annie Johansen, the widow of his son Ulysses, should she come to Bermuda and so long as she remained a widow.

The land around the house has been subdivided and built upon but the old house remains within the family.

Deepdene on Harrington Sound Road was built about 1929 as a winter home for Clinton Ledyard Blair and his wife Florence Jennings Blair (died 1931). The property has been turned into the Manor House condominiums with the main house divided into apartments and numerous units built in the elegant grounds, but a small stone footbridge survives over Harrington Sound Road linking the Boat House to the main property.

Villa Mont Clare to his niece Frances Mary Hill, who later married William Whitney. The Whitneys were major benefactors of St. Mark's Church and Whitney Institute, the school on nearby Flatts Hill (*see chapter 11*). In her will Frances Mary Whitney left Villa Mont Clare to St. Mark's Church for use as a rectory.

Villa Mont Clare was sold by the Anglican Synod about 1978 and enabled the Church to buy Mount Hope, which is adjacent to St. Mark's, as its rectory (*see chapter 11*). Villa Mont Clare is now in private ownership.

The Old Johansen Homestead part way up Town Hill is a late 19th century house with an interesting history. It has descended relatively unaltered through the Johansen family. The house is edged with Greek style moulding typical of the period and has a smooth hip roof and a wooden verandah with a gingerbread balustrade. It was the home of Carl Julius Johansen (1857-1927), who was the coachman to Frances Mary Whitney of Villa Monticello and Villa Mont Clare. She left the house and about 12 acres of land to him in her 1901 will.

The kitchen chimney of the Old Johansen Homestead.

The tower and footbridge over Harrington Sound Road leading to the Boat House of Deepdene are a familiar landmark. *Courtesy Bermuda Maritime Museum.*

The Boat House with its landmark tower and ornate interior was designed by well known American architect, Thomas Hastings (1860-1929). He was a partner in Carrère & Hastings who were responsible for a number of important buildings including the New York Public Library on Fifth Avenue and the Frick Mansion (now Museum) in New York, the House and Senate office buildings in Washington, DC, and the Jefferson Hotel in Richmond, Virginia.

Thomas Hastings and his business partner, John M. Carrère (1858-1911), trained at the École des Beaux Arts in Paris and began their professional career with McKim, Mead & White before leaving to establish their own partnership in 1885. They specialised in the Beaux Arts style which looked to classical roots. There is an extensive collection of their architectural drawings in the Avery Architectural and Fine Arts Library at Columbia University, including those of the work they did at Deepdene.

Although the Boat House was designed by Carrère & Hastings along with the colonnade and several garden features, the main house was planned by Bermuda based architect Frederick P. Hill of Hill & Davis Associates. Hill also designed the extensive additions at Magnolia Hall (see chapter 6). His partner, Herbert E. Davis, was an American born architect who trained at the Massachusetts Institute of Technology and died in Bermuda in 1947. Construction at Deepdene was by Hathway Ltd, builders of Flatts.

Clinton Ledyard Blair (1867-1949), a grandson of American railroad tycoon John Insley Blair, was an investment banker and a founder of Blair & Company at 1 Wall Street, New York. He was a governor of the New York Stock Exchange. Carrère & Hastings also designed his estate Blairsden in Peapack, New Jersey. It had 38 rooms, 25 fireplaces, a sunken pool and Turkish baths. It was sold in 1950 to the Sisters of St. John the Baptist to become a

A view of the famous Boat House

DEEPDENE MANOR

The most luxurious Guest House

On beautiful Harrington Sound

SMITH'S PARISH   BERMUDA

Deepdene Boat House seen from Harrington Sound. The property became a guest house following its sale by C. Ledyard Blair in 1947. *The Bermudian magazine,* January 1948, page 35. *Courtesy family of the late Edmund M. Gosling.*

Catholic convent but has now returned to private ownership.

Deepdene was built on a plot of almost ten acres purchased in 1926 by C. Ledyard Blair from the Synod of the Church of England in Bermuda who owned neighbouring Villa Mont Clare. It is said to have cost US$500,000 to build, an enormous sum at the time. Deepdene was assessed at £20,000 in the Church Vestry Records for 1929, by far the most expensive property in Smith's Parish, Magnolia Hall coming a distant second at £4,000. The cement to build the house was said to have been brought from Mr. Blair's factory in the US but the empty bags were shipped back for a rebate of two cents each.

Deepdene incorporated many expensive interior fixtures removed from the Blairs' New York house opposite the Frick Museum. This house, designed by Carrère & Hastings, was demolished around 1927-1928 to make way for an apartment building.

These fixtures included elaborate carved oak panelling in the great living room at Deepdene said to be done by Grinling Gibbons, perhaps the most famous woodcarver in England. Born in Rotterdam in Holland, Grinling Gibbons (1648-1720) arrived in England about 1670 where he became master carver to patrons such as Kings Charles II,

William III and George I and worked with architect Sir Christopher Wren. His carvings with their elaborate cascades of fruit can be seen at Hampton Court Palace near London, Petworth House in Sussex and at Sudbury Hall in Derbyshire. The panelling was removed when Deepdene Manor was turned into apartments.

The coach house at Deepdene was said to contain 18 carriages, including a glass opera coach, during the time of its ownership by the Blairs.

The interior of Deepdene Boat House is spectacular. Bird's eye cedar and Bermuda limestone have been worked in expert fashion. The ceiling of the main living room is lined in cedar to resemble the upturned bottom of a ship whilst the floor is planked in wide cedar boards caulked to resemble decking. The Bermuda stone is left unplastered and is carved and sculpted with elaborate dentil moulding.

The tower looks as if it should belong to an ancient English church rather than a boathouse. The ironwork design at the top incorporates a crab chasing a lobster, which in turn is chasing a bee. These ironwork animals are said to have represented the initials of C. Ledyard Blair.

There is an unusual copper topped stone umbrella seat (see opposite) on the dock which Blair is said to have called the "wailing tower" since his wife wailed in anguish as she sat there watching her husband's antics with a sailboat on Harrington Sound.

Sadly Florence Blair died in 1931, the year the house was completed, and C. Ledyard Blair is said to have never returned to live at Deepdene. He did remarry in 1936, to Harriet Brown Tailer widow of T. Suffern Tailer. It is said that she did not like the property.

Deepdene was put up for sale but it remained unsold until 1947 when it was purchased by Dorothy Vera Hunter of Harrington House and was turned into an exclusive guest house and named Deepdene Manor.

The Boat House can be seen in the foreground with a glimpse of Deepdene, now the Manor House condominiums, to the rear. The main house was built about 1929 for American investment banker Clinton Ledyard Blair and the Boat House was designed by well known American architect Thomas Hastings, a partner in Carrère & Hastings.

In 1958 it was acquired by Boston-born Godfrey Lowell Cabot (1861-1962), a leading American industrialist and philanthropist who also owned Vagabond in Tucker's Town. Deepdene Manor was leased to Horizons Ltd, which operated Coral Beach, Horizons, Newstead and Waterloo House.

The property changed hands again in 1964 and the hotel closed early in 1978. Meanwhile there were plans to turn it into a luxury spa but ultimately it became a condominium development. The Boat House and its bridge over Harrington Sound Road remain relatively unchanged although the main house has been divided into apartments and the elegant grounds filled with housing units.

Sound's Mouth remains a popular place for people to live. Once the preserve of the Penistons and the Whites, whose house locations are lost in the mystery of time, several historic houses remain but they have been joined by a number of condominium developments.

Deepdene has lost a little of its stately air by its conversion into a guest house and then apartments. The main house and its grounds are cluttered with late 20th century additions and only its classical garden ornamentation and the Boat House remain as important examples of the work of renowned American architect Thomas Hastings.

The old house at Palmetto Grove has gone to be replaced by the purpose built Grove and Palmetto Gardens condominiums, a practical response to the island's housing needs but both are highly visible in their divergence from traditional Bermudian design. 🌴

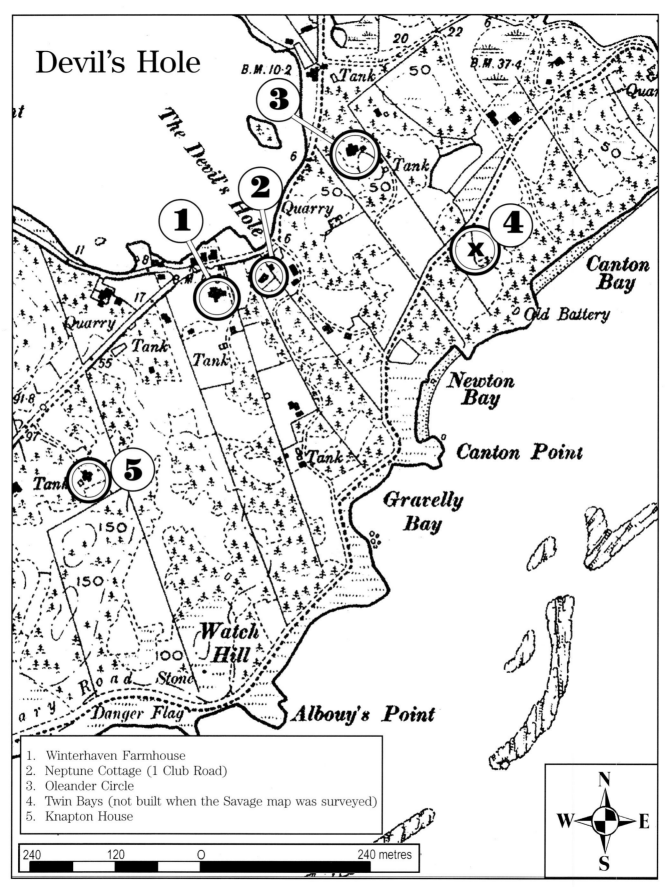

Devil's Hole

1. Winterhaven Farmhouse
2. Neptune Cottage (1 Club Road)
3. Oleander Circle
4. Twin Bays (not built when the Savage map was surveyed)
5. Knapton House

Surveyed and Contoured in 1898-1899 by Lieut. A.J. Savage, RE. Published at the Ordnance Survey Office, Southampton, England, 1901.
Courtesy Works & Engineering.

9
Devil's Hole

A peaceful Devil's Hole photographed by professional photographer William Weiss who worked in Bermuda between 1902 and 1927. *Devil's Hole looking east. Silver print William Weiss. Photography in Bermuda 1839-1939, 1989, page 89.*

Devil's Hole is the name of the area around the Devil's Hole Aquarium on the south side of Harrington Sound. This is a natural feature where fish have long been kept in a sea water pond formed in an ancient cave whose roof has collapsed.

This aquarium is thought to be the island's oldest paying tourist attraction. A charge was first levied on July 26, 1843. In an advertisement dated July 21, 1843, Thomas S.J. Trott in *The Royal Gazette* wrote, "The subscriber has allowed any person to visit his pond for twelve years without charge, al-

though he has frequently been advised to make such; but as the intercourse with strangers has of late increased very much, and he suffers much inconvenience and loss of time of his people in showing it, he has concluded to have a man to attend it, and to make a charge of one shilling for each grown person and half that sum for children, who visit it . . .".

In 1888 naturalist John Matthew Jones in *The Visitor's Guide to Bermuda* wrote of Devil's Hole, "This dreadful name, is given to a cavernous recess filled with salt water on the south side of Harrington Sound, about midway between Walsingham and the Flatts." He described seeing groupers that were "easily recognisable, as they crowd together with open mouths in hopes of a feed when the visitor arrives" and a rarely seen species of ground shark, angel fish "and sundry other fishes; which swim about and can be easily seen as in an aquarium".

The presence of so many apparently tame fish waiting to take the bait has long continued to intrigue children. In the summer of 1927, Alice Cornish aged 13 wrote in her diary of a visit with her sisters Harriet and Susan, "Such fun. These big fish weighing 15 to 30 pounds would jump for the bait and then you could drag them halfway out of the water before they let go. Their mouths would open wide enough to

Fishes in the Devil's Hole. *Bermuda Past & Present, Walter B. Hayward, opposite page 162.*

Bell's Beautiful Bermuda, 1913, page XLVI.

swallow a baseball. The turtles also took part. Harriet got one about halfway out. It certainly made a commotion with its flippers."

The Devil's Hole Aquarium has been overshadowed in recent years by its larger neighbour at Flatts, the Bermuda Aquarium, Museum and Zoo.

With its ready access to Harrington Sound, good planting land and a convenient waterfront for shipbuilding and repair, the area around Devil's Hole was settled early and boasts some wonderful examples of 18th century Bermudian architecture. Oleander Circle, above Devil's Hole, is a hidden and largely untouched treasure and a superb example of a cruciform or cross shaped house. Knapton House, on the hill above, is yet another of Bermuda's cruciform gems whilst the traditional architecture of Winterhaven Farmhouse comes with the added bonus that this property belongs to the people of Bermuda.

Winterhaven Farmhouse faces Harrington Sound opposite the public dock and west of the natural aquarium. It was the home during the first half of the 19th century of the Thomas Trott who first charged admission at the pond, which no doubt started life as a handy spot in which to store the fish catch before the days of refrigeration.

It is a long gable roofed building of Bermudian vernacular design with a chimney at either end and there are two early rear wings. It is symmetrical in appearance with a centred front door. Buttresses are prominent features on

The Devil's Hole natural aquarium, photographed in the early 20th century, was first opened to the public in 1834. *Courtesy Tony Martin.*

Winterhaven Farmhouse was probably built in the late 18th century. Larger windows were installed and buttresses added during the early 19th century.

the front façade. The main house is built over a cellar, which functioned earlier as cooking and service quarters.

An originally detached two storey kitchen and service block was added at the east end, probably early in the 19th century. It has since been joined to the main house.

Thomas Samuel Julian Trott (circa 1787-1857) owned Winterhaven Farmhouse from 1794 until his death, having been left the property when he was about seven years old by his grandfather Thomas Fitt. The house was then home to his family which included his mother Elizabeth Trott (circa 1764-1850), a daughter of Thomas Fitt, and his father Giles Trott as well as a sister and younger brother. The family soon increased by two more brothers and a sister.

His grandfather Thomas Fitt (died 1794) had purchased the land on which Winterhaven Farmhouse stands, around 1768. He owned property in both Hamilton and Smith's Parishes and lived at Leeward in Hamilton Parish (see *Hamilton Parish*) although by the time he died he had moved to Smith's Parish. A blacksmith by trade, he was elected to the House of Assembly in 1774 as one of the members for Smith's Parish.

Giles Trott (died 1814), the father

Winterhaven Farmhouse photographed in the 1970s following its acquisition by the Bermuda Government. It is a traditional one room deep gable roofed house. *The Bermuda National Trust Collection.*

of Thomas Trott, was the brother of President Samuel Trott (1749-1812), the last Trott owner of Walsingham (see *Hamilton Parish*). Not much is known about Giles Trott except he appears in the Smith's Parish records as a juror and churchwarden and acquired the title of worshipful. He died when his son Thomas was about 17 years old although his widow Elizabeth lived on

until 1850, when she died at St. George's.

Thomas Trott spent time in his early manhood in Antigua. Perhaps he left to seek a better living overseas when Bermuda's economy was faltering due to the decline of its carrying trade. He seemed to have returned to live at Winterhaven Farmhouse by 1829. In the Slave Register of 1830 he

Winterhaven Farmhouse

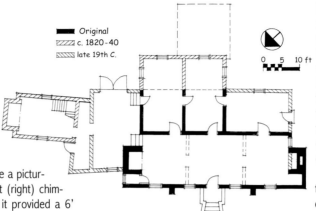

Original
c. 1820-40
late 19th C.

0   5   10 ft

Winterhaven illustrates how outwardly legible early Bermuda houses can be and yet challenging to decipher in full detail. The core consists of a long gable roofed main block now undivided, with an off centre door flanked by four windows, two wall buttresses and two chimneys. Both ends have a closet built into the front side of the chimneys, giving the house a picturesquely uneven shape. The west (right) chimney is larger because originally it provided a 6' wide fireplace for an 8'10" by 12'9" cellar kitchen as well as a heating fireplace for the superior room, just above it. The opposite chimney offered a 5' fireplace for a ground floor east room that once measured about 12' by 13', evinced by a seam in the rear wall and studs between the tie beam and roof collar as well as mortises for the lower studs. Removing the partition coincided with adjusting the location of at least one front window. Whether the west end was divided between a 13' square unheated central space and a second 12' by 13' room depends on the credibility of another tie beam — one of those major structural members that connect front and rear walls at the level of the eaves. If joints in the penultimate west beam are original to this location, the plan was balanced with three rooms. If they only represent the previous use of salvaged old framing, the hall on the west could have been unusually wide: more than 25'. The three room plan seems most plausible.

There are now two parallel rear wings, each with its own gable roof. Both appear original, presumably containing two unheated bedchambers. Initially these rooms were open to the ridge and their rafters whitewashed. They were later lengthened, and the roofs were ceiled off at the collars. Both have simple neoclassical door frames, as does the west closet, which one should balance against the archaic west fireplace finish in considering Winterhaven's original date and evolution.

Most cooking moved out of the cellar when a two storey kitchen quarter was added, perhaps circa 1820-40. The new building was free standing, 16' to the east (left). It contained a 14'4" by 10'4" cookroom with wide fireplace on the ground floor and living quarters above, reached initially by a steep interior stair and later apparently by exterior steps, creating further separation of domestic work and living spaces. The new rooms were drier and better lighted than the cellar kitchen and its adjoining room, both of which were dark, unfinished and thinly plastered.

Some workers must nevertheless have lived on in the cellar at Winterhaven after the new building was put up. Three other cellar spaces, under the east room and the rear wings and accessible from a single low rear door, were roughly plastered. These were lime washed and ochre pigments were occasionally included in the paint, suggesting they continued to be occupied into the 19th century.

By 1900, shed roofed space connected the two buildings, creating a house with a kitchen at the far east end.   *E.A.C.*

Winterhaven Farmhouse: *Floor plan drawn by Steve Conway.*

is listed in Bermuda with house servant Quamina and cook Dick, both from Antigua, as well as Ben, a labourer from Bermuda.

By March 1829 he was taking part in parish affairs and over the following years increased his land holdings to 37 acres and the number of buildings he owned from one to four, one of which was a store. Thomas Trott became a magistrate and also a divisional commander for the North Shore in the marine militia formed by retired naval officer Sir William Burnaby around 1840. He obviously farmed the land around Winterhaven and adopted the innovations of Governor William Reid as ploughs, a harrow and cultivator were amongst his effects at an auction in 1858.

Thomas Trott built a parish Watch House, or lock up, in the angle between Harrington Sound Road and Knapton Hill (*see chapter 11*). It was demolished about 1978.

He married Mary Paynter Musson in 1812 and the couple had two children, Mary Eliza Trott (circa 1820-1900) and Thomas Murray Trott (circa 1823-1898). His will asks his wife to remember, when allocating between the two, that the son would inherit the house, "keeping in mind that as my son Thomas is heir to the house and the piece of land where I now reside . . . that my daughter Mary Eliza should have a greater proportion of the residue so as to make them equal". His wife predeceased him and his son inherited Winterhaven Farmhouse in 1857 and lived there until his death.

Thomas Murray Trott was described at various times as a farmer and vestry clerk. He may also have dealt in property. He left his estate equally between his two sons, Thomas Samuel Julian (born 1857) and Adolphus William Reid (circa 1861-1934). He was in debt when he died and the property was mortgaged by the sons.

In 1902 Reid Trott, who was a successful businessman in Flatts (see *Hamilton Parish*), bought out his brother. The mortgage, however, was not satisfied until he sold Winterhaven in 1920.

The Winterhaven property, which stretched from Harrington Sound to the South Shore, was bought by Henry Stuart Hollis (1876-1942), a Bermudian living in New York. Hollis had done well in business and wanted to build a home in Bermuda as a "winter haven", so his primary interest was the land, on which he built a two storey house, known as Winterhaven, near John Smith's Bay on South Shore Road in which he could spend the winter. The farmhouse at Devil's Hole was in poor condition and

The two storey detached kitchen of Winterhaven Farmhouse, photographed in the 1970s, was probably a later addition in the early 19th century. It provided more acceptable cooking facilities and service accommodation, which was earlier in the cellar.   *The Bermuda National Trust Collection.*

he let it and the farm land for a nominal sum.

Henry Stuart Hollis, known as Stuart, was the eldest son of master mariner Captain Henry Hilgrove Hollis of Bailey's Bay (see *Hamilton Parish*). In his youth Stuart Hollis sailed with his father but after completing his education in England went to New York and joined the firm of A.E. Outerbridge and Co. whose vessels plied between New York, Bermuda and the West Indies. Later he joined the import and export firm of A.D. Strauss & Co. and in 1902 went into partnership with Edward F. Darrell and William P. Lough and formed the firm of E.F. Darrell & Co. with offices in the Produce Exchange Building in New York City.

He retired about 1941 and died the next year. Following his wife's death in the early 1970s the property went to numerous Hollis nephews and nieces who sold it to the Bermuda Government in 1974.

Winterhaven Farmhouse was initially leased for 21 years to the Bermuda National Trust who carried out extensive work to reinforce the cedar roof structure and save the roof slate. It was sub let as a pottery and then as a real estate office.

The lease expired in March 1997 and a new long term tenant was found. Plumbing and electrics were replaced, the kitchen and bathrooms refitted, and battened doors were installed. Winterhaven Farmhouse is now a home

again and the leaseholder received a Bermuda National Trust award in 2003 for the sensitive restoration of the building.

Winterhaven Farmhouse is probably a late 18th century house, built perhaps sometime between 1770 and 1780. It may have been constructed by Thomas Fitt for his daughter Elizabeth and her husband Giles Trott and perhaps changes and additions were made by Thomas Samuel Julian Trott. These would have included the two storey kitchen and service building to the east of the main house, new windows and perhaps the centred front door.

Behind the Harrington Workmen's Club at Devil's Hole is a small house that is currently in a sad state of repair and has been boarded up for some years, but it has a good structure and an interesting history. It is a simple symmetrical one storey building with a kitchen at the rear. It was formerly called **Neptune Cottage** and now goes under the somewhat prosaic name of 1 Club Road. At one time Devil's Hole Aquarium was known as Neptune's Grotto and Knapton Hill was known locally as Neptune Hill.

The land on which Neptune Cottage stands belonged in the late 18th century to Thomas Fitt who in his will written in 1793 left it to his granddaughter Julia Frances Trott (circa 1785-1857). She was an older sister of

Neptune Cottage, built by 1878 by stone mason Benjamin Darrell, behind the Harrington Workmen's Club. It is now derelict, however, it has a traditional symmetrical appearance and there is an elegant fanlight above the front door.

Oleander Circle is an 18th century house overlooking Harrington Sound. There is a front porch projection with scalloped gable ends and welcoming arms steps.

Thomas Samuel Julian Trott of Winterhaven and would have been about eight years old when she received her inheritance.

Within ten years, in 1801, she married John Paynter Musson. The couple moved to Anguilla where two children, John Paynter and Mary Elizabeth, were born. However, Julia Musson returned to her family in Bermuda along with her children as she said she could no longer live with her husband because he kept a mistress and the indignity was more than she could bear. Marine Cottage, which lies not far from the family home at Winterhaven, was built to house Julia and her children.

Neptune Cottage stands on a quarter acre lot on the northeast corner of the land inherited by Julia Musson. In 1852 it was purchased by Benjamin Darrell (circa 1822-1884). He was a stone mason and may have been the slave known simply as Benjamin listed in the Slave Registers of the Musson family.

Benjamin Darrell built Neptune Cottage sometime between 1852 and 1878 when he mortgaged a house and land to Thomas Joseph Pearman (see

This small detached building at Oleander Circle has a Flemish gable roof. *Frederick Hamilton, photographer, Neg.641. Bermuda Archives: The Bermuda National Trust Collection. PA207.*

Hamilton Parish). Darrell, however, died without satisfying the mortgage and the property passed to Pearman. In his 1913 will Pearman left Neptune Cottage to his wife for life and afterwards to his eldest surviving daughter Lucie Spicer, wife of Harry Spicer a surgeon in the Royal Navy.

The property changed hands twice when it was bought back by Eugene Charles Pearman (1873-1946), eldest son of Thomas Joseph Pearman. He

held it until 1944 when it was sold to the trustees of the Harrington Workmen's Club who built a club house on the roadside in front of the cottage. During the 1940s and 1950s it was lived in by Helen Burgess and later Louisa Eve, at which time it was in good condition. It is now uninhabitable.

Oleander Circle stands on a small rise above Turtle Island at Devil's Hole, east of the natu-

ral aquarium. It is in an unrestored state and divided into apartments but it is a magnificent example of an early cruciform house. It contains all the features we think of as typical of an old Bermuda house, massive sturdy chimneys, welcoming arms steps, scalloped gable ends, a projecting porch, windows under the eaves and a multitude of ancient additions.

It would appear to have been built by the Ball family sometime early in the

Oleander Circle

One of Bermuda's least known cruciform houses, Oleander Circle, was probably built by Captain George Ball, who died in 1728, leaving life rights to his second wife Sarah. The Ball house began with three rooms and a porch entry on a single floor above a cellar containing a kitchen on the west (right) under the hall.

Grandson Richard Ball acquired full ownership circa 1751 and he may have added a large rear south room, heated by a sizeable fireplace that shared an exterior chimney with a second cellar fireplace. The elder Ball may have eaten in the hall and slept in the parlour and used the wing as a second bedchamber. The fourth room could have provided Richard Ball with a heated bedchamber and allowed use of the central rear space as a dining room.

An aerial view shows the cruciform shape of the earliest section of Oleander Circle. The wing ending in a massive chimney, right rear, may have been added later in the 18th century. (*See floor plans page 13.*)

The oldest part of the house is treated in a decorative manner outside, with scalloped gables on the four original ends, and with a chubby classical pediment over the front door and rear window of the centre wing. A large west chimney has long stepped shoulders and a stack with grooves expressing the two flues. Its later east mate lacks added breadth of the cellar fireplace and has an unornamented stack, partly rebuilt in the 20th century. The southwest wing was left plain, with a relatively narrow chimney and no parapet. Three small shed roofed spaces at the southeast corner appear service related, per-

haps including a small cooking fireplace added after emancipation.

Most of the early interior finish was renewed in the 20th century, though the upper rooms retain tray ceilings and tie beams, all now cased. The beam at the front of the porch entry has old beaded casing. Original summer beams and joists support the main floor, a single longitudinal summer under the parlour and south addition and crossed summers under the longer hall.

There is a 10'9" by 9'7" ancillary building facing away from the house 17 feet to the northwest. With scalloped parapets and originally open to the roof, it seems more like a buttery than privy, though comparable examples of both are unknown.   *E.A.C.*

Oleander Circle photographed in the early 1920s by John S. Humphreys and described simply as 'House on Harrington Sound'.   *Bermuda Houses, John S. Humphreys, 1923, page 247 plate 135.*

18th century. The Balls are believed to have been engaged in privateering which would have been a likely source of finance for the building of such a splendid house at so early a date.

The earliest confirmed owner of the house now known as Oleander Circle was Captain George Ball (died circa 1728) who wrote his will in 1725. He left his Smith's Parish property to his sons, William and Richard, after the death of their stepmother Sarah.

However, Sarah Ball outlived both the sons and spent a long widowhood in the house, dying perhaps 50 years after her husband. The property was eventually inherited by her step-grandson Richard, the son of William.

Richard Ball (died 1799) was clearly a person of substance and was described as "formerly Justice of Ber-

Twin Bays on South Shore Road was built by entertainer Ross Talbot, known as Blackie. He was a member of the well known Talbot Brothers group. The house originally had two projecting bay windows, hence its name.

muda" when he died and "Esq" in the parish tax assessments. His 1798 will mentions the 1751 valuation of the house and how he paid off the other heirs and occupied the old house on the eastern part of the property in which George and his widow Sarah lived. Some of the enlargements and embellishments to the house may well date to his tenure. There were no surviving children from either of his marriages.

His second wife Mary Ball née Peniston (died circa 1824) outlived her husband by some 25 years. Her will left the house first to her sister Martha Place and then between five Peniston nephews and nieces plus a Musson cousin.

One of these nephews, shipwright William Hugh Peniston (1796-1869), accumulated five sixths of the house. However, he died much in debt and his son and heir, master mariner William Hubbard Peniston, known as Bamboo Billy (1829-1917), was also in financial trouble and at least once sold up and emigrated from Bermuda.

The property changed hands a couple of times around the turn of the 19th and 20th centuries until it was bought in 1921 by retired farmer Benjamin Darrell Talbot (1859-1925). He

had been a large land owner in Tucker's Town but had been bought out by the Bermuda Development Company and purchased Oleander Circle and other properties with the proceeds (*see chapter 11*).

Oleander Circle was left to his adopted daughter Charlotte Salves Smith who had married the Reverend Joseph Daniel Smith. The Reverend Smith, a son of Thomas and Alice Smith, was a pastor in the African Methodist Episcopal (AME) Church.

St. Phillip AME Church was built

on land previously belonging to the Oleander Circle estate. The daughter of the Reverend Smith owned Oleander Circle at the beginning of the 21st century.

Twin Bays on South Shore Road opposite the Marsden Memorial Methodist Church is a 20th century house of individual design that was built on land acquired by the Talbot family from the sale of land in Tucker's Town to the Bermuda Development Company.

It was built by singer and enter-

Oleander Circle, photographed in 1947, is cruciform shaped with a projecting porch and welcoming arms steps.
Frederick Hamilton, photographer, Neg.640. Bermuda Archives: The Bermuda National Trust Collection. PA207.

Knapton House

Two Knapton inventories illustrate that a house with two principal rooms and an enclosed porch on both of two storeys was owned by the family in 1668 and 1703. By 1703 there was also a "dineing roome" with a chamber above it.

It is conceivable that the cross shaped section of the present house was that inventoried in 1703. This is a very substantial house for the era, with a main block, a small front porch projection and a rear wing, all two storeys high covered by single gable roofs. The house faces its property to the north rather than toward Harrington Sound and the South Shore. All the front corners have rustication and the blocks are carried around to the east (left rear) corner, however, in deference to the commanding water view. Both front ends have exterior chimneys providing fireplaces for the ground and upper storeys, and the rear wing has a stack articulated to emphasise its pair of flues.

Knapton House suffered decay in at least one era, before it was purchased and restored by the American Edith Sterling Simon soon after 1929, so the framing system is now fragmentary. It is nonetheless clear that the entry porch was spanned by lightly finished joists, and the floorboards were visible overhead. The entry now opens into a single space, occupying the whole main floor of the principal block. There appears to have been a roughly 13'4" by 14'9" parlour to the west (right) spanned by a summer beam running end to end, and a larger hall to the east (left), the full 22'4" by 14'9" spanned by crossed summer beams.

Four cambered tie beams upstairs are arranged to suggest a narrow (5'3") passage has long separated a slightly wider chamber over the parlour from that over the hall.

Roughly centred, the rear wing contained a sizeable room 17' long and 16'3" wide on both floors. These are plausibly Moses Knapton's dining room and a chamber used for storage in 1703. On the ground floor, it is spanned by a longitudinal summer beam, while upstairs tie beams are confined to the end walls. Framing at the rear end of both spaces, up and down, indicates that the wing extended further to include closets flanking fireplaces on both floors. There is no visible evidence for the square rear room beyond the chimney being contemporary, and there is no corresponding room in Moses Knapton's inventory, unless this was his kitchen. However, his "little room by the parlour" containing a bed worth £6 could be the small existing shed-roofed appendage.

The house was refitted with very academic Bermuda revival woodwork by Mrs. Simon, including delicate neoclassical balusters recycled for a stair in the porch entry. A peculiar small chimney was set in the southwest angle of the porch perhaps in the 19th century to heat the porch at the location now occupied by this stair. Rear additions include 1968 designs by John Kaufmann and 1983 by Beryl E. Brown.

E.A.C.

EARLY 18TH CENTURY
LATE 18TH CENTURY?
20TH CENTURY

Knapton House ground floor plan: *Adapted by Deborah Mackenzie from drawing by Beryl E. Brown.*

---

tainer Ross Talbot, known as Blackie, on a plot he had acquired from his older brother Archibald Maxwell Talbot, known as Archie.

Ross and Archie were members of the famous calypso entertainment group, the Talbot Brothers of Bermuda, who were extremely popular in the second half of the 20th century both in Bermuda and the US. The group, who did much to promote tourism, was made up of brothers Archie, Austin, Dick, Ross and Roy with cousin Mandy.

Hastings Ross Frenshaw Talbot (1918-2000) said, shortly before his death aged 82, that he had built the house himself to a design from his own

head. He was in his late teens when he constructed Twin Bays and let it until he got married about four years later.

Twin Bays was originally built with two projecting bay windows, hence its name, but later a verandah was filled in with a third bay. There are a number of other houses in the area that have copied its style.

The parents of the talented Talbot Brothers were farmer Osmond Charles Frenshaw Talbot and Mamie Susan Augusta Kennedy Talbot née Lambert. She was a church organist and he a gifted dancer, so the brothers grew up in a musical household.

Ross Blackie Talbot is also remem-

bered in an annual golf game, the Ross Blackie Talbot Charity Classic, which has raised large amounts for charity.

Knapton House stands on the eastern slope of Knapton Hill above Devil's Hole. It occupied a two share tract of land, or 49 acres, which stretched from Harrington Sound to the South Shore.

It is a two storey cruciform house with a projecting front porch, ancient chimneys on either end of the cross wings and a chimney on the rear projection. Rear additions of a modern kitchen, family living space and a verandah do not detract from the tradi-

A quiet drive just west of John Smith's Bay, Tuesday, May 19, 1903.　*'The Bluff at Point Knapton', 1903. Deming Album, Neg.3870. Bermuda Archives: The Bermuda National Trust Collection.* PA2004:035.

tional appearance of the front of the house.

It is said to date back to John Knapton (circa 1668) who was one of Bermuda's early silversmiths. However, this is not easy to confirm.

Two inventories exist, one for John Knapton in 1668 which described him as owning "Two shares of land with a faire house" and the other for his son Moses Knapton in 1703. Very few houses in Bermuda survive from the mid 17th century and the history of Knapton House has been varied. It has

suffered from neglect and fire and it is not possible to determine whether the present house is indeed the "faire house" of John Knapton although it is probable that it could have been that of his son.

According to the inventory, John Knapton's house was built over a cellar and contained a hall and "parler" and three upstairs rooms, one of which was over the porch. A "buttrye" and "kichen" are also listed. His house and his possessions were fairly modest.

John Knapton is described in his will as a planter and his inventory confirms this. There was tobacco, a tobacco "wheele", a cheese press and a "milke tubb" in the cellar. In the yard were three "hoggs", a cow and "calfe", a red heifer, two black heifers, a "redd" cow and a steer. In the "buttrye" were five bushells of "casada flower" (probably cassava), one bushel of corn and a pruning hook. However, his ownership of silver appeared to be limited to "one plate cupp" valued at $1.5.0.

According to tradition, John Knapton made what is known as the

Knapton House is a two storey house built to a cruciform plan. A two storey porch projects between two wings flanked by chimneys.

Hubbard-Peniston tankard. This is a sophisticated engraved silver tankard with a hinged lid said to have been made for the marriage of Daniel and Sarah Hubbard née Tucker in about 1700 and it has descended through a Peniston branch of the family.

In 1971 architect Bryden B. Hyde wrote in *Bermuda's Antique Furniture & Silver*, "This tankard is the most important and most controversial piece of silver in Bermuda of possible Bermuda provenance." He continued, "It has always remained in the hands of direct descendants of Daniel and Sarah Hubbard . . . For family funerals it has always been filled with spiced wine and passed among those visiting the house."

Moses Knapton (died 1698), the son of John, was also a planter. The inventory attached to his will, with his possessions listed room by room, describes a house that is probably recognisable as the core cruciform area of the Knapton House we know today. Downstairs there was a porch, hall, parlour, little room by the parlour and a dining room. Above stairs there was a porch chamber, a chamber over the hall, a chamber over the parlour and a chamber over the dining room. There was also a cellar and a kitchen.

His house was better furnished than his father's. He possessed six silver spoons and two silver cups with a total value of £6 although this is fairly minimal compared with the silver listed in the 1699 inventory of Samuel Trott at nearby Walsingham (see *Hamilton Parish*). Moses Knapton owned a considerable number of slaves: five men, two boys and four women. This compares to two on his father's inventory.

Moses Knapton left his wife Mary Knapton, the mansion house and two shares of land as well as a quarter part of the sloop *Mary*. After her death the property was to go to his eldest son, also called Moses.

Mary Knapton (died 1740) outlived her son and was an administrator of his estate. She appears to have stayed in Smith's Parish while mariner Moses Knapton Jr. (died 1714) and his wife Ann had moved to St. George's.

The ownership of Knapton House then becomes somewhat tangled. In May 1727 shipwright Thomas Gilbert and his wife Mary accused widow Mary Knapton of cutting down several timber trees and converting them to her own use. The case went to court and the Gilberts got £27.15.6 in damages. It was difficult to trace the connection between the Gilberts and Mary Knapton, but it is probable that Mary Gilbert was a daughter of Moses Knapton Jr. and therefore a granddaughter of Mary Knapton.

In 1734 Thomas and Mary Gilbert made a joint will in which it was stated that Mary was the sole heir of mariner Moses Knapton of Smith's Parish. They left the westernmost portion of the 49 acre property to their son carpenter John Gilbert and the easternmost to their daughters, Mary, Anne and Sarah.

In 1740 Knapton House became the home of Mary Smith, a daughter of Thomas and Mary Gilbert, who had married Anthony Smith. She left her property to her children, John, Mary, Margaret and Catherine.

Catherine Smith (died 1811), did not marry and left Knapton House to her nephew John Walker (circa 1795-1845). He was to build the house now known as Wistowe at Flatts (see *Hamilton Parish*). However, he ran into financial difficulty and in 1820 advertised for sale or lease his dwelling house and 25 acres of land at Neptune Hill (Knapton Hill) with a valuable standing of timber, a good store and a fish pond on the margin of the Little Sound (an earlier name for Harrington Sound).

The house obviously did not sell and John Walker's debts increased. He died in 1845 at Washington DC, aged about 50, and his executors put first Wistowe and then Knapton House up for sale.

Knapton House was purchased in 1849 for £400 by Thomas Slater (circa 1807-1850). He was a warder of Her Majesty's Naval Yard but did not live long to enjoy his new home as he died the year after its purchase. His widow Catherine Slater née Todd (circa 1816-1884) lived for a time at Knapton House, although by 1881 she appeared to be living in Philadelphia and died in Pembroke.

Her attorney Richard Darrell Darrell wrote to Elizabeth Humphrey, daughter of Catherine Slater, in October 1885 to inform her "the property in Smith's Parish is rented in three parcels. The house is in very bad repair with land between Knapton Hill road and southsea for £40 per annum, the middle land for £7 per annum and the cottage on Harrington Road at 30/- per month."

In 1888 Knapton house was rented to planter Francis Martin. He was obviously struggling financially as in 1896 he mortgaged his chattels and effects and in 1898 he mortgaged his crops of onions, potatoes and lilies. There was a fire about 1919 and not much more than a shell was left of the house.

In 1927 a voting consortium consisting of Eugene Charles Pearman, James Eugene Pearman, William James Howard Trott, Ernest Hugh Watlington, John Hartley Watlington, Joseph Downing Wilfred Carlyle Darrell, William Eugene Meyer, Kenneth Allan Wilkinson, Edward Fairbairn Darrell, Henry

This chimney, set in the angle by the porch, is probably a 19th century addition to Knapton House.

Thompson North, Stephen Righton Wilkinson and Edward Fairbairn Darrell Jr. purchased Knapton House for £2,800. Voting consortiums were formed to acquire property for its voting rights as the right to vote was restricted until 1963 to property owners, who could vote in each parish in which they owned property (*see chapter 10*).

In 1929 American Edith Sterling Simon purchased the house and almost four acres of land. This was the time when Americans were coming to Bermuda and were building or restoring houses in the Colonial revival fashion. She restored Knapton House from its ruinous state, added a kitchen and pantry, cedar fireplace surrounds and panelled doors.

Knapton House changed hands

again in the late 1940s when it was acquired by Murtogh David Guinness (1913-2002), a member of the Irish brewing family and a son of Walter Edward Guinness, the first Baron Moyne.

Murtogh Guinness was a collector of mechanical musical instruments and had one of the rooms at Knapton House lined in velvet to enhance his display. The house was broken into and some of his artefacts were destroyed. He moved to the Bahamas and then to New York City where he amassed one of the most important collections of musical devices in the Western Hemisphere. It is now housed in the Morris Museum at Morristown, New Jersey. The present owners purchased Knapton House in October 1957 and have continued to enhance the property. 🌴

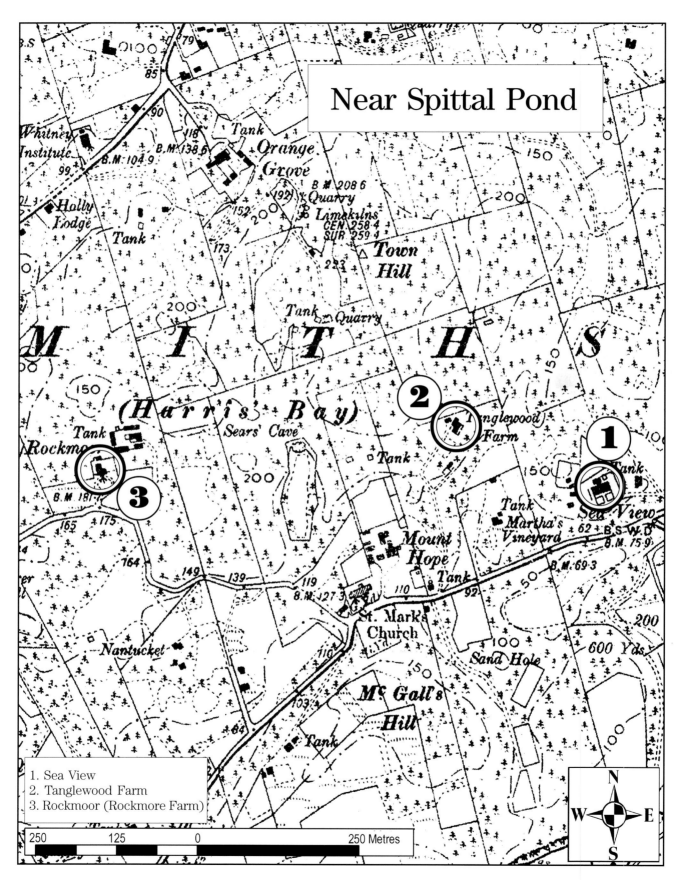

Near Spittal Pond

1. Sea View
2. Tanglewood Farm
3. Rockmoor (Rockmore Farm)

250   125   0   250 Metres

Surveyed and Contoured in 1898-1899 by Lieut. A.J. Savage, RE. Published at the Ordnance Survey Office, Southampton, England, 1901.
Courtesy Works & Engineering.

10
Near Spittal Pond

Land at Spittal Pond was first acquired by Dr. Henry Campbell Wilkinson of the Bermuda Historical Monuments Trust, forerunner of the Bermuda National Trust in May 1946 and the final piece was purchased in 1990. This photograph was taken in the mid 1970s. *The Bermuda National Trust Collection.*

Spittal Pond, earlier known as Peniston's Pond, is a nature reserve in the eastern half of Smith's Parish. The park extends to more than 60 acres and contains a large brackish water pond, a rugged coastline and interesting historic features. It is owned partly by the Bermuda National Trust and partly by the Bermuda Government.

The so-called Spanish Rock, which has an inscription carved on a rocky outcrop overlooking the South Shore, is probably the best known historical feature of the park. In 1962, however, J. Vidago writing in the *Bermuda Historical Quarterly* claimed the letters on the rock were probably "RP" for Rex Portugaliae and were likely to have been carved by a sailor from a wrecked Portuguese ship.

The Spittal Pond Rifle Club was set up in October 1887 when an inaugural meeting was held at Whitney Institute. Its members came from Hamilton, Smith's and Devonshire parishes. A rifle range is marked on the Savage map published in 1901 and the area was used as a military firing range prior to the First World War. They shot from the hill at the west side of the pond towards targets at either the eastern end or to the south.

Peniston's Pond, which was owned by the Peniston family for well over 100 years, was labelled Spittal Pond on the Savage map surveyed 1898-1899. It is not known why or how it acquired this new name.

Sea View, overlooking Spittal Pond, was the home of Clarence Peniston, and was built for him about 1872.

It is a strongly built one storey house over a cellar and is of formal and distinctive design. Unusual features included an imported grey slate roof and wrought iron verandah posts. The posts are similar to the ones on the former Post Office building in Hamilton. (Built about three years before Sea View on the corner of Reid and Parliament Streets, the Post Office now

An aerial photograph of Sea View, built about 1872, shows the main house with its verandah facing the front garden and the South Shore. The old kitchen, with a chimney, is at the rear left and there is a small 20th century addition, rear right.

functions as the Magistrates' Court.) There are Greek revival style mouldings on the house and large keystones over the windows, which have heavy masonry sills.

The former kitchen at the rear with its arched raised cooking fireplace, old bread oven and cedar tie beams, is a particularly interesting feature of the house. Opinions differ as to whether this was an earlier residence or whether

it was built at the same time as the house in a more traditional Bermudian fashion. It is not unusual for service quarters at the rear to be built in a less sophisticated fashion than the rest of the house.

The hurricane of September 1899 did major damage to the house. *The Royal Gazette* of September 16, 1899 reported, "In Smith's Parish Mr. Clarence Peniston, whose residence

Sea View has lost a large area of slating, is perhaps the heaviest sufferer since only two rooms in the house are habitable." The original slate tiles were replaced in 1996 by a white SKB roof, a man made alternative to the traditional Bermuda slate roof fashioned

A close up of the verandah at Sea View with its ornate iron posts, similar to those on the Magistrates' Court (formerly the Post Office) on Reid Street in Hamilton, and the front door with a fanlight above and side lights.

The Royal Gazette, March 20, 1909.

FOR SALE
By Public Auction

Under Power of Sale contained in a
Mortgage

ON THE PREMISES
at 3.00 p.m.

Thursday, 10th Dec. 1936

ALL THAT certain parcel of land situate in Smith's Parish in the Islands of Bermuda containing by estimation sixty acres or thereabouts (be the same more or less) bounded NORTHERLY partly by lands formerly of Richard F. Peniston deceased then of his son Francis Peniston deceased afterwards of Clarence Stuart Peniston deceased and now of his heirs or devisees or their assigns and partly by the South Longitudinal or Church Road EASTERLY by lands of the heirs or devisees of Augustus Peniston deceased or their assigns SOUTHERLY by the Ocean and WESTERLY partly by lands formerly of William Edward Newman deceased then of John William Richard Pearman deceased and now of his heirs or divisees partly by land heretofore of Thomas Spencer deceased and partly by lands formerly of Richard F. Peniston deceased afterwards of his son Francis Peniston and now of his heirs or their assigns OR HOWEVER OTHERWISE the said parcel of land may be bounded may measure or ought to be described TOGETHER WITH the dwelling house known as "Sea View" and the out-buildings thereon erected and the appurtenances thereto belonging.

For further particulars apply to :-
G. C. G. MONTAGU,
Attorney for the Mortgagee.

E. L. PALMER,
Auctioneer.

The Royal Gazette, November 17, 1936.

The old kitchen chimney with bread oven box, right, and its separate chimney stack at the rear of Sea View.

from local limestone.

Clarence Peniston (1840-1908) was one of the many sons of Francis Peniston (circa 1788-1854) of Peniston's, now Magnolia Hall (*see chapter 6*). His father, Francis, and his grandfather, Richard F. Peniston (1760-1826) before him owned the land on which Sea View stands. They may have used the pasture around Spittal Pond to fatten cattle, providing fresh meat to supply the British military.

Susette Harriet Lloyd in *Sketches of Bermuda* published in 1835 wrote, "His (Mr. Peniston's) extremely well kept stalls, in a country like this, where both the cattle and provender must be imported, are well worth seeing. Some of the oxen are very large: and, I believe, are all brought from the United States."

Clarence Peniston farmed the land around Sea View and was a member of the House of Assembly for many years, serving on the Executive Council from 1904. He was also the Provost Marshal General. In 1863 he had married Sarah Almena Conyers (1844-1931) and the couple had seven children, only two of whom continued to live in Bermuda.

In his will Clarence Peniston stated he wished his eldest son Clarence Stuart Peniston to continue to work Sea View Farm until the crops, including the lilies, were harvested. The property was left to his widow and unmarried daughter, Edith Almena, and then was to be sold and the proceeds divided unless his eldest son, Clarence Stuart, desired to purchase the property and retain the estate in the family.

Clarence Stuart Peniston (1872-1930) was the manager of the Bermuda Mineral Water Company. In 1899 he married Ernestine Elise, daughter of Benjamin William Walker, and by 1905 the young couple had moved to Pembroke where she had inherited property from her father.

In March 1909 the furniture at Sea View was put up for auction and it is not known who lived in the house between 1908 and 1936 when Sea View and 60 acres were sold at public auction.

It was reported in *The Royal Gazette* of Saturday, December 19, 1936, "At a public auction on Thurs-

Sea View

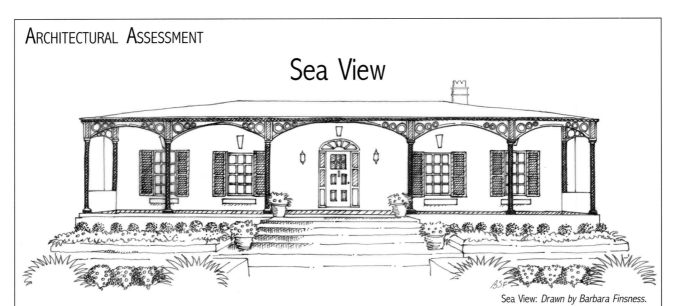

Sea View: *Drawn by Barbara Finsness.*

Sea View, a house built circa 1872 by Clarence Peniston, is a formal house of this era with a complex plan behind rigidly ordered walls designed with details drawn from an eclectic range of sources. The front is five bays wide, the sides four, with a single refined floor above cellars. A front door of neoclassical form and Italianate details opens into a lobby 10' wide by 15' deep, with a heated parlour to the right and a smaller, unheated dining room to the left. Doorways 7'10" wide link the three spaces. Behind these is a narrow longitudinal passage leading to bedrooms on the left (one beyond the dining room) and right. On axis with the dining room and connecting with this passage is an even narrower transverse passage running to the back wall, and now through it, directly into an otherwise detached kitchen.

This is an impressive room, perhaps originally a cookroom and quarters, now undivided 25' long and 13' deep. There are five hanging tie beams, all thin for the length they span. The room is open to the collars and plastered. One would like to know for certain whether this is older than the house, but it appears contemporary in spite of its old open hearth cooking fireplace and ancient general appearance. Clearly it continued to be used in a traditional fashion. The raised work fireplace is 6' wide and 3'2" deep, lined with old red painted brick and spanned by an arch, up to 6' above the recent brick floor. To the left is a contemporary oven, also brick lined, with a cast iron door resembling that at Cotswold (*see chapter 3*).

The house has a very strong Greek revival appearance with crisp and flat walls inside projecting frames formed by cornice, plain pilaster strips and a plain water table. Window sills and peculiar tall and thin keystones project the same distance as these frames, a technique still popular 30 years later. The roof was covered with imported slate until recently replaced with SKB roofing. A low pitched hipped roof reaches down to cover the thin cornice. A small single chimney unobtrusively exits the roof above the parlour. This severity is relieved on the front, overlooking Spittal Pond and South Shore, by a Gothic cast iron porch resembling one at the Old Post Office, now the Magistrates' Court, in Hamilton and on many English railway platforms of the same era.

The three bay kitchen building contrasts completely. Here a hipped roof covered with uneven Bermuda stone extends roughly over exposed rafter ends above uneven stuccoed walls and the large chimney, with high sloped shoulders and the oven, stands almost entirely outside the left end.

Land in front of the house has seen aggressive landscaping, presumably around the era of construction. The immediate front lawn has been relatively flattened, held up by retaining walls, and a lower drive yard is equally level, requiring its own 10' high retaining wall. All the buildings and walls are painted a strong orange and white.

E.A.C.

day afternoon Mr. E.R. Williams, acting on behalf of a syndicate of young businessmen, purchased for $3,800 the estate of the late Clarence Peniston in Smith's Parish known as Sea View. The property comprises about 68 acres of land, the residence and outbuildings … The syndicate's purpose in buying the estate has not been revealed."

It was common at that time for syndicates to purchase a property for its voting rights as owners could vote in each parish in which they owned property of the required value. The principle of one man one vote was not in operation until 1963 and elections were staggered over three days to give property owners the time to visit each parish and vote.

The new owners of Sea View were a group of influential people: Henry Durham Butterfield, Thomas Melville Dill, Edmund Clarence Gosling, Thomas St. George Gilbert, Henry Campbell Wilkinson, Edgar Roderic Williams, Guy Stewart Ridgway, Eldon Harvey Trimingham and Charles Barron Wainwright.

Sea View with 18 acres of land was acquired in 1937 by Edgar Campbell Wilkinson Jr. (1898-1970), who ran a livery stable on Victoria Street in Hamilton as well as stables at Sea View. He lived at Sea View until his death in 1970 when the property was transferred to his three children. Sea View became the home of his daughter in the early 1980s and was sold to its present owners in 1996.

Tanglewood Farm lies to the west of Sea View and is reached from Zuill's Park Road, to the east of St. Mark's Church. It is a charming house in a hidden garden setting.

The house is one room deep and consists of an early front section between two chimneys that contained a hall and chamber either side of a centre passage. The front portion was built over cellars and there is an early wing,

An aerial view of Tanglewood Farm shows the oldest section of the house built in the late 18th or early 19th century, left, between the two chimneys. The wing to the rear with a chimney, centre, is also early. Later 20th century additions are to the right.

with a chimney, to the rear. Tanglewood Farm is gable roofed with decorative stepped Flemish gable ends. A south facing verandah was added in the 19th century. Substantial restoration took place in the mid 20th century when additions were made to the east end of the main house.

It is not easy to state the precise date of its construction. The early portion of Tanglewood Farm may have been built by either Anthony Spencer or his son Thomas. Anthony Spencer (died 1805) was a cordwainer, or shoemaker, and Thomas Gilbert Spencer (circa 1755-1830) was a master shipwright.

Cooking was probably done by slaves in the cellar when the Spencers owned the house. The large double flued chimney at the west end also served a fireplace with an oven, now almost obscured, in the cellar. Food preparation later probably moved upstairs into the rear wing, possibly around the time of emancipation.

In 1870 John William Spencer, a great-grandson of Anthony Spencer, claimed Tanglewood Farm and 17 acres from his grandfather's estate, even though his grandfather had left the house and land to his unmarried daughters.

John William Spencer (1807-1871) was a master shipwright who lived with his brother farmer Rupert Hugh Spencer (1820-1868) at Verdmont (*see chapter 2*). John's eldest daughter, Ella Eliza Spencer (1846-1887) who was also an heiress to the Verdmont estate, inherited Tanglewood Farm (*see also chapter 2*).

In 1876 Ella, who had married Captain James Lusher, sold Tangle-

The verandah on the south facing front of Tanglewood Farm was probably added in the late 19th century by carpenter and farmer Edwin Robert Zuill.

ARCHITECTURAL ASSESSMENT

Tanglewood Farm

Tanglewood Farm appears to have been built as a very straightforward, rational single storey house with a front door opening into a 6' wide central passage between a 19'7" by 15'5" hall on the west (left) and 15'7" by 15'6" chamber on the east (right). A third room in a rear wing on the northeast corner connects with the chamber and served, at certain times, as a kitchen. There is no visible evidence of the rear room being later, and its exterior treatment matches that on the main block: wave-like scalloped parapets terminating the roofs, exterior chimneys with multiple steps at about head level sloping back to narrow stacks with ovolo moulded caps and widely spaced bands. Old photos show the wing with a separate hip at the south end, before a circa 1958 addition to the east.

As at Somerville (*see chapter 4*), cooking was initially done in a sizeable (15'3" by 19'9") kitchen below the hall. There is a 6' by 3'3" work fireplace immediately below the hall fireplace, with the round arched opening for an oven behind it. Food prepared in this low dark space was carried out of a south door and in through the front door to reach diners in the hall.

The rear ground floor room clearly was also employed as a kitchen at some time. Although its 4'11" by 2'9" fireplace is relatively small, a flue from a now lost oven in the northeast corner was carried into the main flue. Either this began as a secondary kitchen or was converted from a chamber into a domestic workroom sometime in the 19th century.

A construction date is important for Tanglewood Farm because it would help chronicle the evolution of kitchens from their grim loca-

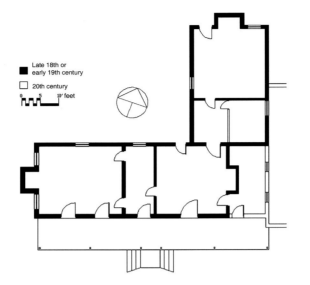

Late 18th or early 19th century
20th century
0   5   10' feet

tion in dark cellars to a relatively superior position above-ground. The lack of virtually all early woodwork makes date guessing difficult, but the long period circa 1770-1820 would be a reasonable proposition.

The house was remodelled in the late 19th century, probably by Edwin Robert Zuill after acquiring it in 1876. He changed front windows to create French doors opening onto a full-length front porch with chamfered posts, a Chinese railing, and exposed rafters. Clearly the porch blocked the old front access to the cellar kitchen, and the Zuills occupied a refined house that nevertheless provided only three rooms, one of them probably used for cooking.

The house was repaired and enlarged by Lurelle Guild, a collector and flamboyant restorer of old houses, soon after he bought it in derelict condition in 1958. He added a kitchen at the northeast corner and an eccentric drawing room with salvaged Ionic pilasters, arches, and niches for sculpture. Guild also added a swimming pool with a high stone wall and entrance through a faux Bermuda buttery, and he rebuilt most of the roof frames and gables on the house. The west and north chimney stacks survive with their early interior finishes hidden above Guild's low tray ceilings, however, and they suggest that originally the rooms were open entirely to the ridge, although the stone partitions now rise only to the roof collar level. Tray ceilings were added, apparently earlier in the 19th century, above first the front spaces, then in the rear room, as there are more layers of yellow ochre, red, and white lime washes surviving above the line of the old tray.   E.A.C.

Tanglewood Farm floor plan: *Drawn by Adam Gauntlett, Ted Gauntlett Chartered Surveyor.*

wood Farm and nine and a half acres to Edwin Robert Zuill (circa 1829-1894).

In 1853 Edwin Zuill married Alice Frances Peniston (born 1829) and the couple had nine children. He was a farmer and carpenter, and may have been responsible for adding the verandah to the front of the house and also changing the windows. The verandah obstructed access from the cellar to the house.

His widow, Alice Zuill, continued to live on at Tanglewood Farm until her death along with his unmarried daughter Ora Ernestine Zuill (1872-1953) who was the first woman registered as

a dentist in Bermuda. She qualified as a Doctor of Dental Surgery at the Philadelphia Dental College in 1897 and was registered as a dentist on June 8, 1911.

The property was owned briefly in 1957 by Edgar Campbell Wilkinson Jr. (1898-1970) of neighbouring Sea View, but the house was by then in ruins and listed in the parish tax assessments as having no value.

In 1958 Lurelle Van Arsdale Guild (1898-1985) bought Tanglewood Farm and was to restore and add on to the house. Lurelle Guild was a well known American industrial designer. He began work in 1927 and became enormously successful, executing more than one

thousand patented designs in one year alone. His most significant achievement was to design the Model XXX vacuum cleaner for Electrolux. He also designed refrigerators for Norge, cookware for Wear-Ever and washing machines for General Electric. During his prolific career, his design clients included Elizabeth Arden, Corning Glass Works, Eastern Airlines, Maytag, Singer and Westinghouse.

Lurelle Guild undertook extensive repairs to the near derelict Tanglewood Farm. He rebuilt most of the roof and added a kitchen and an unexpectedly formal drawing room to the east end of the house as well as a swimming pool.

Tanglewood Farm was in poor condition before it was purchased in 1958 by well known American industrial designer Lurelle Guild. This photograph shows the east end in 1947 before additions were made. *'Tanglewood ',1947. Frederick Hamilton, photographer, Neg. 012. Bermuda Archives: The Bermuda National Trust Collection. PA207.*

This aerial view shows the east side of Rockmoor with its adjoining pool and pool house, foreground. The L-shaped main house can be clearly recognised with the old "packing room" to its rear, right.

The house again suffered neglect in the later years of Lurelle Guild. In 1983 it was purchased by the present owner, who added a porch and updated the kitchen.

Rockmoor is a late Victorian house on St. Mark's Road. It was originally known as **Rockmore Farm** and stood on 97 acres of land stretching from near St. Mark's Church to Jennings Land on the North Shore. It was built for Thaddeus Trott, designed by Edward Peniston and the work carried out by J.D. Gibbons.

It is an L-shaped two storey house with gable roofs, enclosed eaves and bold exterior dentil mouldings. It is built in an ornate Italianate style. The two storey "packing room" at the rear has now been joined to the main house by means of a glass atrium and the chimney with bread oven which once served the kitchen has been cut off at first floor level.

Inside, the imposing Italianate front staircase with its tapered octagonal inlaid newel post is typical of the millwork of Edward Peniston (1838-1903) of Flatts (see page 154). The installation

of a back staircase for the use of servants, or perhaps children, was another feature of many of the late 19th century homes designed by Peniston. He was a brother-in-law of Thaddeus Trott.

Little is known about the builder, except recent renovations in the west bedroom exposed the words "built by J.D. Gibbons – 2 July 1877". Perhaps he was the John Doe Gibbons of Hamilton Parish who married Georgianna DeCoe of Smith's in 1894.

Thaddeus Trott (1838-1924) was the youngest son of William James Trott, grandson of Sarah Trott of Rose Cottage (*see chapter 4*) and great-grandson of William Sears of Orange Grove (*see chapter 7*). In 1863 Thaddeus married Louisa Margaret Pearman (1844-1935), second daughter of John William Pearman of Mount Hope (*see chapter 11*).

The family lived first at Rose Cottage and afterwards at a house then known as Eagles Nest, on the Cable & Wireless property in Devonshire, before building their dream home. According to family tradition, it was called Rockmore Farm because the land consisted of rocks and more rocks.

Helen May Fessenden, second daughter of Thaddeus Trott, in *Childhood Memories of Bermuda in the 70s* wrote, "During the last half of this decade my father and mother embarked on a great adventure, the building of our permanent home (Rockmore Farm)… The new home was an ambitious project; the house was a fine one, first class workmanship, large and lofty rooms, spacious verandahs, numerous bedrooms, our first bathroom and ample tank capacity. As the walls rose the sense of ownership grew within us, we chose our rooms and insensibly dedicated ourselves to the service of this home." The Trotts already had six daughters, aged from three to 14 years, when they moved to Rockmore Farm (later Rockmoor) where four more children were born including their only son William James Howard. The two eldest girls, Eliza (1864-1902) and Helen (1866-1941), were sent to school in England by their uncle Harley Trott of Belmont in Smith's Parish (now Penhurst), so they could educate their younger siblings on their return to Bermuda.

Two of their younger sisters, Hattie

Rockmoor photographed when it was owned by Sir Howard Trott. It was built in 1877 for Thaddeus Trott and was designed in Italianate style by Smith's Parish builder and designer Edward Peniston and constructed by J.D. Gibbons. *Courtesy Penny Cooke.*

Rockmoor has gained a chimney, left, and the verandahs have been altered since the time it was lived in by Sir Howard Trott.

Edward Peniston

Edward Peniston (1838-1903) of Smith's Parish was an important builder and architectural designer in Bermuda during the second half of the 19th century. He kept an up-to-date workshop and was especially noted for the quality and unique design of his woodwork, some of which is stamped with his initials "EP".

Although he is credited with designing and building a number of notable public buildings in the City of Hamilton, Edward Peniston was born and lived in Flatts Village and did a lot of work within the parish. His obituary in *The Royal Gazette*, March 3, 1903, noted, "Among the buildings erected by him may be mentioned the Princess Hotel, the Imperial (demolished 2004), Dr. E.C. Wilkinson's residence (Sofia House on Church Street since demolished), the High School for Girls, the Whitney Institute, the new Phoenix Drug Store (now Aston & Gunn), the Tucker Building (on Reid Street), the Royal Hamilton Amateur Dinghy Club (formerly on Church Street in Hamilton), and a host of others."

The Tower building at Whitney Institute (*see chapter 11*) on Flatts Hill is his most notable landmark within Smith's Parish but he also had a hand in a number of others. He designed Rockmore Farm on St. Mark's Road for Thaddeus Trott. He played a part in the major refurbishment of Mount Hope with Jeremiah Scott Pearman and built pews for St. Mark's Church (*see chapter 11*).

The verandah at Villa Mont Clare (*see chapter 8*) near Flatts Village, with its iron columns and elaborate woodwork, bears the hallmark of his handiwork. There is no proof but it is possible he could have had a hand in the design and in the woodwork in particular of Aldie and Glimmerview on Store Hill. He was also responsible for the addition of the east and west bedroom wings to Orange Grove on Flatts Hill (*see chapter 7*).

Edward Peniston was described as an "architect and builder" in his obituary. It noted, "He studied at Cooper's Institute (probably in New York) and spent some years in America acquiring that intimate acquaintance with the details of his profession to which all

Edward Peniston, architect and builder. *Courtesy Sylvia Panchot.*

his work bears abundant testimony." It continued, "Devoted to his work, and always busy, he took no part in public affairs ... ".

He looked overseas, particularly to America, for his design inspiration rather than to Bermuda with its vernacular tradition. His work shows the influence of the Italianate and also the Arts and Crafts movements. It was characterised by asymmetrical buildings, heavy moulding, bay projections and ornate woodwork.

His woodworking shop was fitted with the latest equipment. In November 1879 he advertised equipment for sale in *The Royal Gazette* and in July 1880 he advertised from his "Steam Wood Works" at Brightside in Flatts that he had fitted his shop with "new Machinery, worked by Steam Power". He added that he specialised in window and door frames, sashes, blinds, doors, cedar rafter feet. He also had "cedar and white pine coffins on hand and finished to order". In February 1889 he was again advertising his equipment for sale as he intended "making a change in his business about the 20th of May".

Edward Peniston lived at Brightside in Flatts. He was the second son of house carpenter Augustus Peniston and his wife Anna Maria North. His father was the son of Ann Peniston, a sister of Richard F. Peniston of Peniston's, later Magnolia Hall (*see chapter 6*). In 1863 Edward Peniston married Adrianna Elizabeth Pearman, a sister of Jeremiah Scott Pearman of Mount Hope.

D.C.

(born 1870) and Emmie (1885-1983), continued to run a school in the packing house. William Edward Sears Zuill, known as Will (1892-1989), of Orange Grove (*see chapter 7*) wrote, "When I was quite young I was sent to school to Aunt Hattie at Rockmore. School was held in the lower part of the building known as the Packing Room. The walls were not plastered but were whitewashed and as I remember it the school was always full."

It was a busy working farm. The house was flanked by barns and stables with a packing room for the farm produce to the rear of the house. Potatoes, onions and tomatoes were grown and exported to New York and Louisa Trott, in the traditional manner of a farmer's wife, raised chickens and geese.

The property was left to their only son William James Howard, who was in 1942 to become Sir Howard Trott, although he probably did not take up residence at Rockmoor until the 1940s.

Sir Howard Trott (1882-1971) was described in an editorial at the time of his death as "father" of the island's thriving tourist industry and indeed he went on to own a large number of local hotels as well as being involved in a multitude of business interests. He was a man of great energy and influence.

A farmer and his family at work. What is now the Pokiok estate, near Spittal Pond, was once the site of a model farm established in the mid 19th century by Governor William Reid. Two agriculturalists, Robert Fox and James McGall, were brought from Britain to superintend the farm and the latest agricultural machinery was imported. *Bermuda through the Camera of James B. Heyl, 1868-1897, compiled by Edith Stowe Godfrey Heyl, page 168.*

He left school aged 16 and took a course in book-keeping and accounting in Belleville, Ontario. His first job was as front desk clerk at the Princess Hotel in Hamilton where his uncle Harley Trott was the majority shareholder.

In 1911 Howard Trott bought the Inverurie Hotel in Paget, now the site of The Wharf development. This was the beginning of Bermuda Hotels Associated, a group united by common ownership and management, including the management of the Princess. In 1919 he bought the Belmont in Warwick in partnership with Dr. Charles Wainwright. They added first a nine hole and then an 18 hole golf course. In 1927 they bought Frascati in Flatts, bringing their hotel bed capacity to 1,300 guests.

In 1915 Howard Trott was made a partner in Pearman Watlington & Co. and his interests expanded to the manufacture of ice, water transporta-

tion and the marketing overseas of Bermuda's agricultural produce.

The Belmont and the Inverurie were sold in 1947 when he bought a controlling interest in Cambridge Beaches in Somerset. His hotel interests also included the Pink Beach in Smith's Parish and the New Windsor Hotel in Hamilton. In 1950 he took over chairmanship of the Bermuda Development Company which owned the Mid Ocean Club, the Castle Harbour and the St. George Hotel. He also had hotel interests abroad and was a shareholder in Half Moon Bay in Jamaica.

His interests were not confined to business. He started the Trade Development Board (now the Department of Tourism) in 1918 and served as a member of the House of Assembly for Smith's Parish from 1925 until 1947 when he became a member of the Legislative Council (the Upper House) and at one time was simultaneously chairman of the Trade Development Board,

the Board of Works and the Board of Agriculture.

He married Elmina Morrison Hutchings (1886-1950) in 1910 and five children were born of the union. He died at his home, Rockmoor, and an obituary in *The Bermudian* magazine observed, "there passed a man who left an indelible mark upon Bermuda, especially upon the development of the tourist trade". Following his death the property was let for some years until it was sold out of the ownership of the Trott family in December 1988.

Sea View, Tanglewood Farm and Rockmoor each stand in countryside, now growing rare in Bermuda. It is interesting that these houses all started existence as family farms but have adapted well to an urban age. Despite the loss of their farms all are still recognisable as the fine – and differing – examples of Bermudian architecture that they are. 🌴

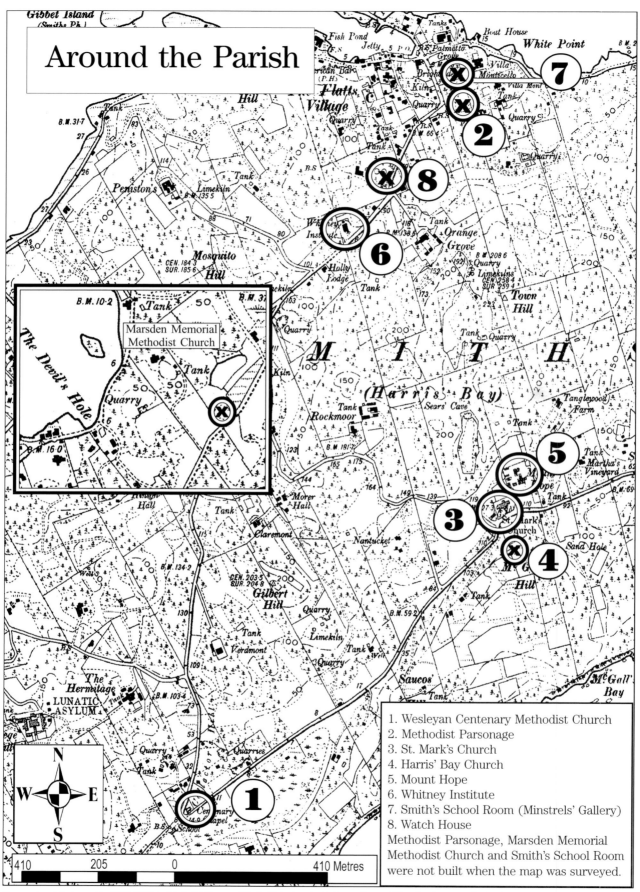

Around the Parish

Marsden Memorial
Methodist Church

1. Wesleyan Centenary Methodist Church
2. Methodist Parsonage
3. St. Mark's Church
4. Harris' Bay Church
5. Mount Hope
6. Whitney Institute
7. Smith's School Room (Minstrels' Gallery)
8. Watch House
Methodist Parsonage, Marsden Memorial
Methodist Church and Smith's School Room
were not built when the map was surveyed.

Surveyed and Contoured in 1898-1899 by Lieut. A.J. Savage, RE. Published at the Ordnance Survey Office, Southampton, England, 1901.
Scale: six inches to the mile. Courtesy Works & Engineering.

11
Around the Parish

A horse and carriage pass by the Wesleyan Centenary Methodist Church which stands on the corner of South Shore Road and Collectors Hill. This peaceful scene was photographed in 1941, a hundred years after the first service was held in the church. *Life Magazine, August 1941, page 62. Courtesy Margie Lloyd.*

Around the parish stand a number of churches conspicuous in their size amidst the rural landscape and in their architecture which borrows little from the Bermudian vernacular tradition. Although Bermudians built their houses in a traditional way, the design of churches seems to have been strongly influenced by Britain, the mother country for many of the early colonists and the birthplace of the Anglican and Wesleyan Methodist faiths.

The Gothic revival style appears to be the most popular choice for church design in Smith's Parish although the circular St. Patrick's Roman Catholic Church on South Shore Road (South Road) is a highly visible 20th century attempt to escape that mould. It was designed by Onions, Bouchard & McCulloch and completed in 1969.

The Anglican church of St. Mark's, although it can boast the oldest congregation, is not by a few years the oldest church building in Smith's Parish. That honour lies with a Methodist church.

The Wesleyan Centenary Methodist Church, which stands at a prominent location on the corner of Collectors Hill and South Shore Road, is the oldest church building in Smith's Parish. Its cornerstone was laid on August 20, 1839, a century after what is generally considered to be the official birth date of Methodism in 1739. The first service was held on Thursday, November 11, 1841.

Today it is a small Gothic revival style church but the original building was a simple rectangular gable roofed hall which forms the core of the present church. Changes were made early in the 20th century to create the Gothic revival church we see today.

Specifications called for the chapel to be 40 by 26 feet and its estimated pre construction cost was £260. It had strip pilasters on its corners and arched windows and doors. The building committee consisted of Thomas A. Smith, Robert W. Gibbons, John Gauntlett and Christopher Jones, who was also the principal stonemason.

Additions were made from 1924 to 1925 when a square tower, buttresses and an extension to include the organ chamber and the choir loft were added to the original building. The windows were replaced with Gothic style ones from St. Mark's Church where they were replaced by stained glass windows. Following these major changes the old chapel became known as Wesleyan Centenary Church.

In 1961 the children of the late Gilbert S.W. Smith and Clara A. Smith, led by Hilda Aitken, donated a cedar pulpit, communion rail and choir screen to the church. Hilda Aitken was one of the first two women to be elected in 1948 to the House of Assembly, the other being Edna Watson. The woodwork was designed by architectural designer C.E. Hinson Cooper (*see chapter 4*), the pulpit made by cabinet maker Alfred Charles Acton, known as Chum, and the rail and screen by Ambard & Company.

The Stephenson Memorial Hall on the east side of the church was completed and dedicated on March 5, 1964.

The Wesleyan Centenary Chapel started life as a simple building with a gable roof. This rectangular hall forms the core of the present church. *Courtesy Norman Noble.*

Wesleyan Centenary Methodist Church with Stephenson Memorial Hall to its rear. The top of the church's square tower is crenelated with Gothic style pinnacles at each of its four corners.

Its design echoed that of the church and it replaced the Popham Hall which stood on the other side of the road on the site occupied at the beginning of the 21st century by the Collectors Hill Apothecary. It was named after the Reverend John Stephenson who in 1799 was the first Methodist Missionary to visit Bermuda.

The Wesleyan Centenary Methodist Church was built on land acquired from John Abraham Skinner and his wife Letitia Cooper Watlington Skinner for the token sum of £10. John Abraham Skinner (1794-1873) was a planter and a wealthy property owner whose ancestors had been shipbuilders. He owned neighbouring Skinner's Farm in Devonshire (see *Devonshire*).

The church was well positioned near the boundary between Smith's and Devonshire to serve the people of both parishes and it stood not far from Tynes Place, the home of Captain Samuel and Nancy Williams, where the congregation met before the chapel was built.

The Methodist Parsonage on Flatts Hill near the junction with Fielders Lane was built in 1904-1905 to serve as the home of the minister of the Bailey's Bay circuit of the Wesleyan Methodist Church of Bermuda.

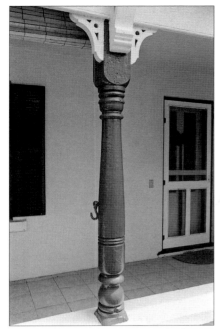

The ornate verandah posts at the Methodist Parsonage were probably the work of carpenter James L. Outerbridge.

The house was built in a conservative fashion with simple Greek style moulding, top hung shutters, decorative turned verandah posts and a barn. It was designed by William Robert Lightbourn with Thaddeus Outerbridge as mason and James L. Outerbridge as carpenter. A stable and carriage house were added in 1921, a bedroom and study in 1930 and garage, patio and new driveway in 1980.

The Reverend Joel Dudley Mader was the first occupant of the Parsonage. He was superintendent of the Bailey's Bay circuit and conducted services for all three chapels within that group: Centenary, Bailey's Bay (see *Hamilton Parish*) and Tucker's Town. The last two have now been converted into private residences.

Marsden Memorial Methodist Church is a small Gothic revival style building which was built early in the 20th century to replace a 19th century church in Tucker's Town. It is located on South Shore Road east of John Smith's Bay and overlooks the old Talbot School house which is home to the Cleveland County Cricket Club.

A remarkable story lies behind this small church as it and its congregation were uprooted from Tucker's Town when that area was turned into an ex-

The Methodist Parsonage stands on Flatts Hill near the corner with Fielders Lane. It was built at the beginning of the 20th century in simple Greek revival style.

clusive development in the 1920s. The predominantly black landowners of Tucker's Town were bought out and many moved to neighbouring Smith's Parish, particularly to the area along the old Military Road (now South Shore Road) between John Smith's Bay and Pink Beach.

Tucker's Town, an isolated peninsular on the main island, was established by Governor Daniel Tucker in the early 17th century as a new town, which never flourished. Rather than being a great New World metropolis which bore his name it became home to a rural community of farmers and fishermen who were said to have numbered about 400 in 1920. It was their

land, all 500 acres, that was desired for an ambitious project designed to fuel Bermuda's developing tourism industry and to obtain a regular shipping service for the export of Bermuda grown agricultural products.

Plans of the Bermuda Development Company in the heady days before the Great Depression included the luxurious Castle Harbour Hotel which was demolished early in the 21st century, two private golf courses and exclusive homes on lots groomed by Olmsted Brothers whose founder had earlier designed New York's Central Park. It was intended as a playground for the rich and famous, transported by ships of the Furness Bermuda Line to escape

Builders of Marsden Memorial Methodist Church

Marsden Memorial Methodist Church would not have looked the way it does if it had not been for the men who built it, one of whom was also intimately connected to the church. Ernest Motyer was the architect and contractor, Louis Petersen the mason and Grenville Darrell the carpenter.

Cyrus Grenville Darrell (1878-1963) was not only the carpenter for the building but he was also an important officer of the church for more than 60 years. He served as steward, trustee,

Grenville Darrell carpenter and trustee of Marsden Memorial Methodist Church. *Courtesy Roland Darrell.*

Ernest Motyer, designer of Marsden Memorial Methodist Church. *Photograph by Walter Rutherford, 1965. Courtesy Arthur Motyer.*

in his obituary of 1983 they knew of "few people who have done so much to further the aims of good architectural practice in Bermuda".

Motyer Construction Company was located in the City of Hamilton, at the eastern end of Front Street, in a building which extended through to Reid Street. Amongst other buildings Ernest Motyer worked on were Wreck House and Blue Flag in Somerset and Tucker's Island House in Southampton which later became part of the US Naval Operating Base.

member of the official board, superintendent of the Sunday School and was a local preacher. It was reported at the dedication ceremony for the church that he donated the communion rail whilst his son Lionel Darrell gave two offertory plates. Grenville Darrell was the son of Joseph George Darrell and his wife Arabelle Adams and was born in Devonshire.

Ernest Motyer (1892-1983) was a contractor who supervised on horseback the building of the Mid Ocean Golf Course during the first year of its construction. He and his family were closely connected with the Wesley Methodist Church in Hamilton and although he worked largely as a contractor he did design a number of houses. Indeed the Council of the Association of Bermuda Architects declared

Unfortunately little could be found out about mason Louis Petersen (1895-1979) except that he was born and died in Pembroke Parish.

An article in *The Royal Gazette* of October, 10, 1923, reporting on the dedication of the church, noted, "Marsden Church is built and slated with Bermuda coral stone. It is fifty-seven feet long, twenty-seven feet wide, with a nine feet square tower with battlements, Gothic windows, and flanking buttresses… To the ridge the building is about twenty-five feet in height, and the tower is some seven feet higher. At the eastern end is a vestibule projecting fifteen feet with a width of twenty feet; within is the minister's vestry and a room for use of the Choir. The interior of the Church is tray-ceiled, with a height of fifteen feet six inches from the floor." *D.C.*

A Methodist missionary preaches to the slaves. This engraving comes from a book written by Joshua Marsden after whom Marsden Memorial Methodist Church is named. *Amusements of a Mission by Joshua Marsden. Bermuda Sampler, William Zuill, facing page 139.*

the restrictions of weather and prohibition in the United States.

The Land Reclamation Act of 1920 laid out the conditions for the clearance of Tucker's Town and the property of the Tucker's Town Methodists was exchanged for land in Smith's Parish and the deal sweetened with a payment of £1,950.

The new church was built with a square crenelated tower, pointed arch windows and doors and flanking buttresses, all in Gothic revival style. Marsden Memorial Methodist Church was dedicated on Sunday, October 7, 1923. A hall was built in the 1940s and choir and organ loft and a new organ were added in the 1950s.

The church was named after the Reverend Joshua Marsden (circa 1777-1837) an English born Wesleyan Methodist missionary who emigrated to Nova Scotia and served in Bermuda from 1808 until 1812. During his time here he formed three branches of the Methodist Society. They were in St. George's, Bailey's Bay and in Hamilton where he acted as architect, supervisor and workman for the Zion Chapel which stood at the head of Queen Street.

Left behind in Tucker's Town when the congregation moved to Smith's Parish was the Tucker's Town Methodist Chapel, the cornerstone of which had been laid in 1861. The Methodist community of Tucker's Town had worked hard to build this chapel with the men giving the proceeds of a day's fishing towards the building fund and the women holding a variety of fund rais-

Marsden Memorial Methodist Church on South Shore Road, which was dedicated in 1923, was built in Gothic revival style. It has a square tower with a crenelated top, pointed arch windows and buttresses.

Harris' Bay Church

Harris' Bay Church stood on the site of the present graveyard of St. Mark's Church. The old church collapsed during renovations in 1846 and St. Mark's was built to replace it. *Southeast View of Harris' Bay Church, Bermuda, J.C.S. Green, 1819. The Bermuda National Trust: Verdmont Museum.*

Harris' Bay Church stood over the road from the present St. Mark's Church. It is no longer in existence but the southwest corner of its foundations were uncovered in the graveyard in an archaeological excavation conducted in 1998.

The old church, which is believed to have been built some time after the hurricane of 1712 and before 1717 collapsed in 1846 whilst work was in progress to repair the roof. It is thought to have been the second Anglican church in Smith's Parish.

Fortunately we have a drawing as well as a description of this old church plus a few artefacts. An 1819 drawing by J.C.S. Green shows a rectangular building running from east to west and standing not far from the northern wall of the graveyard which runs along the side of South Shore Road.

The drawing shows it was a simple structure with a gable roof and sash windows. The 12 over 12 panes of glass in the windows can be clearly seen. An entry porch with simple arched openings was on the south side of the church towards the western end.

In November 1717 the vestry of Southampton sent a delegation to measure Harris' Bay Church as they hoped to rebuild their church, which had been destroyed in the hurricane of 1712, in a similar form but with some modifications. Their findings were written in the Southampton minutes of November 26, 1717.

"The Chancell (of Harris' Bay Church) is twenty foot long, with twelve seats and two Benches. The Body of the Church is forty foot long. On the South Side is four long seats ranging with the Church, and six cross seats. On the North Side between the Chancell and the Pulpit is two seats. Across from the Pulpit to the West end of the same is six ditto. The width from the inside to inside is 24 feet; the height to the wall plate 10 feet. At the west end is a place for the Negros with a Barricade before it that no person can pass to them

with a small door to let them in and out by themselves. At the west end a Vestry eleven feet long and tenn and a half wide from inside to inside. A gallery for the boys over the Negros with three seats. The Vestry is against the Pulpitt. The door is on the east side of the Pulpit. The porch is nine foot from the west end of the church."

From the above description it can be determined that Harris' Bay Church was probably 60 feet long by 24 feet wide and ten feet high to the wallplate. The black congregation was segregated at the west end under a gallery.

The Smith's Parish Vestry minutes report that the Harris' Bay church was repaired in 1760 and again in 1804. In 1830 the rector proposed that the church be enlarged but the vestry felt the expense would be too great.

English governess Susette Harriet Lloyd visited the church at this time and wrote in her book *Sketches of Bermuda*, "On Sunday we went to Harris' Bay Church, which lies at the bottom of a deep valley. It is rather an old building, and not having any steeple, the bell is hung from a fine cedar tree. The church contains an ancient carved cedar screen, and a monument to the memory of Judge Green, who died in 1802."

In 1844 the Assembly had granted £250 for the enlargement of Harris' Bay Church but following its collapse it was decided to abandon the old church and build a new one on the other side of the road. Timber from the old church was used in the construction of the new and some artefacts were removed and placed in the newly built St. Mark's. These included a table and two cedar chairs as well as wall plaques, one commemorating John and Mary Green of Verdmont (*see chapter 2*) and the other Gilbert Salton of The Hermitage (*see chapter 3*). *D.C.*

---

ing events. It was built by contractor Henry Hallett (1817-1901) and has now been turned into a home called Sandcastle.

Left behind too was the burial ground containing ten unmarked graves which now lie in a walled enclosure on the Tucker's Point Golf Course in the middle of a practice driving range. There was also a schoolhouse in which the congregation first worshipped in 1835, just a year after emancipation.

St. Mark's, on the corner of South Shore and St. Mark's roads, is probably the third Anglican church to be built in Smith's Parish. It was a replacement for Harris' Bay Church which was just over the road on the site of the present graveyard (*see On the Side above*). A simple silver chalice dated 1676 is all that remains of the first church which may have stood on common ground on Flatts Hill (*see chapter 7*), according to Richard Norwood's *Book of Survey*

of 1662-3 although the location of this church has yet to be determined.

The cornerstone of St. Mark's was laid on January 19, 1847, the first service held on Easter Day April 23, 1848, and the church consecrated on February 13, 1849. It was built on land given by Sarah Trott and her sister Mary Sears, daughters of William Sears of the property now known as Orange Grove (*see chapters 4 and 7*).

The vestry minutes specified that the new church was to be built to hold about 350 persons and be "of sufficient height (not less than 18 feet from the floor to the wallplate) to admit of galleries being erected hereafter in case of need and the estimate to include one gallery at the west end. The basement of the building to be two feet and the walls 18 inches in thickness."

It was a simple rectangular hall when first built but it has been added to and embellished over the years. The original church was designed and built by William Edward Newman (1795-1869). Not much is known about him except that he owned a great deal of land in the east of the parish and was a Member of the House of Assembly. A plaque was somewhat belatedly erected to his memory following the 50th anniversary of the church in April 1898.

A drawing owned by St. Mark's shows the church as first built with a gable roof with strip pilaster moulding on its corners. It was symmetrical in design with two windows either side of a simple south facing porch.

It was not plastered inside and the congregation was summoned to wor-

St. Mark's Church when first built was a simple rectangular building with a gable roof, arched windows and a simple porch. This building forms the core of the present church. Mount Hope can be seen rear right. *St. Mark's, Bermuda, W.S. Zuill, page 20.*

ship by a bell hanging from a cedar tree and rung by being struck by a stick. The story goes that a woman parishioner was so incensed by the sight of a sage bush sprouting inside the church that she paid the church caretaker Jim

Keele £5 to plaster the interior.

In 1848 Jeremiah Scott Pearman, son of John William Richard Pearman of neighbouring Mount Hope, was the first child baptised at St. Mark's. This was auspicious as he grew up to be a

The tower and spire of St. Mark's were designed by Dr. Henry Hinson and built by mason Julian Tucker. Buttresses and the chancel had yet to be added to the main body of the church. Mount Hope is visible to the right. *Bermuda through the Camera of James B. Heyl, 1868-1897, compiled by Edith Stowe Godfrey Heyl, page 73.*

A chancel, left, was added to St. Mark's in 1884 at the east end of the building. This photograph was taken by Walter Rutherford in the 1930s when the land beside the church was planted with lilies. *The Story of Bermuda, Hudson Strode, 1946, page 205.*

Julian Tucker was the chief mason of the tower and spire of St. Mark's. *Heritage, Kenneth E. Robinson, London & Basingstoke, 1979, page 69. Courtesy Mrs. Rosalind Robinson.*

major benefactor of the church and is remembered in a stained glass window.

St. Mark's remained as a simple country church building for some time as the congregation was locked in a number of parochial battles, firstly with the Reverend Solomon John Stowe who resigned in 1851 following a lengthy hearing at an Ecclesiastical Court and then over the proposed appointment of the Reverend Charles Alfred Jenkins who had married the widow of the Reverend Stowe.

The only addition to the church during this time was in 1860 when a larger and grander porch was added to the south front of the church. This was donated by William Edward Zuill of Orange Grove (*see chapter 7*) along with the square Italian marble floor tiles which came from the cargo of a wrecked ship.

The Reverend George Tucker assumed the position as rector for Hamilton and Smith's parishes in 1869

and under his leadership, combined with the efforts of Jeremiah Scott Pearman, St. Mark's began to develop into an increasingly sophisticated church building.

In 1875 work began on a tower and spire at the west end which would begin to transform the simple country church to the Gothic revival one it is today. The tower and spire were designed by Dr. Henry J. Hinson (1819-1893) of Paget who had trained as a doctor in Scotland where he became interested in architecture and in the Gothic revival style in particular. St. Mark's was the first to be designed by Dr. Hinson who went on to design the spires of St. James' in Somerset and St. Paul's in Paget.

Julian Tucker (1843-1904) was the chief mason on the project. He later built a modified replica of the tower and steeple for St. Paul African Methodist Episcopal Church in Hamilton.

The tower and spire were completed in 1877 at a cost of £489. *The Royal Gazette* of November 27, 1877, reported, "The steeple . . . is in the early English style, modified so as to accord as nearly as possible with the body of the church and is 102 feet high to the cross.

"The tower, 14 feet square, rises to a height of 56 feet and is supported by two buttresses at each of the corners, placed at right angles to each other. These buttresses are carried up in four storeys, each storey being crowned by a plain triangular or pedimental head, except the last which terminates in an hexagonal pinnacle, panelled, but not

---

Notice

TENDERS FOR THE EREC-
TION OF A

Tower and Spire

At St. Mark's Church, Smith's.

TENDERS for the above work will be Received by the Building Committee

Until 31st Present Month,

From Persons wishing to Contract for same.
PLANS and SPECIFICATIONS can be seen on application to JNO. W. PEARMAN.
The Committee do not bind themselves to accept the lowest or any Tender.
For further particulars apply to

Rev. GEO. TUCKER, } Building
JNO. W. PEARMAN, Com-
CLARENCE PENISTON, } mittee.

Smith's Parish, July 14, 1874.—2 pd

The Royal Gazette, July 21, 1874.

The ornate Gothic revival tower and spire rise proudly above St. Mark's Church.

decorated, and from this springs a flying buttress to support the spire also ending in a plain pinnacle.

"From the tower rises an octagonal spire, plain and 46 feet in height, above which is the cross. This cross through some mistake as to dimensions ordered, is set too close to the apex of the spire which gives it a dwarfed appearance. The defect, which was foreseen and pointed out, could have been remedied, but was not upon false principals of economy. Between the but-

tresses are triple and double lancet shaped windows, connected together by dripstones and surmounted by stepped pediments, the highest of which are crowned by crosses.

"The doorways which all open have equilateral shaped arches, chamfered at the edges and quicked, and these give entrance to the lower part of the tower, which forms an open porch. The design contemplated a groined ceiling to this porch, but this has not yet been carried out."

The bell in the tower was the gift of William and Frances Whitney (see chapter 8). It cost £70 and came from Meneely & Co. of Troy, New York, and replaced the old bell hung from a Bermuda cedar tree.

The next additions were the chancel, the section of the church which contains the altar, and vestry on the east end of the church. These were the gift of Adelaide Sarah Trott, wife of Harley Trott and were completed in 1884. At the same time new windows

The addition of the spire to St. Mark's between 1875 and 1877 marked the beginning of the transformation of the simple country church to one of Gothic revival style. *Photograph by Roland Skinner. Bermuda News Bureau.*

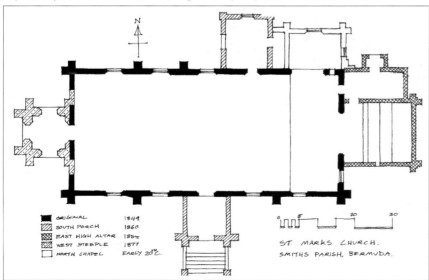

ST. MARKS CHURCH.
SMITHS PARISH, BERMUDA.

ORIGINAL	1848
SOUTH PORCH	1860
EAST HIGH ALTAR	1877
WEST STEEPLE	1877
NORTH CHAPEL	EARLY 20 C.

St. Mark's Church floor plan: *Drawn by Colin Campbell, OBM International.*

were given by the Pearman, Trott and Zuill families. They were made by Ballantine's of Edinburgh.

It is not known precisely when buttresses were added to the main body of the church but their addition would have completed the transformation of the church into a Gothic revival edifice. Attention was now turned to the interior.

New pews were installed in the church in 1901. These were made from mahogany logs sent from the Turks Islands where they had drifted ashore possibly from San Domingo and were shipped to Bermuda aboard HMS *Beta*. The pews were built by Edward Peniston of Brightside (*see chapter 10*) and the ends carved by Arthur Wilkinson (circa 1859-1935) of Bailey's Bay. The total cost was £216.9.6.

In 1907 Jeremiah Scott Pearman donated the iron gates at the entrance to the churchyard and graveyard, the mahogany doors at the porch and the old vestry room, the font stand and the mahogany frontal to the gallery. He also commissioned Arthur Wilkinson (see *Hamilton Parish*) to build a pulpit which was dedicated in 1909. It is notable for its carved panels of flowers. He encouraged the vestry to install a peal of bells as a memorial for Archdeacon the Venerable George Tucker (*see chapter 8*). They were to be the first in Bermuda and caused great excitement when they were first heard on Sunday, March 26, 1911.

In 1923 six new stained glass windows were ordered from Scotland. The old ones were sold to the Wesleyan Centenary Chapel.

There have been a number of minor additions to the church at the northeast corner. These include a second vestry and the small St. Francis chapel, which occupied a space once used for the organ chamber.

The St. Mark's Parish Hall was built in 1973 and in 1978 neighbouring Mount Hope was finally acquired as the rectory whilst Villa Mont Clare (*see chapter 8*) was sold.

The congregation of St. Mark's continues to add to the fabric of their church. Disaster hit during a winter storm of January 11, 1986, when the church was damaged by tornadoes. The window at the east end of the church was sucked out along with its masonry supports and one of the south windows

Mount Hope has been the rectory for St. Mark's Church since 1978. It was built about 1847 by John William Richard Pearman and much altered by his son Jeremiah Scott Pearman. The verandah was probably designed and built by Edward Peniston.

blew in. The church was restored and a new window in the chancel installed. It was designed and made by Bermudian artist Vivienne Gardner. It is a replica of the original and incorporated pieces of stained glass salvaged from the ruins.

Mount Hope was built as a private home about 1847 by John William Richard Pearman (1817-1896). He was a ship builder and farmer who later became a Member of Parliament for Smith's Parish.

The two storey house which stands to the northeast of St. Mark's behind the parish hall has been subject to a number of changes. It started life as a one storey dwelling somewhat similar to the original house at Magnolia Hall (*see chapter 6*) or to Villa Monticello (*see chapter 8*) with a symmetrical façade and a walled garden.

Jeremiah Scott Pearman (1847-1932), the only surviving son of John William Richard Pearman, inherited Mount Hope and made substantial

The rustic cedar gazebo designed by Jeremiah Scott Pearman served as a pavilion for tennis at Mount Hope.

Mount Hope

It is believed that Mount Hope was built for John W.R. Pearman in 1847 and enlarged for Jeremiah Scott Pearman, possibly by Edward Peniston in or after 1896. A photo of adjoining St. Mark's Church in *Bermuda through the Camera of James B. Heyl, 1868-1897* (*see page 163*) shows it as a single storey house with a hipped roof and enclosed yard, so presumably the old house constitutes part of the present fabric.

The basic form was used throughout the 19th century, but this building is draped with an eclectic array of details that Peniston used elsewhere to distinguish his buildings from the plain vernacular houses then dominant. The main block has a symmetrical five bays, with a hipped roof that carries out over small two storey projections at both ends. The roof also extends over a substantial T-shaped porch, with panelled masonry piers supporting the central projection and cast iron panelled columns as the main lower structure. Upstairs there are turned classical balusters between chamfered posts. Original finished and painted framing of the upper porch floor is now sheathed. There is an original polychrome tile floor. Hard edged stucco was scored to resemble ashlar, with masonry straps at floor and chair rail level on the wings. There are stone eaves except where rafter feet are exposed in less visible locations, including parts of the main block hidden by porch and wings.

It is a centre passage house, one room deep. Double Eastlake doors with miniature panels open into the passage dominated by a small stair made bold by its mahogany balustrade. A reeded rail rises

MR PEERMANS RESIDENCE

Mount Hope, the home of Jeremiah Scott Pearman, was described as "Mr. Peerman's Residence" in this early 20th century postcard. *Donald E. Stephens Collection, Bermuda Maritime Museum.*

from a grand tapered and turned column carved with a barley sugar twist pattern and rosettes. The same twisted shape is used for the balusters, originally two per step, now one. The stair has strong neoclassical form and Italianate elaboration in spite of its modest size: curved junctures with curved panels at the first landing and with curved stringers there and where it reaches the upper floor. The style is made more emphatic by the presence of a round headed niche beside the landing, a neoclassical flourish popular by the 1810s. Trim consists of baseboards - no chair rails or cornices - and symmetrical frames with carved corner blocks on the doors and windows. Passage partitions now have round headed doorways with 20th century doors and side lights with privacy glass. The left first floor room has a faceted, glazed bay and there is a square bay to the right, the latter with a front door and perhaps originally intended as a lobby. Upstairs most of the trim was replaced in the late 20th century and the plan has been somewhat altered. The rooms have tray ceilings and hewn tie beams, perhaps alterations in pursuit of Bermudian quality. The house is built against a hillside, and two rear rooms are upstairs, largely unexcavated below.

Down the hill at right front is a picturesque octagonal gazebo with root and vine bench backs and a concave roof covered with Bermuda slates, built by Jeremiah Scott Pearman (1847-1932), an amateur cabinet maker, who made the rustic benches of the same character that are now at Orange Grove.   *E.A.C.*

changes. These included excavation to create two storeys at the front of the house. He also changed most of the interior trim, installing woodwork in the then fashionable Charles Eastlake style.

The verandah forms a prominent feature of the house and was added by Jeremiah Scott Pearman. It is believed to have been designed and built by his brother-in-law, builder and designer Edward Peniston of Brightside (*see chapter 10*). It has cast iron pillars and is similar to one at Villa Mont Clare (*see chapter 8*).

Jeremiah Scott Pearman was a senior partner of commission agents Pearman, Watlington & Company along with John Cox Watlington and Henry J. Cox. He was a member of the House of Assembly from 1897 and for several years prior to his death was Deputy Speaker. He was also a gentleman farmer and keen gardener and was active in St. Mark's Church and in the parish as a whole. He lavished time and money on charity. The care of neighbouring St. Mark's Church was his particular concern. Jeremiah Scott Pearman was a bachelor and lived at Mount Hope with his unmarried sister Catherine Pearman, known as Kate (1850-1948).

Kate Pearman lived at Mount Hope until her death and in 1950 the house,

its eight outbuildings and more than six acres of land were sold by the many beneficiaries of Jeremiah Scott Pearman's estate to Anthony Soares Marirea, John Franklyn Peniston and Vivian Burrows.

The house was seriously damaged by fire and required extensive renovation when purchased by the church in 1978 along with four surrounding buildings. The rectory had earlier been at Villa Mont Clare on Harrington Sound Road near Flatts (*see chapter 8*).

Whitney Institute was built in the late 19th century on donated land and has at the beginning of the 21st century become a government aided middle school serving a wider area than just the parish.

The oldest part of the school, the Tower, stands as a prominent landmark on the top of Flatts Hill. It was built in an ornate Italianate style and was, along with its northern addition, designed by Edward Peniston of nearby Brightside in Flatts. Italianate was a style of architecture popular in the 1840s to 1880s and evolved from a romantic interpretation of the villas of Tuscany, Umbria and Lombardy. Square towers and verandahs were features of this style.

Edward Peniston (1838-1903) was a joiner and building contractor who designed and built a number of other notable public buildings (*see chapter 10*). He was the brother of Ameria Ann Pearman of Sunnyside in Shelly Bay (see *Hamilton Parish)* who together with her husband Thomas Joseph Pearman donated the land on which the original portion of the school stands. She had inherited the property from her father Augustus Peniston of Bridge House (*see chapter 8*).

The founder trustees of the school were all prominent men in the community. They were rector of Smith's and Hamilton parishes the Reverend George Tucker, the Worshipful Justice Edwin Peniston, Edward Peniston, doctor Aggeus Outerbridge, merchant Jeremiah Scott Pearman, master mariner Alonzo Peniston, and planters Thaddeus Trott, John William Richard

Whitney Institute on Flatts Hill opened as a school in September 1884 with just 17 students. The Tower was photographed in 1885. *Courtesy Board of Trustees Whitney Institute.*

Several additions have been made to the original Whitney Institute Tower building and can be seen in this aerial photograph taken in the 1950s. A wing was built to the rear in 1889, the tower was adapted to take a clock and bell in 1901 and two verandahs were added to the east and west sides in 1923. The building to the right is the Vesey wing and houses classrooms. *Courtesy Board of Trustees Whitney Institute.*

Pearman, John Newbold Smith, Edwin Robert Zuill, Arthur Outerbridge, Algernon Rees Outerbridge, Herbert Albouy Peniston and William Hugh Peniston, plus Daniel Robert Tucker who was described simply as a gentleman.

The Smith's Parish Friendly Association was formed to oversee the building of the school with the Reverend George Tucker as chairman and Jeremiah Scott Pearman as secretary. Progress was delayed by the storm of August 29, 1880, which destroyed the partially completed building. It was finished through the generous contributions of William and Frances Mary Whitney of nearby Villa Mont Clare and Villa Monticello (*see chapter 8*). Frances Whitney also left an endowment legacy of US$10,000 to be used towards repairs and maintenance.

The school finally opened its doors as Whitney Institute in September 1884 with 17 students, all white. Its first teacher E.C. Pfeiffer from New England only lasted a few months. He was replaced by Reginald Aubrey Fessenden when the school reopened in September 1886. Reginald Aubrey Fessenden (see *Hamilton Parish*) was to become a pioneer in radio science.

Reginald Fessenden was succeeded by Alfred Hedley Cotton and then in 1890 James Carters McLaughlin (*see chapter 4*) began his long association with the school which lasted, with one interruption, until his death in 1929. An assistant teacher, Florence B. Peniston, was hired in 1891 and by January 1898 the school had 75 pupils.

The Tower building provided an auditorium for concerts, dances and other community events and has been added to over the years. In 1901 Jeremiah Scott Pearman donated a clock which is said to have come from the estate of William Pitt, although whether it was from the estate of William Pitt, the first Earl of Chatham, or his son William Pitt the younger, both of whom were British prime ministers, is not known. The clock was placed in memory of John William Richard Pearman, a former trustee and father of Jeremiah Scott Pearman. The Tower was adapted to house the clock and a bell. The clock is still in place.

In 1923 two verandahs, designed by architect and surveyor William Downing Wilkinson, known as Bill, were added to the east and west side of the Tower building. They were donated in memory of the two sons of the Reverend George Tucker who died within two weeks of each other in Flanders during the First World War. Bill Wilkinson, who trained in Toronto in Canada, also designed Cedar Grove on Trinity Church Road and the tower and spire at Holy Trinity Church in Hamilton Parish (see *Hamilton Parish*). Numerous additions have been made to the school complex over the years to bring it to the level it is today when it serves about 350 pupils.

Having built a school for the white children, the vestry of St. Mark's now turned its attention to one for the black children of Smith's Parish. This was at a time when education in Bermuda was segregated. The two Sunday Schools were to remain separate until 1963.

Smith's School Room or **Flatts Mission Hall** was built in 1903 halfway down Flatts Hill on land owned by the rector, the Reverend George Tucker, who lived in neighbouring Palmetto Grove (*see chapter 8*). It was 50 feet by 20 in Gothic revival style with a gable roof and pointed arch windows and doors and strip pilasters on its corners. The land was given, according to the terms of the Reverend Tucker's will, in trust "to permit the coloured church people of Smith's Parish . . . to use the said building as a Sunday School and for a Day School".

The first teacher was William Nathaniel Adolphus Percival who had been at Cripplegate School from 1900 to 1903 (see *Hamilton Parish*).

In 1963 the Sunday Schools from the Smith's School Room and from Whitney Institute moved to St. Mark's Parish Hall and the School Room was leased by Government as a temporary post office while the Flatts Post Office

Staff and pupils of Whitney Institute in 1945 when the headmaster was J.M. Rosenwarne and fees averaged about £8 a year. *Beautiful Bermuda, Frank R. Bell, tenth edition 1947, Beautiful Bermuda Publishing Company, Inc., New York, page 256.*

The Italianate style Tower building of Whitney Institute with its clock and bell tower presents an imposing presence on Flatts Hill. It is used for administrative offices with a library upstairs.

The old Smith's Parish Watch House, or parish lockup, stands on Middle Road immediately east of the Flatts Post Office. It originally consisted of two separate buildings joined by a wooden bridge but was badly damaged in a fire in April 1899. It was renovated in 1936.

G   **R**

GOVERNMENT NOTICE

The Royal Gazette and Colonist Daily, May 17, 1922.

was rebuilt next to Whitney Institute.

The School Room was somewhat dilapidated by 1971 when it was rented by Charles Zuill and Desmond Fountain as an artists' studio. It was purchased by sculptor Desmond Fountain in 1975 and converted into a home known as Minstrels' Gallery which retained the Gothic revival character of the original Smith's School Room.

A Watch House, or parish lock-up, still stands on Middle Road immediately east of the Flatts Post Office. It is a small somewhat unusual two storey structure and at one time consisted of two separate buildings each with a chimney and joined at the upper level by a wooden bridge. The building to the west, nearest the Post Office, is the larger of the two and has the biggest chimney.

It is not known why there were two buildings. The larger may have provided accommodation for the parish constable or may have served as a poor house, as care of the indigent was one of the responsibilities of the parish vestry.

The Watch House was badly dam-aged by a fire set by an arsonist on April 26, 1899, and may have stood derelict and roofless for some time because it is drawn in outline only on the Savage map surveyed from late 1897 to 1899.

There are reports of an inquest into the cause of the fire in *The Royal Gazette* of May 2 and 9, 1899. Neighbours Clarence Darrell of Clarendon and Arthur Outerbridge of Dean Hall (*see chapter 7*) were first on the scene but found it impossible to save the burning section of the building. The fire occurred in the western portion and to prevent it spreading to the eastern part "Mr. Darrell cut down the bridge".

The inquest concluded, "That on the morning of the 26th day of April 1899, one of the two buildings known as the Watch House or Poorhouse in Smith's Parish, was set on fire by some person or persons unknown; and the jury is unable to find any evidence as to who committed the arson, or who is suspected of having committed, or attempted to commit, such arson."

The Flatts Watch House was built on land donated in 1834 by the Worshipful Francis Peniston of Peniston's, now Magnolia Hall (*see chapter 6*). One hundred years later, in March 1934, the Smith's Parish Vestry conveyed to the Government "the parcel of land with the building known as the Watch House". It was renovated in 1936 for use as a Petty Sessions courthouse when the interior was converted to a single space. It is now used for meetings of the Smith's Parish Council and other parish organisations.

The Flatts Watch House was one of at least two such neighbourhood lock-ups in Smith's Parish. A second one at Devil's Hole stood on a small jib, or triangular, lot west of the junction between Harrington Sound Road and Knapton Hill near Winterhaven Farmhouse (*see chapter 9*). It was damaged by the hurricane of 1895 but was still in existence until about 1978.

The people of Smith's have always exhibited a strong community spirit which is exemplified in the many fine buildings, religious, educational and practical, constructed to serve the parish. The land on which these buildings stand was most often donated and the money to construct them raised by the people of the parish. 🌴

Minstrels' Gallery on Flatts Hill was built in 1903 as the Smith's School Room or Flatts Hill Mission Hall in Gothic revival style. It was converted into a residence in the 1970s.

Glossary

ABUTMENT • Solid masonry used to counteract the thrust of an arch or vault.

ARCHITRAVES • Linear ornamental mouldings and bands that surround a window, door or other opening. The lowest element in an entablature.

ARTS AND CRAFTS • A late 19th and early 20th century taste for design emphasising hand workmanship and based on the study of regional traditions. William Morris (1834-1896) was the greatest English exponent.

ATRIUM • A rectangular shaped open patio around which a house is built. The central open area of a Roman house.

BAKE OR BREAD OVEN • A masonry chamber used for baking, usually located or adjoining a kitchen fireplace.

BALUSTER • A short pillar that supports the handrail and encloses the side of a staircase.

BAY • The division of the façade of a building into discrete units based on the number of openings. A house with four windows and a door would be described as a five bay building.

BAY WINDOW • An angular or curved projecting window.

BEAD • A small round moulding.

BEAUX ARTS STYLE • Elaborate planning as fostered by the École des Beaux Arts in late 19th century Paris, France, based on study of old-world architecture, primarily classical.

BED CHAMBER • A room furnished and used primarily for sleeping.

BOLECTION • A moulding that projects beyond the face of an adjoining frame or panel, often used to frame fireplaces in Bermuda.

BRACE • A subsidiary timber set diagonally to strengthen a timber frame.

BRACKET • Projecting wooden or masonry support members, sometimes decorated.

BUNGALOW • A detached single storey house in its own plot of land, originally used for simply constructed dwellings with verandahs for English officials in India and later for similar buildings, often with broad gables and porches, built in England and America.

BUTTERY • A service room for the storage of household provisions and implements for food preparation. Surviving Bermuda butteries are detached and generally have a pointed roof.

BUTT HINGES • Simple hinges with rectangular leafs attached to the edge of a door leaf and rebate or a doorframe.

BUTTRESS • A masonry support that gives additional strength to a wall.

CAMBER • A slight upward curve in a horizontal beam.

CHAIR OR DADO RAIL • A wooden moulding on an interior wall at the height of the back of a chair.

CHAMBER • A room generally used to designate a sleeping space.

CHAMFER • A bevel or thin oblique surface formed by cutting off a square edge. Summer beams in refined Bermuda spaces are often chamfered.

CHANCEL • That part of a church containing the altar.

CHIMNEY SHAFT • The upper part of a chimney.

CHINESE RAILING • A railing incorporating Oriental inspired motifs, usually rectangular pieces assembled like a fret.

CHOIR • The part of a church where divine service is sung, usually part of the chancel with pews or stalls for the singers.

CLOSED STRING STAIR • The outer edge of a stair is known as a string. If the edges of the treads and risers are enclosed, it is known as a closed string stair.

COLLAR BEAM • A horizontal cross beam in a roof that ties a pair of rafters together at a level above the wallplate.

COOKROOM • A space where food is prepared, a kitchen.

CORBELLED • The projection of masonry, sometimes in a stepped series.

CORNICE • A horizontal moulded projection crowning the wall. It is the top element in an entablature.

COVE • A moulding with a concave profile.

CROSSETTE • A lateral projection of an architrave moulding at the head of a lintel used in classical design, found most commonly in door and window surrounds and chimneypieces. The projection is also known as an ear.

CRUCIFORM HOUSE • A modern term designating a building with an enclosed porch projection at the front, two rooms per floor in the main block and a rear wing often containing a stair, and or a third room.

CUPOLA • A polygonal or circular projection at the centre of a roof, used for observation, a belfry or as an eyecatching terminus on a pretentious building.

CYMA • A double curved moulding with an S-shaped profile.

DENTIL • A small rectangular block closely set in a row. Part of a cornice.

DORIC • A classical order characterised by a plain capital or head and heavily fluted columns.

DOUBLE PARLOURS • Pairs of entertaining rooms linked by wide doorways; were increasingly common among fine 19th century Bermuda houses.

DOUBLE PILE • A double pile dwelling is two rooms deep, from front to rear.

EASTLAKE, CHARLES (1836-1906) • Architect, furniture designer and writer. Born in Plymouth in England but his writing was particularly influential in the US.

ENCLOSED EAVES • A manner used in Bermuda from about 1830 to 1930 whereby the rafter feet at the eaves were enclosed in masonry mouldings. Regained popularity in the 1990s.

ENTABLATURE • The upper part of a classical order consisting of architrave, frieze and cornice.

FAÇADE • The principal face or front elevation of a building.

FANLIGHT • A semi-circular window over a door, often with radiating glazing bars suggesting a fan.

FLEMISH GABLE • A gable end decoratively scalloped or otherwise shaped and raised slightly above the roof level.

FOYER • An entrance space between the outside and inside rooms of a building, often used in a theatre. A small lobby.

FRAMING • The timber structure of a building.

GABLE • The vertical triangular section of wall at the end of a pitched roof between the eaves and the ridge.

GARRET • A room within the roof space of a house used for living or working.

GEORGIAN STYLE • Strictly 1714-1830 but in Bermuda the style arrived later for general use. Characterised by symmetry and balance.

GINGERBREAD • A popular term for decorative woodwork, usually fretwork.

GOTHIC • A style of architecture popular in Europe from the 12th to the 16th century, characterised by the use of the pointed arch, ribbed vaulting and buttresses.

GOTHIC REVIVAL • A revival of the Gothic style influential among Bermuda churches in the late 19th and early 20th century.

GREEK REVIVAL • A revival of Greek classical architecture, influential in Bermuda in the second half of the 19th and early 20th century.

H-HINGE • A wrought iron hinge made with two parallel legs in the form of an H and joined in the centre by a knuckle. Called a side hinge in the 18th century.

HALF-ROUND TRANSOM • A fanlight.

HALL • The principal multipurpose room of a dwelling.

HEAD • The uppermost member of a structure.

HIP ROOF • A roof with four sloping sides.

HL-HINGE • A variety of H-hinge with a horizontal leg either at the top or bottom of the vertical leg that is attached to the door or shutter.

IONIC • One of the five orders of classical architecture, more elaborate than Doric.

ITALIANATE OR ITALIAN VILLA STYLE • An architectural style characterised by asymmetrical composition, square towers and generous verandahs. Popular for rural and suburban houses in 19th century Britain and US and used in Bermuda and elsewhere on symmetrical buildings.

JAMB • One of the vertical sides of a doorway, window or other wall opening.

JOINED STOOL • Backless seating with four legs and stretchers, mortised and tenoned together.

JOISTS • Horizontal timber beams that support floorboards or a ceiling.

KEYSTONE • Wedge shaped stone used at the apex of an arch, or centre of a flat head. Placed above many Bermuda windows.

KICK RAFTER • A short extension at the bottom of a rafter used to extend the eaves.

KNEE • A right angled corner brace at the top of masonry walls.

LANCET WINDOW • A tall narrow window with a pointed arch.

LATH • A thin strip of wood used in roofing, placed at regularly spaced intervals across the rafters and carrying slates.

LATH AND PLASTER • Thin strips of wood used in walling and nailed to frames with gaps used as a base for plaster.

LEAF • One of two or more wooden, moving parts of a door or shutter. Plural leaves.

LIME WASH • A simple type of matt paint made from slaked lime and water. Colours are obtained using alkali-resistant pigments, particularly metal oxides from natural earths.

LOBBY • A small hall or corridor connected with a larger room or series of rooms and used as a passageway or waiting space.

LUG • The lip on the underside of a tile.

MASONRY STRAP • A bead or projecting masonry.

MODERNISM • A 20th and 21st century idiom concerned with functionalism and new technology, rejecting most ornament and aspiring to create new solutions for architecture and urban design. It is characterised by asymmetrical compositions, mass produced materials and open plan interiors.

MORRIS, WILLIAM (1834-1896) • English designer, poet and political theorist who influenced architects through designs for furnishings for his firm Morris & Co., the founding of the Society for the Protection of Ancient Buildings (SPAB) and the architecture of his own house, Red House, designed by Philip Webb which inspired the Arts and Crafts style using traditional building crafts and local materials.

MORTICE • A recess, socket or hole cut into a piece of timber or other material to receive a tenon.

MOULDING OR MOLDING • A decorative band applied or cut into a surface, often obscuring a joint between pieces.

MUNTINS • Small moulded bars of wood that hold the edge of glass panes in a window sash.

NEOCLASSICAL • Revival of largely domestic Roman decorative motifs, particularly influential in Bermuda woodwork after about 1780.

NEWEL • A post that forms the support and axis of a stair.

OUTLET • A term used in Bermuda for a small peripheral room, often at the rear of a house and used for storage space as well as sometimes having a bed.

OVOLO • A wide convex moulding stepped at the top and bottom.

OXFORD MOVEMENT • A high church revival movement in the Church of England led by Oxford clerics dissatisfied with the decline of church standards. It started in 1833 and stressed the historical continuity of the church, its standards and ceremony.

PALLADIAN • Design incorporating temple fronts and three-part centrally arched windows, after the Italian Renaissance classicist architect Andrea Palladio (1508-1580).

PARAPET • A low protective and sometimes decorative wall enclosing the edge of a roof.

PARLOUR • A multipurpose entertaining and family sitting room located on the principal floor, secondary to the hall.

PASSAGE • A long narrow space providing access to various rooms or parts of a building.

PEDIMENT • A low triangular gable with a horizontal cornice and raking cornices.

PEG • A wooden pin driven through a hole in order to hold two or more parts of a structure together. Also used for hanging clothes, sometimes in passages and closets.

PIER • A vertical masonry support, usually square or rectangular.

PILASTER • A flat rectangular column attached to a wall.

POCKET DOOR • A door that slides into a pocket, or specially constructed space inside the wall.

PORCH OR STOOP • A covered entrance to a building, enclosed or semi-enclosed. See stoop.

PRE-RAPHAELITE • This style of painting and glassmaking is characterised by exaggerated attention to detail in work by a group of artists formed in London in 1848 which espoused a closer study of nature and of method and spirit of artists before Raphael (1483-1520).

QUOIN • Articulated corner stones. Rusticated quoins were stones or stucco projecting beyond the surface of the wall, generally with bevelled edges.

RABBET (REBATE) • A long recess or groove that receives a door leaf or window sash. Some early Bermuda doors lack rabbets.

RAFTER • The sloping timber used to support the roof.

RAFTER FEET • Lower ends of rafters.

REED • A small convex moulding.

REFINED SPACE • The most elegant spaces in a house, usually those used for entertaining.

RIDGE • The upper edge of two sloping surfaces of a roof. The apex of a roof.

ROMAN CLASSICISM • A style of architecture where the wall is the essential element, built up with the use of rounded forms, such as the arch, vault and dome, and decorated with porticos and colonnades.

RUSTICATED • Stonework that had deep sunk joints between blocks to create a bold effect. Quoins are rusticated corner blocks.

SASH WINDOW • A window with glazed sashes that slide up and down, one in front of the other.

SHEATHING • Boards nailed to wall studs or rafters to provide a base for the finished covering or left as an exposed surface.

SHED ROOF • A roof which slopes one way only, used for verandahs and minor additions.

SHINGLES • Thin pieces of wood overlapping to provide a rainproof finish for a roof or wall.

SLATE • The Bermuda term for limestone slabs used as roof covering.

SOFFITT • The exposed underside of an arch, balcony, beam or other architectural element.

SPINDLE FRIEZE • A decorative band below the cornice with turned elements forming a railing or screen at the top of a porch.

STACK • The upper shaft of a chimney.

STOOP • A raised uncovered platform before the entrance of a house approached by means of steps.

SUMMER BEAM • A large horizontal beam spanning space and supporting joists. Also called a bridging beam.

TIE BEAM • The principal transverse framing member connecting the front and rear wallplates.

TRAMMEL BARS • Iron or wood bar used to suspend pots or kettles in a fireplace.

TRANSVERSE • Lying in a cross direction, front to back rather than end to end.

TRAY CEILING • A modern term for a raised ceiling with plaster carried along the underside of rafters up to their collars.

TRUSS • A rigid triangular roof framework for spanning between two load bearing walls.

VAULTED • An arched ceiling or roof.

VERNACULAR ARCHITECTURE • Traditional local style of building.

VERNACULAR REVIVAL • The return to traditional Bermudian architecture beginning in the 1920s and 1930s.

VICTORIAN STYLE • A popular and loose designation for several 19th century styles, including Gothic and Italianate. Styles are generally flamboyant.

WALLPLATE • A horizontal longitudinal member placed on top of a wall to support the rafters, traditionally timber.

WHITEWASH • A finish composed of slaked lime and water. It was the earliest finish on the outside and interior of Bermuda buildings. See lime wash.

ZIGGURAT • A rectangular tower in the form of a pyramid built in diminishing stages.

Sources: Department of Architectural Research, Colonial Williamsburg Foundation; *An Illustrated Glossary of Early Southern Architecture and Landscape*, ed Carl R. Lounsbury; *Bermuda's Architectural Heritage: Sandys*; *Old House Dictionary*, Steven J. Phillips; *The Visual Dictionary of American Domestic Architecture*, Rachel Carley; *The Anatomy of a House*, Fayal Greene; *The Penguin Dictionary of Architecture*, John Fleming and others; *Shorter Oxford English Dictionary*, 3rd edition, editor C.T. Onions.

Verdmont: Inventory of John Dickinson
December 14, 1714

An Inventory and Appraisment taken and made the day and year above written of the Goods Chattels and Psonall Estate of Mr. John Dickinson late of Smiths Tribe Deced. by us who names are here unto Subscribed.

Viz

In the Hall

	£.	s.	d.
To 1 Oval Table	2	15	0
To 1 Do Lesser	2	0	0
To 1 Small Do	1	5	0
To 1 Settle	2	10	0
To 1 Couch and Furniture	1	10	0
To 1 Doz.Cain'd Chairs	6	0	0
To 1 Large looking Glass	3	0	0
To 12 Picktures all at	6	0	0
To 2 Small hand Guns	2	10	0

In the Parlour

	£.	s.	d.
To one Low bedstead bed and Furniture	4	0	0
To one Large Cedar Chest with Lock and Key	2	0	0
To one Smaller Do.	1	15	0
To one Cedar Press	4	0	0
To one Chest Draws	2	0	0

	£.	s.	d.
To one Woren Trunk	-	6	0
To one Small Table wth Draws	1	0	0
To one Less Do.	-	10	0
To two Arm'd Chairs with Cushions	1	0	0
To one High and three low Bass chairs all at	-	15	0
To one Cabinett	1	5	0
To 1 Looking Glass	1	5	0
To 1 Pair Tables etc	-	8	0
To Parcell of Books	10	0	0
To 1 Woren Cain'd Chair	-	3	0
To 1 Pair and irons	-	8	0
To 1 Watch	5	0	0
To 2 Peices Chinz qt. 36 yds	5	0	0
To 1 Small Case of Knives	-	5	4
To 1 Pair money Scales & Weights	-	10	0
To one Large Ditto	-	10	0
To 2 Do. Smaller	-	10	0
To 19 Glasses	1	10	0

	£.	s.	d.
To 11 yds Fustain at 2/8 pr. yd.	1	10	0
To Earthen ware	0	8	0
To 229 ounces Plate at 6/10 pr. ounce	78	4	0

In the Northermost Chamber

	£.	s.	d.
To Severalls all praised at	50	0	0

In the Dining Room

	£.	s.	d.
To 5 Brass Candle Sticks	1	10	0
To A Ceder Chest	-	10	0
To 1 Deal Do.	-	10	0
To one Small Table	-	10	0
To 10 Woren Bass Chairs	2	0	0
To Chocolatt Stone & Pin	-	10	0
To 6 Pair Smoothing Irons	1	0	0
To 1 Bell mettle Spice morter & Pestle	-	8	0
To 1 Standard and Joyn Stoole	-	2	0
To the Leafe of a woren Table	-	5	0
To 1 Pair Bellows and Tongues	-	2	8

Continued...

Inventories: Explanatory Notes

Standardised spelling is a modern requirement. Variations in spelling were common throughout the period covered by these inventories. If a word appears unfamiliar, attempt to say it and then consider how you would spell it. Some of the less familiar terms are given below.

Aloes tub: A tub used to boil aloes to make purgative medicine.

Bushel: A dry measure equivalent to 8 gallons.

Chafing dish: A utensil for keeping food warm.

Close chair and pan: Commode or chamber pot consisting of a pan enclosed in a box to keep the smell in.

Counterpane: A quilted coverlet.

Damask: A patterned, solid coloured fabric with figures in warp faced satin and background in weft faced satin weave. The pattern is created by the difference in light reflection between the warp faced and weft faced areas.

Diaper: Twilled white linen cloth woven with geometric patterns, used as towels or napkins.

Dimity: A stout cotton fabric, woven with raised stripes usually employed undyed for bed coverings and bedroom hangings, and sometimes for garments.

Do: Ditto, as above.

Dowlas: Coarse linen calico fabric, sackcloth, probably for clothes for the slaves.

Fustian: A fabric made of a blend of cotton and linen.

Doz: Dozen, 12.

Gallipot: A small glazed earthenware jar used to hold ointments or medicine.

Guglet: A vessel, or juglet, similar to an unlipped jug.

Hambrois sheets: Hamborough, a fine woolen cloth originating in Hamburg.

High chairs: High backed chairs.

Hogshead: A cask with variable volume measure, eg 54-60 galls rum.

Holland sheets: A fine textile, originally imported from Holland, made of linen and cotton glazed with oil and starch, used for luxury sheeting.

How: Hoe.

Huckaback: Stout linen or cotton fabric with rough surface, for towels.

Lanthorn: Lantern or portable light, which might be carried on a stick, with metal walls and panels of horn enclosing a candle.

Marcella/Marceils Marseilles: A heavy, corded cotton fabric with a pattern woven in the goods; usually white, it resembled hand quilting. Used primarily for bed coverings from the late 18th to the early 20th century also used for petticoats and vesting in the mid 19th century.

Oznabrigg Osnaburg: A coarse, durable cloth used to make loose fitting work clothes for slaves. Named from Osnabruck, a town and district in North Germany, noted for its manufacture of linen.

Peck tub: A vessel or dry measure equivalent to 2 Imperial gallons.

Pile Tray: Mould for striking coins.

Pillowbere: Pillow case.

Pnywt: An alternative abbreviation for pennyweight. See Troy weights.

Porringer: A small basin, probably with a lid, from which soup or children's food was eaten.

Princes linen: A corded linen cloth.

Puncheon: A large cask with a varying capacity, eg 90-100 galls rum.

Sconce: A lantern, or candlestick with a screen to protect the light from wind and with a carrying handle.

Shapes: Moulds.

Snuffers: Scissors for putting out candles and trimming their wicks, with a case.

Spud: A digging or weeding instrument with a narrow blade.

Tieles: Tiles.

Troy weights: Traditional British standard of weights for precious metals, ie 1 pound (lb) = 12 ounces; 1 oz = 20 pennyweights; 1 pwts = 24 grains.

Truckle bedstead: A low bed running on small rollers or wheels which could fit under a standing bed when not in use.

Waiter: A salver or small tray.

In the Chamber over the Hall

To a High Bedstead bed & Furniture Compleat	11	0	0
To 1 Quilt	2	10	0
To 1 Do.	2	10	0
To 1 White Cotton Coverlid	1	10	0
To 1 Do. Fustain	1	0	0
To 2 pair Holland Sheets	3	0	0
To 1 Do. & one odd Sheet	7	0	0
To 3 Hambrois Do.	1	0	0
To 20 Towels	1	0	0
To 2 Damask Table Cloths	2	0	0
To 2 Do. Diaper	3	10	0
To 7 Hugaback Do.	5	5	0
To 12 Pair & one Pillowbers	5	0	0
To 8 Do. Less	-	10	0
To 1 Doz: & 1/2 hugaback napkins	1	7	0
To 1 Doz: Diaper Do.	-	12	0
To 1 Chest Drawers vernished	3	10	0
To 1 Table and Carpet	1	5	0
To Dressing Box & Glass	1	5	0
To 1 Looking Glass	1	5	0
To 10 High Bass Chairs	4	14	0
To Low Do. wth. Cushions	-	8	0
To Glasses and earthenwave	1	0	0
To 1 East India Bowle	-	2	0
To 1 Pair Bellows	-	2	0

In the Storeroom over the Parlour

To one High bedstead and bed and Curtains	6	0	0
To 1 Piece thin Duck	4	0	0
To 1Doz. Knives and Forks	1	0	0
To 5 Pictures	-	16	0
To a halfe Barrell Flowr	2	0	0
To 2 Remnts. brown Ozenbrigs	2	0	0
To Parcell Silver fringe	-	15	0

In the Chamber over the Dining room

To 1 high Bedsted and bed & Furniture Complet	10	0	0
To 151 pound Pewter at 12d. a pound	7	11	0
To A parcell of worn Tin Ware	-	17	0
To Cedar Chest with lock key	1	7	8
To 9 Old chairs	-	16	0
To 1 Small table and carpet	-	12	6
To a Warming pan	1	10	0

In the Room over the Nothermost Chamber

To 1 Bestead bed and furniture Compleat	6	0	0
To 1 Chest drawers	1	10	0
To 1 Small Plain table	-	10	0
To 1 Press	2	0	0
To 2 High cain chairs one low Do.	1	3	0

In the Garrett

To Low bedstead bed and furniture	2	0	0
To 1 old Close Stoole and Bed pan	-	5	0
To 1 Speaking Trumpet	1	0	0

In the Out Store Room and Kitchen

To 1 Copper Kettle and 1 pott	10	0	0
To 1 Old chest with glass and lead etc.	2	0	0
To 20 Worn corne casks and other casks	3	10	0
To 1 Brass kettle little Do.	2	0	0
To 2 Small Cooper kettles	2	5	0
To Wooden ware	2	2	0
To 1 Grid Iron	-	5	4
To 1 Baking Stone	-	10	0
To 2 Iron potts and pott hoocks	2	10	0
To 1 Frying Pan	-	4	0
To 3 Iron Spitts and Andirons	1	0	0
To 1 Chafing Dish	-	5	0

Outroom and Buttery

To 1 Whip saw	2	5	0
To 1 Iron Spudd	0	10	0
To A Servants lodgings	1	0	0
To Severalls in the Buttery	0	14	0
To Firewood and other wood in the Cabbin	5	10	0

In the Field

1 Black Horse	4	5	0
1 Red Do.	2	10	0
1 Mare	2	10	0
1 Stagg	6	0	0
6 Cowes	12	0	0
1 Do. Fatt	3	0	0
2 Bulls	3	0	0
1 Young stear	-	15	0
1 Ewe sheep	-	8	0
3 Calves	3	5	0
2 Goats	-	10	0

Slaves

1 Negro man called Sambo	25	0	0
1 Do. called Prince	30	0	0
1 Do. Robin	35	0	0
1 Do. Peter	35	0	0
1 Woman called Ruth	20	0	0
1 Do. Beck	25	0	0
2 Corn mortars and Pestle iron	1	0	0
1 Worn corn mill	1	0	0

In the Sea

Two Sailed Boat etc.	25	0	0
To 400 £ lead @ 3d. pr. £	5	0	0
Parcell of glass bottles	-	12	0

In the Outlett and 3 cellars – North Side

Parcel single ten nails	1	10	0
Parcel double Do.	3	0	0
Do. eight penny Do.	1	5	0
1 Iron chain	2	10	0
Mallassos	1	10	0
Parcel house timber and lime kiln wood	7	0	0
A parcel firewood	5	0	0
To Do. ordinary timber	3	0	0
To sloop Eliz and Mary	400	0	0
Cash reced of Henry Carneby	40	10	0
Worm and still etc.	12	10	0
2 Doz. Pewter Plates	2	0	0
5 Worne Hows	2	0	0
Iron Mill	3	0	0
	£1074	17	10

Sam Sherlock
Len White
John Darrell

To a debt due from Capt. John Roe of Antigua, merchant, not yet received 136 14 0
To several other debts not reced. the certain quantity unknown

• This inventory was found in the Book of Wills, volume 5, starting on page 51 (W5:51). It was transcribed from the original by Betty Hollis.

Verdmont: Inventory of Perient Spofferth and Elizabeth his wife
September 13, 1733

To	£. s. d.
1 Oval Table	3 0 0
3 Cained chairs	1 18 0
1 Chest of Drawers	5 0 0
Half the books	5 0 0
1 Worn Cained Chair	- 6 0
1 pr. Scales & Weights, old	- 1 4
1 Bras Candlestick, old	- - 6
5 Half worn Bass Chairs	- 13 0
3 Smoothing Irons	- 2 0
1 High Bedstead Bed & Furniture	5 0 0
2 Chests with Lock & Key, ceder	5 5 0
1 Copper Kettle	- 12 0
1 Spit & Andiron	- 2 8
1 Negro man Prince	28 0 0

1 Do. woman Sue	25 0 0
2 Do Boys Both Called Jack	17 10 0
2 Do. 1 Tom & other Sam	14 0 0
2 Cows	6 10 0
1 Calf	- 18 0
1 Bull	3 10 0
1 Horse	5 0 0
2 Shoats (young pigs)	1 4 0
6 Napkins, 1 Table Cloth & 1 Towel	2 9 0
12 Plates	1 0 0

1 Silver Cup ⎤
1 Do. Porringer ⎟
1 Do. Salver ⎬ wt. 36.14.17 @ 5/10 p/oz — 10 14 2½
1 Do. Salt Cellar ⎟
3 Do. Spoons ⎦

1 Saddle & Bridle	3 8 0
1 Looking Glass	1 0 0
1 Frying pan	- 13 6
	157 1 8½

Benj. Harvey
John Tucker
John Wingood

• *This inventory was found in the Book of Wills, Volume 6, on pages 333 and 334 (W6:333). It was transcribed from the original by Ted Cart.*

Verdmont: Inventory of the estate of Thomas Smith
December 1782

In the Hall as follows Vizt.

	£. s. d.
1 Doz. Mahogany Chairs	9 0 0
2 Square Do. Tables	8 0 0
1 Card Table	3 10 0
2 Candle Stands	3 0 0
1 Harpsicord	30 0 0
1 Brass Hearth Tongs and Shovels	7 10 0
3 Prints	3 0 0
2 Looking Glasses	8 0 0
1 Large Picture	- 13 4

In the Parlour as follows Vizt.

1/2 dozen Mahogany Chairs	8 0 0
1 Tea Table	2 13 4
1 Safe	1 4 0
1 Small Round table	- 16 0
2 Square Mahogany Tables	7 0 0
17 Prints	12 0 0
2 Looking Glasses	7 10 0
2 Winsor Chairs	1 10 0
1 Clock	16 0 0
1 Grate and Tongs	2 0 0
2 Spying Glasses	3 0 0

In the Chamber below stairs Vizt.

8 Cedar Chairs	6 8 0
1 Chest of draws	15 0 0
1 Cupboard	- 13 4
1 Dressing Table	4 0 0
1 Small Case of Draws	7 0 0
1 Bed and Furniture	10 0 0

11 Prints	2 6 8
1 Looking Glass	2 13 4
1 Two Arm'd Chair	2 13 4

In the Dining Room as follows Vizt.

5 Small Windsors	1 0 0
3 Old Low Chairs	- 4 0
1 Round Cedar Table	3 0 0
1 Deal Chest	3 0 0
1 Do. Table	- 2 8
1 Cupboard	- - -

In the Chamber over the Parlour

1 Bedstead and Furniture	32 0 0
1 Mahogany Cabinet	24 0 0
1 Looking Glass	4 0 0
1 Two Arm'd chair	4 0 0
2 Mahogany Tea Tables	2 13 4
1 Japan Tea Kettle	- 12 0
1 Japan Coffee Pot	- 5 4
2 Do. Waiters	1 10 0
2 Do. Bread Baskets	- 16 0
1 Tea Box	- 13 4
2 Cedar Stand	- 10 0
8 Prints	3 0 0
6 Mahogany Chairs	8 0 0
2 Windsor Chairs	1 10 0
1 Cedar Chest	3 10 0
1 Mahogany Waiter	1 10 0

In the Chamber over the Chamber below Stairs

1 Bedstead and furniture	12 0 0
1 Old Chest of Draws	2 5 0
1 Mahogany Table	2 13 4
1 Dressing glass	1 16 0
6 Mahogany chairs	4 0 0
2 Small cedar Do.	1 0 0
4 Prints	1 10 0
1 Camera Obscura	- 5 0

In the Chamber over the dining Room

2 Bedsteads and Furniture	10 16 8
3 Mahogany Chairs	3 0 0
1 Cedar Table	- 10 0
1 Looking Glass	- 5 4

Chamber over the Hall Vizt.

1 Bedstead and Furniture	24 0 0
1 Mahogany Cabinet	26 0 0
1 Looking Glass	4 0 0
1 Cedar dressing Table	- 13 4
1 Mahogany Writing Table	1 10 0
6 Mahogany Chairs	3 0 0
2 Arm'd Chairs	3 6 8
2 Windsor Chairs	1 6 8
6 Framed Prints	1 6 8

In the Garrett as follows Vizt.

2 Bedsteads	5 0 0
1 Screen	- 13 4
5 Cedar Chairs	1 0 0

Item	£	s	d
1 Speaking Trumpet	-	6	8
2 Maps	-	-	-
1 Pair Scales	2	13	4
4 Demi Johns	-	10	8
14 Jugs	2	2	0
1 Looking Glass	-	3	4
1 Microscope	1	6	8
1 Lanthron	-	5	4
1 Saddle Chest	-	1	4
1 Bed pan	-	5	4
1 Warming pan	1	0	0
3 Shapes and two Water Pots	1	10	0

Plate

Item	£	s	d
1 Coffee pott	14	0	0
1 Tea Pott	7	13	0
1 Set of Castors	22	0	0
4 Salts with Ladles	3	19	0
2 Butter Boats	10	10	0
1 Waiter	13	0	0
3 Pair plated Candlesticks	5	8	0
1 Soup Spoon	2	16	0
1 Marrow Do.	-	9	0
2 Cases of Silver handle Knives and Forks with 11 Spoons	13	0	0
1 Doz. and eight Tablespoons	18	0	0
2 Doz. and four teaspoons	5	13	4
3 pair of Sugar Tongs, 2 strainers	1	15	0
1 pair of Snuffers and 1 Stand and 1 Ladle	7	0	0

China

Item	£	s	d
13 Dishes	6	6	8
2 Doz. and 11 Soup Plates	5	0	0
4 Doz. and 2 shallow Do.	6	12	0
1 Guglet and Bason	1	0	0
1 Do. without Bason	-	4	0
9 Bowls	7	0	8
4 Pint Do.	-	13	4
2 Half Pint Bowls	-	2	0
1 Turine	1	10	0
1/2 Doz. large Cups and Saucers	-	12	0
2 Quart China Mugs	-	10	0
1/2 Doz. Coffee Cups and Saucers	-	13	4
Doz. Do. without saucers	-	12	0
2 Doz and 4 Tea Cups and Saucers	2	0	0
1 China Tea Pot	-	1	4
2 Slop Bowls	-	10	8
1 Canister	-	1	8
6 Chocolate mugs	1	0	0
1/2 Doz. blue and wte china cups & saucers	-	6	8

Glass

Item	£	s	d
3 Doz. and 11 Wine Glasses	4	0	0
7 Wine and Water Do.	1	3	4
11 Ale Do.	-	13	4
1/2 Doz. Washing Do. with saucer	-	16	0
1 Doz. Do. Do. without Do.	1	0	0
5 Tumblers	-	5	4
1 large Glass with handles	-	6	8
1 Do, Do, without Do.	-	6	8
10 Decanters	4	8	0
2 Cruets	-	4	0
1 Guglet	-	2	8
4 Candle Shades	4	0	0
1 pair Candlesticks	1	0	0
1 Pyramed with Jelly Glasses	3	12	4
1 Do. without	1	4	0

Queens Ware

Item	£	s	d
12 Dishes	4	10	0
22 Plates	-	16	8
5 Fruit dishes	-	4	0
1 Turine	-	16	8
1 Do. small	-	8	0
2 Cups for Pickles	-	2	8
1 Stand for Do.	-	4	0
6 Fruit Dishes	1	6	8

Pewter

Item	£	s	d
16 Dishes	8	0	0
1 Do. melted	-	2	0
3 Doz. and 4 Plates	5	0	0
4 Water Dishes	4	10	0
1/2 Doz. Water Plates	3	12	0
1 Tea Dish with a cover	1	10	0
12 Basons	3	0	0
4 Tin Pans	-	2	8
Pate pans	-	6	0

Linens etc.

Item	£	s	d
1 Pair of holland Pillow Cases	3	10	0
5 Breakfeast Cloths	2	10	0
7 Damask Table Cloths	12	0	0
5 Huckaback Do.	4	10	0
8 Common Do.	2	8	0
1 Large Diaper Do.	2	5	0
4 Pair Holland Sheets	10	0	0
11 Damask Napkins	3	6	0
1 Large Diaper Towel	-	6	8
9 Coarse Do. Do.	1	6	8
3 Cotton Counterpanes	8	0	0
1 Marcells Do.	5	6	8
1 Chints Do.	4	5	0
8 Pair coarse Sheets	5	0	0
2 Odd Do.	1	6	8
2 Pair common Pillowcases	-	4	0
7 Princes Linen Towels	-	7	0
4 Blankets	2	13	0
1 Suit Curtains	5	10	0
1 Old Quilt	1	0	0

Kitchen Stuff

Item	£	s	d
2 Pair Racks	-	16	0
2 Copper Fish Kettles	1	16	0
3 Bell metal Skillets	6	0	0
1 Dutch oven	-	13	4
2 Pair Pot Hooks	-	4	0
6 Iron Pots	4	0	0
6 Trivits	1	10	0
2 Gridirons	-	5	4
1 Dozen Skewers	-	2	0
3 Tea Kettles	2	13	4
2 Pair Steelyards	-	18	0
1 Brass spice Morter	-	13	4
1 Marble Do.	-	10	0
4 Spits	1	0	0
2 Large Brass Kettles	4	10	0
6 Pair smoothing Irons and Stands	-	16	8
1 Pair small Racks	-	6	8
1 Chafing Dish	-	6	0
3 Pair Brass Candlesticks	2	14	0
1 Pair flat Do.	-	6	8
1 Frying pan	-	5	0
2 Deal tables	-	-	-

Wooden Ware

Item	£	s	d
3 Pails	-	16	0
3 Washing Tubs	-	15	0
2 Small Pails	-	4	0
3 Small Tubs	-	16	8
1 Peck Tub	-	4	0

Men Slaves

Name	£	s	d
Bacchus	30	0	0
Daniel	73	0	0
Mell at Sea	75	0	0
Joe	90	0	0

Women

Name	£	s	d
Rachael	35	0	0
Sue	45	0	0
Marian	45	0	0

Boys

Name	£	s	d
Nat	35	0	0
Sam	35	0	0
Davy	28	0	0
Jim	25	0	0
Tom	15	0	0

Girls

Name	£	s	d
Tish	25	0	0
Sall	25	0	0

Cattle

Item	£	s	d
3 Horses	17	0	0
1 Bull	15	10	0
7 Cows	113	0	0
1 Steer	10	0	0
1 Hefer	9	0	0
A Parcel of Paper hangings	1	0	0
2 Glass Cruets	-	3	4
1 China Tea pott	-	1	4
A Parcel of Sash Glass	3	0	0
1/2 Doz. wash Glasses with saucers	-	16	0
2 Old silver Poringers	3	11	4
1 Doz. Knives and forks Ivory	2	0	0
23 Candle Moulds	1	6	8
10 Common Knives and forks	-	10	0
1 pr. Scales and Weights for Gold	1	4	0
1 Grinding Stone	-	8	0
3 Pine tables	1	6	8
4 Hoggs	8	0	0
2 Sheep	4	0	0
2 Goats	3	0	0
200 Tieles	4	0	0

	£	s	d
3 Jarrs	1	0	0
A Parcel of Empty Bottles	1	0	0
2 Morters and one Iron Pestle	1	10	0
3 Hoes and 4 Axes	1	0	0
2 Pitt Axes	-	8	0
1 Grinding stone	-	13	4
1 Hand saw	-	4	0
1 Pine Table	-	2	8
A Parcel of Books	32	6	8
1 Earthen Pott	-	2	0
1 Dust pan and Brush	-	6	8
1 Mahogany Water	-	5	4

At the Custom House

	£	s	d
2 Large looking glasses and sconces	2	13	4
4 Views of London, two of the Glasses broken	1	10	0

	£	s	d
2 Round Tables 1 Mahogany & the other Cedar frame	4	0	0
2 Cedar Candle stands	-	13	4
1 Dozen Cedar Chairs	4	0	0
1 Book Case, Glass doors	22	0	0
1 Clock	13	0	0
2 Large Pieces Mahogany	8	6	0

At Mr. Atwood's, St. George's

	£	s	d
1 Clock	14	0	0
1 Card table	2	13	4
Case of draws, Glass doors	16	0	0
1 Square Tea Table	1	4	0
1 Round Do.	1	0	0

At the Custom House

	£	s	d
A 30 Inch Box and Counter beam & Copper Seals	6	0	0

	£	s	d
A Pile of Troy Weights in a Case 128 ounces			
A Do. weights and grains			
1 pair of 8 Inch neat flat brass Scals and 32 oz Pile Troy 10s. in Mahogany Case	2	10	0
Triangles with Scales and Weights	5	0	0
A Complete Set of the Statutes at large	17	0	0

Appraised by us December 1782
Mich. Burrows
Benjamin Harvey
William Wingood

• *This inventory was found in the Book of Inventories, Volume 1, part 1, starting on page 46 (INV1:1:46). It was transcribed from the original by Betty Hollis*

APPENDIX 4

Verdmont: Inventory of John Green
June 15, 1803

£. s. d.

	£	s	d
1 Set of dinner China	12	10	0
2 Cases with Ivory handle knives & forks and one dozen Silver Spoons	14	0	0
1 Large Mahogy tea Waiter	1	0	0
2 Japan Waiters	2	10	0
1 Mahogany knife Tray	-	6	8
1 Large pine & Cedar Writing Desk	1	13	4
1 Small writing Case	2	10	0
1 Backgammon Table	1	6	8
1 Flute case contg. 2 Flutes	1	13	4
3 Dressg. Tables with 1 Toilet	2	6	8
1 Tea Chest	-	13	4
2 Dressing Glasses	-	10	0
3 Doz. & 2 Wine Glasses	3	0	0
15 Claret Glasses	1	6	8
8 Wine & Water Glasses	-	13	4
8 Quart Decanters	1	6	8
6 Pint Ditto	-	16	8
	48	3	4
2 Water Guglets	-	3	4
17 Irish Glasses	1	8	4
1 Pair plated Candlesticks	1	6	8
1 Pair Tin Do. Do.	-	-	6

	£	s	d
12 Pair Sheets 8 pr only	20	0	0
4 Pair fine Pillow Cases	2	6	8
4 Do. Coarse Do.	1	13	4
4 Damask table cloths	9	17	4
4 Diaper Do.	2	0	0
16 Diaper Towels	2	0	0
6 Linnen Do.	-	2	0
6 Oznabrugs Do.	-	1	0
21 Doiles	-	3	6
1 Bed, Bolster & 2 Pillows without feathers	5	0	0
1 Suit of Curtains	12	0	0
1 Large copper Irish kettle	4	0	0
1 Still	6	0	0
1 Tin Dutch Oven	-	13	4
	68	16	0
1 Eppurn	7	10	0
Some Books	2	12	0
Some prints say 6	12	0	0
One Horse	33	6	8
One Cow	8	0	0
	63	8	8

Negroes

	£	s	d
Brutus a Boy	40	0	0
Prince a Do.	40	0	0
Philis a Girl	25	0	0
	285	8	0

Saml. Trott, Administrator
Jo Hinson
Saml. S. Trott
James Musson Junr.

• *This Inventory was found in the Probate Record Inventories, Book 5, starting on page 210 (INV5:210). It was transcribed from the original by Betty Hollis.*

Verdmont: Inventory of Samuel Trott
June 1835

Inventory of the Personal Effects of the late Hon Samuel Trott of Smith's Parish, deceased. Viz:-

	£.	s.	d.
2 Cotton Quilts	4	0	0
1 India Chintz Coverlit	2	0	0
3 Pair Linen Sheets	2	17	0
3 Damask Table Cloths	5	0	0
2 Breakfast ditto	-	18	4
1 Doz. Damask Towels	2	0	0
1 Suit Bed hangings	-	13	4
2 yds Silk damask of no value	-	-	-
3 Blankets	2	0	0
3 Feather Beds with 3 bolsters &			
8 Pillows	18	0	0
1 Mattress	7	0	0
3 Bolsters ⎤ see above	-	-	-
8 Pillows ⎦	-	-	-
1 Pine Press	5	0	0
1 Cedar Chest of Drawers	3	0	0
2 Bureaus with glass fronts			
at £10 each	20	0	0
2 Mahogany Chest Drawers £4 & £3	7	0	0
1 Clock (old)	-	-	-
6 Bedsteads (Do.) 20/- 40/- 133/4			
& 60/	12	13	4
1 Cot	-	-	-
1 Basin Stand	-	8	4
2 Toilet Tables	-	13	4
1 Toilet	-	-	-
2 Knife Cases	-	6	8
2 Large easy chairs	3	0	0
18 Mahogany ditto	12	0	0
14 Cedar ditto	5	6	8
12 Windsor ditto	5	6	8
1 Rocking Chair	1	0	0
1 Settee	2	0	0
2 Cedar Chests	6	0	0
Lot of Prints and Paintings (in the Garret)	6	13	4
Lot of Books			
2 Old Bibles 30/-			
2 Vols. Johnson's dict. £5			
3 Vols. Chambers Do. £5			
4 vols Blackstone 20/-			
lot old books $2	20	10	0
4 Pier Glasses	8	0	0
1 Floor Clock	2	13	4
2 Card Tables	4	0	0
Set, Dining Tables (in 3 parts)	6	13	4
1 Round Cedar ditto	1	5	0
Lot of old smaller Tables	-	-	-
1 China Dinner Service	7	0	0
2 .. Tea ditto	1	0	0
A quantity China plates, mugs, ⎤			
cups & saucers	3	10	0
& 1 large China Bowl ⎦			
A Lot of Broken China	1	0	0
16 Cold. Glass finger basins	-	13	4
Lot of old Dish Covers	-	6	8

	£.	s.	d.
4 quart and 6 pint decanters	1	5	0
carried forward	57	16	8
Lot of inferior Decanters	-	15	0
Lot of Wine Glasses (4 doz.)	-	16	0
.. Tumblers (1 & 3/12 doz.)	1	0	0
4 Coasters	-	3	4
1 Pr. Shades	1	6	8
Lot Jelly Glasses	2	0	0
1 Silver Coffee Pot			
2 Cruet Stands			
6 Salts			
1 Pr. Snuffers and Stand			
43 Table Spoons 256 oz at			
28 Tea Spoons 6/8 per oz.			
4 Salt Spoons	85	6	8
1 Marrow Spoon			
1 Tea [illegible]			
1 Strainer			
1 Punch Ladle			
1 Soup Ladle			
1 Pr. sugar tongs			
(Plated) 6 handled Knives & forks 0	1	0	
4 3/12 Doz. Ivory handled ditto 0	11	0	
1 Epergne (valued as plated)			
(but if silver 140 oz at 6/8 per oz)	5	6	8
8 Candlesticks	2	0	0
1 Liquor Stand (plated)	4	0	0
1 Rummer	-	5	0
Lot Pewter plates (with warmers)	3	6	8
1 Copper Clothes Kettle	1	0	0
A 1/2 gall: pint & 1/2 pint measures	-	6	8
2 Copper Skillets 50/- &			
Tea Kettle 10/- 1 pr dogs 0	3	0	0
2 Iron Spits ⎤			
2 .. Pots ⎬	1	6	8
Lot Skewers ⎦			
1 Large mortar and pestles	1	6	8
2 Marble do ditto	2	0	0
1 Knife Stone	-	13	4
1 Cedar Table Frame	-	6	8
1 ditto (for milk)	-	5	0
1 Copper Coffee Urn	-	13	4
1 Cedar Horses	-	6	8
1 Japan & 1 wooden Tea Tray	-	10	0
2 Waiters	-	6	8
1 Pair wine coolers	-	10	0
2 Pr. scales and weights £3.6.8 small £2			
	4	0	0
1 Pr. money Do.	-	13	4
1 Horse Net	1	0	0
1 Letter Desk 5/- 1 Bird cage 2/6	-	7	6
Lot old Window Blinds	-	13	4
Old Trunk containing Lot old articles	-	-	-
Lot of Jars & Lot remnants			

of paper hangings   (See paper apart)
Lot Sundries not worth enumerating but
supposed to be of value of (see notes)

	£	s	d
	12	10	0
	£364	2	2

Negroes   Man Tom
          Man Dick
          Man Prince
          Woman Nancy
          Boy Geoffrey

Or the compensation money for the same when
received

Smith's Parish   June 1835.
Sarah Trott
Administratrix

Thomas S.I. Trott
John P. Musson
William R. Peniston

Paper Apart: Hon. S. Trott
Valuation of Articles included in the Item of Sundries not worth enumerating

	£	s	d
1 Broken Grate etc	3	0	0
1 Small Yew Table	1	6	8
1 China Jar (cracked)	-	10	0
2 Knife cases	1	13	4
A Spy Glass — broken	1	0	0
Lot of Miscellaneous articles	5	0	0
	£12	10	0

July 9th 1835
Sarah Trott

Note: There are some family pictures (about nine
in number) which, having been held by the late
Hon. Saml. Trott, may be considered a part of his
Personal Estate; but have not yet been put in the
Inventory; as it is desirable that they should re-
main, with other family pictures at Verdmont.

• *This was found in the Book of Inventories 7,
page 357 (INV7:357).*
It was transcribed by Hilary Tulloch.

Somerville: Will of John Gilbert (fragment)
1699/1700

Bermuda Is
Somer Islands

In the Name of God Amen. I John Gilbert of Smiths Tribe in the Island aforesaid being att Present Sick and weak of Body but of Memory Sound and Perfect thanks bee to almighty God and calling to Remembrance the uncertaine Estate of this Transitory Life, and that all Flesh must Yeild to Death when please God to Call; do make Constitute Ordaine and Declare this my Last Will and Testament In manner and forme Following Revokeing and annulling by these Presents, all and Every Testament and Testaments, Will and Wills heretofore by mee made and Declared Either by Word or Wrighting and this Onely to bee Taken for my Lawful Will and Testament and none Other.

Inprimess; I Commit my Soule into the hands of Almighty God my Saviour and Redemer In whom and by the Merritts of Jesus Christ, I Trust and beleive assuredly to bee Saved; and my Body to bee buried in Such Place as itt Shall Seeme fitt to my Executors hereafter named to appoint; and for the wordly Estate that God hath been Pleased to Bless mee with I Do Give and bequeath in manner and forme Following.

Item, I Give and bequeath unto my Sonn, John Gilbert my now Dwelling house in Smith's Tribe, with all out houses thereon (the Store House by mee built by the Sea Side with Six foot of Ground for Priveledges round about the Said Store House & Also a Convenient Priveledge for Landing Puting in and takeing out of Goods in the Said Store House Excepted) Together with all That Thirty and Two Acers of Land one which the Said house Standeth formerly bought of John Wentworth abutting Easte on Land in Possession of Severaine Vickars or his assignes West on Land Formerly belonging to John Young Senr. or his assignes North on the north Side Sea, South on Land of John Righton or his Assignes and also the Three Acers of Land bought of William Young Ajoying

one the Weste Side of the Said Land to him and to his heires for Ever after my Decease in manner and Forme Following.

I Also Give unto him my Said Sonn my Long Table Nine Joynt Stooles One Joynt Forme belonging the Said Table, the Settell Cubbard Two Chests Two Armed Chares now belonging and Standing in the Hall, one Small Table in the Northermost Chamber, with my Silver Hilted Sword and Belt, my Silver headed Cane, the half of my Wareing apparrell, my Largest Silver Tankerd my Silver Sack cupp, Three Silver Spoones marked I E Provided my Said Sonn John Leaves unto my Sone Joseph Gilbert the Long Table and Cubbard; and the next Best Short Table all now Standing in ye house which my Said Sonn John now Dwells in Devens Tribe

Item I Give and bequeath unto my aforesaid Sone Joseph Gilbert my house and Fourteene Acers of Land in Deven Tribe bought of Samuel Wise Senr. now in Possession of my Said Sonn John Gilbert with the Long Table, Cubard and Short Table above Expressed (the Said Land abutting East on the School Land, West on the Land in Possession of Capt. John Tucker, North on Land in Possession of Samuel Wise Junr. South on the high way by ye Pond) and to his heires for Ever, in maner and forme Following. I also Give and bequeath unto him my Said Sonn Joesph Eighty pounds mony; and all the Debts hee now Oweth mee and the One Moiety or half of the Storehouse and Priveledge above Expressed, the Said Eighty Pounds money to bee Paid within Six Months after my Decease by my Executors here after named, and hee my Said Sonn Joseph to hold the Said half Part of ye Said Store House and Privlidge to him and his heires for Ever; I also Give and bequeath to him, my Said Sonn Joseph my Molatta Woman Called Hanna, Bought of Richard Appowen Senr. and my Other Silver Tankerd

marked as above my Silver Mugge without marke; three Silver Spoones marke as aforesaid and my hand Gun and the other half of my weareing apparell..

Item; I Give and bequeath unto my Daughter Presila Tatem all that Hundred Pounds money Shee had Lately of mee Towards payment of her Land Shee bought of John Bullock; and I also Give and bequeath unto her my Said Daughter the Sume of forty Pounds money beside to bee paid out of my Estate as Yett undisposed of to bee paid within one Yeare next after my Decease or Sooner (if itt may bee) by and att the Discresion of my Executors hereafter named; and I also Give to her my Said Daughter my Silver bason, One Large wrought Silver dram Cupp with three Silver Spones marked as abovesaid,

Item, my will is that Neither of my aforesaid Sonns John Gilbert nor Joseph Gilbert Shall Possess the houses and Lands afore Given untill they shall build and Erect, or Cause to bee builded and Erected one house of Stone on my Share of Land in Smiths Tribe bought of Nicholas Trott Esqr. formerly belonging to Coll: William Sayle one the Dimentions hereafter Expressed one Such a Place on the Said Land as my now wife Mary Gilbert Shall Chuse and appoint.

The hall Twenty and One foot Long the Parlor fifteene foot Long Sixteen Foot Brode Each, Two back Chambers Each forteene foot Squaire & with Entry proportionable; and Porch Twelve foot Square with Celler under the Hall Parlor and Porch, with Two Chimnys Suitable and hearths and one of the Cellers and Chimney most Convenian Fitted for Kitchen, and itt is my Will that my Servants bee Constantly aiding and assisting ....(REST MISSING)

- *This will was found in the Book of Wills, volume 2 (W2,1:115).*

Hinson Hall: Inventory of Samuel Spofferth
February 26, 1771

A true and perfect Inventory of all and Singular the Personal Estate of the honorable Samuel Spofforth Esq. late of Smith's Tribe in these Islands deced. Viz:

At his dwelling House at Harris Bay Vizt.

In the Little Chamber £. s. d.

1 Glass doored Bureau	20	10	14
1 Mahogany dressing Table with draws			
	5	15	0
1 Cedar Chest	4	12	6
1 Bed, Bedstead & red & white callico Furniture	23	2	6
1 Looking Glass with Mahogany Guilt Frame			
	8	0	4
6 Mahogany Cushion Chairs	6	6	8
1 Hand Brush	-	1	4
1 Small hair Trunk	-	11	7½
1 Portmenteau Do.	-	4	4
1 Small red Trunk	-	4	4
1 Smaller Do.	-	3	4

In the Closet Chamber Viz:

1 Bed, Bedstead & blue & white Callico Furniture	7	13	4
1 Old Colostool chair and pan	-	12	0
1 Old looking Glass	-	2	6
1 Small Do. with a Mahogony Frame	-	12	9
1 Old Japan'd Cabinet	-	3	2
1 Old Sconce	-	1	0

In the great Chamber Viz:

1 Bed Bedstead with red & white Chinz Furniture	9	0	0
1 Yellowwood Chest of draws	2	16	3
1 Large looking Glass	1	15	0
1 Do.	3	10	8
1 Bureau	6	2	6
1 Yellowwood Desk	2	10	0
1 Japanned Corner Cupboard	-	7	0
1 Round Cedar Table	-	19	0
1 Do. Mahogony Do.	1	4	6
1 Small Do. Tea Table	-	5	4
6 Cedar Cained Chairs	4	16	0
1 Flower Peice in a Frame	-	6	8

In the Entry Viz:

1 Large Deel Chest	1	4	0
1 Do.	1	4	0
1 Smaller Do.	-	5	8
1 Round Mahogony Table	1	10	0
1 Old hair Trunk	-	3	4
8 Old Leather Cushioned Chairs	3	0	0
1 Old Cedar Bedstead	-	5	4

In the Hall Viz:

3 Large guilt Mahogony framed looking Glasses	24	1	0
1 Large Mahogany round Table	6	10	0
1 Do. Cedar Do.	4	0	0
1 Square Mahogany carved Tea Table	2	11	3
1 Round Do. Tea Table	2	0	0
1 Cedar Chest	5	7	6
18 Cedar Cained Chairs	18	0	0
2 Large armed Do.	2	13	4
1 Pr. Glass Sconces	-	-	-
1 Tea Board	-	8	0

Plate Viz:

1 Silver Tea pott and Stand 23oz. @ 7/6			
	8	12	6
1 Do.Milk pott, 3 Do. & 5 pnywt % 6/8	1	1	8
1 Silver Spoon Tray 3oz 8 pnywt @ 7/-	1	3	9½
8 Do. teaspoons 3oz @ 6/8	1	0	0
1 Pair Do. Tongs	-	7	8
2 Cases contg. 1 doz. Silver handle knives & forks	22	7	0
1 Doz. Silver Table Spoons	12	0	0
7 Silver Table Spoons 16 oz 4 pnywt @ 7/-	5	13	4¾
1 Do. Saucepan	5	6	8
1 Do. Porrenger 8oz 12 pnywt at 5/10	2	10	2
2 Do. Tea Cannisters 12 oz 9 pnywt @ 7/6	4	13	4½
1 Do pair Salts & Shovels 5 oz 6 pnywt at 7/6	1	19	9
1 Do. large Soup Spoons 6 oz 4 pnywt at 7/6	2	6	6
1 Do. Pepper Box 4 oz 16 pnywt at 5/10	1	8	0

China Viz:

1 China Tea Pott and Stand	-	8	4
1 Do. and Do.	-	4	0
1 Doz. & 2 Tea Cups and Saucers	1	4	6
1 Half Gallon China Mug	-	6	8
1 Quart Do. Do. Broken	-	-	-
1 Pint Do. Do.	-	-	8
1 Glass painted quart Do. Crakt.	-	-	8
1 Large China Gallon Bowl Crakt.	-	3	4
2 Quart Do.	1	0	0
1 Pint Do.	-	6	8
1 Doz. China Soup Plates	1	12	6
11 Blue & white Plates Do.	-	13	4
2 Sallad Dishes	-	10	8
2 Small flatt Do.	-	12	0

1 Large flatt China Dish crakt.	-	3	0
1 Bread and Butter Plate	-	1	4
7 Red and white China Plates	-	12	4
1/2 Doz. red and white Coffee Cups & Saucers	-	6	8
2 China Flower potts	-	3	4
1/2 Doz. Water Plates	-	6	0
1 Blue & white Tea pott Stand	-	-	4
1 Do. Spoon Tray	-	-	8
1 Patty Pan	-	-	8

Earthen Ware Viz:

1 White Stone Dish	-	2	8
1 Earthen Soup Do. Broke	-	-	-
1 Large fish Do.	-	4	8
1 Small Do. Do.	-	1	8
3 Large Earthen Plates	-	2	0
Blue and white Do.	-	-	8
4 Half pint Earthen Cups	-	1	4
2 Pint Do.	-	1	4
1 Quart Stone Do.	-	-	8
1 Earthen Teapott	-	-	8
1 White Stone milk pott	-	-	4
1 Green Do.	-	-	6
8 Milk Plates Some Broke	-	1	4
4 Milk Basons Some Broke	-	2	0
1 Large Earthen Gallipott Crakt	-	-	8
1 Creem pott	-	1	0
4 Earthen hand basons Some broke	-	1	4
1 White Stone Mustard pott	-	-	4
1 Stone water Pitcher	-	2	0
3 Stone Sugar Potts	-	8	0
4 Small Do., 1 Smaller Do	-	4	0
2 Large Earthen panns	-	1	8
2 Chamber potts broken	-	-	-
10 Stone Juggs	2	0	0
1 Small Do.	-	2	0

Glass Ware Viz:

1 Doz. and 5 Wine Glasses	-	11	0
2 Punch Do.	-	1	0
2 Wine and Water Do.	-	4	0
2 Small Tumbler Do. one broke	-	-	4
1 Large Do. with a Cover	-	2	0
1 Pint Flint Tumbler	-	1	4
1 Glass Pipe	-	1	4
1 Vinegar and Oyl Glass	-	1	0
1 Doz. Wash Glasses	-	10	0
5 Wash Glasses with Saucers	-	10	0
11 Jelly Glasses	-	1	4
6 Small flowered Tumbler Glasses	-	1	0
9 Do. plain Do.	-	2	4
10 Sellabub Do.	-	3	4
4 Sweetmeat Do.	-	1	4

Item	£	s	d
1 Mustard Do.	-	1	8
1 Sugar Do.	-	2	8
2 Quart Decanters	-	8	0
1 Pint Do.	-	2	0
3 Glass Salts	-	5	4
1 Vinegar Cruet	-	1	0
6 Tea Bottles	-	4	0
6 Pickle Do.	-	2	0
5 Green flasks	-	1	4
10 Pint Bottles	-	1	8
4 Doz. quart Do.	-	12	0
1 Case with 6 2-gallon flasks	1	2	6
3 Common cases with a doz. flasks in each	1	4	0
3 Half gallon Flasks	-	2	0
3 Large 5 gallons Bottles	-	8	0
8 Demi Johns	1	1	4
1 Open mouthed Flask	-	-	8

Pewter & Tin Ware Viz:

Item	£	s	d
1 Large deep Pewter Dish	-	10	0
2 Small Do.	-	9	0
2 Large flatt Do.	-	17	6
5 Smaller Do.	1	3	4
3 Small Do.	-	4	0
1 Doz. flatt Plates	1	4	0
11 Do.	-	11	0
9 Soup Do.	-	9	0
1 Terene	-	10	0
2 Doz. Candle Molds	1	4	0
1 Pewter quart Pott	-	-	8
1 Do. pint Do.	-	1	0
1 Tin Cheese Toaster	-	-	8
2 Do. Cake pans	-	1	4
19 Tea Canisters	-	1	8
3 Doz. Nap bisquet panns	-	1	4
1 Large Tin cannister	-	-	8
1 Do. funnel	-	-	4
1 Plate Cover	-	-	8

House Linen & Bed Furniture Viz:

Item	£	s	d
4 Bed Blankets	3	0	6
1 Large white Quilted Coverled	1	16	0
1 Large Callico Do.	2	0	0
1 Smaller Do.	-	6	8
1 White tufted Do.	1	2	6
1 French quilting Do.	-	7	4
9 Pairs of fine Holland Sheets, 5 pairs Bgt £18.15.0 & 4 Ditto £3.15.0	22	10	0
4 Pair Coarser Do,, 3 pr Bgt £8.2.0 & 1 Do. 6/8	8	8	8
10 Pair Pillow Cases	1	16	0
3 Large Damask Table Cloths	3	4	0
2 Damask Breakfast Cloths	-	18	0
2 Huggoback Table Cloths	-	10	0
2 Diaper Do.	-	6	8
2 Dowlas Do.	1	6	8
2 Princes Linnin Do.	-	8	0
1 Doz. new Damask Napkins	2	8	0
15 Old Do.	1	4	0
5 Huggoback Towels	-	10	0
7 Diaper Do.	-	14	0
6 Princes Linn Do.	-	8	0

Item	£	s	d
4 Ozenbrig Do.	-	5	4
2 Diaper Table Napkins	-	1	8
1 Pc. Blue & white Callico & a remnant to make up a Bed Pillow	16	13	4
12 Doz. Binding for Do.	2	15	0
2 Ironing Blankets	-	2	0
1 Remnant Sail Cloth	1	4	0
1 Sail Duck Floor Cloth	1	0	0
1 New Bed Tick Bolster and 2 Pillows	5	5	0
5 Yds brown Broad Cloth	5	12	6
10 Yds Do.	11	5	0
31/2 Yds superfine light Col'd Do. with 7 Yds Silk for lining and Trimmings	10	1	4
A small Bundle of Thread	-	4	0
10 new Ozenbrig's Bags	1	0	0
3 old Do. Do.	-	-	8
1 Doz. new Ivory Handle knives and Forks	3	0	0
1 Doz. green Do. Do.	2	15	0
1 Carving knife and forke	-	5	4

Kitchen Furniture Etc:

Item	£	s	d
1 large Iron dripping pann	1	0	0
1 Copper Stew pann	-	16	0
1 Bell Mettal Skillet	1	0	0
1 Iron Do.	-	2	0
1 Large Copper Cloaths Kettle	3	0	0
1 Smaller Do. Do.	-	10	0
1 Baking Iron	-	12	0
2 Pair large Bell Mettal Candlesticks	3	5	0
3 Common Do.	-	11	0
1 Chafing Dish	1	4	0
1 Old Do.	-	2	8
1 Warming Pan	1	4	0
1 Waffle Iron	-	6	8
2 Pr. Smoothing Irons	-	4	0
3 Large Iron Potts	1	1	4
1 Small Do.	-	2	0
1 Large Iron Kettle	-	13	3
2 Small Iron Kettle	-	7	0
1 Small frying Pan	-	2	0
2 Iron Spitts	-	2	8
3 Do. Trevets	-	7	0
1 Gridiron	-	-	4
1 Pair hand Irons	-	4	8
1 Iron Tea kettle	-	10	0
1 Copper Do.	-	15	0
1 Do. (broken)	-	5	4
1 Marble Spice Mortar	-	13	4
1 Ligniem Vita Do. and pestle	-	2	8
1 Bell Metal Spice Mortar and pestle	-	5	4
1 large Mortar and 2 Iron Pestles	1	7	10
1 Small hair Seive	-	-	10
2 Large Washing Tubs	-	15	0
1 Large Pail	-	5	4
1 Small Do.	-	2	6
1 Bread Tub	-	4	8
1 Half Bushel Do.	-	3	4
1 Hand Do.	-	2	8
8 Alloes Tubs	1	6	8
1 Large Cedar Kitchen Table on a Frame	-	6	0
1 Do. pine Do.	-	5	0
2 Small Ironing Do.	-	9	4

Item	£	s	d
2 Deal Buttery Do.	-	11	6
1 Mahogany Tea Table (at Mrs. Cobbs)	-	2	10
1 Iron fender	-	3	4
1 Flesh fork	-	1	4
1 Bed Pan	-	10	0
2 Small Sugar Reggs with heads	-	2	8
1 Large Do.	-	2	0
1 Milk Pail	-	2	0
1 Brass Door Lock	-	3	4
2 Marble Image with a Stand	-	2	0
1 Old Brass Coffeepott	-	2	0
1 Large pair Steelyards	1	4	6
1 Pr. large Brass Scales with Weight	-	3	8
1 Case with a pair of Plate Scales and Weights	1	4	0
1 Do. with a pair of Gold Do. & Do.	-	5	4
1 Do.	-	8	0
1 Large Broad ax	-	6	8
1 Small Do.	-	2	0
2 Wood Do.	-	10	0
2 Hatchets	-	3	4
2 Cross Cut Saws	2	10	0
1 Hand Saw	-	6	8
1 Large Vicar Cloaths Basket	-	4	0
1 House Bell	-	7	0
68 Books (most of them old and much hurt)	3	5	6
1 Safe	-	18	8
4 Brass Cocks (one at the Island)	-	10	0

In the Cellar Viz:

Item	£	s	d
12 Cedar Boards	2	0	8
3 Short Do.	-	6	8
2 Deal Do.	-	2	0
1 Small Iron Pott with Turpentine	-	1	8
Some Boat Timbers	-	1	0
1 Pick Ax	-	5	4
1 Empty pipe	-	3	0
1 Small Grindstone	-	2	8
4 Doz. old Iron hoops & some broken ones	-	4	0

In the Store House Cellar Viz:

Item	£	s	d
13 Ps. Timber	2	10	0
9 Mahogony Boards	3	16	8
1 Cedar Do.	-	2	4
18 Ps. Cedar Beams & Stern	26	2	0
9 Ps. Timber under Do.	-	6	0
Part of a Bbl. Tar	-	1	4
Do. of a Bbl. Lime	-	-	-
1 Pc. Sheet Lead	1	1	0
1 Large Stern Post out of doors	3	15	0

At Mrs. Peniston's Viz:

Item	£	s	d
1 High Bedstead	-	12	0
1 Truckle Do.	-	10	0
2 Small feather Beds	6	0	0
1 Old Cedar Press	1	0	6
1 Pc. Dbbl. fortified fourpounders (at Coln. Trotts)	30	0	0
A Box contg. some Match Powder Horns and Cartridge Boxes (in the loft)	-	4	8

At the Island Viz:

Item	£	s	d
10 Squared Rafters only five	-	3	4
2 Ps. Wallplate	-	4	0
4 Beams	-	4	0
4 Cedar Gutters	-	11	0
2 Old pine Boards	-	1	4
16 Ps. of Roughd Ships Timber only Nine	3	1	4
1 Pc. Do. (in the Grounds)	-	3	8

In the Cellar Viz:

Item	£	s	d
1 Pipe with some Vinegar Empty	-	2	0
1 Empty Pipe	-	2	0
1 Iron bound Hogshead	-	6	8
4 5 Gall. Bottles	-	10	8
1 Dim John	-	2	8
2 Old empty Boxes	-	1	0
A few Shingles	-	1	4
Some old Boards	-	2	4
1 Water Jar (in the Buttery)	1	1	0

In the House Viz:

Item	£	s	d
1 Brass Compass	1	4	0
1 Old Cedar Dressing Table	-	6	8
1 Old broken Chair	-	-	-
A Small parcel of Shingles	-	-	-
50 Bricks	-	2	4

In the Yard

Item	£	s	d
1 Old Grindston	-	-	-
1 Pine Board	-	1	4

In the Kitchen Viz:

Item	£	s	d
2 Iron Potts	-	8	8
1 Iron bound Puncheon, 4 Iron hoops	-	6	8
1 Wooden bound Puncheon with one head	-	-	-
1 Old Cedar Cupboard	-	5	11
1 Mortar & Pestle	-	18	0
1 Hatchet	-	2	0
1 Pine Crib	-	6	8
1 Old small Arm	-	8	4
1 Old Cedar Teastor	-	2	8
1 Curry Comb	-	-	8
8 Pitchpine Boards	-	12	4
1 Cedar Pail	-	1	4
1 Old Pewter Plate	-	-	-
2 Gun carriages	3	5	0
1 Worm & Ladle	-	4	0
34 Four pound Shott	1	1	6

At Mr. Bascome's Viz:

Item	£	s	d
1 Barrel 40d. Nailes	16	1	9
1 Bbl Do. not quite full, 1 Bbl 30 d. Do. about a quarter out (sold before appraised)			
8 Ps. Timber llying at Mr. Saul. Tatems	-	10	8
1 Pc. Do. near Do.	-	3	4
1 Pc. near Mr. Boyers	-	5	4

Horses & Cattle Viz:

Item	£	s	d
1 Larger bull	7	0	0
1 Young Do.	1	11	9
1 Stear	3	15	0
3 Milch Cows	11	13	0
1 Heiffer	2	2	6
The White Horse	10	0	0
1 Mans Saddle, Bridle & Furniture	1	10	0

Negros Viz:

Item	£	s	d
1 Negro Man called August at Sea	75	0	0
1 Do. Jacob	56	5	0
1 Do. Lewis	61	5	0
1 Do. John	35	0	0
1 Do. Tom	30	0	0
1 Negro Boy Sam	32	10	0
1 Negro Wench Sarah	47	0	0
1 Do. Ephy	41	0	0
1 Do. Janey	10	0	0
1 Small Boat at the Island	1	4	6
1 Large Do. with Grapnel and Chairs	11	10	0
By estimation 100 Bushels of Lime in the Limekiln at the Island	6	13	4
1 Copper Hogshead Pump	1	0	0
A Parcel of Sawed Stone 75c	5	0	0

Sundry Goods in the Hands of sundry persons not as yet accounted for

Sundry outstanding debts the amount unknown

NB there are sundry small articles which it was the joint desire of the Children might not be added to the foregoing Inventory but might be disposed of by their Mother such as Mr Spofforths Wearing apparel and Watch The grey horse and side saddle and Mr Spofforths Sword and Cain

Appraised by Us

Willm. Wingood

Joseph Jennings

Anthony Peniston

Benjn.Harvey

- This inventory was found in the Book of Wills, Volume 8, starting on page 523 (W8:523) and was transcribed by Joan McKendry.

Source Notes

Research for this book was done by a team of volunteers. The bulk of the work was done in the Bermuda Archives and in the Registry General but extended to the Bermuda National Library, law and bank offices and homes. Each researcher produced a narrative summary of their findings to aid in the writing of the book, as well as an ownership chain and source notes which are published below. Research papers (copies or extracts of deeds, wills, assessment records, newspaper extracts etc.) are kept on file at the Bermuda National Trust.

A chain of house ownership is given at the start of each house source note. A new owner's relationship to the previous one is given when the house has been inherited (see key to family relationships). The date of ownership is listed in the centre column and documentary proof on the right. In some instances the lists begin with the ownership of the land or a prior building on the site, and a 🏠 has been inserted to show when it is thought the present house was built. The ownership chain generally concludes at the end of 2002, not the publication date of this book.

In the case of public buildings such as churches or schools, where ownership probably remained in the same hands, dates of significant change to the structure are listed above the source notes.

Juniperhill Press publications were invaluable for our genealogical research.

Key to Abbreviations in Smith's Parish

1727Ass	1727 tax assessment (available PRO:CO 37/12 Bermuda Archives)		PWD	Public Works Department plans and surveys (Bermuda Archives)
1789Ass	1789 tax assessment (Bermuda Archives, transcribed BHQ 1946 three issues)		RG	*The Royal Gazette* and other early newspapers (Bermuda National Library)
19CCR	*19th Century Church Registers of Bermuda*, indexed by A.C. Hollis Hallett, 1997		RS	Register of Ships (Bermuda Archives)
ADMIN	Book of Administrations (Bermuda Archives)		SM/A1	Smith's Parish Vestry Old Assessment Book 1930-1950 (Registry General)
BA	Bermuda Archives		SM/A2	Smith's Parish Vestry Assessment books 1950-1970 (Registry General)
BHQ	*Bermuda Historical Quarterly*			
BI	*Bermuda Index 1784-1914*, compiled by C.F.E. Hollis Hallett, 1989		SM/CV1	Smith's Parish Vestry book Church minutes 1867-1897 (Bermuda Archives)
C	Customs Records, Inwards and Outwards (Bermuda Archives)		SM/CV2	Smith's Parish Vestry book Church minutes 1897-1955 (Bermuda Archives)
CR	Colonial Records (Bermuda Archives)			
D	Book of Deeds (Registry General)		SM/LT(V)	Smith's Parish Vestry Land Transfer papers 1950-1971 (Registry General)
D/AD	Book of Alien Deeds (Registry General)			
D/OWN	Deeds in possession of owner (or owner of a neighbouring property)		SM/LT(G)	Smith's Parish Land Transfer papers 1972- (Government Records - Registry General)
DBBP	Deeds, Bonds, Bills, Protests (Bermuda Archives)		SM/PVA1	Smith's Parish Vestry book 1750-1811 (Bermuda Archives)
EBR	*Early Bermuda Records 1619-1826*, compiled by A.C. Hollis Hallett, 1991		SM/PVA2	Smith's Parish Vestry book 1812-1838 (Bermuda Archives)
			SM/PVA3	Smith's Parish Vestry book 1838-1850 (Bermuda Archives)
Est	Estate of		SM/PVA4	Smith's Parish Vestry book 1857-1867 (Bermuda Archives)
FN	*Family Narrative*, Hereward T. Watlington		SM/PVB1	Smith's Parish Vestry book Parish minutes 1867-1890 (Bermuda Archives)
FR	Freeholders' Register 1867-1942 (Bermuda Archives)			
INV	Book of Inventories (Bermuda Archives)		VC	Voluntary Conveyances (Registry General)
M	Book of Mortgages (Registry General)		W	Book of Wills (Bermuda Archives). Double dates indicate written/proved
Memorials	*Memorials of the Discovery and Early Settlement of the Bermudas or Somers Islands 1515-1685*, Vols 1 & 2, compiler J.H. Lefroy, 1981			
M/Z	Genealogical notes, compiled by Julia Mercer & W.E.S. Zuill (Bermuda Archives)			Volume number, where applicable, and page number follow abbreviations
				Names of books, newspapers, magazines and ships are in italics
Norwood	'Book of Survey of 1662-3', in Lefroy's *Memorials* Vol 2, Appendix XV. 1981			Names of articles in newspapers and magazines are in quotation marks

Key to Family Relationships

br/o	brother of	gd/o	granddaughter of	np/o	nephew of		
ch/o	children of	gs/o	grandson of	s/o	son of		
d/o	daughter of	h/o	husband of	sis/o	sister of		
f/o	father of	m/o	mother of	w/o	wife of		
gch/o	grandchildren of	n/o	niece of	wd/o	widow of		

INTRODUCTION: READING THE BUILDINGS OF SMITH'S PARISH

I thank all the Bermuda residents who gave access to their buildings and those who worked with us on the measured drawings. Further appreciation is due to Diana and Nigel Chudleigh and Margie and Peter Lloyd for generously housing, entertaining and transporting me throughout the project.

Dell Upton transcribed most of the early Bermuda probate inventories over 20 years ago and donated the transcriptions to Colonial Williamsburg in 2001, making possible the functional analysis of late 17th and early 18th century houses. Additional transcribed inventories were supplied by Smith's Parish researchers. Susan Buck, Cary Carson and Jeff Klee read a draft of the introduction and provided helpful comments.

There were useful interviews including those with Henry Laing, 31 Jul 2004 (Hereward T. Watlington and restoration of Rose Cottage); Yeaton D. Outerbridge, 8 Dec 2004 (changes to Villa Monticello); Aileen Morrison, 16 Nov 2004 (room arrangements at Aldie); Gloria McPhee, 17 Nov 2004 (Clarence Orester Darrell's house and stores); Wayne Jackson, 30 Nov 2004 (construction of 20th century houses); Colin Campbell, 2 and 3 Dec 2004 (Lawrence Smart and Wilfred Onions); William Zuill, 13 Oct 2003 and 14 Jan 2005 (Orange Grove, Somersall, and the Bermuda National Trust); Louis Mowbray, 8 Dec 2004 (Timberly); David Wilkinson, 6 Jun 1991 (Dr Henry C. Wilkinson) and Ronica Watlington, 25 Feb 2003 (Stilwell).

Sources: *Bermuda Cottage Plans*, The Historical Monuments Trust; *Residence in Bermuda* with preface by Hervey Allen; *Of Consuming Interest: The Style of Life in the Eighteenth Century*, Cary Carson, Ronald Hoffman and Peter J. Albert; *The Framed Houses of Massachusetts Bay, 1625-1725* and 'Three Hearths: A Socioarchitectural Study of Seventeenth Century Massachusetts Bay Probate Inventories', both by Abbott Lowell Cummings; 'Household Stuffe: Material Culture and Identity in the Seventeenth Century Anglo-Colonial World', Mary Ellin D'Agostino; *Bermuda Houses*, John S. Humphreys; *Housing Culture: Traditional Architecture in an English Landscape*, Matthew Johnson; 'Temporal Patterning in House Plans from the 17th Century Chesapeake', Fraser D. Neiman; *Another World: Bermuda and the Rise of Modern Tourism*, Duncan McDowell; 'Housing for Planters, Servants and Slaves in the Early Chesapeake Colonies', Cary Carson, 2005; Bermuda Historical Quarterly, Spring 1945, p16 'A Perticular Account of the Inhabitants . . . from 1 January 1697 to 1 January 1698' (house numbers and roofing materials); Report of Governor Day CO37 2:194 BA (population); will of John Gilbert (W21:115,226 1699/1700).

Additional information was provided by the following researchers: Linda Abend (Knapton House, Outerlea, Edward Peniston, Rose Cottage, St. Mark's Church, Stilwell), Ted Cart (Channelway, Channelway Cottage, Somerville, Verdmont), Barbara Hutchings Cooper (George Houston Hutchings), Fay Elliott (Cotswold, Villa Mont Clare, Villa Monticello), Betty Hollis (inventories), Suzanne Judah (Hinson Hall), Margie Lloyd (Glimmerview, Oleander Circle, Winterhaven), Lark Lombardo (Aldie), Joan McKendry (inventories), Cecille Snaith Simmons (Wesley Centenary Methodist Church), Hilary Tulloch (Orange Grove, Somersall).

Edward A. Chappell

CHAPTER 1 SMITH'S PARISH

Smith's Parish

Bermuda's Story, Terry Tucker, p119 (parish jingle); *Sketches of Bermuda*, Susette Lloyd, p33 (parish names); *The Adventurers*, Henry Wilkinson, pp57, 79, 184-185 (Sir Thomas Smythe); *Rich Papers*, Vernon Ives, p393 (Sir Thomas Smythe); Crown Lands Box 458 1872, SM/PVB1 (John Thomas Smith); *Bermuda Islands Guide*, map 16 (height of The Peak); *Marine Ecology of Harrington Sound*, Martin Thomas, pp3-12, *Natural History of Bermuda*, Martin Thomas, pp177-182 (Harrington Sound); *The Visitor's Guide*, J.M. Jones, p70 (Smith's Marsh); *Bermuda Forts*, Edward Harris, pp97, 98 (forts); *Memorials* 1:201 (village or town development); *Memorials* 2:664-671 (number and type of houses); *Rich Papers*, Vernon Ives, p241 (shares of Sir Thomas Smythe); 1761 Roads Act, *Bermuda in the Old Empire*, Henry Wilkinson, p336 (roads); *The Bermuda Railway*, Colin Pomeroy, p95 (railway).

Archaeology: Smith's Parish Uncovered

Bermuda Forts, Edward Harris, pp98-99; 'Found: First St. Mark's Church', M. Kostro and P. Nascar; 'Archaeological Excavations at the Winterhaven House, Smith's Parish, Bermuda', Dwayne W. Pickett, The Colonial Williamsburg Foundation, October 1997.   Researcher: Richard Lowry

On the Side: The Savage Survey

Information on the life and career of Lieutenant Savage came from England. School lists for Haileybury and Army Lists were consulted at the UK National Archive, his obituary found in the *Royal Engineers Journal* from the RE Library, Chatham, Kent, and a memoir from *Who's Who*. Family information and the photograph of the young Arthur J. Savage were generously provided by his grandson, Major P.J.A. Savage, RE, who also worked in military survey.

The background to setting up the Bermuda Survey was obtained from the *Journals of the House of Assembly* and *Acts of the Legislature*. Savage's commission to survey Bermuda, recorded by Henry Wilkinson and Hereward Watlington in Bermuda and in the *Royal Engineers Journal*. Notice of the arrival of the survey team appeared in the *Bermuda Royal Gazette*. The methods used to conduct the survey were taken from the accounts of Savage or his superior officer printed in *The Bermuda Almanack* from 1897 to 1903.

Sources: *Haileybury Register, 1862-1891*, p283; *Haileybury Register, 1862-1946*, p141; Army List, Jan-Mar 1894, p247 and Jul 1895, p786; *RE Journal*, 1933, p294; *Who's Who*, 1932, p2863; *Journals of the House of Assembly*, 1893 Session 2, p98; *Acts of the Legislature, Vol.III, 1884-1895*; *Bermuda from Sail to Steam*, Henry Wilkinson, p908; 'Maps and Surveys of Bermuda', Hereward Watlington, BHQ, Winter 1975, pp65-68; 'Bermuda', C.E.E. Sloan, *RE Journal* Vol 92, p4; *Bermuda Royal Gazette*, 9, 16 Nov 1897, 7, 14 Dec 1897; *The Bermuda Almanack* 1898, p255 and 1900, pp249-254, 266-268 and 1901, p238 and 1903, p243.

Additional information: *Bermuda Forts*, Edward Harris (Major Andrew Durnford).   Researcher: Hilary Tulloch

Chapter 2 Verdmont

Verdmont and Cottage, 4, 6 Verdmont Road

Owner (relationship)	Date owned	Source
Capt (Gov) William Sayle	c1663-1671	Norwood 27, land only
Mary (Mrs Edward) Audley (gd/o William Sayle)	?-1688	D3:162
Nicholas Trott	1688-c1694	D3:162
🏠 (House built by John Dickinson between 1696 & 1714)		
John Dickinson	c1694-1714	D3:162
Elizabeth Dickinson (wd/o John Dickinson) & Elizabeth Spofferth (d/o Elizabeth Dickinson)	1714-1733	W6:327 1733/1733, co-listed 1727Ass
Elizabeth Dickinson	1733-bef1747	W5:48 1714/1714, house & 50 acres
Elizabeth Spofferth Brown (d/o Elizabeth Spofferth)	c1747-1755	W6:327, M/Z, W12a:182 1752/1753, SM/PVA1 1st husband Robert Brown died 1753
Hon Thomas Smith (Collector, 2nd h/o Elizabeth Brown)	1755-1781	M/Z, SM/PVA1, BHQ Summer 1967 p59
Elizabeth Smith (wd/o Hon Thomas Smith)	1781-1789	SM/PVA1, 1789Ass
Hon John Green & wife Mary (d/o Hon Thomas Smith & stepd/o Elizabeth Smith) & Est	1789-1810	BHQ Summer 1967 p59, SM/PVA1, plaque St. Mark's
Samuel Henry Trott (np/o Mary Green) & Est	1811-1830	SM/PVA2
John Henry Trott (s/o Samuel Henry Trott)	1831-1860	SM/PVA2-4, FN pp275-278
Rupert H. Spencer & Est (by purchase)	1860-1876	SM/PVA4, SM/PVB1, W22:291 1868/1868, D28:169
Stafford Nairn Joell (h/o Emma Spencer n/o Rupert H. Spencer)	1876-c1912	SM/PVB1, D28:169, house & 28+ acres
Emma Spencer Joell	c1912-1919	D40:52, W33:193
Lillian Wood Joell & Irene Churchill Joell (ch/o Stafford Nairn Joell & Emma Joell)	1919-1920	W33:193
Lillian Wood Joell	1920-1951	VC2:119
Alan Paul Joell (np/o Lillian Wood Joell) (by purchase)	1951	D59:20
Bermuda Historical Monuments Trust (by purchase)	1951-1970	D/OWN, house & 2.2 acres
(Opened as museum)	1957	RG 22 Nov 1957
The Bermuda National Trust	1970-	Owner 2002

Deeds, wills, assessments, genealogies, maps, previous studies and only a little historical imagination were needed to construct an unbroken line of ownership dating back to Governor William Sayle in 1663. The tenure of Verdmont's builder John Dickinson and his Spofferth/Smith descendants (c1694-1789) and precise description of his properties appeared in wills and assessments; the 50 acre Verdmont portion stretched south to the sea. The names Spofferth and Spofforth occur equally often in the records. For the sake of consistency Spofferth has been used throughout this book. Further assessments and prior studies established and extended ownership to Collector Thomas Smith's son-in-law John Green and the Trott family (1789-1860). Information on the Spencer/Joell years (1860-1951) mostly depended on assessments but Ives' account, 'The Spencer-Joell Family at Verdmont', provided a time saving collation of documentary research; a Spencer division of land in 1876 gave Verdmont a South Road boundary and 29 acres. The Bermuda National Trust was cheerfully cooperative in providing information and its owners' deeds showing the buildings enclosed by a little over 2 acres.

Additional information: *Of Consuming Interests*, Cary Carson et al, 1994, pp631-633 (architectural information and changes); *An Illustrated Glossary*, Carl Lounsbury, 1994, (architectural definitions); *Bermuda in the Old Empire*, Henry Wilkinson, pp63-66 (Amity); 'Administration of Custom Finance', Bermuda Archives Government Records, John Adams, p402; *Bermuda Her Plants & Gardens 1609-1850*, Jill Collett, p29 (plant collection. She gives John Dickinson Letters 1700 Sloane Manuscripts, British Museum 4063 ff 14, 33, 63 as the British Museum reference); Historical Society of Pennsylvania, Philadelphia (John Green letter of Sep 1773 to Thomas Smith); 'Verdmont', Hereward Watlington; *Bermuda from Sail to Steam*, Henry Wilkinson, pp28, 58, 112-118, 216, 219 (John Green), 515, 516 (slaves); *Bermuda Gazette*, 11 Sept 1802 (John Green's death); *Sketches of Bermuda*, Susette Lloyd, pp153, 154 (visit to Mrs Trott); 'The Spencer-Joell Family at Verdmont', Vernon Ives; 'Bermuda Historical Monuments Trust', Hereward Watlington; 'Verdmont', Elizabeth Taylor, *The Bermudian*, August 1939 pp14, 15, 24 & 25 (death of Kate Trott from typhoid, water pump); Bermuda Historical Monuments Trust, Minutes, BA; *The Royal Gazette Weekly*, 17 Nov 1957 (cost of restoration); RG 22 Nov 1957 (opening date). Researcher: Ted Cart

On the Side: William Sayle

Inventory of Colonel William Sayle W1:145 17 Nov 1671, transcribed by Betty Hollis; *Memorials* 2:669 & 670; *Guide to Verdmont, Historic Bermuda House*, undated, pp21 & 22; 'The Legacy of Preacher's Cave', James Ziral. Researcher: Diana Chudleigh

Architectural Assessment: Verdmont: Site and Form

Background research by Ted Cart.

Architectural Assessment: Verdmont: Interior Finish and Evolution

Background research by Ted Cart.

On the Side: Born into Slavery

Inventories and will transcribed by Betty Hollis and Ted Cart: inventory of John Dickinson 1714, W5:51; will of John Dickinson W5:48 1714/1714; inventory of Thomas Smith December 1782, INV1,1:46; inventory of John Green 1803, INV5:210; and Slave Registers of Bermuda, 1821, 1827, 1830, 1833-1834. Researcher: Diana Chudleigh

CHAPTER 3 DOWN COLLECTORS HILL

Introduction

Bermuda Journey, William Zuill, p140 (Collectors Hill); Government Records Documenting Finance and Regulation of Commerce, 402.1-5, BA (collection of duty on imports); *Bermuda from Sail to Steam,* Henry Wilkinson, pp368, 369 (Gilbert Salton); INV1,1:46 (inventory of Thomas Smith).

Greenbank (formerly Watkins house), 23 Collectors Hill

A report by Edward A. Chappell, made following a visit on 21 Feb 2003, is kept on file by the Bermuda National Trust.

Owner (relationship)	Date owned	Source
Joseph Watkins (h/o Winifred Hill) & Est	bef1789-1811	SM/PVA1
Mary Watkins, Ann Homeyard Taylor, Elizabeth Davis, Sarah Watkins, Grace Peniston Watkins (ch/o Joseph Watkins)	1811-1868	Deed 1811 (M/Z 'Watkins'), RG 21 Nov 1867
Marcus Harvey (by purchase)	1868-1883	SM/PVB1
Sarah Jane Harvey (wd/o Marcus Harvey)	1883-1913	W25:176 1879/1884, SM/CV2
Est of Marcus Harvey	1913-1927	SM/CV2
Charles Harvey White (adopted s/o Marcus Harvey)	1927-1947	W25:176 1879/1884, 1/2 land & house, SM/CV2, FR
Charles Wesley White & Isobel I. Harvey (ch/o Charles H. White)	1947-1967	W46:127 1946/1947, 1/2 land & house
Ruth Virginia White & Fay Alfreda White (ch/o Charles W. White)	1967-present	VC15:110 1967, 0.2484 acres & part of house,
2003 joint owner/occupiers		
Sheila Etoile Harvey & Arthur Hamley Harvey (ch/o Isabel Harvey)	1967-1986	SM/LT(V) 0.2484 acres & part of house, W78:214 1962/1965
Sheila Etoile Harvey & Est Arthur Hamley Harvey	1986-1990	W156:24, ADMIN, probate 1990
Sheila Etoile Harvey & Helen Irene Francis (sis/o Arthur H. Harvey)	1990-1991	W156:24, ADMIN, probate 1990
Nadine Helen Francis (d/o Helen Francis)	1991-present	VC55:206 1991, 0.354 acres & part of house,
2003 joint owner		

In the 1789 assessments, Joseph Watkins (died 1813) owned 4 acres and a house in Smith's. This estate was deeded in 1811 to his five daughters (M/Z 'Watkins'). Information on the Watkins family came from the 'Journal of J.H. Darrell'.

The assessments show in 1869 Marcus Harvey (c1831-1883), a planter, owning the house and in his will (W25:176) he left his estate to his wife Sarah and daughter Alice and then to his adopted son Charles Harvey (White) who in his will (W46:127) left half of the estate with the house to his son Charles Wesley White and daughter Isobel Irene Harvey and half to his sons Marcus Harvey White and Alfred Carlington White.

Marcus Harvey White of Devonshire Parish (died 1968) in his will (W88:72) left two lots in Smith's Parish to son Marcus Eugene White and daughter Winifred Pauline White. Alfred Carlington White of Smith's Parish (died 1976) sold to his daughter Joycelyn (White) Darrell the eastern portion of the estate in 1969 (SM/LT(V)103/69) and son Dudley the western portion (SM/LT(V)102/69). Isobel Irene Harvey in her will (W78:214) left her part of the estate on Collectors Hill to son Arthur Hamley Harvey and daughter Sheila Etoile Harvey. Charles Wesley White (died 1969) transferred by deed of gift to his daughters Ruth Virginia and Fay Alfreda (VC15:110) in 1967.

Arthur Hamley Harvey died intestate in 1986 and his sisters Sheila Etoile Harvey and Helen Irene Francis were granted entitlement to his estate (W156:24, ADMIN Probate 25 May 1990). In 1991 the sisters gave their section of the property to Nadine Helen Francis (VC55:206). The house, known now as Greenbank, is jointly owned by Fay and Ruth White and Nadine Helen Francis.

Researcher: Fay Elliott

Cotswold, 21 Collectors Hill

Owner (relationship)	Date owned	Source
Mary Packwood	c1727-1744	1727Ass, land only
Sarah Gibbons Smith (gd/o Mary Packwood)	1744-1804	W12b:128 1744/1746, SM/PVA1
🏛 (House may have been built for Sarah Smith)		
Est of Sarah Gibbons Smith	1804-1805	Chancery Court 101/5:114 (BA)
Benjamin Harvey Morgan & wife Jane (by purchase)	Aug 1805	RG 20 Apr 1805, house & 5 acres
Honora Place (by purchase)	Oct 1805	Also 1 acre 1 rood from father William Wingood
Robert Adams & wife Honora (Place)	Jan 1809	Private papers of Jean Lyles
🏛 (Or house may have been built by Thomas W. Smith)		
Thomas W. Smith (by purchase)	1809-1835	House & 6 acres 1 rood
Isaac Smith (s/o Thomas W. Smith)	1835-1870	W16:34 1835/1836, SM/PVA2
Eliza Smith (wd/o Isaac Smith)	1870-1878	W22:437 1870/1871
Adolphus Smith (s/o Isaac & Eliza Smith)	1878-1908	W22:437 1870/1871
George Ernest Smith (s/o Adolphus Smith)	1908-1950	Subject to life interest of father
Joseph John O'Brien & wife Isabelle Sadie (d/o George E. Smith)	1950-1961	VC5:51 house, shop, store & 5 acres
John W. Butterfield (by purchase)	1961-1965	House & 0.592 acres
Gelston & Madelyn Wood Hardy (by purchase)	1965-1969	SM/LT(V)21/65
Joyce Olive Lusher (by purchase)	1969-1993	SM/LT(V)100/69
Sue Lusher Plathe (d/o Joyce Olive Lusher)	1993-	Owner 2002

The land on which Cotswold was built was given to Sarah Gibbons by her grandmother Mary Packwood, who clearly owned property as she appears in the 1727 assessments, in her will (W12b:128). Sarah married, becoming Sarah Smith, and was assessed in 1803 for a house and land. It is not known when Sarah built the house and it is most likely that she was only a child when given the land. Unfortunately no assessments can be found for Sarah Smith before 1803. She died intestate in 1804 and her real estate was sold to pay off her debts (ADMIN3:259). Benjamin Harvey Morgan, a merchant from St. George's, bought the property for £200 in August 1805 and promptly sold it in October to Honora Place for £270. Robert Adams and his wife Honora Place sold in January 1809 for £320 to Thomas William Smith of Devonshire including 1 acre 1 rood of land given to Honora by her father William Wingood. Thomas W. Smith (1783-1835) was the grandson of Nathaniel Tynes of Devonshire, "one of the celebrated ship builders to His Majesty in the Island" (BI:1423). Thomas' mother Elena, the daughter of Nathaniel, married William Smith who died in 1796. Nathaniel was made guardian of his grandson Thomas after his father died (ADMIN3:81) and Thomas was left money in his grandfather's will (W13:48 1807/1807). Thomas' grandmother Rebecca died in 1808 "struck by lightning while preparing bread and butter for her grandchildren" (BI:1423). Thomas Smith owned Cotswold for 26 years leaving it to his son Isaac (1807-1870) in his will (W16:34). Isaac and his wife Eliza Smith had 13 children (private papers of Jean Lyles) but only five were alive at the time of their mother's death. Isaac left the estate to his wife and then to his eldest son Adolphus Smith (1832-1916). In 1908 Adolphus conveyed the property to his son George Ernest Smith subject to a life interest. George Smith was the first to plant Canary Island bananas (*Life on Old St. David's*, p64). In 1950 George and Jessie Smith conveyed the property to their son-in-law and daughter, Joseph (Jack) and Isabelle O'Brien. In 1961 the house passed out of the Thomas W. Smith family after over 150 years. The property is now only 0.592 acres. Wills, deeds and Chancery Court proceedings were consulted in the research for this house. It was difficult to trace ownership in the Smith's Parish assessments as there were gaps.   Researcher: Fay Elliott

Architectural Assessment: Cotswold
Background research by Fay Elliott.

Tynes Place, 11 A.P. Owen Road (Ap Owen Road)

Owner (relationship)	Date owned	Source
John Tynes Sr	died 1774	SM/PVA1
John Tynes Jr (s/o John Tynes Sr)	1774-1792	W12b:303 1774/1774
Est John Tynes Jr	1792-1794	SM/PVA1
Robert Jones	1794-1797	SM/PVA1
Henry Roberts	1797-1808	SM/PVA1
Est John Tynes Jr	1808-c1816	SM/PVA1
Capt Samuel Williams	c1816-1867	SM/PVA2-4, RG 12 Feb 1828
Capt Benjamin Abraham Williams (s/o Samuel Williams)	1867-1890	D/OWN, SM/PVB1
Matthew Richey Smith (by purchase)	1890-1932	D/OWN, D35:701
Beryl Boorman (d/o Matthew Richey Smith) & estate	1932-1978	D/OWN
Roderick L. DeCouto (by purchase)	1978	D/OWN, M49:440
Larry Thomas & Nancy Suzanne Dennis (by purchase)	1978-	D/OWN, owners 2002

Although the owners were convinced the house was once owned by John Tynes Sr, it was not easy confirming his ownership. In the late 1700s there was a John Tynes living in Devonshire and another living on Middle Road in Smith's Parish. Following the change of owners in the assessments was also very tenuous as the Smith's Parish assessors were not always precise. To underscore the importance of seeing owners' deeds, although Matthew Richey Smith purchased the property in 1890, the assessments continued under the name of Benjamin Abraham Williams until after 1894. The researchers wish to thank Mr & Mrs Dennis for their cooperation and enthusiastic support.   Researchers: Joy Wilson-Tucker & Linda Abend

Architectural Assessment: Tyne's Place
Background research by Joy Wilson-Tucker & Linda Abend.

On the Side: The Hermitage
M/Z44 'Salton' (letter to William Zuill and biographical account of Gilbert Salton by Evan Aubrey Jones); D45:371, 1921 (land transfer between Jeremiah Scott Pearman and Henry Thomas Harvey); Slave Register, 1827, p65 (Elizabeth Tynes).   Researcher: Linda Abend

CHAPTER 4 HEART OF SMITH'S

Introduction
Bermuda Journey, William Zuill, p107.

Somerville, 21 Middle Road

Owner (relationship)	Date owned	Source
John Young	1663-1678	Norwood 25, land only
William Young & Alice Axtell (ch/o John Young)	1678-1689	W1:278 1678/1680
John Gilbert	1689-1700	W2,1:115, 226 1699/1700, M/Z 'Gilbert', land only
Mary Gilbert (wd/o John Gilbert)	1700-?	W2,2:144 1700
🏛 (House built for Mary Gilbert circa 1700)		
Josiah & Elizabeth Smith	?-1732	M/Z 'Gilbert'
Anne Smith (by purchase, no relation to Josiah Smith)	1732-1762	M/Z 'Gilbert', SM/PVA1
John Burtell (2nd h/o Anne Smith, gs/o Mary Gilbert)	1762-1775	M/Z 'Gilbert', SM/PVA1
Capt William Williams (by purchase)	1775-1786	M/Z 'Gilbert', SM/PVA1

Henrietta Williams (wd/o Capt William Williams	1786-1818	M/Z 'Gilbert', SM/PVA1-2
John Harvey Tucker (by purchase)	1818-1868	M/Z 'Gilbert', SM/PVA2-4 & SM/PVB1 Wings added, called Somerville
George Somers Tucker & Louisa Bryan Tucker (ch/o John Harvey Tucker)	1868-1888	W22:302 1859/1868, SM/PVB1
John William Richard Pearman (by purchase)	1888-c1894	M/Z 'Gilbert' & 'Pearman', SM/PVB1, FR
Thomas Heber Outerbridge & wife Mary Eleanor (d/o John William Richard Pearman)	c1894-1942	M/Z 'Gilbert', SM/CV2, *The Bermudian* Sept 1933. Residents from 1888, house & land additions
Bertha Loutrelle Outerbridge, Kate Langdon (Mrs Freer) Cox, Benjamin C.C. Outerbridge (ch/o Thomas H. Outerbridge)	1942-1957	M56:112, property subdivided
George Henry Russell (by purchase)	1957-1968	M56:112, SM/LT(V)53/57, house & 1.736 acres
Robert Fitzhugh Lee (by purchase)	1968-1975	D/OWN
Robert Fitzhugh Lee & Barbara Ann Lee	1975-	D/OWN, owners 2002

Extant wills, deeds, assessments and secondary notes covered most of the house history. Mercer/Zuill notes filled blanks with digests of unattainable original documents, including a lost Outerbridge file tracing ownership back to 1689 (M/Z 'Gilbert'). However a close look at the three surviving pages of John Gilbert's twelve page will (W2,1:115, 226) challenged the familiar story that Somerville is the house he ordered built for his wife. The 1699 will gives construction details (almost exactly like Somerville's) for the house to be built on land acquired from Nicholas Trott. Trott's 1696 deed to Gilbert (D3,1:68) is for a share elsewhere in Smith's. Had Gilbert's instructions been carried out to the letter, Somerville is a model for or of a building that no longer stands, but records of that share (Norwood 23) argue against this possibility. Gilbert owned Somerville's site as well. His widow's discretion as legal guardian of their newborn son (W2,2:145) plus a look at the will's nine missing pages might explain and excuse the executor's disobedience. Conventional wisdom is jostled but not dislodged.

John Gilbert wrote his will 19 Feb 1699/1700. This is actually 1700 in modern dating. He could not have died until 1700.

Josiah Smith, who owned Somerville until its sale in 1732 to Anne Smith, was a descendant of Thomas Smith, a substantial landowner in South Carolina. There was no documentation as to how and when he obtained the property from the Gilbert family.

Anne Smith, known as Annie, may have been the widow of Seth Smith who died in 1732 (M/Z 'Smith':92). Her second husband, John Burtell, was a grandson of Mary Gilbert for whom the house was built.

Additional information: 'The question of the Bahama jurisdiction over the Turk's Islands discussed in a letter to the Honourable Speaker & Gentlemen of His Majesty's colonial assembly of the Bermuda or Somer's Islands, London 1803', reproduced in BHQ, Spring 1944, p21; *Family Narrative*, Hereward Watlington, p234 (Mary Tucker letter); *The Bermudian* magazine, September 1933, p10 (detached kitchen); *Bermuda Journey,* William Zuill, p108 (rubber tree); *The Bermudian* magazine, January 1935, p10, 11 (Dr Outerbridge). Researchers: Diane Price & Ted Cart

Architectural Assessment: Somerville

Background research by Ted Cart.

Rose Cottage, 3 Kilderry Drive

Owner (relationship)	Date owned	Source
Capt Richard Jennings	c1663-1669	Norwood 32, CR5A:144 (Garrod transcription) land only
John Jennings (s/o Richard Jennings)	1669-1684	W1:128 1669/1669
Est of John Jennings	1684-1701	DBBP4,3:325
(House probably built)		
Edith Butterfield (d/o John Jennings)	1701-1758	W3,1:32 1684/1688, DBBP4,3:325
Heirs of John Tucker (s/o Edith Jennings Butterfield)	1758-1807	1789Ass
William Sears	1807-1830	W15:219 1827/1830, SM/PVA2, D/OWN
Mary Sears & Sarah Trott (ch/o William Sears)	1830-1853	SM/PVA3-4
Sarah Trott	1853-1864	SM/PVA4
Melville Trott (gs/o Sarah Trott)	1864-1868	W21:481 1859/1864
Carrie & Leila Trott (ch/o Melville Trott)	1868-1915	SM/CV2
Dr Thomas Heber Outerbridge (by purchase)	1915-1942	SM/CV2
Bertha Loutrelle Outerbridge, Kate Langdon (Mrs Freer) Cox, Benjamin C.C. Outerbridge (ch/o Thomas H. Outerbridge)	1942-1948	D/AD80:28, SM/A1
John Thomson Donaldson & Eric Walter Pasold (by purchase)	1948-1962	D/AD80:28, SM/A1
M.A. Gibbons, L.P. Gutteridge & Mrs Elsa Gosling (by purchase)	1962-1964	D/AD80:28
Henry D.W. Laing (by purchase)	1964-	Owner 2002, SM/LT(V)7/65

Much of the history of Rose Cottage was provided by the current owner who in 1965 painstakingly restored a ruin fated for demolition. The wills of Richard Jennings, his son John Jennings and William Sears along with the discovery of DBBP4,3:325 confirmed transfers of the property through to 1830. Although Rose Cottage was assessed under the estate of Sarah Trott from 1864 until 1893, it was traced to Leila Trott in 1911/1912. Information on the tenancy of Whitney headmaster James McLaughlin was found in the school's archival material made available by then headmistress Mrs Gail Graham. Bertha Loutrelle Outerbridge of Somerville, Kate Langdon (Mrs Freer) Cox of Mayflower in Devonshire and dairyman Benjamin Chauncey Curling Outerbridge of Outerlea inherited Rose Cottage from their father. D/AD80:28, the sale from Donaldson and Pasold to Gibbons, Gutteridge and Gosling, provided information on the Outerbridge family ownership. Mr Henry D.W. Laing generously shared old photographs, architectural drawings and family folklore.

Additional information: 'Rose Cottage', 18 May 1966, updated 25 Feb 1996, Henry D.W. Laing; 'Childhood Memories', Helen Fessenden (Christmas at Rose Cottage); M/Z47:77 Orange Grove (Sarah Trott); Andrew Cooper, Peggy Harris and Elizabeth Harriot (information on Hinson Cooper).

Researcher: Linda Abend

Architectural Assessment: Rose Cottage

Background research by Linda Abend.

Hinson Hall (formerly Hinson's), 12 Hinson Lane

Owner (relationship)	Date owned	Source
Capt (Gov) William Sayle	bef1663-1671	Norwood 28, land only
Mary (Mrs Edward) Audley (gd/o Capt [Gov] Sayle)	?-1688	D3:162, land only
Nicholas Trott	1688-c1694	D3:162, land only
John Dickinson	c1694-1714	W5:48 1714/1714, land only
Elizabeth Dickinson (wd/o John Dickinson)	1714-1733/1747	W5:48, W6:327 1733/1733, land only, life interest
🏛 (House built sometime between 1743 & 1771)		
Mary Dickinson Spofferth (d/o John Dickinson & w/o Samuel Spofferth)	1733/1747-1789	Mary & Samuel married in 1743, Samuel died 1770/1
Joseph Hinson Sr (by purchase)	1790/1791-1809	D26:274, SM/PVA1
Margaret Hinson (wd/o Joseph Hinson Sr)	1809-1835	W13:230 1808/1810, life interest, D26:274
Joseph Hinson Jr & William Walter Kelly (s/o & gs/o Joseph Hinson Sr)	1835-1851	W13:230 1808/1810, D26:274 (see notes below)
William Walter Kelly & Catherine Hinson (gs/o Joseph Hinson Sr & wd/o Joseph Hinson Jr)	1851-1862	W13:230 1808/1810, D26:274
John Wood Hinson & Mary Jane Hinson (ch/o Joseph Hinson Jr)	862-1872	W22:429 1843/1870, D26:274
Mary Jane Hinson Peniston (d/o Joseph Hinson Jr)	1872-1903	D26:274, W28:112 1903/1903, W28:95 1898/1902
Alice Beatrice Rogers (d/o Mary Jane Peniston)	1903-1911	W28:112 1903/1903 (see notes below)
Alice Beatrice Rogers & Ada Winthrop Vesey (ch/o Mary Jane Peniston)	1911-1917	W28:112 1903/1903
Alice Beatrice Rogers & heirs of Ada Winthrop Vesey	1917-1921	D/OWN
Alice Beatrice Rogers	1921-1924	D/OWN
William James Howard Trott (by purchase)	1924-1937	D/OWN
Roy Bryan Greyson Peniston (by purchase)	1937-1945	D/AD2:227, D/OWN
Henry John Balkwill Dunkley (by purchase)	1945-1947	D/OWN
Mabel Gray Kugima (by purchase) (d/o Henry J.B. Dunkley)	1947-1983	D/OWN
Stanley Henry Kugima (wd/o Mabel Kugima)	1983-1993	D/OWN
Mary Frances Gray Gaglio (gd/o Henry J.B. Dunkley)	1993-2000	D/OWN
Paragon Trust as trustee of the Noslo Trust (by purchase)	2000-	D/OWN, owners 2002, house & 1.131 hectares

Ted Cart's research on Verdmont, the deeds supplied by the then owner of Hinson Hall and the find in Registry General of D26:274 told the whole story of Hinson Hall.

However some explanation of the story of the house as set out above is necessary. Joseph Hinson Sr bequeathed all his property, after the death of his wife, to be equally divided among his children, Nicholas, Joseph, Patsy, Bernard Albouy and Peggy Glaspy or their heirs. Margaret died in 1835 having seemingly outlived all of her children (bar Joseph Hinson Jr) and her grandson William Walter Kelly, the only/eldest son and heir-at-law of Peggy Glaspy Hinson Kelly.

Joseph Hinson Jr's first born child, also Joseph, died aged 22 in Antigua in 1839, four years before Joseph Jr made his will in 1843 and he, Joseph Jr, bequeathed his share in Hinson Hall, after his wife's death, to his two surviving children John Wood and Mary Jane Hinson.

By the time of the death of Mary Jane Hinson Peniston, she had become the sole owner of Hinson Hall and its 20 acres of land. She bequeathed the house to the use of her unmarried daughter Alice Beatrice as long as she remained unmarried, subject to a provision in favour of her married daughter Ada Vesey in the event of her (Ada) becoming a widow during the celibacy of Alice. In that event she bequeathed the house and its land equally between the two. Ada's husband Nathaniel Vesey died in 1911 and it wasn't until 29 Dec 1917 that Alice became Mrs William Rogers, Ada having died some 9½ months earlier on 15 Mar 1917. So in 1911 the estate was divided between the two sisters. By an indenture dated 10 Nov 1921, Alice purchased her sister's share of the property and became the sole owner of the house and 20 acres.

Additional information: *Bermuda in the Old Empire*, Henry Wilkinson, pp125 (privateering, cardinal, sage), p138 (surveyor general), p139 (Hinson's Island), p165 (away at sea), p232 (peace), p327 (Crow Lane); Book of Commissions, Vol 5, p117 (*Mary Ann*); Book of Grants Vol 1, circa p13 (Hinson's Island); *The Bermudian* magazine, Sept 1939 (perfume).

Researcher: Suzanne Judah

Architectural Assessment: Hinson Hall

Background research by Suzanne Judah.

Chapter 5 Down Store Hill

Introduction

Bermuda Journey, William Zuill, pp99, 100; will of William Sears W15:219 1827/1830; PWD/SM/8 1830 (location of store).

On the Side: Julia Elizabeth Mercer

RG 3 Aug 1932 and M/Z 'Mercer' (obituaries); M/Z 'Mercer' (letter from Edith Vickers).

Archivist Karla Hayward explained, "The Zuill family kindly permitted the Bermuda Archives to microfilm the notes in 1989 where they remain freely available for public research."

Researcher: Lark Lombardo

Aldie, 5 Aldie Drive

Owner (relationship)	Date owned	Source
William Sears	?-1830	Land only: W15:219 1827/1830
Frances Perot Hinson & Sophia Angelina Zuill (ch/o William Sears)	1830-?	One half each, PWD/SM/8
Sophia Angelina Zuill (Mrs William Edward Zuill)	?-1873	Her death
Fanny Louisa, Julia Elizabeth & Sophia Sears Zuill (gch/o Sophia & William Edward Zuill)	1873-various	W23:141 1873/1874
Sophia Sears & husband Edgar Campbell Wilkinson	various-1896	SM/PVB1, 19 acres
🏛 (House built before 1897)		
Julia Elizabeth & husband Elmore Reid Mercer (by purchase)	1896-1920	D/OWN, D36:285, 5 acres, he died 1920
Julia Elizabeth Mercer (wd/o Elmore Reid Mercer)	1920-1932	Her death, W38:243
Thomas William, Howard Campbell, Archibald Reid & Anne Mercer (ch/o Julia Elizabeth Mercer)	1932-1943	W38:243, FR
George Hill Wingate (by purchase)	1943-1963	D/OWN, D51:90
George Hill Wingate & wife Aileen Dora Grace Beatrice Wingate	1963-1981	SM/LT(V)5/63
Aileen Dora Grace Beatrice Wingate	1981-1982	VC33:168 1.592 acres
Aileen Rose Morrison (d/o George Hill Wingate)	1983-	Owner 2002

Aldie was already built in April 1897 when Elmore Reid and Julia Elizabeth Mercer mortgaged the house and its 5 acres for £450 (M14:231). Originally part of William Sears' estate known as Bostock's, the land was divided among the three daughters of Sophia Angelina Zuill. Although no deeds or other conveyances could be found, the vestry minutes of January 1892 (SM/PVB1) indicate that Edgar Campbell Wilkinson purchased his wife's sisters' shares. In 1896 the Mercers purchased the 5 acres from Wilkinson who owned two undivided third parts and his wife Sophia Sears Wilkinson who owned the remaining one third part. Although Aldie's architect is not known, the Mercers lived for several years in Montclair, New Jersey, and it is thought that Aldie was styled after a house there. The owner Mrs Morrison was very helpful in providing ownership history.

Additional information: 'Perpetual Picnics, A family holiday in the 1920s', William S. Zuill.

Researcher: Lark Lombardo

Architectural Assessment: Aldie

Background research by Lark Lombardo.

Glimmerview, 16 Store Hill

Owner (relationship)	Date owned	Source
William Sears	?-1830	D/OWN, W15:219 1827/1830
Frances Perot Hinson & Sophia Angelina Zuill (ch/o William Sears)	1830-?	D/OWN, one half each, PWD/SM/8
Sophia Angelina Zuill (Mrs William Edward Zuill)	?-1873	19CCR:335 her death
Fanny Louisa, Julia Elizabeth & Sophia Sears Zuill (gch/o William Edward Zuill)	1873-various	D/OWN, W23:141 1873/1874
Fanny Louisa & husband William Leander Zuill (one third)	1874-1896	D/OWN, sold to E.C. Wilkinson
Julia Elizabeth & husband Elmore Reid Mercer (one third)	1874-1891	D/OWN, sold to E.C. Wilkinson
Sophia Sears (one third) & husband Edgar Campbell Wilkinson (two thirds)	1874-1899	D/OWN, sold to Skinner
🏛 (Skinner built Glimmerview between 1899 and 1904)		
James William Musson Skinner & wife Eliza Estelle (sis/o E.R. Mercer, by purchase)	1899-1904	D/OWN
Eugenius Foggo Zuill (by purchase)	1904-1930	D/OWN
Edmund Zuill (np/o Eugenius Zuill) & wife Frances	1930-1981	D/OWN, W37:429 1928/1930
William & Carole Mayo (by purchase)	1981-1983	D/OWN
Ian & Veronica Clarke (by purchase)	1983-1994	D/OWN
Andrew & Lucy Martin (by purchase)	1994-	D/OWN, owners 2002

The deeds of the house (kindly provided by the current owners) trace the ownership of the land from the 1827 will of William Sears. It was part of a tract of "about 48 acres commonly called Bostock's". But even at the time of the 1898/9 Savage map there was no house on the site of Glimmerview. The deeds show that it was built by James William Musson Skinner between 1899 when he bought the land with one house on it (presumably the old house Bluxworth near the North Shore Road) for £600 and 1904 when he sold it to Eugenius Foggo Zuill for £1,100 with two houses.

A letter written by Sir John Cox to Elizabeth Zuill Cart in 1986 records that his uncle Eugenius Zuill and his new wife moved into Glimmerview after returning from their 1903/1904 marriage trip. It recounts their kindness to him as a small child and her early death. Further information about Eugenius Zuill came from his obituaries in *The Bermudian* magazine Dec 1930 and *The Royal Gazette* 13 Nov 1930.

The deeds record that after Eugenius Zuill's death it went to a nephew Edmund Zuill. He and his wife Frances, daughter of Dr William E. Tucker, lived there throughout most of their married life. A letter dated Aug 2000 from Felicity Zuill Simpson (daughter of Edmund) relates her memories of the house during the 1930s, 1940s and 1950s.

Oral tradition says that the same man built Glimmerview as built Aldie but whether this refers to builder/owner or builder/architect is not clear. Aldie was built by James Skinner's brother-in-law and they might well have used the same builder/architect and he might well have been Edward Peniston (died 1903) but there is no proof of this.

Additional information: *Devonshire*, p66 (James Musson Skinner); BHQ, Autumn 1980, p47 (Poinciana); 'Perpetual Picnics, A family holiday in the 1920s', William S. Zuill.
Researcher: Margie Lloyd

Architectural Assessment: Glimmerview

Background research by Margie Lloyd.

Outerlea, 13 Store Hill

Owner (relationship)	Date owned	Source
William Sears	?-1830	Land only: D/OWN, W15:219 1827/1830
Frances Perot Hinson & Sophia Angelina Zuill (ch/o William Sears)	1830-?	D/OWN, one half each, PWD/SM/8
Frances Perot Hinson (Mrs Cornelius C. Hinson)	?-1864	W23:259 1873/1875, D49:111, 9 acres
William Richard Peniston & wife Felicia (d/o Frances Perot Hinson)	1864-1891	D49:111, SM/PVA4
John Ruthven Peniston (s/o William Richard Peniston)	1891-1898	W27:416 1898/1898, he died 1898
Felicia Peniston (wd/o William Richard Peniston)	1898-1913	D49:111, Felicia died 1913, W31:20 1906/1913
Alonzo Peniston & Frederick William Peniston (ch/o William Richard Peniston)	1913-1914	D49:111, Frederick William died 1915
Alonzo Peniston & William Cornelius Peniston (s/o Frederick William Peniston)	1914-1917	D49:111
William Cornelius Peniston	1917-1928	D49:111
Benjamin Chauncey Curling Outerbridge (by purchase)	1928-1978	D49:111
🏛 (House built circa 1932)		
Est of Benjamin Chauncey Curling Outerbridge	1978-1984	
William & Mary DeSilva (by purchase)	1984-	Owners 2002

Originally part of William Sears' estate, the property known as "Bostock's" was divided between his two daughters, Sophia Angelina Zuill and Frances Perot Hinson. The Outerlea property is part of the eastern 19½ acres inherited by the two daughters of Frances Perot Hinson. Eudosia Hinson (the wife of Phares Cooper) received the 10 acres south of Middle Road (on which Windy Bank house was built) and Felicia Hinson (the wife of William Richard Peniston) received the 9+ acres on the north side (W23:259). The 1928 deed recorded in the Registry General as D49:111 gave the ownership history of the land before it was purchased by Benjamin Chauncey Curling Outerbridge from the great grandson of Frances Perot Hinson. Information on dairyman B.C.C. Outerbridge (1880-1978) was found in Bell's 1946 edition of *Beautiful Bermuda* and *The Royal Gazette* of 20 Mar 1978.

Additional information: An account of George Houston Hutchings was written by his daughter Barbara Hutchings Cooper, 24 Jan 2004; *The Bermudian* magazine, April 1933, p10 (Outerlea). Childs Frick (1883-1965) of Castle Point, or Frick's Point house, was the naturalist who funded the famous Murphy/Mowbray expedition that in 1951 rediscovered the cahow.
Researcher: Linda Abend

Millwood, 9 Store Hill

Owner (relationship)	Date owned	Source
Eugenius Foggo Zuill	1904-1930	Land only, part of Glimmerview property
Edmund Eugenius Zuill, Ormond Cox Zuill & Margaret Adelaide Gilbert (np/o, br/o, sis/o Eugenius Foggo Zuill)	1930-1933	D/OWN, W37:429
Edmund Eugenius Zuill, Ormond Cox Zuill	1933-1935	D/OWN
Dora Millwood Smith (n/o Eugenius Foggo Zuill)	1935-1958	D/OWN, W38:341
🏛 (House built in 1936 by Cyril Hilton Smith)		
Dora Millwood Smith & husband Cyril Hilton Smith	1958-1961	D/OWN, VC8:211, SM/LT(V)43/58
Jeffrey C. Astwood & Joyce M. Astwood (by purchase)	1961-1966	D/OWN
John A.B. Nicholson (by purchase)	1966-1971	D/OWN
Arthur D. Spurling & William R. Kempe (by purchase)	1971-1974	D/OWN
Margaret Peniston Berk (by purchase)	1974-1988	D/OWN, VC21:134
Ian & Anna Fulton (by purchase)	1988-	D/OWN, owners 2002

Cyril Hilton Smith designed and built Millwood on land given to his wife Dora Millwood Smith by her mother Margaret Adelaide Gilbert, a sister of Eugenius Foggo Zuill of Glimmerview. Mrs Sally Madden (the Smiths' daughter) provided family history and generously shared old photographs taken before the renovations and additions made in 1992 by Dr and Mrs Fulton.
Researcher: Linda Abend

Channelway, 5 Store Hill
Channelway Cottage, 3 Store Hill

Owner (relationship)	Date owned	Source
Eugenius Foggo Zuill	1904-1930	Land only, part of Glimmerview property
Ormond Cox Zuill (br/o Eugenius Foggo Zuill)	1930-1936	
🏛 (Channelway built by Cummings Vail Zuill in 1936)		
Cummings Vail Zuill (s/o Ormond Cox Zuill)	1936-1976	VC3:281, M27:37, FR
🏛 (Channelway Cottage built in 1950s)		
Est Cummings Vail Zuill	1976-1981	Elizabeth Cart (d/o C.V. Zuill)
Robert D. Steinhoff (by purchase)	1981-	D/OWN, owners 2002

    Tracking the history of this 20th century house (1936) was uncomplicated thanks to the pleasant and full cooperation of the family of its builder, the late C. Vail Zuill, CBE, JP; specifically his widow Janette R. Zuill, MBE, daughter Elizabeth Cart and son Cummings V. Zuill, Jr. Thanks go as well to Channelway's equally cooperative present owners, Mr and Mrs Robert D. Steinhoff.

    Additional information: Many thanks to Andrew Trimingham for the information on Byllee Lang; RG 10 May 1976 (obituary Vail Zuill).

Researcher: Ted Cart

CHAPTER 6 ALONG NORTH SHORE

Introduction

    Bermuda Journey, William Zuill, p100 (causeway); *Slavery in Bermuda,* James E. Smith, pp35-37, 85-86; 'The Flatts - A Centre of Early Colonial Life', E.C. McLaughlin; *Memorials* 2:25, 26.

On the Side: Jennings Land Burial Ground

    The late Donald Leach and Margaret Doyle of Jennings Land, are to be commended for their care of this burial ground. Louis Mowbray remembers the graves from when he walked to school at Whitney Institute over what was then a golf course from his home at Timberly, on the next share to Jennings Land.

    Additional information: conveyance to Bermuda Historical Monuments Trust 1 Sep 1953 (BA BNT 5); Minutes of the Bermuda Historical Monuments Trust (BA); *Memorials* 1:689; *Memorials* 2:671, 668, 670, 703; W2.2:14 (1691/1692 inventory Richard Jennings); D8:436/438 (Richard Downing Jennings & Joseph Clayton Jennings); Peniston Papers 12, BA (old mansion house).   Researchers: Linda Abend, Hilary Tulloch

Magnolia Hall (formerly Peniston's), 38-40 North Shore Road

A report of Peniston's Shipyard by Edward A. Chappell, made following a visit on 11 Oct 2003, is kept on file by the Bermuda National Trust.

Owner (relationship)	Date owned	Source
western portion – land only		
Hugh Wentworth	1663	Norwood 21
John Gilbert, carpenter	?-1700	W2,1:115 1699/1700
Heirs of John Gilbert	1700 - 1741	W7:134, Peniston Papers(BA)
Alice & Sarah Gilbert (ch/o John Gilbert, mariner)	1741-c1796	Peniston Papers
John Gilbert Peniston (s/o Sarah Gilbert)	c1796-1797	Peniston Papers
Richard F. Peniston (by purchase)	1797-1826	Peniston Papers
eastern portion – land only		
Matthew Batson	1663	Norwood 21
Richard Vickers	died c1691	King's Bench Papers 1803 (BA)
Mary Gibbons (d/o Richard Vickers)	c1691-c1770	King's Bench Papers
William Gibbons (s/o Mary Gibbons)	c1770-c1789	King's Bench Papers
Timothy Taylor (son-in-law of William Gibbons)	c1789-1809	Peniston Papers
Mary Taylor (w/o Timothy Taylor & d/o William Gibbons) & Thomas Gibbons (son-in-law of Mary Taylor)	1809-1811	Peniston Papers
Richard F. Peniston (by purchase)	1811-1826	Peniston Papers
🏛 (House built by Richard F. Peniston circa 1815)		
Frances Peniston (wd/o Richard F. Peniston)	1826-1829	W15:155 1826/1826
Francis Peniston (eldest s/o Richard F. Peniston)	1829-1854	D9:428
Mary Ann Gilbert Peniston (wd/o Francis Peniston)	1854-1884	W19:347 1853/1854
Ida & Anna Maria Peniston (ch/o Francis Peniston)	1884-1894	W25:235 1876/1884
Anna Maria Peniston	1894-1899	W25:235
Est of Francis Peniston	1899-1905	FR, SM/CV2
Ormond Cox Zuill (by purchase)	1905-1923	FR, SM/CV2
Ormond Ralph Loblein (by purchase)	1923-1926	
🏛 (Major additions to house after 1926)		
Leslie Workman Howarth (by purchase)	1926-1952	FR
Mary Littlejohn (d/o Leslie Howarth)	1952-2000	W50:145
Bermuda Trust Company (Littlejohn family)	2000-	Owners 2002, Fred Littlejohn

Peniston Papers deposited in the Bermuda Archives provided original deeds not filed in the Registry General. Richard F. Peniston purchased 15 acres from distant relative John Gilbert Peniston, 12¼ acres from Mary Taylor and her son-in-law Thomas Gibbons and 7 acres from Alice Gilbert Peniston's estate. Although there was a large dwelling house on John Gilbert Peniston's property (RG 11 Feb 1797) it would appear that Richard F. Peniston built a new house in the centre of his 34+ acres. Also found in the Peniston Papers were a series of plats commissioned by Francis Peniston and drawn by Daniel Prudden in 1829 describing the vast landholdings of Richard F. Peniston. RG 20 Mar 1900 advertised for sale the household furniture in the four bedroom house. Wills and assessments confirm that the property remained in the Peniston family until it was purchased by Ormond Cox Zuill.

Magnolia Hall as an osteopathic sanitarium was mentioned in *Beautiful Bermuda* 1913 p164, RG 5 Dec 1911, 25 Jan 1912 and 2 Jan 1917. Information on J.J. Moniz's tenancy and tomato canning factory was provided by Jessie Moniz and also by Gwendolyn Steed Smith whose father farmed for J.J. Moniz. An article on the canning plant of 1918 by Jerry DeCouto published in *Bermuda's Heritage 1980* was helpful. Photos of the original one storey house were provided by Elizabeth Cart and William Starr Peniston.

Additional information: *Family Narrative*, Hereward Watlington, pp214, 215; *The Royal Gazette* 30 May 1837, 19 June 1838, 24 March 1840 (shipbuilding); *The Jackson Clan,* Vernon Jackson, pp18-20, 23-29; Jesse Moniz (Moniz family). Researcher: Linda Abend

On the Side: Goods and Chattels

'Goods & Chattels', Mary Ellin D'Agostino; and inventories transcribed by Betty Hollis and Joan McKendry: inventory of John Dickinson 1714, W5:51; inventory of Thomas Smith 1782, INV1,1:46; inventory of Samuel Spofferth 1771, W8:523. Researcher: Diana Chudleigh

Stilwell (formerly Vancefort), 24 North Shore Road

Owner (relationship)	Date owned	Source
John Young	1663-1678	Norwood 25, land only
William Reynolds & wife Sarah (d/o John Young)	1678-1690	W1:278 1678/1680
John Reynolds (s/o William Reynolds)	1690-?	W2,2:32 1690/1691
John Gilbert	?-1700	M/Z 'Gilbert'
Est of John Gilbert	1700-c1766	M/Z 'Gilbert'
Capt John Steed Sr	c1766-1788	PWD/SM/6
Elizabeth Steed (d/o John Steed)	1788-1791	SM/PVA1
Capt John Steed Jr (s/o John Steed)	1791-1801	SM/PVA1, RG 7 Nov 1801
James Tynes (by purchase)	1801-1833	SM/PVA2, PWD/SM/1 & 8
Est of William Sears	1833-c1882	SM/PVA3-4, SM/PVB1
Henry James Zuill (gs/o William Sears)	c1882-c1915	FR
William E.S. Zuill (s/o Henry James Zuill)	c1915-?	FR, SM/CV2
W.E.S. Zuill, B.C.C. Outerbridge, Kate Pearman & trustees of Jeremiah Scott Pearman Est	?-1938	D/AD2:252
Marjorie Critten (by purchase)	1938-1954	D/AD2:252
Henry Ponsonby Watlington (by purchase)	1954-	D/AD3:436, SM/LT(V)20/54, owners 2002

We cannot be certain but it is possible that the core building of Stilwell was the dwelling house of William Reynolds. The house was enlarged by James Tynes whose ownership could be traced through the assessments from 1801 until his death. Further confirmation was found in M4:306, INV8:331 (BA), RG 1 Oct 1833 and Chancery Court Records (BA). The house and 9 acres were lost in the extensive landholdings of William Sears' estate and then of his son-in-law William Edward Zuill. There are no deeds or voluntary conveyances and the transfers to Henry James Zuill and William E.S. Zuill were found in the Freeholder's Register but the dates may not be accurate. Ownership for the period 1915-1938 remains cloudy. Biographical information on long-time tenant Col William Thomas Wood was provided by his great-granddaughter, Elisabeth L. Wood.

Additional information: PWD/SM/8 (James Tynes' building place). Researchers: Jinny White & Linda Abend

Architectural Assessment: Stilwell

Background research provided by Linda Abend.

Spruce Cottage, 22 North Shore Road

A report by Edward A. Chappell, made following a visit on 11 Oct 2003, is kept on file by the Bermuda National Trust.

Owner (relationship)	Date owned	Source
Nathaniel Tynes	c1795	SM/PVA1
🏛 (Storehouse built early 19th century)		
James Tynes (s/o Nathaniel Tynes)	1797-1833	SM/PVA1-2, PWD/SM/1 & 8
Est of James Tynes	1833-1834	RG 1 Oct 1833
Joseph Jauncey Outerbridge	1834-1857	Held mortgage, M4:306, SM/PVA3
Mary Jauncey Outerbridge Ewing (gd/o Joseph J. Outerbridge)	1857-1866	W20:185 1847/1857
Thomas Fowle Ewing (f/o Mary J.O. Ewing)	1866-1867	W22:150 1866/1867
Frances Fowle Tucker (sis/o Thomas Fowle Ewing)	1867	W22:150 1866/1867
Robert Alexander Tucker (s/o Frances Fowle Tucker)	1867-1886	SM/PVB1
Thomas Jackson (by purchase)	1886-1910	SM/PVB1
Sarah Ann Jackson (d/o Thomas Jackson)	1910-1929	SM/CV2
Benjamin Chauncey Curling Outerbridge (by purchase)	1929-1979	D49:107, SM/A1
Margaret & Bruce Barker (by purchase)	1979-1993	Oral
Margaret (Barker) Ingham	1993-	Owner 2004

Built on the northeastern boundary of William Sears' property then known as Bostock's (W15:29 1827/1830), the early history of Spruce Cottage is still not clear. It could not be determined how or when Nathaniel Tynes acquired the small lot. Information on the shipbuilding activities of James Tynes was found in Wilkinson's *Bermuda from Sail to Steam*, pp250, 281, 355. M4:306 and Chancery Court records describe his financial difficulties. After Tynes' death the property was easily traced through the parish assessments up to the present time.   Researcher: Linda Abend

CHAPTER 7 FLATTS HILL

Introduction
Mid-Ocean News 16 Aug 1922 (obituary Clarence Darrell).

Orange Grove, 11 The Peak Road
Calabash Cottage, 7 The Peak Road
Sandbox Cottage, 9 The Peak Road

Owner (relationship)	Date owned	Source
Sir Thomas Smythe	1618	Norwood 18, land only
Valentyne Markham		CR8:75
Dr Gabriel Barber		CR8:75
Gabriel Barber (s/o Dr Gabriel Barber)		CR8:75
Perient Trott of London		CR8:75
John Somersall	1654-1674	CR8:75
🏚 (House built by 1662-3 for Somersall on part of Norwood 18)		
Est of John Somersall	1674-1677	CR8:77
William Maligan (steps/o John Somersall)	1677-1690	CR8:77, W1:183 1671/1674
Est of William Maligan	1690-c1697	W3,1:113 1689/1690
James Maligan (s/o William Maligan)	c1697-1701	W3,1:113, came 'of age'
Est of James Maligan	1701-c1721	W2,2:153 1698/1701
Miriam Maligan (later Corbusier, d/o James Maligan)	c1721-c1746	W2,2:153, married or 'of age'
Est of Miriam Maligan Corbusier; Henry Corbusier (wd/o Miriam)	c1746-1764?	Henry Corbusier appears to have paid assessments until his death in 1764
James Corbusier (s/o Henry & Miriam Corbusier)	1746?-1766	No will found for Miriam Corbusier
Est of James Corbusier	1766-1777?	Assessments paid by his widow Ann
Henry Corbusier (s/o James Corbusier)	1771?-1783	W12a:287 1765/1766, 'of age'
Mary Corbusier (sis/o Henry Corbusier)	1783	M/Z48:7-8, sold to her, mansion house & 12 acres, 5/6 Mar 1783
Samuel Trott Jr (cousin/o Mary Corbusier) & James Musson Sr (f-in-law/o Samuel Trott Jr) (by purchase)	1783	M/Z48:7-8, 28/29 Mar 1783
Bridger Goodrich (by purchase)	1783-1788	M/Z48:7-8, 7/8 Aug 1783
William Sears (by purchase)	1788-1830	D3:64
Est of William Sears	1830-1843	W15:219 1827/1830
🏚 (Orange Grove newly built by 1855)		
Sophia Angelina Zuill (d/o William Sears) & husband William Edward Zuill	1843-1872	W15:219, W23:56 1869/1872
Sophia Angelina Zuill	1872-1873	W23:56
Est of William Edward Zuill	1873-1915	W23:56
Henry James Zuill (gs/o William Edward Zuill)	1915-1916	W23:56
Est of Henry James Zuill	1916-c1930	W32:132 1916/1916
William Edward Sears Zuill (s/o Henry James Zuill)	c1930-1988	D/OWN, SM/CV2
William Sears Zuill (s/o W.E.S. Zuill)	1988-	VC52:311, owner 2002

William Edward Sears Zuill wrote many articles for the *Bermuda Historical Quarterly* including a series on the history of his home Orange Grove (BHQ, Summer 1972-Winter 1974). This provided the basis for research.

Ownership was traced back using: Smith's Parish assessments and vestry records (SM/PVA2-4 and SM/PVB1); the wills of William Edward Zuill (W23:56), William Sears (W15:219), James Corbusier (W12a:287), William Maligan (W3,1:113) and John Somersall (W1:183); deeds (D6:64) between Bridger Goodrich and William Sears; Colonial Records (CR8:75, 77); Lefroy's *Memorials* 2:667 and the Mercer/Zuill genealogical notes.

The ownership of the property was relatively straightforward but perhaps the 18th century period should be elaborated upon. William Maligan, in his will (W3,1:113), left his house to his wife Miriam for her life and after to their son James. Wife Miriam Maligan died shortly after her husband while James was still a minor. The estate was held in trust for James who 'came of age', ie was 21 years old, in 1697. The following year he made his will which was granted probate in 1701, after he had been lost at sea. James Maligan's will (W2.2:153 1698/1701) left his estate between his wife Frances and daughter Miriam (c1701-1746), the latter's share put in trust (W3:169 1706/7) until she married or came of age. Miriam Maligan married Henry Corbusier and their first child, James, was born in 1722. It has therefore been assumed that Miriam Maligan inherited the property on her marriage about 1721, although she may have inherited earlier on the death of her mother as her step-father, Captain John Gilbert (died c1733), became her guardian in 1719. Miriam (Maligan) Corbusier died in 1746 (no will found) and her husband Henry Corbusier continued to pay the assessment until his death in 1764. James Corbusier (1722-1766) the eldest son inherited the Maligan family home. He had married Ann Outerbridge in 1748. James' will (W12a:287) left his house to his wife Ann for her widowhood and then to his son Henry Corbusier (1749-1783). It is not clear whether Henry took on responsibility for the property when he became 21 because his mother Ann continued to pay the assessments until 1777, six years later. M/Z48:18 notes that she died in 1782. Henry Corbusier died the following year having sold the property to his sister Mary. The house and land passed in a period of six months through several family members by purchase until it was sold to Bridger Goodrich in August 1783. It is thought that these family deals were carried out to break the entail from James Corbusier's will, eventually allowing the property to be sold out of the family. During this period the house was used to accommodate soldiers. The Minutes of Council of 8 April 1783 include, "That there is a House near the Flatts belonging to the Hono'ble Samuel Trott Junr: Esquire which is in tenantable Repair and has lately been inhabited by Mr. Henry Corbusier and if it could be procured would be an immediate provision for the Reinforcement lately arrived from New York. Mr Trott thereupon signified to the Board that he will let the House Cistern Outhouses (except the Westermost) Yards and Gardens commonly used with the same at such Monthly hire as the Governor and Council shall think him Reasonably entitled to. Resolved accordingly." (*Bermuda Journal of Archaeology and Maritime History* Vol 13, 2002, p187). At the meeting ot 29 April 1784 Mr Trott stated that the troops had occupied his house from 10th April to 10th December 1783, and the Council authorised that he should be paid £64 (*Bermuda Journal of Archaeology and Maritime History* Vol 15, 2004, p147). One can only assume that Bridger Goodrich did not take possession of the house in a hurry and that he and Trott sorted out the rent between them.

Genealogical information was taken from vital records (Registry General), memorials in St. Mark's Church and churchyard, Smith's Parish, and Great Saling Parish Register (Essex Record Office, England, D/P311 1/1).

Additional sources on the Zuill family included: Orange Grove: *The Bermudian* newspaper, 17 Jan–2 May 1855 (advertisement); M/Z47:47, 86, 88, 120-1 (alterations); PWD/SM/12 1842 (survey); W15:219 & codicil, W23:56, M/Z76 referring to D15:189 and ANG/SM/PVA2 (Sophia Angelina Zuill inheritance and buyout); M/Z47:86 and *The Bermudian* newspaper, 1 Jan 1851, p2, c1 (named Orange Grove, citrus orchards); M/Z47:86 (tropical trees planted). William Edward Zuill: M/Z47:13, M/Z76, W14:288 1818 (and William James Sears); M/Z47:14 (wedding); M/Z47:15; M/Z76 (to Demerara); RS2.5, M/Z47:88, C12.14, C15.7-9, C15.11-12 (brig *Herald*). William Sears Zuill: *The Bermudian* newspaper 23 May 1855, RG 22 May 1855 (marriage); M/Z76 (death); W32:13-19 (will). Henry James Zuill: W23:56, M/Z47:88 (trustees); M/Z47:120-1 (E. Peniston letter 2 May1883); M/Z47:88, 90, 109-110 (family social life); M/Z47:88, 120-1 (1883 rebuild); M/Z47:90, 92, 94 (children); M/Z47:94 (rubber tree); W32:132-5 (will); ANG/SM/CV2 (1921 survey). William Edward Sears Zuill: RG 3 Feb 1943, p16 and 11 Jul 1989, p6 (biography); *The Royal Gazette and Colonist Daily* 3 Dec 1942, M/Z76 (public service); *The Bermudian* magazine, Jan 1938 p10 and May 1946 (author and historian); RG 11 Jul 1989, p6 (obituary).

Sources used for earlier owners included: John Somersall: *The Adventurers*, Henry Wilkinson, 2nd ed, p403 and *Memorials* 1:644-5, 2:202 (public life); *Memorials* 2:671.33 (house and family); CR8:77 (prenuptial agreement); CR5A:194-5 (Garrod trans.); W1:297 1679 (will disagreement). William Maligan: CR8:101 (and Indian John); W3.1:130 (inventory). Miriam Maligan: W3:169 1706/7, W5:23 1719 (guardians); CR9:134 (death). James Maligan: W2.2:153 1698/1701 (will). Henry Corbusier: M/Z47:66; *Bermuda in the Old Empire*, Henry Wilkinson, p440 (biography); W12a:231 1763/1766 (will); M/Z48 (public service). Bridger Goodrich: M/Z47:70, M/Z48:8-9, *Family Narrative*, Watlington (purchase); 'Archival Assessment of Bridge House', Michael Jarvis, p49 (business); D3:64, D9:60 (sale). William Sears: M/Z47:53 (went to sea); RS2/1-2, C9/1, C10/1-4 (ships); M/Z46 & 47, BI:1170 & 1574, RG 27 Mar 1824 (family); 1789 assessment, ANG/SM/PVA2 (wealth); M/Z47:28-31 (inventory).

William and Joyce Zuill generously provided further evidence and anecdotes from family papers.

Additional information: Court of Assizes AZ102/11 (1782 trial of Henry Corbusier); 'William Sears', BHQ, Winter 1973, p99 (£40).

Researchers: Jean Jones & Hilary Tulloch

Architectural Assessment: Orange Grove

Background research by Hilary Tulloch.

Family Story: Mid 19th Century Changes to Orange Grove

Background research by William Zuill.

Architectural Assessment: Somersall, 12 The Peak Road

Owner (Relationship)	Date owned	Source
🏠(House built 1958)		
William Sears Zuill	1958-2001	Owner
Rebecca Zuill Brady (d/o William Sears Zuill)	2001-	Owner 2003

William and Joyce Zuill together with their daughter Rebecca Brady kindly recounted the history.　　Researcher: Hilary Tulloch

On the Side: Folly Tower, 24 The Peak Road

Notes on the Zuill family were made when researching the history of Orange Grove and Rockmoor. Dates were taken from vital records in the RG, information and anecdotes from copies of the Mercer/Zuill genealogical notes (M/Z47 & 76) at BA and from Hereward Watlington's account of the families in *Family Narrative*. William S. Zuill kindly recounted the family perspective and he and Charles Marshall generously made it possible to view the architecture of the building.　　Researcher: Hilary Tulloch

Dean Hall (formerly Deane Hall), 76 Middle Road

Owner (relationship)	Date owned	Source
Peter Gallagher	c1768-1808	D/OWN, SM/PVA1
Est of Peter Gallagher	1808-1809	W13:249 1802/1811
🏠 (House probably built circa 1811)		
Henrietta Gallagher (d/o Peter Gallagher)	1809-1811	D/OWN
Henrietta Gallagher & husband William Henry Dean	1811-1818	William Henry's death
Henrietta Dean	1818-1845	D/OWN, SM/PVA2
Mary Alice Dean & Eliza Susan Wood Outerbridge (ch/o Henrietta Dean)	1845-1882	D/OWN, Mary Alice's death

Eliza Susan Wood Outerbridge & husband		
John Downing Outerbridge	1882-1879	D/OWN, John Downing's death
Eliza Susan Wood Outerbridge	1879-1890	D/OWN, SM/PVB1
Arthur Outerbridge (eldest s/o Eliza Susan		
Wood Outerbridge)	1890-1911	D/OWN, inherited one-half share and bought remaining half from siblings
Algernon Rees Outerbridge (br/o Arthur		
Outerbridge)	1911-1912	W30:261 1901/1912
Maria Williams Outerbridge (w/o Algernon		
Rees Outerbridge)	1912-1934	W44:161
Lillian Rees Peniston & Enith Urma		
Outerbridge (ch/o Maria Williams Outerbridge)	1934-1967	W88:62 1959/1967
Lillian Rees Peniston	1967-1973	W102:254 1948/1973
Lucy Dean Caton & Elsie Leeuwin		
Butland (ch/o Lillian Rees Peniston)	1973-1976	VC24:216
Lucy Dean Caton and children Ann Peniston Kirpalani, Michael Gorman Peniston Caton, Elizabeth Deane		
Peniston Caton	1976-1991	VC24:216
Est Lucy Dean Caton	1991-1994	D/OWN
Michael & Margaret Caton	1994-	D/OWN, owners 2003

Dean Hall was traced back to Irish tailor Peter Gallagher who came to Bermuda sometime before 1767. According to the assessments a structure of some sort stood on the property by 1768. The 1788 deed to neighbouring Orange Grove refers to Gallagher's land to the north (D3:158). A plan of the area as surveyed by D.R. Prudden in 1837 confirms that the property was "formerly Peter Gallagher but now Mrs Dean" (BA). Although the property was assessed from 1818 until 1893 as William Dean's estate, various wills and vestry entries confirm it descended from Henrietta Dean to her children and now her great-great-great-grandchildren. Margaret and Michael Caton generously shared old family documents which included deeds and wills not otherwise available.

Additional information: *Chronicle of a Colonial Church*, A.C. Hollis Hallett, p265 (Smith's Parish church).　　　Researcher: Linda Abend

Architectural Assessment: Dean Hall

Background research by Linda Abend.

Travellers' Rest, 61 Middle Road

Owner (relationship)	Date owned	Source
Richard Peniston	?-1803	W12:151 1803/1803, mariner of Flatts, who is not to be confused with Richard Peniston of Smith's who also died in 1803
Frances Peniston (d/o Richard Peniston & w/o Richard F. Peniston)	1803-1827	D9:356, land only
Nicholas Peniston (s/o Frances Peniston)	1827-c1846	SM/PVA2-3
Augustus Peniston (by purchase)	c1846-1876	SM/PVA4
🏛 (House built around 1861)		
Ameria Pearman (d/o Augustus Peniston & w/o Thomas J. Pearman)	1876-?	W24:66 1872/1877, SM/PVB1
Jeremiah Scott Pearman (no relation, by purchase)	?-1921	Whitney Institute Archives
Trustees of Whitney Institute (by gift)	1921-	Owners 2002

The transfer of the 12½ acre property from Richard Peniston to his daughter and then her son was documented by wills and deeds. Augustus Peniston's ownership was confirmed by his will (W24:66). No deeds could be found but the documents made available by Whitney Institute's headmistress Mrs Gail Graham contained a mention of the gift of Travellers' Rest by Jeremiah Scott Pearman of Mount Hope.

Thanks are expressed to the family of Ann Zuill Williams for permission to quote from her book *The Back Yard.*　　　Researcher: Linda Abend

CHAPTER 8 SOUND'S MOUTH

Introduction

Memorials 1:169 (bridge already erected); *Memorials* 2:407 (repair of bridge, Anthony Peniston); AZ102/6 (Court of Assizes).

Bridge House, 104 Middle Road

A report by Edward A. Chappell, made following a visit on 30 June 2004, is kept on file by the Bermuda National Trust.

Owner (relationship)	Date owned	Source
Anthony Peniston	bef1674-c1710	*Memorials* 2:407 bridge keeper in occupation
Elizabeth Peniston (wd/o Anthony Peniston)	c1710-aft1733	BHQ 1949-1952 & Winter 1946
Anthony Peniston	bef1763-1788	Grants Vol 1:181 1772
Est Anthony Peniston	1788-1801	D10:144
Samuel Trott & wife Catherine (d/o Anthony Peniston)	1801-1822	W10:276 1778/1788
🏛 (Present house built by 1823)		

Augustus Peniston (by purchase)	1822-1876	D/OWN, SM/PV
Est Augustus Peniston (wife Anna Maria in occupation)	1876-1880	W24:66
Thomas J. Pearman & wife Ameria (d/o Augustus Peniston)	1876-1920	D/OWN, W24:66 1872/1877, FR
Henry James Tucker & wife Nella Tucker (by purchase)	1920-1950	D/OWN, FR
Henry James Tucker Jr & Robert Noel P. Tucker (ch/o Henry James & Nella Tucker)	1950-1978	W48:289 1941/1950
Henry James Tucker Jr	1978-1983	W115:125 1965/1978
Judith Trott Tucker Denney (d/o Henry James Tucker Jr)	1983-1987	VC35:113
Frederick & Judith T.T. Denney	1987-	VC45:53, owners 2002

Information regarding the holding of a Council of War in Apr 1696 and Council Meetings during the years 1702-1709 at Anthony Peniston's house now called Bridge House was obtained from the *Bermuda Historical Quarterly* (various issues 1949-1952). In September 1717 a Council meeting was held at widow Elizabeth Peniston's house in Flatts. Further meetings were held at Elizabeth Peniston's house during the years 1717 to 1728 (BHQ, various issues 1949-1952). The Judges held Court at widow Elizabeth Peniston's house at Flatts during 1726-1733 (Court of Assizes AZ102/6).

Much of the information about the Peniston family was taken from the pre-1920 work of Colonel William H. Corbusier, available in the Bermuda Archives (PA48, BA).

Anthony Peniston (died c1710), mariner, was the son of Thomas Peniston (died c1655) who was one of the earliest settlers in Bermuda. Anthony was described by Hereward Watlington as "one of the Pioneers in Bermuda of shipbuilding which through his achievement made the name of Bermuda famous in the shipping world for nearly two centuries". (*Family Narrative*, Watlington, p209).

Anthony Peniston (died 1788), great-grandson of Thomas Peniston, was granted a water lot at Flatts in 1772 which was probably land which has since been dredged across the road from the Bridge House property which he already owned. In his will he left his estate to his wife Elizabeth and then to his children. Catherine Trott his daughter, second wife of Samuel Trott, inherited the Bridge House property. They sold to Augustus Peniston in 1822. But there is no proof as to which of them built Bridge House.

In the early 20th century occupants included Fannie and Gertrude Trott, spinster aunts of Henry James Tucker Sr.

Additional information: *Man of Stature*, J.R. Williams; *Bermuda Sampler*, William Zuill, p337.   Researcher: Fay Elliott

On the Side: Palmetto Grove
Palmetto Grove (later Palmetto Bay Hotel and since demolished), 1 Harrington Sound Road

Owner (relationship)	Date owned	Source
Anthony Peniston	c1763-1788	SM/PVA1
Elizabeth Peniston (w/o Anthony Peniston)	1788-1799	
Est of Elizabeth Peniston	1799-1801	D10:142
Paynter Musson & wife Ann (d/o Anthony Peniston) & Est	1801-1838	D10:142, D10:144, ADMIN5:12
Samuel Paynter Musson & Frances Musson (ch/o Paynter Musson)	1838-c1840	Chancery Court Records Apr 1838, RG 30 Apr 1838
🏛 (House built circa 1838 by Samuel Paynter Musson)		
Samuel Paynter Musson	c1840-1847	SM/PVA3
Frances Musson & Susannah Musson (sis/o Samuel P. Musson)	1847-1873	In occupation, M/Z, D26:196
Samuel Musson (h/o Susannah Musson) & children Anna Trott, Eliza Musson, Susan Paynter Musson & Georgiana Sauer	1873-1881	
Anna Trott (d/o Samuel & Susannah Musson)	1881-1883	D30:32, D31:502
Harley & Thaddeus Trott (ch/o Anna Trott and husband William James Trott	1883-1893	W25:101 1874/1883
Rev George Tucker (by purchase)	1893-1908	SM/PVB1
Anna Emmeline Tucker (wd/o Rev George Tucker)	1908-1949	W47:200 1938/1949
William Eldon Tucker & Henry James Tucker (s/o Rev Tucker)	1950	W29:320 1906/1908
Henry James Tucker	1950	D56:280
Palmetto Bay Co Ltd (by purchase)	1950-1970	SM/A1-2
Palmetto Bay Club Co Ltd (by purchase)	1970-2000	SM/A2 100/70
		Demolished 2000

The house was built on land acquired by Ann Musson (1760-1824) in the 1801 subdivision of her father Anthony Peniston's estate (died 1788). Samuel Paynter Musson (c1794-1873) son of Ann and Paynter Musson obtained administration of his father's estate in 1838 and auctioned the estate to pay off the remainder of his father's debts. His sister Frances, a spinster, bought the estate and sold it back to him. Sometime after 1838 Samuel Paynter Musson built Palmetto Grove. By a deed dated 1847 (M/Z 'Musson':161) he gave real estate including Palmetto Grove, which he said was "lately erected by him", to his sisters Frances and Susannah, wife of Samuel Musson, to be held in trust for them for life. In 1852 he set up a trust fund for Susannah and Samuel Musson and in his will he left his estate ultimately to Harley and Thaddeus Trott, sons of his niece Anna (W24:92 1872/73).

Samuel Paynter Musson was a merchant in Bridgetown, Barbados. His business grew and he "rose to a position of eminence amongst the merchants of Bridgetown having more vessels consigned to him than to any other". He had a reputation for integrity and "scrupulous exactness" in business. In private life "he was equally esteemed as a kind-hearted, benevolent man, ready to do anyone a service. His purse was always open for the relief of the distressed, and as in everything else it was done without ostentation." (Obituary, Barbados 15 Nov 1873 M/Z).

Additional information: *Bermuda Journey*, William Zuill, p178 (mahogany tree); *Bermuda from Sail to Steam*, Henry Wilkinson, p855; *Family Narrative*, Hereward Watlington, p253.
Researcher: Fay Elliott

Villa Monticello (formerly Harrington Retreat), 4 Harrington Sound Road

Owner (relationship)	Date owned	Source
Matthew Lowe	?	CR5A:41 (Garrod trans.)
John Stowe	prior 1658	CR5A:41 (Garrod trans.) purchased 50 acres
🏛 (Earlier house on share 17)		
Lieut Anthony White	1658-c1673	Norwood 17
Honora White (wd/o Lieut Anthony White)	c1673-1677	W1:168 1672/1673
Anthony White (s/o Lieut Anthony White)	1677-c1709	W1:168
Elizabeth White (wd/o Anthony White)	c1709-?	W4:42 1707/1709
Leonard White (s/o Anthony White)	?-1732	W4:42
Est Leonard White	1732- ?	M/Z
Anthony White (of New Jersey)	?-1743	M/Z
Jeremiah Peniston (by purchase)	1743-?	M/Z75 'White', Bond Jan 1743/1744
Anthony Peniston (s/o Jeremiah Peniston)	bef1763-1788	W9:1 1768/1771, Peniston Family Tree p42 (PA48, BA)
Elizabeth Peniston (wd/o Anthony Peniston)	1788-1799	W10:276 1778/1788, SM/PVA1
Est of Elizabeth Peniston	1799-1801	D10:142
🏛 (Present house built)		
Robert Spencer Musson & wife Miriam (d/o Anthony Peniston)	1801-1828	D10:142
Robert Spencer Musson Jr (s/o Robert S. & Miriam Peniston)	1828-1864	SM/PVA2-4 purchased additional lot from Elizabeth Hill (d/o Anthony Peniston)
Miriam Musson (m/o Robert Spencer Musson Jr)	1828-1852	W21:516 1847/1864, in occupation
Dorcas Musson (wd/o Robert Spencer Musson Jr)	1864-1869	In occupation
Frances D. Atwood & Elizabeth E.M. Musson (ch/o Robert Spencer Musson Jr)	1869-1871	W21:516 1847/1864
Anthony Burgess Hill (by purchase)	1872-1877	D26:255
Frances Mary Whitney (sis/o Anthony Burgess Hill)	1877-1901	W24:123 1877/1878, SM/CV1
Anna Maria Outerbridge	1901-1928	W27:714 1890/1901, SM/CV2
Est Anna Maria Outerbridge	1928-1951	W37:19, for use of Belle Townsley Outerbridge (n/o Anna Maria Outerbridge)
Percy Clisdell Outerbridge (cousin/o Anna Maria Outerbridge)	1951-1963	W37:19
Outerbridge Investment Co Ltd	1963-1968	SM/LT(V)94/63
Yeaton Duval Outerbridge	1968-1993	SM/LT(V)36/68
Peter Devine (by purchase)	1993-2000	Oral
The Hammond (Bermuda) Trust (by purchase)	2000-	Owner 2002

Norwood's Survey of 1663, no 17, shows a dwelling house on 49 acres of land in Smith's Parish. This is the first recorded house on the site on which Villa Monticello was built in the beginning of the 19th century. It was bought from John Stowe prior to 1658 by Lieutenant Anthony White. In his will Anthony White left his "Dwelling House" to wife Honora and then to his eldest son Colonel Anthony White. It was quite easy to trace the succession of the property through the White family via wills. The property moved out of the White family in 1743 when according to a bond mentioned in the M/Z notes but not found in the public record Jeremiah Peniston bought it and it passed on through the Peniston family to Robert Spencer Musson who was the husband of Miriam Peniston daughter of Anthony Peniston.

The house became known as Harrington Retreat when owned by the Mussons (RG 1 Sep 1863). In 1872 by purchase the property came into the Hill family and was left to Frances Mary Hill who married William Whitney, US deputy consul.

An added help to the research of the house were inventories showing each room; also wills and assessments were consulted to trace Villa Monticello to the present owners.

Additional information: *The Adventurers*, Henry Wilkinson, p306; *Memorials* 2:102 (drinking); *Bermuda from Sail to Steam*, Henry Wilkinson, p757 (reduced circumstances); *Bermuda in the Old Empire*, Henry Wilkinson, p65 (*Amity*). Researcher: Fay Elliott

Architectural Assessment: Villa Monticello
Background research by Fay Elliott.

Villa Mont Clare, 10 Harrington Sound Road

Owner (relationship)	Date owned	Source
Anthony Peniston	1765-1788	SM/PVA1, land only
Elizabeth Peniston (w/o Anthony Peniston)	1788-1799	W10:276 1778/1788, SM/PVA1
Est of Elizabeth Peniston	1799-1801	
Frances Mary Hill (d/o Anthony Peniston)	1801-1811	D10:142, land only
John Burgess Hill (h/o Frances Mary Peniston Hill)	1811-1817	SM/PVA2
🏛 (House built for John Burgess Hill circa 1812)		
Est John Burgess Hill	1817-1851	W14:220 1813/1818, Bl:617, D19:124
Anthony John Hill (s/o John Burgess Hill)	1818-1865	W14:220
Frances Mary Whitney (n/o Anthony Burgess Hill)	1865-1901	D24:332
The Synod of the Church of England in Bermuda	1901-1978	W27:714 1890/1901
		Rectors of St. Mark's Church in occupation

Ernest David DeCouto & Phyllis Violet DeCouto (by purchase)	1979-1998	D/OWN 19 Mar 1979
R & H Trust Co (Bda) Ltd (by purchase)	1998-2003	D/OWN 23 Nov 1998
Paragon Trust Ltd	2003	D/OWN 24 Mar 2003, owner 2003

The ownership of Villa Mont Clare can be traced from the Peniston family through to the Hill family via marriage from wills and assessments. The original land was given by Anthony Peniston to his daughter Frances Mary, first wife of John Burgess Hill who built the house in about 1812. John Burgess Hill's assessments increased from 1812 to 1815 which suggests when Villa Mont Clare was built.

Anthony John Hill son of John Burgess Hill inherited Villa Mont Clare in 1818. Although he lived only a year after retiring from a successful business career, and totally blind, he devoted himself to helping the poor and afflicted in his own parish and adjacent Smith's Parish. He was an active member of Trinity Church and when he died a memorial service was held in his honour RG 23 Nov 1901 (obituary of Mrs William Whitney).

After Frances Mary Whitney left Villa Mont Clare to St. Mark's Church to be used as a rectory, Henry James and Nella Louise Tucker lived in the house. Henry James Tucker was the son of the Reverend George Tucker and their son Henry James was born in 1903 at Villa Mont Clare (*Man of Stature*, J.R. Williams, p5).

Additional information: *St. Mark's Church*, William Zuill. Researcher: Fay Elliott

Architectural Assessment: Villa Mont Clare

Background research by Fay Elliott.

The Old Johansen Homestead, 19 Town Hill Road

Owner (relationship)	Date owned	Source
Frances Mary Whitney	1865-1901	W27:714 1890/1901, earlier history is the same as Villa Mont Clare and Villa Monticello
🏛 (House built before 1890)		
Carl Julius Johansen	1901-1927	FR, SM/CV2 cottage & 12 acres
Almira Julia Eddison Johansen (wd/o Carl Johansen)	1927-1936	W36:427 1921/1928
Samuel Raymond Wayson Johansen (s/o Carl Johansen)	1936-1968	W36:427 1921/1928, D50:62
Elizabeth Ardney Johansen (wd/o Samuel R.W. Johansen)	1968-1991	W88:315 1960/1968
Vincent Darrell Johansen (s/o Samuel R.W. Johansen)	1991-	W88:315 1960/1968, owner 2002

The ownership of this property can be easily traced through wills. Frances Mary Whitney left to Carl Julius Johansen who left his estate to his wife Almira Julia Eddison Johansen and then to his 11 children, but he left his dwelling house known as "the homestead" to his son Samuel Raymond Wayson Johansen who in turn left to his son, the present owner Vincent Darrell Johansen who lives abroad. The property has been rented since 1990 to the present time.

Many thanks to Hon. C.V. (Jim) Woolridge for background information on the Johansen family. Researcher: Fay Elliott

The Boat House (now part of Manor House apartments, formerly Deepdene Manor, Deepdene Boat House), 7 Harrington Sound Road

Owner (relationship)	Date owned	Source
The Synod of the Church of England in Bermuda	1901-1926	D/AD:194, land only
Clinton Ledyard Blair	1926-1927	D/AD:194
Clinton Ledyard Blair & Florence Jennings Blair	1927-1931	D/AD1:206
🏛 (House and boat house built circa 1929)		
Clinton Ledyard Blair	1931-1947	Florence Blair died 1931
Dorothy Vera Hunter (by purchase)	1947-1953	M36:48, SM/A2
Deepdene Manor Hotel Co Ltd	1953-1958	SM/LT(V)116/53
Godfrey Lowell Cabot & Est	1958-1964	D/AD4:414, SM/LT(V)115/58, he died 1962
Deepdene Manor Hotel Co Ltd	1964-1965	D/AD6:220, SM/LT(V)17/64
Deepdene Ltd	1965-1980	Hotel closed early 1978, RG 6 Apr 1978
Manor House Properties Limited	1980-?1981	RG 22 Mar 1980, 23 Jul 1980
Jeannine Lucette Galene (The Boathouse)	1981-1988	D/AD16:8, leaseholder
John Downing Outerbridge (The Boat House)	1988	SM/LT(G)89/2, leaseholder 2002

It was not possible to see the deeds and the early chain of ownership was largely discovered from records in the Registry General, from the books of Alien Deeds and Land Transfer papers. *The Royal Gazette* was the source of information from 1965.

Many thanks to W. Barry Thomson of the Blairsden Association Inc. for his information on C. Ledyard Blair and architects Carrère & Hastings. The Blairsden Association was a non profit organisation which made a bid to purchase and restore Blairsden, the house built for C. Ledyard Blair in New Jersey. This attempt failed and the house is now in private hands.

Additional information: 'Carrère & Hastings', C.C. Blake, (Carrère and Hastings); *The Bermudian* magazine, July 1952 p24; 'The Truth about Blair's Folly' in *Mid-Ocean News* 17 Mar 1962; 'Splendour on the Shore', Diana Chudleigh. Researchers: Diana Chudleigh, Linda Abend

CHAPTER 9 DEVIL'S HOLE

Introduction

RG 21 Jul 1843, *The Bermudian* magazine May 1977, *The Visitor's Guide*, J.M. Jones, p54, 'Perpetual Picnics, A family holiday in the 1920s', William S. Zuill (Devil's Hole Aquarium).

Winterhaven Farmhouse, 84 Harrington Sound Road

Owner (relationship)	Date owned	Source
Samuel Newton	?-1663-?	Norwood 3, no link found to Mary Savage
Mary Savage	c1758-1768	W11:57 1793/1794 of Thomas Fitt
🏛 (House probably built circa 1770-1780)		
Thomas Fitt (by purchase)	c1768-1794	SM/PVA1, his death from W11:57
Thomas Samuel Julian Trott (gs/o Thomas Fitt)	1794-1857	Fitt's will said Trott's mother was not to be dispossessed
Thomas Murray Trott (s/o Thomas Samuel Julian Trott)	1857-1898	D/OWN, W20:214 1842/1857, D31:38
Thomas Samuel Julian Trott Jr & Adolphus William Reid Trott (ch/o Thomas Murray Trott)	1898-1902	D/OWN, A.W. Reid Trott bought out his brother in 1902, M13:455
Adolphus William Reid Trott (2nd s/o Thomas Murray Trott)	1902-1920	D/OWN, M13:455
Henry Stuart Hollis (by purchase)	1920-1946	D/OWN
Ethel MacKay Hollis (wd/o Henry Stuart Hollis)	1946-1973	D/OWN
Hollis (multiple) heirs	1973-1974	D/OWN
Government of Bermuda (by purchase)	1974-	Owners 2002

The earliest deed which refers to Winterhaven Farmhouse is the 1880 one (D31:38) whereby Thomas Murray Trott broke an entail. Thereafter the title is covered by the deeds. They also cover various other pieces of land, some of which are not now part of the property and some of which cover land further south added later to the property and not part of the farmhouse 15 acres.

That 1880 deed referred back to Thomas Fitt's 1793/4 will which said he had bought this land and house from Mrs Savage. Mrs Savage's presumed Christian name Mary was obtained from the parish assessments but considerable effort has failed to establish a link between the ownership of Samuel Newton in 1663 and Mary Savage in the 1760s.

Elyston Haycock, Tony Martin (quoting oral information from Amy Clendenen and lending newspaper clippings) and Eddie DeMello provided background information on the 20th century.

Additional information: *Bermuda from Sail to Steam,* Henry Wilkinson, p555 (marine militia); RG 24 Aug 1942 (Hollis obituary). 'Archaeological Excavations at the Winterhaven House, Smith's Parish, Bermuda', Dwayne W. Pickett, The Colonial Williamsburg Foundation, October 1997.

Researcher: Margie Lloyd

Architectural Assessment: Winterhaven Farmhouse

Background information by Margie Lloyd.

Formerly Neptune Cottage, 1 Club Road

Owner (relationship)	Date owned	Source
Samuel Newton	?-1663-?	Norwood 3, no direct link has been traced between Newton & North but both are connected to the Heesom family
Martha & Mary North	?-?	Reference in W11:57 1793/1794
Thomas Fitt (by purchase)	?-1794	W11:57 1793/1794
Julia Frances Trott (gd/o Thomas Fitt)	1794-1801	Her 1801 marriage to John Paynter Musson
Julia Frances Musson & daughter Mary Elizabeth Musson	1801-1852	1879 vestry minute refers to 1852 deed
🏛 (House built between 1852 and 1878)		
Benjamin Darrell (by purchase)	1852-1884	1879 vestry minute refers to 1852 deed, M8:71
Thomas Joseph Pearman (by mortgage)	1884-1916	D51:353
Ameria Pearman & Lucie Spicer (w & d/o T.J. Pearman)	1916-1921	W32:156 1913/1916
Frederick Brunell Spurling & Frederick Alexander Spurling (by purchase)	1921-1923	D51:353
Joseph Repose Moniz (by purchase)	1923-1929	D51:353
Eugene Charles Pearman (s/o T.J. Pearman, by purchase)	1929-1944	D51:353
Harrington Workman's Club (by purchase)	1944-	D51:353, owners 2002

The deeds of the house were not made available but a registered deed (D51:353) recording the 1944 sale to Harrington Workman's Club gave the history back to 1921. Working backwards, T.J. Pearman's 1913 will (W32:156, proved 1916) established his ownership and named the house as Neptune Cottage. An 1878 mortgage (M8:71) showed that Benjamin Darrell had owned a house and land which he mortgaged to Pearman. This mortgage was never satisfied so presumably Pearman acquired the property after Darrell's 1884 death. In 1879 the vestry records show that Benjamin Darrell, a stone mason (from his death record in the Registry General), produced deeds dating back to 1852 showing that he had bought the land (just over ¼ acre with apparently no house on it) from Julia Musson and her daughter.

It seems likely but cannot be proved that Benjamin Darrell was the coloured slave Benjamin shown as a slave of the Mussons in the Slave Registers. His age as stated then was two years different from his stated age when his death was registered. From the death record his parents were Peter and Grace and they were probably the Peter and Grace shown in the Slave Registers as slaves of the nearby Mercer family (of the property now known as

Mercer Heights, 13 Harrington Sound Road). If so, Benjamin had been with Julia Musson since he was a small child and she might well have sold him a piece of land.

Information on Julia Musson came from the Mercer/Zuill notes.

Researcher: Margie Lloyd

Oleander Circle, 96 Harrington Sound Road

Owner (relationship)	Date owned	Source
Samuel Newton	?-1663-?	Norwood 3, no link found to George Ball
(House probably built by George Ball)		
George Ball	?-1728	W6:146 1725/1728
Sarah Ball (2nd w/o George Ball)	1728-?	W6:146, W12:5 1798/1800, life interest
Richard Ball Jr (gs/o George Ball)	?-1799	W12:5 1798/1800
Mary Ball (w/o Richard Ball Jr)	1799-c1819	4 acres, W15:71 1819/1824
5 Peniston & 1 Musson heirs	c1819-various dates	
William Hugh Peniston (by various means acquired 5/6th)	c1819-1869	SM/PVA3, War Dept deeds (BA)
N.C. & E.S.H. McCallan (by mortgage? purchase?)	1849-?	SM/PVA3-4 (a share of the 5/6 share)
William Hubbard Peniston (s/o William Hugh Peniston)	1869-1882	Inherited 5/6 with debt
George Barnett Hollis (by purchase)	1882-?	SM/PVB1, 5/6 house & 7 acres, M9:216, FR
Robert William Lorenzo Gibbons (by purchase)	?-1892	M12:108
Daniel Trimingham & Hilton A. Pitt (by mortgage)	1892-1906	M12:108
E.A. Trimingham & E.E. Trimingham (ch/o D. Trimingham)	1906-1913	D44:235 (applies to land of AME church but covers Oleander Circle)
Robert Fisher (by mortgage? Lilian R. Peniston had some interest)	1913-1921	D44:235, M18:15, M18:99
James Reginald Conyers	1921	D44:235, W35:489 of B.D. Talbot
Benjamin Darrell Talbot (by purchase)	1921-1925	W35:489 1924/1925
Charlotte Salves Smith (adopted d/o Benjamin Darrell Talbot)	1925-1946	W35:489
Rev Joseph Daniel Smith (wd/o Charlotte Salves Smith)	1946-1952	VC5:288
Eula Alice Douglas (d/o Charlotte Salves Smith)	1952-	Owner 2002

The deeds of the property have not been seen but it was possible to construct the history from records in the public domain. Early information about the Ball family came from *Bermuda in the Old Empire*, Henry Wilkinson, p441, and Hereward Watlington, BHQ, Spring 1959, p24. The House of Assembly assessment of 1789 showed Richard Ball with 41½ acres in Smith's but with no indication how much was associated with Oleander Circle. Subsequent ownership was traced through wills. That of Richard Ball (W12:5 of 1798/1800) records that the house had been valued at £110 in 1751. Assessments supplement the wills from 1819 but while the will of Mary Ball (proved 1824) made clear who was to inherit the house it was difficult to follow the six shares of her heirs through the records.

Some information about the Peniston ownership came from records in the War Department files in the Bermuda Archives. Envelope 200 includes a plan and shows the Oleander Circle tract owned by William Hubbard Peniston and Mortimer Outerbridge. In 1872 a small part of it was compulsorily purchased for the South Coast Military Road and some land on the shore. The deed recounts how the father of William Hubbard Peniston, William Hugh Peniston, who had a 5/6 share of the property by the time he died in 1869, had a mortgage from his son-in-law William Edward Newman which was never registered but which meant that Newman's widow in equity had a claim on the proceeds of the sale. Mortimer Outerbridge had the other 1/6 share which he had bought from John William Spencer, another son-in-law of William Hugh Peniston, in 1868. This 1/6 share has not been shown in the ownership list or pursued further.

When William Hubbard Peniston inherited the property he also seems to have inherited many of his father's financial problems. In 1878 he and his wife and children went to Australia hoping to settle there (see *Letters from Grenfell*, G.J. Butland) but things did not work out and they returned to Bermuda in 1879. An article in the *Bermuda Maritime Museum Quarterly*, Vol 4, No 2, of Summer 1991 gives details of a distinguished career at sea in spite of the financial problems.

Information about Benjamin Darrell Talbot came from Mrs Sylvia Simons, a long time resident of the area, whose mother Mrs Helen Burgess was a sister of the Rev Joseph Daniel Smith.

Researcher: Margie Lloyd

Architectural Assessment: Oleander Circle

Background information by Margie Lloyd.

Twin Bays, 2 Talbot Lane

Owner (relationship)	Date owned	Source
Gerald Dupont Hollis	1881-?	SM/PVB1, land only
Archibald Maxwell Talbot (by purchase)	?-1940	M28:161
(House being built in April 1940)		
Hastings Ross Frenshaw 'Blackie' Talbot (br/o Archibald Talbot)	1940-2000	SM/A1, VC3:525, died 2000
Bryan Talbot (s/o H.R.F. Talbot)	2001-	Owner 2003

Most of the information about this house came from a conversation with Mr Ross (Blackie) Talbot when he was 82 shortly before his death in November 2000. The date of the building and source of the land was confirmed from parish assessments in the Registry General, a voluntary conveyance and two mortgages.

Additional information from the sleeve of *Bermuda Holiday*, recording of the Talbot Brothers, and Mr Talbot's obituary in RG 25 Nov 2000.

Researcher: Margie Lloyd

Knapton House, 40 Knapton Hill

Owner (relationship)	Date owned	Source
John & Elizabeth Knapton	1657-1668	Norwood 4, CR2:278, W1:120 1662/1668
Moses Knapton (s/o John Knapton) and wife Mary	1668-1689	W2,1:58 1698/1698, inventory W2,2:235 1703
Moses Knapton Jr (s/o Moses Knapton)	1689-1714	W5:55 1714, died intestate
Mary Knapton Gilbert (d/o Moses Knapton Jr & w/o Thomas Gilbert)	1714-1740	W12a:428 1734/1740 joint will Thomas & Mary
Mary Gilbert Smith (d/o Mary Knapton Gilbert)	1740-1792	W11:1 1788/1792
Catherine Smith (d/o Mary Gilbert Smith)	1792-1811	W13:353 1806/1812, SM/PVA1
John Walker (np/o Catherine Smith)	1811-1845	W17:223 1838/1845, SM/PVA2
Est of John Walker	1845-1849	SM/PVA3
Thomas Slater (by purchase)	1849-1850	D17:358
Est of Thomas Slater	1850-1927	SM/PVA4, PVB1
E.C. Pearman, J.E. Pearman, W.J.H. Trott, E.H. Watlington, J.D.W.C. Darrell, W.E. Meyer, K.A. Wilkinson, E.F. Darrell, H.T. North, S.R. Wilkinson, E.F. Darrell (by purchase)	1927-1929	D45:360
Edith Sterling Simon (by purchase)	1929-c1949	D/AD1:256
Hon Murtogh Guinness (by purchase)	c1949-?	SM/A1
Nicholas Bayard Dill (by purchase)	?-1957	SM/LT(V)72/57
John Stanhope Gladwin (by purchase)	1957	SM/LT(V)72/57
Warren A.H. Brown (by purchase)	1957-	SM/LT(V)74/57, owner 2002

John Knapton has long been associated with Knapton house and the family's ownership was easily traced through the Colonial Records, wills and inventories. Moses Knapton Jr died intestate in 1714 and it was only through his sister Sarah Thomas' will (W5:251 1717/1718) that we learned of his daughter Mary, the wife of Thomas Gilbert. The Court of Assize case (AZ102/6) and Mary Gilbert's will (W12a:428) then confirmed her connection to Moses Knapton. The Smith family ownership was traced through wills and the assessments. *Bermuda Gazette* 15 Jul 1820 and *The Royal Gazette* 23 Jan 1849 highlighted John Walker's continuing financial difficulties. After Thomas Slater's death the property was advertised for rent in RG issues 6 Oct 1863 and 8 Sep 1885. The Mercer/Zuill notes provided copies of correspondence between barrister Richard Darrell Darrell and the children of Thomas Slater, as well as the lease signed by planter Francis Martin in 1888. Darrell's letters mention that the house was in serious disrepair. It would appear that Martin was still the tenant in 1898 when he mortgaged his crop of onions, potatoes and lilies (M13:328). His wife Philomena died on Knapton Hill in 1912 (BI). Between 1911 and 1918 the property, assessed under Martin, dropped in value from £500 to £250. An abstract of title for the neighbouring Palmetto Vale house (since demolished) was provided by Knapton House's current owners. This revealed the deed of sale to a voting consortium from John Colin Campbell and Mabel Patterson who were Thomas Slater's grandson and great-granddaughter-in-law (D45:360). Oral history has it that a fire and obvious neglect caused the house to be in a very derelict condition when purchased by American Edith Sterling Simon (also known as Edith Fitzhugh Simon) in 1929. The period of ownership for Murtogh Guinness is unclear; the only reference found was in the assessment ledger for 1949 and 1950. The researchers wish to thank Mr and Mrs Warren A.H. Brown for their interest and assistance.

Additional information: Mrs A.F. Smith's 'Bermuda Silversmiths and Their Silver', pp162, 163, 176, 177; M/Z45 (Richard Darrell Darrell correspondence).

Researchers: Simon Baillie & Linda Abend

Architectural Assessment: Knapton House

Background information by Linda Abend.

Chapter 10 Near Spittal Pond

Introduction

Spittal Pond Management Plan, circa 1986; 'Portuguese Epigraphy in Bermuda', J. Vidago; *The Naturalist in Bermuda*, J.M. Jones, pxviii; *The Visitor's Guide*, J.M. Jones, pp64-65; RG 4 Oct 1887 (Rifle Club); D56:374 25 Feb 1950; RG 4 Oct 1887; Conveyances dated 23 May 1946; D48:153 28 Dec 1949; SM/LT(V) 23/50; Reports of the Department of Agriculture 1952, 1953, 1966, 1975.

Researcher: Hilary Tulloch

Sea View (formerly Sea View Farm), 4 Seaview Lane

Owner (relationship)	Date owned	Source
Capt Thomas Albouy	?-c1796	PWD/SM/9, 1789Ass
Est of Capt Thomas Albouy	c1796-c1802	*Bermuda Gazette* 9 & 16 Jan 1802
Richard F. Peniston (by purchase)	c1802-1826	Peniston Papers (BA)
Est of Richard F. Peniston	1826-1830	D9:428
Francis Peniston (s/o Richard F. Peniston)	1830-1868	D9:428
🏠 (House built circa 1872)		
Clarence Peniston (s/o Francis Peniston)	1868-1908	SM/PVB1
Est of Clarence Peniston	1908-1936	W29:364 1900/1908
Sea View Syndicate — H.D. Butterfield, T.M. Dill, E.C. Gosling, T.StG. Gilbert, H.C. Wilkinson, E.R. Williams, G.S.Ridgway, E.H. Trimingham, C.B. Wainwright (by purchase)	1936-1937	RG 17 Nov 1936 & 19 Dec 1936, FR
Edgar Campbell Wilkinson Jr (br/o Henry Campbell Wilkinson, by purchase)	1937-1970	SM/A2 house & 18½ acres

Henry Campbell Wilkinson	1970-1971	SM/A2
Edgar Campbell Wilkinson, David Edmund Wilkinson & Sandra Outerbridge (ch/o Edgar Campbell Wilkinson)	1971-1996	VC17:237, SM/LT(V)30/71 house & 17½ acres
James Morrison Macdonald & Jan Elizabeth Macdonald (by purchase)	1996-	House & 0.532 acres (lot B), owner 2002

The map of 1787 (PWD/SM/9) and 1789 assessments confirmed that Capt Thomas Albouy owned a house and 20 acres. The property was advertised for sale in 1802 and was purchased by Richard F. Peniston. An 1802 draft version of his will mentioned the house and 25 acres purchased from Rebecca and Thomas Albouy, the children of Capt Thomas Albouy (Peniston Papers). During the early 1800s Peniston began amassing his vast real estate holdings (by 1819 he owned 282 acres in Smith's Parish). In 1829/1830 surveyor Daniel R. Prudden was commissioned by Peniston's eldest son Francis to map the many tracts of land. As well as inheriting the family home, Peniston's (later Magnolia Hall), Francis also acquired "the south-side house". In 1868 Francis' youngest son, Clarence Peniston, was given the old house, assessed for only £100, and 60 acres. Clarence built the present house, possibly incorporating the old kitchen building and in 1873 the house value jumped to £400 (SM/PVB1).

Additional information: *Sketches of Bermuda*, Susette Lloyd, p156.   Researcher: Linda Abend

Architectural Assessment: Sea View
Background research provided by Linda Abend.

Tanglewood Farm, 2 Wilderness Lane

Owner (relationship)	Date owned	Source
🏛 (House built late 18th or early 19th century)		
Anthony Spencer	?-c1795	1789Ass, SM/PVA1, PWD/SM/5
Thomas Spencer (s/o Anthony Spencer)	c1795-1830	SM/PVA2, W15:280 1828/1831
Est of Thomas Spencer	1830-1870	SM/PVA3-4, M/Z 'Spencer'
John William Spencer (gs/o Thomas Spencer)	1870-1871	SM/PVB1
Ella Eliza Spencer (d/o John William Spencer)	1871-1876	SM/PVB1, W23:188 1868/1874
Edwin Robert Zuill (by purchase)	1876-1895	SM/PVB1
Est of Edwin Robert Zuill	1895-1957	W27:144 1892/1895
Edgar Campbell Wilkinson Jr (by purchase)	1957-1958	SM/A2:59/58
Lurelle Van Arsdale Guild (by purchase)	1958-1983	D/AD4:351
Lucetta Elizabeth Jones Ashurst (by purchase)	1983-	D/AD17:187, owner 2003

In 1789 cordwainer Anthony Spencer (died 1805) was assessed for two houses and 46 acres. One house and approximately 23 acres were located on the western half of Norwood Share 15, the area of Tanglewood Farm. It could not be determined if the present house is the 1789 one or if it was built slightly later by Anthony's son, master shipwright Thomas Spencer (c1755-1830). In 1795 Thomas was assessed for property valued at £900. According to a PWD plan in the Bermuda Archives, the heirs of Anthony Spencer owned 24 acres; however the plan's date 1787-1820 covers a wide time frame (PWD/SM/5). The Mercer/Zuill notes indicate that Thomas may even have purchased the property from his uncle John Spencer (died 1774/1780); however there are no deeds to substantiate this.

Watlington's *Family Narrative* says that Thomas' eldest son, Joseph Young Spencer (c1775-1840) lived at Tanglewood Farm with his wife Martha Pickering Peniston (c1785-1863) and their two sons Rupert Hugh and John William. Between 1838 and 1875 the house fluctuated in the assessments with a value of between £90 and £150 so it could never have been considered a grand house.

In 1870 John William Spencer claimed Tanglewood Farm and 17 acres with his grandfather's will (W15:280) even though Thomas Spencer left the house and land to his unmarried daughters Esther Eliza, Sarah Harriet and Rachel Young Spencer. John William Spencer died in 1871 aged 64 and his eldest daughter Ella Eliza inherited the property (W12:188). In 1876 Ella sold Tanglewood Farm and 9½ acres to Edwin Robert Zuill, to whom she was related by marriage. Edwin Robert's daughter Ora Ernestine Zuill sold the by then almost derelict property to Edgar Campbell Wilkinson in 1957. The following year Tanglewood Farm with less than one acre of land was sold to American Lurelle Van Arsdale Guild. Although the house was again in a derelict condition when purchased by the present owner in 1983, it has been sensitively restored.

The information on the registration of Ora Zuill was obtained from Dr John Cann, Chief Medical Officer, Department of Health; information on Lurelle Van Arsdale Guild from the internet.   Researchers: Pat Waltham & Linda Abend

Architectural Assessment: Tanglewood Farm
Background research provided by Linda Abend.

Rockmoor (formerly Rockmore Farm), 9 St Mark's Road

Owner (relationship)	Date owned	Source
Richard Downing Jennings & Est	c1789-1858	SM/PVA1-2
Thomas Melville Dill (by purchase)	1858	SM/PVA4
Harley Trott (by purchase)	1858-1875	SM/PVA4
🏛 (House built by Thaddeus Trott around 1877)		
Thaddeus Trott (br/o Harley Trott, by purchase)	1875-1924	SM/PVB1, SM/CV1
William James Howard Trott (s/o Thaddeus Trott)	1924-1956	W35:215 1913/1924
William James Howard Trott Ltd	1956-1971	SM/LT(V)71/56, SM/A2
Est of William James Howard Trott	1971-1988	W96:189 1967/1971
Peter Frederick Wilson (by purchase)	1988-1993	D/AD21:295

John Edmund McFaul & Charmaine Lise McFaul (by purchase)	1993-1996	D/AD24:275
Nicholas Mark Cooke & Penelope Atteline Cooke (by purchase)	1996-2001	D/AD26:142
Nicholas & Seraphina Hoskins (by purchase)	2001-2004	Oral
The Planter Trust	2004-	Owners 2004

Ownership was traced through the Smith's Parish assessments and vestry records (SM/PVA2-4, SM/CV1), the wills of Thaddeus Trott (W35:215) and Sir W.J. Howard Trott (W96:189) and the Book of Alien Deeds (Registry General).

Genealogical information was taken from 19CCR, vital records (Registry General) and memorials in St. Mark's Church and churchyard.

Background information is from 'Childhood Memories', Helen Fessenden; *Family Narrative*, Hereward Watlington; *Bermuda from Sail to Steam* Vol 2, Henry Wilkinson; Mercer/Zuill notes; *The Royal Gazette* 26, 27, 31 Jul 1971; *Mid-Ocean News* 25 Apr 1964, 6 Nov 1965; 'Agriculture in Bermuda', W.J.H. Trott; M/Z47:81, 90 (Aunt Hattie's school).

Mrs Penelope Cooke kindly provided an early photograph of the house. Researcher: Hilary Tulloch

On the Side: Edward Peniston

The Royal Gazette, 3 Mar 1903 (obituary). Researcher: Linda Abend

CHAPTER 11 AROUND THE PARISH

Wesleyan Centenary Methodist Church (formerly Wesleyan Centenary Chapel), 1 South Road

Owner/Additions to building/Major events	Date	Source
Wesleyan Methodist Trustees: John Stephens, James Richardson, Robert W. Gibbons, William T. Steed, Thomas A. Smith, John W. Smith, Samuel White, John Gauntlett	1839	Deed 23 May 1839 (PA100:96, BA)
🏛 (Chapel built 1839-1841)		
Cornerstone laid	20 Aug 1839	RG 27 Aug 1839
Wesleyan Centenary Chapel opened for divine service	11 Nov 1841	RG 9 Nov 1941
Wesleyan Methodist Trustees of Smith's Parish Body No 1	1923	Methodist Church Act 1923
Addition of tower & buttress & enlargement of choir loft & organ chamber	?1924-1925	Notes of Norman Noble
Renamed Wesleyan Centenary Church	1925	Notes of Norman Noble
Stephenson Memorial Hall completed & dedicated	?	Notes of Norman Noble

Information on Wesleyan Centenary Methodist Church was generously provided by Norman Noble who has committed himself to the study of his church. Report on the laying of the foundation stone was found in *The Royal Gazette* of 27 Aug 1839.

Additional information: *Wesleyan Centenary Church, Foundation Stone*, 1939; *Wesleyan Methodist Church*, N. Noble; *A Methodist Epic*, C. Munro, pp8, 15-16.

The roof of the church caved in during April 2005 and the timber and slate had to be removed. The congregation met in the church hall whilst repairs were taking place. *The Royal Gazette, 7 May 2005.*

Also in 2005 the church changed its name to Centenary Methodist Church, following affiliation with the United Methodist Church of America.

Researcher: Cecille Snaith-Simmons

Methodist Parsonage, 96 Middle Road

Owner	Date	Source
Thaddeus Trott, Dudley Cox Trott & others	bef1904	Land only
🏛 (House built in 1904-1905)		
Wesleyan Methodist Trustees of Smith's Parish: Matthew Richey Smith, George Ernest Smith, R.L. Popham, J.D. Gibbons, W.R. Lightbourn	1905-1923	
Wesleyan Methodist Trustees of Smith's Parish Body No 1	1923-	Owners 2002

The Parsonage was designed by Smith's Parish resident William Robert Lightbourn and built by mason Thaddeus Outerbridge of Flatts and carpenter James L. Outerbridge of Bailey's Bay. The house together with a barn was completed in Jan 1905.

Information was provided by Mr Norman Noble. Researcher: Cecille Snaith-Simmons

Marsden Memorial Methodist Church (formerly Marsden First United Methodist Church),
151 South Road

Owner/Additions to building/Major events	Date	Source
William Franklin Outerbridge	?-1915	Land only: D43:226 1923
Charles Mortimer Outerbridge (br/o William Franklin Outerbridge)	1915-1920	D43:226
Elma Winifred Cooper (by purchase)	1920-1922	D43:226
Bermuda Development Co Ltd (by purchase)	1922-1923	D43:226
Smith's Parish Trustees Body No 2	May 1923	D43:226

Marsden Church dedicated	7 Oct 1923	RG 6 Oct 1923
Trustees: Simeon Trott, Grenville Darrell, O.C. Lambert, Jonathan Smith, Humphrey Smith, Lionel Darrell, Floyd Hollis, George Burgess, Seaward Smith, Andrew Smith		RG 6 Oct 1923
Marsden First United Methodist Church	Sep 2001	*Bermuda Sun* 27 Jun 2001, *United Methodist News Service* 3 June 2002

Marsden Church was dedicated on Sunday, 7 Oct 1923. This was announced in *The Royal Gazette* of 6 Oct and reported on 10 Oct 1923.

Additional information: *Another World,* Duncan McDowall, p82-85 (Tucker's Town); *United Methodist News Service*, 3 June 2002 (Tucker's Town); *Chronicle of a Colonial Church,* A.C. Hollis Hallett, pp252-256 (Joshua Marsden); *St. George's*, Michael Jarvis, pp150, 151 (Tucker's Town); *A Methodist Epic,* C. Munro, pp7, 21, 35, 36.　　　　　　　　　　　　　　　　　　　　　Researcher: Linda Abend

On the Side: Builders of Marsden Memorial Methodist Church

Thanks to Roland Darrell for information on his grandfather Grenville Darrell and to Arthur Motyer for information on Ernest Motyer. The dedication of the church was in RG 10 Oct 1923 and the obituary of Ernest Motyer in RG 20 Jul 1983.　　　　　　Researcher: Linda Abend

On the Side: Harris' Bay Church

'Found: First St. Mark's Church', M. Kostro and P. Nascar, p14; Minutes of parish meeting Southampton Tribe, 28 Nov 1717; *Chronicle of a Colonial Church*, A.C. Hollis Hallett, p272; ANG/SM/PVA2-4 (repairs and collapse of church); *St. Mark's*, W.S. Zuill, pp11, 12.　　　　Researcher: Linda Abend

St. Mark's Church, 60 South Road

Owner/Additions/Major events	Date	Source
John Somersall	c1623	Norwood 18, land only
Harris' Bay Church	1655	CR2:256, old church and present graveyard
Sarah Sears Trott	1846	SM/PVA2-4, D17:149, land only
ᵐ (New church built 1847-1849)		
Foundation stone laid	1847	RG 19 Jan 1847
First service	1848	RG 3 May 1898
Consecration	1849	RG 20 Feb 1849
Porch added	1860	SM/PVA4
Tower & steeple started	1875	SM/PVB1
Tower & steeple completed	1877	RG 27 Nov 1877, SM/PVB1
Buttresses added	1877	*St. Mark's*, W.S. Zuill, p28, RG 27 Nov 1877
Chancel & vestry added	1884	SM/PVB1

The history of St. Mark's Church is well documented in the Smith's Parish vestry books in the Bermuda Archives (SM/PVA1-4, PVB1, CV1-2). A booklet entitled *St. Mark's Bermuda* by W.S. Zuill was very helpful. Additional information was found in *The Royal Gazette* of 3 May 1898. Rev Robert Thacker cheerfully assisted by pointing out old church foundations in the graveyard and highlighting interior church features.

The square marble floor tiles donated by William Edward Zuill for the south porch were very likely from the wrecked British brig *Uhla* from Italy (BHQ, Summer 1957, pp61-65).

Additional information: *Bermudian Images,* John Adams, p70; *The Royal Gazette*, 27 Nov 1877 (tower and steeple); ANG/SM/CV2 (cost of pews).　　　　　　　　　　　　　　　　　　　　Researcher: Linda Abend

Mount Hope and Cottages, 13 Mount Hope Lane

Owner (relationship)	Date owned	Source
Col Charles Walker	early 1700s	M/Z, land only
Joseph Young	?-1731	W6:252 1730/1731, M/Z
Rachel Young (d/o Joseph Young)	1731-1783	M/Z
Rachel Spencer & Thankful Tatem (ch/o Rachel Young)	1783-1819	PWD/SM/5, M/Z, FN:282
Elizabeth Pearman (d/o Thankful Tatem)	1819-c1821	M/Z
Josiah D. Pearman (wd/o Elizabeth Pearman)	c1821-1839	SM/PVA2, held in trust for son
ᵐ (House built by John W.R. Pearman in 1847)		
John William Richard Pearman (s/o Josiah D. Pearman)	1839-1896	SM/PVA3-4, PVB1
Jeremiah Scott Pearman (s/o John W.R. Pearman)	1896-1932	W27:325 1893/1897
Est of Jeremiah Scott Pearman	1932-1950	SM/A1, SM/A2
Anthony Soares Mareira, John Franklyn Peniston & Vivian Burrows (by purchase)	1950-1978	SM/LT(V)
St. Mark's Church	1978-	*St. Mark's*, W.S. Zuill

Mount Hope has an uncomplicated ownership history. The assessments prove it was built in 1847 and stayed in the Pearman family until the death in 1948 of Miss Kate Pearman, sister of Jeremiah Scott Pearman, known as 'the father of Smith's Parish' for his many donations. Mount Hope's close proximity to St. Mark's Church made it an ideal choice for the rectory. Pearman's beneficiaries offered it to the Church Vestry in 1954 (SM/CV2) but funds were not available until 1978.

Additional information: RG 30 June 1932 (obituary); *St. Mark's,* W.S. Zuill, pp33, 34, 46.　　　　　　　　　　Researcher: Linda Abend

Architectural Assessment: Mount Hope

Background research provided by Linda Abend.

Whitney Institute, 59 Middle Road

Owner/Additions to building/Major events	Date	Source
Ameria Ann & Thomas J. Pearman	1876-1878	Land only, earlier ownership same as Travellers' Rest (see Chapter 7)
Trustees: Rev George Tucker, Edwin Peniston, Edward Peniston, John W.R. Pearman, John Newbold Smith, Aggeus Outerbridge, Edwin Robert Zuill, Algernon Rees Outerbridge, Herbert A. Peniston, William Hugh Peniston, Alonzo Peniston, Daniel Robert Tucker	1878	D30:110, D31:18
Grand opening of Smith's Parish School	1883	RG 16 Oct 1883
Opening of Whitney Institute	1884	
Northern additions built	1889	
Enlargement of building and alteration of tower for bell donated by J.S. Pearman	1901	
East and west verandahs added	1923	

Former headmistress Mrs Gail Graham generously made available the school's archival material. The early minute books provided details on the early history of the building. Deeds for the transfer of the property from the Pearmans to the trustees are recorded in the Registry General. The account of damage done by the hurricane of 1880 was reported in *The Royal Gazette* of 7 Sep 1880. Subsequent stories on the school were found in newspaper issues of 2 and 6 Sep 1884, 24 Aug 1886, 16 Aug 1887, 1 Jan 1898.

Additional information: *Beautiful Bermuda*, Frank R. Bell, 1947, p256; *St. Mark's, Bermuda*, W.S. Zuill, pp33, 34.   Researcher: Linda Abend

Minstrels' Gallery (formerly Smith's School Room and Flatts Hill Mission Hall), 100 Middle Road

Owner	Date	Source
Rev George Tucker	c1893	Land only
(Smith's School Room built in 1903)		
Synod of Church of England in Bermuda	1908-1975	W29:320 1906/1908
Desmond Hale Fountain & Miranda Mary Campbell Fountain (by purchase)	1975-1992	*The Bermudian* Dec 1977, SM/LT(G)21/75
Charles & Lesley Hall (by purchase)	1992-	Owner 2002, Lesley Hall

The building known as 'The Flatts School' had already been built when Archdeacon Tucker wrote his will in 1906 (W29:320). The 1903 Education Department Report on schools (BA) mentioned the new 50 ft x 20 ft building and teacher William Percival who had taught at Cripplegate School in Bailey's Bay from 1900-1903. *The Royal Gazette* of 24 Dec 1904 advertised entertainment at Smith's School Room by the children of the day school and young men of the night school. A notice in *The Royal Gazette* of 17 Mar 1922 advised that the Police Magistrate would hold court at the School Room on Flatts Hill. It has been a private residence since the mid 1970s.

Additional information: *St. Mark's*, W.S. Zuill, pp40, 41, 46.   Researcher: Linda Abend

Watch House, 65 Middle Road

A report by Edward A. Chappell, made following a visit on 30 Jun 2004, is kept on file by the Bermuda National Trust.

Owner	Date	Source
Smith's Parish Vestry	1843	SM/PVA2-3, land given by Francis Peniston inherited from his maternal grandfather Richard Peniston
Destroyed by fire	1899	RG 2 & 9 May 1899
Government of Bermuda	1934	Owner 2002

Francis Peniston's two acre property was described as being 'partly in Smith's and partly in Hamilton Parish and bounded on the south by the public road and land on which stands the watch house of Smith's Parish' (D9:364 1827). This watch house was possibly the one resolved to be built in Smith's Parish in 1789 (SM/PVA1) and probably stood near the present one (SM/PVA2). Whatever was still standing of the Watch House was destroyed by the hurricane of 1880 (RG 31 Aug 1880). In 1843 Francis Peniston offered the parish a piece of land for the purpose of building a new watch house (SM/PVA3). The 1899 fire was reported in RG 2, 9 May 1899. Curiously, there is no mention of either the hurricane damage or the fire in the vestry minutes. The Ministry of Works and Engineering kindly provided the deed recording the transfer to Government.   Researcher: Linda Abend

Bibliography

Acts of the Legislature of the Islands of Bermuda 1690 to 1895, Vol III, 1884 to 1895. 1896.

Adams, John, *Bermudian Images The Paintings of Bruce Stuart*, Bermuda, Hamilton: Windjammer Gallery Ltd. 1989.

Allen, Hervey, 'Preface' in *Residence in Bermuda*, Bermuda, Hamilton: Bermuda Trade Development Board. 1936.

Bell, Euphemia Young, *Beautiful Bermuda, The Standard Guide to Bermuda*, 5th ed. New York and Bermuda: Bermuda Tourist and Advertising Bureau. 1913.

Bell, Euphemia Young and Frank R. Bell, *The Standard Guide to Bermuda. Beautiful Bermuda. The Bermuda Blue Book, Official Directory and Buyer's Guide*, 9th ed., New York and Bermuda: Beautiful Bermuda Pub. Co. 1946. 10th ed. 1947.

Benbow, Colin H., *A Century of Progress, A History of the Bermuda Telephone Company Ltd., 1887-1987,* Bermuda: Bermuda Telephone Co. Ltd. 1987.

Bermuda's Architectural Heritage: Devonshire, Bermuda National Trust. 1995.

Bermuda's Architectural Heritage: Hamilton Parish, Bermuda National Trust. 2002.

Bermuda's Architectural Heritage: St. George's, Bermuda National Trust. 1998.

Bermuda Cottage Plans, Bermuda: The Historical Monuments Trust. 1948.

Bermuda Islands Guide, The, Clarion Enterprises. 1982.

Bicknell, A.J., and Comstock, William T., 'Detail, Cottage and Constructive Architecture', reprinted in *Victorian Architecture: Two Pattern Books*, Watkins Glen, New York: American Life Foundation and Study Institute. 1976.

Blake, Curtis Channing, 'The Architecture of Carrère and Hastings, Columbia University', unpublished Ph.D. dissertation. 1976.

Blouet, Olwyn, 'Governor Reid in post-emancipation Bermuda, 1839-46: An Advocate of social and economic change', in *The Journal of Caribbean History*, Vol 9, May 1977.

Butland, Gilbert J., *Letters from Grenfell: From a New South Wales Goldminer in the 1870s*, Australia: Sydney University Press. 1971.

Calnan, Patricia, *The Masterworks Bermudiana Collection*, Bermuda, Hamilton: The Bermudian Publishing Company Ltd. 1994.

Carley, Rachel, *The Visual Dictionary of American Domestic Architecture*, New York: Henry Holt and Company Inc. 1994.

Carson, Cary, Ronald Hoffman & Peter J. Albert, eds., *Of Consuming Interests The Style of Life in the Eighteenth Century*, Charlottesville and London: United States Capitol Historical Society by the University Press of Virginia. 1994.

Carson, Cary, 'Housing for Planters, Servants, and Slaves in the Early Chesapeake Colonies', unpublished paper. 2005.

Chappell, Edward, 'Interpreting Bermuda's Architecture', *Bermuda Journal of Archaeology and Maritime History*, vol 6. 1994.

Chudleigh, Diana, 'Splendour on the Shore', in *Bermuda Homes & Gardens*, Jan/Feb 1993, p30.

Collett, Jill, *Bermuda Her Plants & Gardens 1609-1850*, Bermuda, Hamilton: Bermuda National Trust, and London: Macmillan. 1987.

Cummings, Abbott Lowell, *The Framed Houses of Massachusetts Bay, 1625-1725*, Massachusetts, Cambridge: Harvard University Press. 1979.

Cummings, Abbott Lowell, 'Three Hearths: A Socioarchitectural Study of Seventeenth-Century Massachusetts Bay Probate Inventories', in *Old-Time New England*. 1997.

D'Agostino, Mary Ellin, 'Goods & Chattels: Comparing Probate Inventories from 17th Century Plymouth Colony, Maryland & Bermuda', paper presented at Society for Historical Archaeology conference, Richmond, Virginia. 1991.

D'Agostino, Mary Ellin, 'Household Stuffe: Material Culture and Identity in the Seventeenth-Century Anglo-Colonial World', dissertation, University of California, Berkeley. 1998.

Darrell, John Harvey, 'Journal of J.H. Darrell', unpublished journal at Bermuda Archives.

DeCouto, Jerry, 'Canning Plant in Smiths Parish 1918', in *Heritage* magazine, compiler Reginald E. Ming. 1980.

Fessenden, Helen M., 'Childhood Memories of Bermuda in the '70s', in *Bermuda Historical Quarterly*, Vol 5, pp22-38, Spring 1948.

Fleming, John, Hugh Honour and Nikolaus Pevsner, *The Penguin Dictionary of Architecture*, Fourth edition, London: Penguin Books. 1991.

Greene, Fayal, illustrations by Bonita Bavetta, *The Anatomy of a House A Picture Dictionary of Architectural and Design Elements*, New York: Doubleday. 1991.

Hallett, A.C. Hollis, compiler, *Early Bermuda Records 1619-1826: A Guide to the Parish and Clergy Registers with some Assessment Lists and Petitions*, Bermuda: Juniperhill Press. 1991.

Hallett, A.C. Hollis, *Chronicle of a Colonial Church 1612-1826 Bermuda*, Bermuda: Juniperhill Press. 1993.

Hallett, A.C. Hollis, indexer, *19th Century Church Registers of Bermuda*, Bermuda: Juniperhill Press. 1997.

Hallett, C.F.E. Hollis, compiler, *Bermuda Index 1784-1914: An index of births, marriages, deaths, as recorded in Bermuda newspapers*, 2 Vols, Bermuda: Juniperhill Press. 1989.

Hallett, C.F.E. Hollis, compiler, *Early Bermuda Wills 1629-1835: Summarized and indexed A genealogical reference book,* Bermuda: Juniperhill Press. 1993.

Hallett, C.F.E. Hollis, compiler, *19th Century Bermuda Wills 1835-1913 Summarized and indexed A genealogical reference book*, Bermuda: Juniperhill Press. 2000.

Harris, Edward Cecil, *Bermuda Forts 1612-1957*, Bermuda: Bermuda Maritime Museum Press. 1997.

Hayward, Walter B., *Bermuda Past & Present A Descriptive and Historical Account of the Somers Islands*, New York: Dodd, Mead & Company. 1911. 2nd ed. 1923.

Heyl, James B., *Bermuda Through the Camera of James B. Heyl 1868-1897*, compiled by Edith Stowe Godfrey Heyl, Bermuda, Hamilton: The Bermuda Book Stores. 1961.

Humphreys, John S., *Bermuda Houses*, Boston, Massachusetts: Marshall Jones Company. 1923.

Humphreys, John S., *Bermuda Houses*, Facsimile Edition, Bermuda: Bermuda Maritime Museum. 1993.

Hyde, Bryden B., *Bermuda's Antique Furniture & Silver*, Bermuda: Bermuda National Trust. 1971.

Ives, Vernon A., editor, *The Rich Papers: Letters from Bermuda 1615-1646,* Bermuda: Bermuda National Trust. 1984.

Ives, Vernon A., *Guide to Verdmont*, Bermuda: Bermuda National Trust. Undated.

Ives, Vernon A., 'The Spencer-Joell Family at Verdmont', unpublished study at the Bermuda National Trust. 1976.

Jackson, William Vernon, *The Jackson Clan: The Story of a Bermudian Family*, Bermuda: published privately. 1991.

Jarvis, Michael, 'An Archival Assessment of Bridge House (1657-1971), St. George's, Bermuda', A Report prepared for the Bermuda National Trust, August 1993.

Johnson, Matthew, *Housing Culture: Traditional Architecture in an English Landscape*, London: UCL Press Ltd. 1993.

Jones, John Matthew, *The Naturalist in Bermuda, A Sketch of the Geology, Zoology, and Botany,* London: Reeves & Turner. 1859.

Jones, J. Matthew, *The Visitor's Guide to Bermuda With a Sketch of its Natural History*, London: Reeves & Turner; Bermuda: S. Nelmes. 1888.

Journals of the House of Assembly of Bermuda 1891-1893, Session 2, 1893.

King, Norman C., ed., *Haileybury Register, 1862-1946*, 7th ed., England, Hertford: Haileybury and Imperial Service College. 1946.

Kostro, Mark & Nascar, Paul C. 'Found: First St. Mark's Church', in *MARITimes*, the magazine of the Bermuda Maritime Museum, Vol11, No.3, p14. 1998.

Lefroy, J. H., *Memorials of the Discovery and Early Settlement of the Bermudas or Somers Islands 1515-1685 compiled from the colonial records and other original sources*, 2 Vols, (originally published London 1877 & 1879, reprinted 1932), Bermuda: Bermuda Historical Society, Bermuda National Trust. 1981.

Lloyd, Susette Harriet, *Sketches of Bermuda*, London: James Cochrane and Co. 1835.

Lounsbury, Carl R. ed., *An Illustrated Glossary of Early Southern Architecture and Landscape*. Prepared at the Colonial Williamsburg Foundation. Charlottesville and London: University Press of Virginia. 1994.

McCallan, E.A., *Life on Old St David's*, Bermuda, Hamilton: Bermuda Historical Monuments Trust. 1948. 2nd ed. Bermuda: Bermuda Historical Society. 1986.

McDowall, Duncan, *Another World Bermuda and the Rise of Modern Tourism*, London: Macmillan Education Ltd. 1999.

McLaughlin, E.C., 'The Flatts — A Centre of Early Colonial Life', in *The Bermudian* magazine, March 1934, p15.

Mercer, Julia E., *Bermuda Settlers of the 17th Century: Genealogical Notes from Bermuda* (originally published serially in *Tyler's Quarterly Historical and Genealogical Magazine*, Vols XXIII-XXIX as 'Genealogical Notes from Bermuda'), Maryland, Baltimore: Genealogical Publishing Co Inc. 1982.

Milford, L.S. ed., *Haileybury Register*, 1862-1891, 2nd ed., England, Hertford: Stephen Austin & Sons. 1891.

Munro, Clayton A., *A Methodist Epic, An historical record of the Methodist Church in Bermuda*, authorized by the Synod of the Wesleyan Methodist Church of Bermuda, 1949, amendments and addendum by Joseph J. Outerbridge, 1966. 1985.

Neiman, Fraser D., 'Temporal Patterning in House Plans from the 17th-Century Chesapeake', in Theodore R. Reinhart and Dennis J. Pogue, *The Archaeology of 17th Century Virginia*, Virginia, Richmond: Archeological Society of Virginia. 1993.

Noble, Norman, *Wesleyan Methodist Church 160th Anniversary Service*, service sheet. 1999.

Norwood, Richard, 'Norwood's Book of Survey of 1662-3', Appendix XV, pages 645-717, Lefroy, J. H., *Memorials of the Discovery and Early Settlement of the Bermudas or Somers Islands 1515-1685*.

Phillips, Steven J., *Old-House Dictionary An Illustrated Guide to American Domestic Architecture 1600 to 1940,* New York: J. Wiley & Sons, Inc. 1994.

Photography in Bermuda 1839-1939, Bermuda: The Bermudian Publishing Company Limited. 1989.

Pomeroy, Colin A., *The Bermuda Railway — Gone But Not Forgotten!* Bermuda: privately published. 1993.

Raymond, Stuart A., *Words from Wills and other probate records 1500-1800 A Glossary,* England, Lancashire, Bury: The Federation of Family History Societies. 2004.

Reports of the Department of Agriculture, 1952, 1953, 1966, 1975.

Rider, Fremont, editor, *Rider's Bermuda — A guide book for travellers*, compiler Frederic Taber Cooper, New York: Henry Holt. 1923.

Robinson, Kenneth E.*, Heritage,* London: Macmillan Education Limited. 1979. 2nd ed. 1985.

Royal Engineers Journal, The, 'Obituary of Colonel Arthur Johnson Savage D.S.O.', p294. 1933.

Ruck, O.E., Major RE, 'Survey of Bermuda' in *The Bermuda Pocket Almanack Guide and Directory 1898*.

Savage, A.J. Lieut. RE, 'Survey of Bermuda Addendum' in *The Bermuda Pocket Almanack Guide and Directory 1900*.

Savage, A.J., Lieut. RE, *Islands of Bermuda Surveyed and Contoured in*

1898-9, England, Southampton: Ordnance Survey Office. 1901.

Sloan, C.E.E., Capt. RE 'Bermuda' in *The Royal Engineers Journal* Vol 92, p4. 1978.

Smith, Mrs. Allan F., 'Bermuda Silversmiths and their Silver; in *Bermuda's Antique Furniture & Silver*, Bryden B. Hyde, p155. Bermuda: Bermuda National Trust. 1971.

Smith, James E., *Slavery in Bermuda,* New York: Vantage Press. 1976.

Spittal Pond Management Plan, papers of the Bermuda National Trust, undated, c1986.

Stark, James H., *Stark's Illustrated Bermuda Guide*, Boston: Stark; London: Sampson Low, Marston; Hamilton: S. Nelmes. 1897.

Stevenson, Kevin ed., *150th Anniversary of Photography. Celebrating the First One Hundred Years of Photography in Bermuda, 1839-1939*, Bermuda: The Bermudian Publishing Company Limited. 1989.

Stevenson, Kevin, ed., *Early Colour Photography in Bermuda 1939-1960 Emeralds on a Silver Zone*, Bermuda: The Bermudian Publishing Company Limited. 1992.

Strock, George, 'Old Bermuda Honeymoon Isles become U.S. Defense Bastion' in *Life* magazine, Vol 11 No.7 p67, 18 August 1941.

Strode, Hudson, *The Story of Bermuda* with photographs by Walter Rutherford, New York: Harrison Smith and Robert Hass. 1932. 2nd ed., New York: Harcourt, Brace and Company. 1946.

Taylor, Elizabeth, 'Verdmont — Smith's Parish, the home of Miss Lillian Wood Joell' in *The Bermudian*, August 1939, p14.

Thomas, Martin L.H., *Marine Ecology of Harrington Sound Bermuda*, Bermuda Zoological Society Scientific Reports. 2003.

Thomas, Martin L.H., *The Natural History of Bermuda*, Bermuda Zoological Society. 2004.

Trott, W.J.H., 'Agriculture in Bermuda' in *Empire Digest*, magazine, pp70-3. 1944.

Tucker, Terry, *Bermuda's Story Today and Yesterday 1503-1973*, Bermuda, Hamilton: The Bermuda Book Stores. 1959. Reprinted eight times until 1980.

Verrill, Addison E., *The Bermuda Islands*, reprinted from the *Transactions of the Connecticut Academy of Arts and Sciences*, published privately. 1903.

Vidago, J. 'Portuguese Epigraphy in Bermuda, 1543', *Bermuda Historical Quarterly*, Vol 19, p53, Summer 1962.

Watlington, Hereward T., 'Bermuda Historical Monuments Trust, The First 30 Years, 1937-1966', Bermuda, Hamilton: The Trust. 1967.

Watlington, Hereward T., 'Verdmont' in *Bermuda Historical Quarterly*, Vol 24, p56. Summer 1967.

Watlington, Hereward T., 'Maps and Surveys of Bermuda 1511-1973', Part IV, in *Bermuda Historical Quarterly*, Vol 32, pp65-8, Winter 1975.

Watlington, Hereward T., *Family Narrative*, Bermuda: published privately. 1980.

Wesleyan Centenary Church, Foundation Stone Laid August 20th, 1839, A narrative of matters associated with this event, 1939.

Who's Who, 1932, p2863.

Wilkinson, Henry C., *The Adventurers of Bermuda A history of the island from its discovery until the dissolution of the Somers Island Company in 1684*, London: Oxford University Press. 1933. 2nd ed. 1958.

Wilkinson, Henry C., *Bermuda in the Old Empire A History of the Island from the Dissolution of the Somers Island Company until the end of the American Revolutionary War: 1684-1784*, London: Oxford University Press. 1933. 2nd ed. 1950.

Wilkinson, Henry C., *Bermuda from Sail to Steam The History of the Island from 1784 to 1901*, 2 Vols, London: Oxford University Press. 1973.

Williams, Ann Zuill, *The Back Yard A Bermuda Childhood*, London: Macmillan Caribbean. 1988.

Williams, J. Randolf, *Man of Stature: Sir Henry James Tucker*, Bermuda, Hamilton: Camden Editions. 1987.

Williams, Ronald John, *Bermudiana*, Bermuda: The Bermudian Publishing Company. 1936. 2nd ed., New York: Rinehart & Company Inc. 1946.

Ziral, James, 'The Legacy of Preacher's Cave', in *The Bermudian*, December 1992, p34.

Zuill, William E.S., *Bermuda Sampler 1815 1850*, Bermuda, Hamilton: The Bermuda Book Stores. 1937.

Zuill, William E.S., *Bermuda Journey: A Leisurely Guidebook*, New York: Coward-McCann. 1946. 7th Impression, Bermuda, Hamilton: The Bermuda Book Stores. 1974.

Zuill, William E.S., 'The Story of Orange Grove' in *Bermuda Historical Quarterly*, Vol 29, pp168, 203, 243, Vol 30, pp11, 53, 75, 99, Vol 31, pp34, 63, 95, Summer 1972 - Winter 1974.

Zuill, William S., with chapters by Rev Ernest Redfern and Anthony Pettit, *St. Mark's Bermuda,* Bermuda, Smith's Parish: St. Mark's Vestry. 1986.

Zuill, William S., *The Story of Bermuda and her People*, 3rd ed., England, London and Basingstoke: Macmillan Education Ltd. 1999.

Zuill, William S., 'Perpetual Picnics, A Family holiday in the 1920s' in *The Bermudian* magazine, May 1977.

Periodicals published in Bermuda, various editions:

Bermuda Gazette

Bermuda Historical Quarterly

Bermuda Journal of Archaeology and Maritime History

Bermudian, The, magazine

Bermudian, The, newspaper

Royal Gazette, The

Royal Gazette and Colonist Daily, The

Mid-Ocean News

Index